NITY AND AL

THE UNIVERSITY OF LEEDS

Theatre and religion

MANCHESTER
UNIVERSITY PRESS

Theatre and religion

Lancastrian Shakespeare

edited by
Richard Dutton,
Alison Findlay
and Richard Wilson

Manchester University Press

Manchester and New York

distributed exclusively in the USA by Palgrave

Copyright © Manchester University Press 2003

While copyright in the volume as a whole is vested in Manchester University Press, copyright in individual chapters belongs to their respective authors, and no chapter may be reproduced wholly or in part without the express permission in writing of both author and publisher.

Published by Manchester University Press
Oxford Road, Manchester M13 9NR, UK
and Room 400, 175 Fifth Avenue, New York, NY 10010, USA
www.manchesteruniversitypress.co.uk

Distributed exclusively in the USA by
Palgrave, 175 Fifth Avenue, New York,
NY 10010, USA

Distributed exclusively in Canada by
UBC Press, University of British Columbia, 2029 West Mall,
Vancouver, BC, Canada V6T 1Z2

British Library Cataloguing-in-Publication Data
A catalogue record for this book is available from the British Library

Library of Congress Cataloging-in-Publication Data applied for

ISBN 0 7190 6362 0 *hardback*
   0 7190 6363 9 *paperback*

First published 2003

10 09 08 07 06 05 04 03   10 9 8 7 6 5 4 3 2 1

Typeset in Sabon
by SNP Best-set Typesetter Ltd., Hong Kong
Printed in Great Britain
by CPI Bath

For Ernst Honigmann

'They say he is already in the Forest of Arden,
and a many merry men with him.'

Contents

Notes on contributors   *page* ix

Acknowledgements   xiii

1   Introduction: a torturing hour – Shakespeare and the martyrs   *Richard Wilson*   1

2   Bare ruined choirs: remembering Catholicism in Shakespeare's England   *Eamon Duffy*   40

3   Shakespeare's Jesuit schoolmasters   *Peter Milward S. J.*   58

4   Jesuit drama in early modern England   *Robert S. Miola*   71

5   Richard Verstegan and Catholic resistance: the encoding of antiquarianism and love   *Donna B. Hamilton*   87

6   Catilines and Machiavels: reading Catholic resistance in *3 Henry VI*   *Randall Martin*   105

7   'This Papist and his Poet': Shakespeare's Lancastrian kings and Robert Parsons's *Conference about the Next Succession*   *Jean-Christophe Mayer*   116

8   Catholic exiles in Flanders and *As You Like It*; or, what if you don't like it at all?   *Carol Enos*   130

9   Requiem for a prince: rites of memory in *Hamlet*   *Gerard Kilroy*   143

10   Richard Topcliffe: Elizabeth's enforcer and the representation of power in *King Lear*   *Frank Brownlow*   161

11   Learned pate and golden fool: a Jesuit source for *Timon of Athens*   *Sonja Fielitz*   179

12   *Cymbeline* and the sleep of faith   *Margaret Jones-Davies*   197

13   Shakespeare and Catholicism   *Arthur F. Marotti*   218

14   The cultural politics of Maybe   *Gary Taylor*   242

Index   259

Notes on contributors

Frank Brownlow was born in Northern Ireland and educated at Wallasey Grammar School, Liverpool University and The Shakespeare Institute. He is currently Gwen and Allen Smith Professor in English at Mount Holyoke College, and his most recent book is *Robert Southwell*.

Eamon Duffy is Professor of Divinity at Magdalene College, Cambridge, and is author of numerous important publications on Catholicism and on early modern English religious history, including *The Stripping of the Altars* (1992), *The Voices of Morebath: Reformation and Rebellion in an English Village* (2001) and *Humanism, Reform and the Reformation: The career of Bishop John Fisher*, which he edited with Brendan Bradshaw (1989).

Richard Dutton is Professor of English at Lancaster University, where he has taught since 1974. He has published widely on early modern drama, particularly on questions of censorship and authorship in *Mastering the Revels: The Regulation and Censorship of English Renaissance Drama* (Macmillan, 1991) and *Licensing, Censorship and Authorship in Early Modern England: Buggeswords* (Palgrave, 2002). He has recently finished editing, with Jean E. Howard, four *Companion* volumes of new essays on Shakespeare's *Comedies, Tragedies, Histories* and *Problem Plays, Late Plays and Poems* (Blackwell, forthcoming). He is General Editor of the Palgrave Literary Lives Series and of the Revels Plays. He has recently edited Ben Jonson's *Epicene* (Manchester University Press, 2003) and is currently editing *Volpone* for the forthcoming new Cambridge Ben Jonson.

Carol Curt Enos is a retired high-school English teacher who lives in Lawrence, Kansas. She holds a bachelor's degree in education from the University of Kansas, an MST in French from SUNY-Binghamton, and a master's degree in English from the University of Kansas. A revised version of her master's thesis, *Shakespeare and the Catholic Religion*, was published by Dorrance Publishing Company in 2000.

Sonja Fielitz is Professor of English Literature at the University of Munich. She is currently working on a project concerning the role of the Jesuits' Provincia Germaniae Superioris for the early Jesuit mission in England. Her further academic interests and publications include a book on the role of Ovid's *Metamorphoses* in the cultural discourses in England between 1660 and 1800, several articles on Elizabethan and Jacobean drama and also on children's literature.

Alison Findlay is Reader in Renaissance Drama at Lancaster University. Her publications include *Illegitimate Power: Bastards in Renaissance Drama* (Manchester University Press, 1994), *A Feminist Perspective on Renaissance Drama* (Blackwell, 1998). She is co-director of an interdisciplinary research project on early modern women's drama, and co-author of *Women and Dramatic Production 1550–1700* (Longman, 2000). She has written on *Much Ado About Nothing* for the *Companion to Shakespeare: The Comedies*, edited by Richard Dutton and Jean E. Howard (Blackwell, forthcoming), and is currently working on *Women in Shakespeare* for the Athlone Shakespeare Dictionaries series.

Donna B. Hamilton is Professor of English at the University of Maryland. Her publications include *Virgil and The Tempest: The Politics of Imitation* (Ohio University Press, 1990); *Shakespeare and the Politics of Protestant England* (Harvester Wheatsheaf, 1992); *Religion, Literature and Politics in Post-Reformation England, 1580–1680*, edited with Richard Strier (Cambridge University Press, 1996); an edition of *The Puritan Widow*, in *The Complete Works of Thomas Middleton*, edited by Gary Taylor (Oxford University Press, forthcoming). Hamilton's recent work on English Catholic writers includes *Anthony Munday and the Catholics* (forthcoming from Ashgate).

Margaret Jones-Davis, after teaching for fifteen years at the Université de Lille III (1970–85), is now Maître de Conférences at the University of Paris-Sorbonne (Paris IV). Co-author of *Le Roman en Grande Bretagne depuis 1945* (PUF, 1981), she has since specialized in Shakespeare studies. She has edited *Richard II* (Folio-Théâtre, Gallimard, 1998) and *Cymbeline* (Editions Théâtrales, 2000), and is now preparing the edition of six plays for the new Pléiade, Gallimard, and a book on Shakespeare and nominalism.

Gerard Kilroy is finishing a doctorate at Lancaster University on Shakespeare, Edmund Campion and the literary *memoria* of the recusant community. Educated at Magdalen College, Oxford, he is Head of English at King Edward's School in Bath, where he also organizes a monthly Café Philo and a biannual Shakespeare Symposium.

Arthur F. Marotti is Professor of English at Wayne State University. His extensive publications include a wealth of writing on early modern literature and Catholicism. He is author of *Manuscript, Print, and the English Renaissance Lyric* (Cornell University Press, 1995) and editor of

Catholicism and Anti-Catholicism in Early Modern English Texts (Macmillan, 1999). He has co-edited and contributed to *Print, Manuscript and Performance: The Changing Relations of the Media in Early Modern England* (Ohio State University Press, 2000), *Catholicism and Anti-Catholicism in Early Modern English Texts* (Macmillan and St Martin's Press, 1999) and *Texts and Cultural Change in Early Modern England* (Macmillan and St Martin's Press, 1997).

Randall Martin, Professor of English at the University of New Brunswick, has recently edited *3 Henry VI* for the Oxford Shakespeare. He is currently working on a book about women, murder, and equity in early modern crime pamphlets, and editing *Every Man Out of His Humour* for the Cambridge *Works of Ben Jonson.*

Jean-Christophe Mayer is a Senior Research Fellow employed by the Centre National de la Recherche Scientifique (CNRS), France. He is also a member of the Institute for Research on the Renaissance, the Neoclassical age and the Enlightenment (IRCL) at Université Paul Valéry, Montpellier. His publications include an edition and translation of Henry Porter's *Two Angry Women of Abingdon* (Gallimard), a volume of essays on William Shakespeare's *Antony and Cleopatra* which he has edited (Rennes University Press), and the recent *Breaking the Silence of the Succession: A Sourcebook of Manuscripts and Rare Elizabethan Texts (c.1587–1603)* (Montpellier University Press, 2003) which he has also edited. He is currently working on a book to be entitled *Shakespeare, Catholicism and the Stage.*

Peter Milward is Emeritus Professor of Sophia University, Tokyo, and Director of the Renaissance Institute, Tokyo. Born in London, in 1925, he studied at the Jesuit High School, Wimbledon College and Campion Hall, Oxford, before taking an MA in Classics and English. He entered the Society of Jesus and went out to Japan in 1954, and was ordained in 1960. He taught English Literature at Sophia University 1962–96. He is the author of books on Shakespeare, Hopkins, Eliot and Chesterton, published in England, America and Japan, notably *Shakespeare's Religious Background* (Sidgwick and Jackson, 1973), *Religious Controversies of the Elizabethan Age* (Scolar Press, 1977) and *The Jacobean Age* (1978).

Robert S. Miola is Gerard Manley Hopkins Professor of English and Lecturer in Classics at Loyola College in Maryland. He has written on the classical backgrounds to Shakespeare, has edited Jonson's *Every Man Out of His Humour* for the Revels Plays, and is currently compiling an anthology, *The Catholic Renaissance.*

Gary Taylor is Director of the Hudson Strode Program in Renaissance Studies at the University of Alabama. He is general editor of *William Shakespeare: The Complete Works* (1986) and *The Collected Works of Thomas Middleton* (forthcoming); author of *Reinventing Shakespeare*

(1989), *Cultural Selection* (1996), and *Castration: An Abbreviated History of Western Manhood* (2000). He is currently at work on a book on the publisher Edward Blount.

Richard Wilson is Professor and Director of the Shakespeare Programme at Lancaster University. He has published numerous essays on Shakespeare and his contemporaries, and is author of *Will Power: Essays on Shakespearean Authority* (Harvester Wheatsheaf, 1993) and editor of *Christopher Marlowe* (Longman Critical Readers, Longman, 1998). He co-edited *New Historicism and Renaissance Drama* (Longman, 1991) with Richard Dutton. His most recent research has been on Shakespeare, secrecy and Catholicism.

Acknowledgements

We are grateful for the generosity of all those who assisted in the organization of the 'Lancastrian Shakespeare' conference and exhibition at Hoghton Tower and the University of Lancaster in July 1999. In particular, we would like to thank Sir Bernard and Lady Rosanna de Hoghton, whose hospitality and enthusiasm made the conference such an outstanding success. For their invaluable support we are also indebted to the Council of the Duchy of Lancaster, and the Clerk of the Council, Mr M. K. Ridley; the late David Fraser and Granada Television; Peter Robinson and the members of the Blackburn Partnership; Gary Bates and Paul Heathcote of Heathcote's Restaurant; the music director and staff of Lancaster Priory; Professor Pierre Iselin and the Sorbonne Scholars; Anthony Holden; Dr Robert Poole; Tristram Quinn and the BBC *Newsnight* team; Lindsay Newman and the Librarians of Lancaster University; and Matthew Frost and Manchester University Press.

Introduction: a torturing hour – Shakespeare and the martyrs

> What revels are in hand? Is there no play
> To ease the anguish of a torturing hour?
> > *A Midsummer Night's Dream*, 5.1.36–7

On Friday 9 October 1874 at University College, London, the New Shakspere Society was presented with a paper by the critic Richard Simpson on 'The politics of Shakspere's historical plays' which, as Gary Taylor points out, was one of the first historicist interpretations of English literature and a founding document of historicism in Shakespeare study.[1] Simpson had laid the ground for this revolutionary moment with a talk in July on 'The political use of the stage in Shakspere's time', which argued – in terms that resonate with new historicism – how

> In Elizabeth's days . . . drama occupied not only a literary position, but a po-
> litical one . . . Statesmen wanted the stage to be a mere amusement, to beguile
> attention from graver matters; but the stage poets had a higher mission, and
> from their wooden pulpit, clad in their surplice of motley, they preached a
> varied body of philosophy, such as no other pulpit ever equalled.[2]

This picture of the playwright exchanging the vestments of a priest for those of a player was not incidental, since Simpson's Althusserian theme was that the Shakespearean stage did not merely reflect historical reality but shaped the history by which it was shaped, exactly as the clergy had once dominated ideas. Theatre, in Simpson's astonishingly modern analysis, was, in effect, the 'Ideological State Apparatus' of Elizabethan England, wresting from preachers 'the development of political thought'.[3] But what made this 'political Shakespeare' so deeply disturbing to Victorians was Simpson's theory that the reason why ecclesiastics opposed the actors so much was that they broke the ideological monopoly of the Church of England with plays which subverted the established authorities, making 'kings fear to be tyrants' (as Philip Sidney wrote) 'and tyrants to manifest their tyrannical humours'. Far from merely mirroring magistrates, the playhouse was 'a bearpit of angry controversy', where majesty was mocked, and

'malcontents whose ideas were not realised in the actual government . . .
responded to the eager passions of the audience' by intervening in 'the questions of the hour'.[4] In both radical tragedy and coded comedy, Elizabethan
theatre was inherently oppositional, Simpson argued; but to recognize this
fact was instantly to raise the question how Shakespeare himself used the
theatre for his own personal political purposes: 'where his sympathies lay,
and what opinions he advocated in those dangerous days, when words and
even thoughts might make a man a traitor':[5]

> The very perfection of his artistic powers has led to a depreciation of his per-
> sonality. He is regarded rather as a mirror in which nature is perfectly reflected
> than as a person actuated by common motives . . . It would be a good deed
> to remove him from this Epicurean heaven of moral indifference, and to show
> that he took, as a reasoner, a decided part in the affairs which engrossed the
> minds of the day.[6]

A true criticism, according to the recent formulation of Pierre Bourdieu,
is one that

> far from annihilating the creator by reconstruction of the social determina-
> tions that exert pressure on him, and reducing the work to the product of a
> milieu, allows us to understand the specific labour the writer had to accom-
> plish, both against these determinations and thanks to them, to produce
> himself as creator, that is, as the *subject* of his own creation.[7]

Bourdieu is writing of Flaubert and the nineteenth-century 'invention of the
pure aesthetic' of artistic autonomy; but, once again, post-modern theory
was anticipated by Simpson's claim, at the very dawn of art-for-art's-sake,
that Shakespeare's famed invisibility and disinterestedness were themselves
politically *revealing* and *interested*, since 'the emphatic repudiation of all
politics, or of any definite policy . . . the entire freedom from all political
allusions, in that dangerous time, was itself political'.[8] No wonder, then,
that in the weeks preceding his paper Simpson suffered a crisis of confidence, since his arguments that 'a play is not an isolated literary effort,
but part of an organic system, like an article in a newspaper', and that
Shakespeare's work existed in manuscripts which were constantly revised,
undermined the investment of the New Shakspere Society in the stability of
the texts and the writer's authorial control.[9] Nor that, since no one was
more committed to the consecration of Shakespeare as 'the great professional artist, who combined freedom from conformity with the rigour of
the scientist',[10] than the Society's own Chairman, it was to Frederick James
Furnivall that Simpson (despite calling him 'an absolute ignoramus')[11]
turned for advice. In the event, however, when Furnivall read 'The politics
of Shakspere's historical plays' he reported that he did not agree with a
single word of it, while confessing his total ignorance of sixteenth-century
politics.[12] So, when Simpson addressed the Society he was heard in a stony

silence, and Furnivall's Olympian obliviousness was imitated studiously by the members, who preferred the Bard in their own complacent self-image to the conflicted Shakespeare the paper described:

> There was a political current in Shakespeare's mind which in the days of Elizabeth led him into opposition. If he welcomed the accession of James, he was soon undeceived, and the winter of his discontent had become gloomier than before . . . We see him in his earliest works choosing stock examples of weak princes ruined by their favourites and ministers . . . Then we find him dilating on the miseries of the just rebellion . . . Then, in *Henry V*, we have a manifesto of the political scheme of the friends of Esssex. Finally, in *Henry VIII*, we have the conclusion of the drama of the fall of the English nobility. First comes a period when the memory of Leicester's preponderance is fresh, then a period of impatience at the dodges of Cecil . . . Then a time when his hopes were raised for the success of Essex, and lastly a time of reaction, when he began but did not finish a picture of the condition of England under the Tudors.[13]

The portrait Simpson presented in his interpretation of the histories was of an author strategically disengaged from the political issues of his time, but negotiating his professional position-taking through technical decisions that were more ideological than any overt didactic commitment. Thus, Simpson confronted the modern myth of creative genius, at the moment of its birth, with an account of Shakespeare's plots in relation to their sources, not to expose the writer's indebtedness but to show how alterations can be read as signs of intentionality, or even the text's 'political unconscious'. So, in *Richard III*, the Machiavellianism of the usurper makes him the ironic model for the Tudors; in *King John*, changes highlight the similarity of the medieval despot to Elizabeth I, and the 'Suicided' Arthur to Mary Stuart; in *Henry VI* and *Richard II*, focus on upstarts strikes at the oppressiveness of Leicester and Cecil; in *Henry IV*, conflation of the Percy story sharpens parallels with the Northern Rising of 1569; in *Henry V*, invention of the army and courtship scenes is keyed to Essex's project of religious toleration; and lastly, in *Henry VIII*, updating of the Tudor system figures the development of absolutism under James I. Wary of Furnivall's scorn of biographical criticism, Simpson was pioneering a method that carefully avoided the traps of either exclusively external or internal interpretation, suggesting instead a dialectical tension between Shakespeare's formal choices and historical determinants. In the opinion of David Carroll, the Victorian specialist who is one of the very few modern commentators ever to take Simpson's criticism seriously, what distinguished his methodology was precisely this combination of historicism with the formalism preferred by Furnivall, 'seeing both activities as constitutive of a larger process . . . a skill rare in English criticism'.[14] The shock of his critique of the histories, therefore, was to situate Shakespeare's inscrutability, which had become such a totem for the Romantics, in relation to the 'mystical and hidden allusion' in 'the "opposition" literature of Elizabeth's reign', and to show how these plays would have been racked for meaning by a public of 'intelligencing interpreters'.[15] Many years before this became a hermeneutic cliché, Simpson saw the affinities between the Renaissance playhouse and the torture chamber, and depicted a secretive Shakespeare whose art was indeed to hide his face from his inquisitors (like the players of *A Midsummer Night's Dream*) behind successive mediations of historical reality.

Shakespeare's apparent freedom from historical inquiry – 'Out-topping knowledge', in Matthew Arnold's idolizing expression[16] – was the supreme instance, Simpson inferred, of the Elizabethan 'habit of covert allusion to matters which, if openly treated, might have subjected authors and speakers to all kinds of punishment'.[17] It was the playwright's very silence on his own times, therefore, that became, by this light, the real subject of his plays and the source of his abiding mystery. This was an argument which strikingly prefigured Bourdieu's thesis that the freedom from commission that would be a precondition of modern art did indeed originate in the Elizabethan theatre, where 'an intellectual order in a true sense began to define itself in opposition to the economic, political and religious powers';[18] but it entirely depended, like the sociologist's study of Flaubert, upon a painstaking tracking-down – or 'thick description' – of all the political, social and cultural environments within which Shakespeare's creative project evolved. In the 1874 meetings of the Society, as Carroll relates, 'the members were both overawed by the magnitude of the task that Simpson had defined . . . and unwilling to see the bard assimilated so thoroughly to the contemporary'.[19] For Simpson's focus on the author's point of view necessitated paying detailed attention to his geographical origins and location in social space, and what alarmed the Society was that this inquiry pointed towards aristocratic backers whose religious affiliations were Catholic or even treasonable. Simpson had, in fact, flagged his findings on Shakespeare's recusant patronage networks twenty years earlier, in a series of articles for the journal *The Rambler*, where his analysis was simply too incendiary for a Protestant academy to allow. Since he was himself a Catholic, it was easy to denigrate his discoveries as partisan, and, when the mighty *Edinburgh Review* savaged Simpson as an 'angry zealot' of a faith which 'fettered the intellect and crippled the will', his research was condemned to remain the greatest story never told about Shakespeare, eclipsed by Arnold's Man of the Millennium, who was still being hailed as 'an impenetrable enigma' (with a 'view of the world' which was, however, transparently 'sceptical, secular and humanist to the core') in the same inane terms as late as 1999.[20] The *Edinburgh Review* is worth quoting because its vacuousness remains that of journalists today, who continiue to maintain that we can know nothing about Shakespeare:

As a man of true nobility of soul . . . to take up a strong position was incompatible with his temperament which had nothing in common with that of the martyr. So he kept to the even tenour of his way, presenting in his works opinions which no system-monger can squeeze into a formula . . . Above the narrow janglings and bickerings in which he lived, his 'easy numbers' rise to the full diapason of a more than earthly music.[21]

While his contemporaries were 'lurching between Geneva and Rome,' sermonized *The Edinburgh Review*, 'Shakespeare became impatient with the harbour to which he was moored by accidents of birth, and set sail for the wider ocean of humanity.' The metaphor of the ship – familiar from *Shakespeare in Love* – would recur in bardolatry as a symbol for the slippage by which the universal genius breaks free of 'narrow and jangling' circumstance on to 'the wider ocean', bound for 'secular and humanist' shores which look, in fact, very much like America. In the film the voyage worked to heterosexualize the plays out of the pederastic playhouse; and in the journal it did so to purify them of the equivalent Victorian phobia, of Catholicism. Shakespeare's 'universality' is always a 'middle way' conformable to the Church of England; and the best evidence *The Edinburgh Review* could deploy against Simpson was therefore that in the end 'Shakespeare's remains were interred in the chancel . . . of the church at Stratford'.[22] Unlike modern Stratfordians who reiterate this fact, the nineteenth-century reviewer could not know what historians have shown, that interment in consecrated ground was one of the many privileges exercised, as Puritans complained, by crypto-Catholic gentry in the Midlands.[23] He should have known, however, that it was expressly because he 'died a Papist', according to the seventeenth-century clergyman Richard Davies, that on his tomb Shakespeare had laid 'a curse on any one who shall move his bones'.[24] But determination to claim exclusive rights in the Bard for Protestantism – in the name of a 'wider humanity' – would be the undeclared aim of many who accused Simpson of religious mania, without actually examining his position or acknowledging their own.[25] For he was, in fact, arguing not that Shakespeare lived and wrote as a Catholic but that 'there was a great battle in Warwickshire' between rival faiths during the Elizabethan period; that if evidence suggested that 'the poet's family, patrons and friends were Catholic', pressure of 'royal passions and popular prejudice' pushed the London stage in a contrary Protestant direction;[26] and that the plays could be properly interpreted only if they were situated in the context of this fierce ongoing contradiction:

as our knowledge of Elizabethan politics is very one-sided, through the victorious cause having thoroughly effaced the conquered, it will be necessary to understand the drift of the opposition literature of the period. It is not enough to know only the final result which our histories give us, but its birth and growth, the throes of labour, the ebbs and flows of success, the high hopes dashed, the terrors which proved baseless. The dramas were written amidst these changes, and the poet kept his finger on the pulse of the time.[27]

The Shakespeare of Simpson's interpretation was far more complex, he believed, than the 'fossil' excavated by Furnivall, or 'the dry husk' of the biographers.[28] It had been the rich historical background of George Eliot's novels which guided him, Simpson explained to the historian Lord Acton, and it was significant that it was another historian, Samuel Gardiner, who was most enthusiastic about his critical method.[29] Historians responded to his theory that Shakespeare's signature ambiguity came from the collision of his Catholic context with his need to conform to 'national feeling, so skilfully played on by the statesmen of Elizabeth'.[30] For though critics have ridiculed Simpson as (in the single sentence of Samuel Schoenbaum) a 'bardolatrous amateur' intent on burying the Bard in a Franciscan habit,[31] what he actually wrote was that 'Shakespeare was an accomplice in the conspiracy of tyranny and talent . . . to poison all the traditions of the age with the perversions of Protestantism . . . he was a prime and powerful agent in that conspiracy, perhaps the most powerful, for he was, is, and ever will be, a popular poet'; but that the tortuousness of Shakespeare's text proves that 'his complicity in that conspiracy' was because 'he conceived himself under a necessity'.[32] The story Simpson told, that is to say, was one of apostasy, not unlike the struggle between head and heart related by John Carey in his account of how John Donne, 'the kinsman of martyrs, committed mortal sin against the Faith', when he betrayed his 'father's spirit' and deserted Catholicism, yet by rebelling against his own heritage created an 'apostate art' out of 'self-doubt, divided loyalty, sundering of ties, spiritual estrangement, and loss of trust'. 'Though he forsook the Roman Church', Donne 'never escaped its grasp', Carey concludes, 'his Catholic upbringing marked him indelibly'; but he also reminds us that this was in fact the plight of an entire generation of Elizabethans who confronted what the poet and martyr Robert Southwell called 'the dreadful moment' of collaborationist choice, 'whereupon dependeth a whole eternity.'[33] As Simpson wrote, the surprise would be if Shakespeare were as simple-mindedly Anglican as claimed by proponents of the National Poet, since his generation were not 'torchbearers of Protestantism' but 'the last lights of Catholicity'. Until 1558 Catholicism had, after all, been the official state religion; so the 'real question is not what they were when they wrote, but what they were when they were educated'.[34] Like Carey (or the Marxist historian Christopher Hill with his diagnosis of the 'double heart' of Andrew Marvell), Simpson saw revolutionary literature as a product of social fissure and psychic fragmentation;[35] and the Shakespeare he presented was the prototype, therefore, of the artist as split personality, torn between his Catholic upbringing and the 'national detestation of the Holy See' after the Pope declared a *fatwa* on the Queen.[36] In an age of religious terrorism and torturing interrogation, deception and dissimulation were matters of life and death for the dramatist, by this light, which meant that the caricature of the cynical collaborator 'commodity' in *King John* was actually Shakespeare's own self-portrait, Simpson suggested, put into the mouth of the forked-tongued Bastard:

> ... that same purpose-changer, that sly devil,
> That broker that still breaks the pate of faith,
> That daily break-vow, he that wins all ...
> That smooth-faced gentleman, tickling commodity ... (*John* 2.1.567–73)

'Utterly unscrupulous as to truth', in plays such as *King John* and *2 Henry VI* Shakespeare 'distorts and falsifies the facts of history in a most unprincipled manner', Simpson conceded, so as 'to pander to popular prejudices as to the "domination" of Rome'.[37] If the 'sly devil' who 'breaks the pate' of monkish faith was born a papist, this was hardly a hagiography for a Franciscan brother, but it was an apt tribute for a dialogic dramatist, and Simpson conjectured a primal scene of fratricidal betrayal to explain the 'break-vow' compulsion he identified with the poet's lying genius. For in October 1583 the 'smooth-faced gentleman' of nineteen had come very close indeed to the subterranean world of the Catholic *jihad*, when his family was fatally entangled in a conspiracy to assassinate the Queen. The Throckmorton Plot was named after the Warwickshire aristocrat whose mansion near Stratford was the headquarters, but the marksman actually trained to shoot Elizabeth was a twenty-three-year-old squire named John Somerville, married to a daughter of Edward Arden, the head of Shakespeare's mother's clan. Intellectual and argumentative, Somerville had been primed in the Jesuit theory of tyrannicide by a priest disguised as Arden's gardener, and he was escorted on the ride towards London by one of Arden's pages, who later testified how he had seemed so 'tormented of mind' that he deserted him before he was shopped to magistrates by a suspicious publican near Oxford.[38] This boy, Simpson hinted, was possibly Shakespeare himself, who, he speculated, Somerville made his secretary in the weeks when he paced Arden's library, book in hand, torn 'between fear and resolution', and so became 'the original of Hamlet'.[39] Though we know the dramatist stayed close to the jackal's brother, such a fantasy was far-fetched and did the critic harm; but it highlighted what must truly have been a traumatic crisis for Shakespeare's neighbourhood, when Arden's Protestant supplanter as High Sheriff, Sir Thomas Lucy, and officers from the Privy Council ransacked the homes of suspected plotters hunting for incriminating evidence. Tortured in the Tower of London, the would-be regicide confessed how he had been supplied with papist propaganda 'containing exhortation to his wicked enterprise', so the investigators were under orders from Lord Burghley to bring back the proof that this 'furious young man of Warwickshire' had been 'enticed by certain traitorous persons, his allies and kin'.[40] What the pursuivants had to report, though, was that, as if by plan, Somerville's relatives 'alleged that since Midsummer he had been affected with a frantic humour grown of jealousy conceived of his wife', and that, unless the Rackmaster, Thomas Norton, extracted more hard evidence from his torture of the prisoners, it would be impossible to make further arrests:

> Unless you can make Somerville, Arden, Hall the priest, Somerville's wife, and his sister, speak directly to those things which you desire to have discovered, it will not be possible for us to find out more than is found already; for the Papists in this county do generally work upon the advantage of clearing their houses of all show of suspicion, and therefore, unless you can charge them with matter from the mouths of your prisoners, look not to wring any thing from them by finding matter of suspicion in their houses.[41]

'Like Hamlet', Simpson thought, the suicide attacker 'concealed his determination to kill the prince under the mask of an alienated mind', and at the torturing hour, as the Ardens were being racked in the Tower, their friends and relations saved their necks with the fiction that it was through sexual jealousy that he had fallen 'Into the madness wherein he now raves / And all we mourn for' (*Hamlet* 2.2.150).[42] There was a deep complicity, the critic inferred, between Shakespeare's creative imagination and his community's necessity to 'throw dust in the eyes of the watchful Puritans',[43] and the Somerville disaster taught the dramatist a lesson he never forgot, in the perils (suggested by the terrorist's very name) of standing 'too much i'th' sun' (1.2.67) of a criminal trial. Thus, with the searchers' efforts to 'pluck out the heart' of the townsmen's allegiance (3.3.336), and their own panic to ensure that it was not possible to 'wring any thing' from them, this Stratford tragedy could be seen as the template for all of Shakespearean drama, in which, over and again, the scene was set by the sovereign's despotic allegiance test – to find out 'Which of you shall we say doth love us most' – and the subject's desperate refusal to 'heave heart' into mouth (*Lear* 1.1.49; 89). So, between despotism and desperation, public acclaim and private anguish, or what was displayed and what could never be disclosed, the catastrophic events of 1583 plunged Shakespeare into the secrecy that would make his work so enigmatic, Simpson concluded, and motivate his art. Shakespeare had been described as the son of a butcher in John Aubrey's seventeenth-century account, who 'When he killed a calf would do it in high style, and make a speech', the critic recalled; but was not this legend an allegory of the dramatist's own relationship to religious terrorism, and of an art which displaced the burning question of the day – 'Whether to suffer the slings and arrows' of outrageous oppression (like some medieval saint), or take arms, 'And, by opposing, end them' (like a modern martyr) (*Hamlet* 3.1.59–61) – by ritualizing the violence on stage?[44] Hence, as Edward Arden was disembowelled and hanged at Tyburn, and John Somerville mysteri-

ously strangled in his Newgate cell (to prevent, it was said, a scaffold confession incriminating his controllers), Shakespeare played the fool when the
investigators called, and, in the great crisis of his young life, learned how
to act in order to survive.

Though it has been ignored by almost every biographer, the Somerville
episode was interpreted by Simpson as a crucial turning-point of
Shakespeare's life, and he even wondered whether Aubrey's story that 'there
was another butcher's son in the town . . . held not inferior to him for natural
wit, that died young', might not refer to the appointed assassin.[45] Whatever
the likelihood of such a twin, this phantom double did vividly illustrate
Simpson's theme, that there was in the writer's development, as with all his
Warwickshire contemporaries, a historic choice between resistance and collaboration, and that the plays derived their tension from this counterpoint
of the chosen road to London with a never-taken path to Rome. As the
Rambler essays repeatedly stressed, there was no question that Simpson
'imagined Shakespeare to be a fervent Catholic . . . on the contrary', the
evidence suggested, 'he went orderly to church'; but the plays would be
enriched, the critic asserted, if they were read contrapuntally, as products
of the 'interior exile' that contemporaries termed church papistry: the 'schis-
matic' attitude of those 'Catholics at heart' who conformed outwardly to
the official religion, but kept their true loyalties hidden from the world.[46]
There was a strange affinity, in other words, between critics and inter-
rogators when it came to exposing Shakespeare's shadowy affiliations; but
just what dangers these might have led him into, if the Stratford search had
been successful, would become clear only in 1757, when the very evidence
for which the Sheriff hunted was uncovered by a bricklayer, concealed
'between the rafters and the tiling' of the Shakespeares' Henley Street house.
The incriminating material was a pamphlet of six pages, purporting to be
the 'Spiritual Testament' in fourteen articles of the signatory, who was none
other than Shakespeare's own father John. In this pseudo-legalistic pledge
the testator swore his true faith not to any earthly ruler but to 'God, the
Blessed Virgin, the archangels, angels, patriarchs, prophets, evangelists,
apostles, saints, martyrs, and all the celestial court and company of heaven';
vowed to 'suffer violence of pain and agony . . . like to a sharp cutting razor'
rather than forsake the 'Catholic, Roman and Apostolic Church'; beseeched
his 'dear friends, Parents, and kinsfolks, by the bowels of our Saviour', to
pray to deliver him from the 'pains and torments' of Purgatory; bequeathed
his soul to be 'entombed in the sweet and amorous coffin of the side of
Jesus Christ, there to bless for ever and ever that direful Iron of the Lance';
and formally appointed 'the glorious and ever Virgin Mary', together with
his own patron, Saint Winifred, as 'Chief Executress' of his will.[47] As
Simpson noted, the fact that this baroque document had been secreted in
the roof, rather than burned 'when the persecution became prying', was in
itself a 'standing protest' of commitment;[48] but the questions its discovery

provoked were: where had it come from and in what circumstances had it
been signed?

John Shakespeare's 'Spiritual Testament' embarrasses the Shakespeare
establishment, with its unholy alliance of traditionalists who claim the
dramatist for a patriotic Protestantism and modernists who insist he had
no politics or personality at all. Sceptics, like Schoenbaum, have been able
to retreat, however, into a 'secular agnosticism' towards the document,[49]
since the original was lost as soon as it was printed in 1790 by Edmund
Malone. Simpson suspected that it had, in fact, been deliberately destroyed
precisely to cast doubt upon its authenticity, in response to the disquiet it
provoked. Certainly, it has been easy for sophists who think there is nothing
outside the text to use its disappearance to rest assured that 'awkward questions about its date or provenance and the possibility of forgery, cannot
now receive definitive answers'.[50] Yet it is because we can now give much
more definite answers about its date and provenance than its discoverers
were able to provide that the authenticity of the testament can be assumed
beyond reasonable doubt. Once again, it was Simpson who began to supply
a context for the 'Spiritual Testament', when he was the first to point out
that the sequence of articles followed very closely a devotional exercise, *The
Testament of the Soul*, devised by Carlo Borromeo, the fanatically zealous
Archbishop of Milan and doctrinal dictator of the Counter-Reformation.
Shakespeareans had debunked the text as a concoction; but Simpson must
have been one of the very few Victorians to know that 'Every day this Saint
Carlo made certain "protestations" to his angel-guardian', of which 'the
form was precisely the same' as that of the Henley Street find. He knew,
moreover, that Borromeo had circulated his exercise as a formulary during
an epidemic in 1576, and that, though no copy of this text was thought to
survive, it had been issued to priests during the Cardinal's audiences.[51]
Simpson knew all this because, parallel to his Shakespeare articles, he was
deeply into his life's work, which was to be a biography of Edmund
Campion, the charismatic Jesuit who in 1580 led a doomed mission to
England from Prague *via* Milan, where the missionaries had been briefed
in a week-long seminar, at the end of which they were presented with *The
Testament of the Soul* from its author's hands. What Simpson did *not* know
initially, however (and would learn only during later research), was that,
having arrived separately at Dover, the Campion suicide squad had made
directly for the house of Sir William Catesby (the father of the Gunpowder
conspirator, Robert Catesby, and another kinsman of Edward Arden), at
Lapworth Park, just north of Stratford-upon-Avon itself.

It was Simpson's work for his Campion biography that gave him, in contrast to other Shakespeare critics, such privileged access to the world of
Catholic militancy in which copies of Borromeo's 'Spiritual Testament'
would have been subscribed. He came to understand, for instance (what
has never quite been acknowledged by literary scholars), that the reason

why the missionaries went straight to Stratford was that they were heading
for a place described by the historian Patrick Collinson as 'essentially
a Catholic stronghold'; by Antonia Fraser as 'at the centre of the map of
recusant England'; and by Sir John Neale as 'a bastion of church papists'
encircled by firebrand Calvinists.[52] His inquiry into the religious warfare
in the area, between reformers – Lucys, Grevilles and Combes – and conservatives – Ardens, Catesbys, Cloptons, Somervilles and Throckmortons – alerted
him to what has been confirmed by Roger Manning in his book on rural
revolt: that the Shakespeares were bound to side with relatives in a region
where 'religious factionalism caused the Puritans and Catholics to take
exceptionally hostile positions to one another', which were more die-hard
than in any other part of England.[53] And his investigation of the patronage
networks which hosted the Jesuits made him aware that, as Anne Hughes
has shown, in Shakespearean Warwickshire Catholic politics were a function of 'seigneurialism', since 'most recusants were clients or "servants" of
the elite group', so in the towns and villages dominated by magnates such
as the Throckmortons recusancy was practically mandatory.[54] All the evidence, in other words, which Simpson found to explain why Campion went
immediately from Italy to Stratford coincides with the research of modern
historians, to establish not only why Shakespeare's father might have signed
a Catholic pledge of faith but also why it would actually have been surprising, given his connections, if he had not done so. Thanks to reports filed
by Campion's Jesuit partner, Robert Parsons, the critic also had a date for
the Shakespeare 'Testament', which, being handwritten by one of the cell,
must have been sworn in autumn 1580, before the priests imported printed
copies; and even a picture of the intense and dangerous occasion, possibly
at Henley Street, at which the will would have been signed by the dramatist's father, whose eldest son might have been enjoined to aid him in his
afterlife, as the most important of the 'dear friends, Parents, and kinsfolk'
beseeched to 'Swear . . . swear . . . swear' (*Hamlet* 1.5.157–82):

> We entered as kinsfolk of some person within, where putting ourselves in
> priest's apparel, we had secret view and conference with all the Catholics that
> might come, whom we caused to be ready that night late for Confession, and
> next morning very early we had Mass and after an exhortation.[55]

Like the confession box, also inaugurated by the cardinal in 1576, John
Shakespeare's 'Testament' was a perfect example of the genuflecting 'forms,
files, receipts and regulations' invented by Borromeo, as John Bossy has
remarked, to 'bureaucratize the soul' by making 'self-examination available to everyman'.[56] But equally, like Faustus's pact or Shylock's bond,
Borromeo's 'Testament' was a product of the 'all-pervading contractarian-
ism' of the age, and prompted a riposte in the Protestant Bond of Association drafted by ministers in 1584, which similarly required signatories to
swear allegiance to the Queen (of England, not of heaven), and 'pursue by

force of arms' and 'all other means of revenge' any who 'devilishly sought to harm Her Majesty', and 'never to desist from forcible pursuit against such persons, to their utter extermination'. Historians characterize the Bond as a resort to 'lynch law', and 'a naked appeal to the most primitive instincts of its signatories', but in all Protestant parts of England Shakespeare's contemporaries queued up to sign it at church meetings, six at a time kneeling bareheaded to make their marks.[57] Literary critics who find it hard to imagine Shakespeare's father signing the 'Testament' underestimate, therefore, the extent to which the French wars of religion had inspired a mania of mutual destruction, when fundamentalists across Western Europe vied to sign up to pacts, on one side or the other. In his Campion book Simpson was able to situate the swearing of the Borromeo pledge precisely, in fact, as one of the initiation rituals practised by the Jesuit mission to institute an English 'sodality' of sworn vigilantes, in imitation of the French Catholic League.[58] The stubborn collective denial of the admissiblity of the Shakespeare 'Testament' depends not only, therefore, on the notion that it could have been fabricated by an eighteenth-century forger with access to another copy of the Borromeo exercise that even Simpson did not possess, because it was also afterwards destroyed, but on a wilful disregard for what we do now know. Simpson's identification of the 'Testament' was vindicated, in any case, by the discovery in 1923 of a 1661 Spanish version printed in Mexico City, and finally, as late as 1966, of a printed English one of 1638.[59] Meanwhile, his theory has been substantiated in detailed commentaries by a Jesuit scholar, Herbert Thurston, and James McManaway;[60] with the result that, as Stephen Greenblatt concludes, there is now 'a clear implication to be drawn' from this document, which is that 'the playwright was probably brought up in a Roman Catholic household in a time of official suspicion and persecution of recusancy'. But if in 1580 John Shakespeare's 'Spiritual Testament' was sworn seriously, and if Shakespeare himself later conformed to the Church of England, there is, Greenblatt adds, a further implication, also anticipated by Simpson: that twenty-one years later, when he buried him, the 'playwright was haunted by the spirit of his Catholic father', pleading to him from the grave.[61]

'Did his kinsfolk help him afterwards with their prayers, alms, and Masses?' Simpson wondered, when he described how John Shakespeare had very likely been buried without any monument because of his obstinate recusancy, in contrast to the temporizing that secured his son an honoured tomb.[62] If there are, as Jonathan Bate declares, 'good reasons to suppose that the "Spiritual Testament" is authentic', upon Simpson's question hangs not just 'irresistible biographical speculation' but crucial issues about 'the whole range of Shakespeare's plays'. Since 'we know that John Shakespeare was fined for non-attendance at church, a fact which supports the inference that he died a Catholic', as Bate asserts, and that 'as a faithful Catholic he would believe that he would do penance in Purgatory until he could gain remission through the prayers of those he left on earth', the dramatist's relationship to this Catholic 'cult of the dead' suddenly becomes central to our interpretation of the Shakespearean stage.[63] It does so because, as Greenblatt explains, at moments like the close of *A Midsummer Night's Dream*, when the Fairies return to bless the house, or when Edgar quotes Jesuit exorcists in *King Lear*, the plays are 'haunted' by the ghosts of their Catholic past, 'by rituals and beliefs that have been *emptied out*' or abandoned, 'leaving only vivid empty ceremonies' behind.[64] Thus, it is as if Simpson's question itself returns to haunt the critics of a secular age; and Greenblatt has recently made Shakespeare's own haunting by his recusant father the focus of a commentary on the 'Spiritual Testament', *Hamlet in Purgatory*, where he elaborates his thesis that theatre stole its props and rituals from the church, but now in the context of old Hamlet's claim to be in a Catholic Purgatory, like that envisioned by Borromeo:

> I am thy father's spirit,
> Doomed for a certain term to walk the night,
> And for the day confined to fast in fires
> Till the foul crimes done in my days of nature
> Are burnt and purged away.   (1.5.9–13)

The Ghost's cry from the grave – 'Adieu, adieu, remember me' (91) – becomes so significant, in this account, because Shakespeare's entire drama is seen by Greenblatt as a case of *bad faith*: a perversion of papistry into poetry, spirits into actors, and, as Prospero puns (in the last lines of the last play), prayers into praise (*Tempest*, Epilogue 16–20). Solemnly sworn to witness his father's will, Shakespeare's dramatic career was nothing but a faithless betrayal, if the oath had any meaning, of the beliefs he had promised to remember and uphold.[65]

Ever since John Dover Wilson adduced that 'the Ghost *is* Catholic: he comes from Purgatory', critics have begun to agree with James Joyce in reading *Hamlet* as the tragedy of a Protestant author who bought literary immortality by cruelly denying 'Our Father who art in Purgatory'.[66] Joyce was, perhaps, reacting to the posthumous edition of Simpson's notebooks published in 1899 by Henry Bowden, which sought to show Shakespeare's doctrinaire fidelity to Rome.[67] But these notes were never meant for publication, and Bowden's rehash has been described as having eviscerated their meaning.[68] For Simpson maintained in print that the son avoided his father's ruin precisely because 'we cannot suppose Shakespeare to have been so uncompromising a Catholic'. As the first to realize that John's claim to be absent from church out of fear of 'process of debt' was 'the common excuse of recusants', and that 'mortgage of the greater part of his property' was 'a recognised means of evading the iniquitous robberies of the penal laws', Simpson grasped just how much the playwight's father had risked when he was twice 'called to account for his recusancy to Sir Thomas Lucy'.[69] He

also perceived what is confirmed by historians, that the vicious social conflicts which split Stratford – such as the 1607 enclosure riots; the 1601 corn
dispute, in which Shakespeare's friend Richard Quiney was killed by
Greville thugs; and the legendary poaching from Lucy, when the poet was said
to have been whipped out of town – were all expressions of sectarian hate.[70]
'Deer-poaching was no mere lark,' Simpson observed, 'but an act of ret-
ributive justice or revenge';[71] but the teenager who avenged his dead cousins
by raiding their persecutor's park learned his lesson from their tragedy, in
this account, and never again courted a suicidal end. Speculating that the
Stratford glover was one of those 'Catholics who had great difficulty in
bringing up their children to follow their religion', Simpson deduced that
John lost control of his son the instant he fled to 'the dissipations of
London', where 'a strict and troublesome religion, involving persecution
and hardship, was scarcely likely to be openly professed by fast young men'.
Seeking 'safety from continual change of residence', Shakespeare spent his
whole adulthood, according to the Victorian critic, in the constant effort to
live down his bloody fundamentalist affiliations, escaping the holy war for
which he had been trained in the refuge of a profession that was a standing mockery of martyrdom:

> Luckily for himself, he was but a poor despised player, to whom as much
> license on matters of state was allowed as to Motley himself; and still more,
> who was necessary to the amusement of the persons who might have hanged
> him if he had been a more important personage.[72]

'An you should do it too terribly you would fright the Duchess . . .
and that were enough to hang us all': the actors' tactic, rehearsed in *A
Midsummer Night's Dream*, to 'leave the killing out' so as not to offend
the 'ladies' (2.1.61; 3.1.12) provided the dramatist with his own survival
strategy, we infer from Simpson's description of a career in which 'his
"motley" saved him, because he was necessary to the Queen's amusement'.[73]
We do not know whether Shakespeare was personally present, in fact, to see
Arden hanged, or witnessed the martyrdom in 1581 of Campion himself,
though the critic argued that 'we cannot suppose that he was less moved
than the rest of the London crowds at the harrowing barbarities practised'
at Tyburn.[74] Yet, as Graham Greene complained, his decision to 'leave the
killing out' means there is 'one whole area of the Elizabethan scene that we
miss' on Shakespeare's stage, where 'the kings speak, the adventurers speak,
the madmen and the lovers, the soldiers and the poets, but the martyrs are
quite silent'. Francis Bacon, the novelist observed, had been one of the
lawyers in attendance when papists were racked, but 'if Shakespeare had
sat where Bacon sat and given orders for the torture, one wonders whether
into the great plays which present so smooth and ambiguous a surface, there
would have crept a more profound doubt than Hamlet's, a love deeper than
Romeo's'. Instead, from the absence of the martyrs, objected Greene, 'one

might have guessed there was a vast vacuum where the Faith had been: the noise of pilgrimages has been stilled: we come out of the world of Chaucer into the silence of Hamlet's court . . . out of the colours of Canterbury into the grey world of Lear's blasted heath', where characters speak as stoics or 'pay lip service to Venus'. 'How far removed', the Catholic writer regretted, these plays seem 'from the routine of the torture chamber';[75] and the same disgust at Shakespeare's effacement of Elizabethan violence was expressed by the cultural materialist Francis Barker, who theorized that it was the dramatist's project to occlude the barbarism of Tyburn and the Tower, by 'making violence into a spectacle of the exotic . . . in another time, in another place, among other people'.[76] Yet, as Simpson wrote, what is striking about Shakespeare's muteness on the Elizabethan regime is how it also goaded rivals, such as Henry Chettle, into deploring his refusal 'to dissemble, flatter and lie' to praise a tyrant he may have despised.[77] Shakespeare's famed canniness was not, therefore, a modern invention, but had always been the subject of scandal and resentment, as from the very first his critics voiced dismay with what he wrote, in contrast to their hopes of what he might. Shakespeare criticism starts precisely from this disappointment, Simpson thought, and the surprise among his earliest readers that, by 'leaving out the killing' on the scaffold and the rack, this 'smooth and ambiguous' writer had failed to live up to their expectations of becoming the great religious poet of his time.

Richard Simpson's researches into Shakespeare's Catholic origins established, with a wealth of archival detail, the inescapable horizon for a historicist reading of the plays, which only a criticism sunk in what Michel Foucault termed the 'historically well-determined little pedagogy' of 'the death of the author' continues to reject.[78] Yet rediscovery of his Catholic terrorist associations meant not only that critics had more cause for confidence about where, geographically and ideologically, Shakespeare was coming from in the 1580s. It also meant that they began to grasp more of where he was going, in contrast to the itinerary which might have been expected. As Taylor summarizes it, all the evidence suggested that 'for much of his life Shakespeare was a church papist' or occasional conformist to the state religion; that 'once he began dividing his life between Stratford and London, he might have become a recusant', absenting from the Church of England; but that 'like a majority of English Catholics, he had no appetite for martyrdom'.[79] The question for commentators who followed Simpson, then, was, how far down the Roman road taken by his father did Shakespeare go before he diverged from the calvary of the martyrs? How much of the dark and violent narrative of Elizabethan Catholicism, of which Shakespeare did *not* speak, could be projected, that is to say, into the bright spectacular spaces of which he did? And this question was pressing because it appears to have been raised by no less a judge than the martyred poet Southwell himself. This theory, developed by the Jesuit Christopher

Devlin, depends on the dedication of the martyr's bitter poem of betrayal, 'Peter's Plaint', to 'My worthy good cousin, Master W.S.', with a reproach that 'W.S.' is wasting wit 'distilling Venus' rose', rather than penning 'Christian works'. The scorn seems to be for *Venus and Adonis*, though Southwell also cites *A Midsummer Night's Dream*, arguing that, instead of making 'a poet, a lover, and a liar' all identical, 'W.S.' should imitate Christ, when he staged his Last Supper as a Passion Play.[80] Finally, punning on his names – 'will seek peer' – Southwell conjures a theoretical future for the writer he calls the 'sweetest' as his own equal and companion, in what seems to be the first of so many critical attempts 'desperately seeking Will' for a career as a fully committed and signed-up Catholic propagandist:

> License my pen to seek a peer;
> Your heavenly sparks of wit show native light,
> Cloud not with misty loves your orient clear;
> Sweet flights you shoot, learn once to level right.
> Favour my wish, well-wishing works no ill;
> I move the suit, the grant rests in your will.

Southwell's picture of 'Master W. S.' as a Robin Hood, shooting at the 'right' target by the light of love, projects the future the dramatist might have, if reoriented by his good 'will'. The implication, if this shaft is Shakespeare's, is that the young archer had indeed signed the testament that now 'rests' on his word. And the 'grant' who waits on 'Will's word' in this marching order might well be John Grant, Somerville's brother-in-law, and a kinsman, Devlin demonstrated, of both Shakespeare and Southwell, whose farm at Snitterfield near Stratford was used to hide the guns and ammunition in a string of Catholic plots.[81] Grant would destroy himself in the Gunpowder conspiracy, blinded in an explosion to which *Macbeth* may refer in lines about treason being blown back into the eyes of its perpetrators by Christ: 'like a naked new-born babe, / Striding the blast' (1.7.21). This image is a retort to Southwell's best-known poem, in which the holy 'babe all burning bright / Did in the air appear' like some incendiary device;[82] and it marks for all time Shakespeare's rejection of the plea made in 'Peter's Plaint', which might have involved riding in one of the 'well-wishing' pilgrimages led by Grant to St Winifred's Well in Wales. As Winifred was his patron, it seems likely that John Shakespeare did make a pilgrimage to Holywell, beside his Arden, Catesby and Vaux in-laws, to dedicate himself to her cause. This was the pilgrimage taken by the Gunpowder Plotters in 1605;[83] but, whether or not the son also followed his 'native light' to Snitterfield and Wales, Southwell's handshake pulled him into the same 'tight-knit circle of interlocking relationships', where, as Fraser puts it, 'everyone was related to everyone else.'[84] It was a network of papist *refuseniks* based on houses such as that of John Trussel at Billesley, where Shakespeare is said to have used the library, which conceals a priest-hole behind panelling. Trussel, himself a poet, historian and printer of Southwell, was a business partner of the Shakespeares;[85] but, as Simpson noted, Shakespeare's Arden connection also made him a junior of the Throckmorton clan, and so kin to his crucial patron, the Earl of Southampton. This put him near the centre of the 'web of blood relationships' that bound Essex's 1601 Revolt, seen by Simpson as a strike for Catholic toleration, but by historian Mervyn James as a vehicle for 'ultramontane Catholic crusaders' such as Robert Catesby.[86] No wonder, then, that as late as 1613 the survivors of the Gunpowder Plot were prosecuted in Star Chamber for staging *King Lear* and *Pericles* as a provocation in their Pennine redoubt.[87] All through his life, it seems, Shakespeare was writing just a wall away from the secret cell of Catholic extremism, studiously oblivious to the violent preparations going forward in the room beyond.

If Shakespeare was resented, even in life, for 'striding the blast' of politics, then, as Simpson wrote and Taylor reiterates, that neutrality cannot, given his terrorist associations, have been unintentional, since 'vacuums have to be carefully constructed and maintained', and 'any act so bizarre and sustained' as this author's 'apparent invisibility is not a simple fact: it is a motivated action and a performance'.[88] Whether he participated or not, he could not have been unaware, for example, of the clandestine education system that was devised in Warwickshire during his boyhood as a nursery of resistance to the Tudor state. This was an operation managed from Park Hall, the mansion in the Forest of Arden where the Ardens ran an illicit school for Catholic boys, imaged by Devlin as 'a counter-reformation in minature', with the manic Edward Throckmorton as a star. Two years older than his cousin Shakespeare, Throckmorton departed Stratford in 1580, bound for early death in Rome; but a eulogy of this 'angelical boy' by Southwell suggests the *curriculum vitae* the dramatist might have had, if he had answered the call.[89] In any case, the dramatist was probably among those 'school-fellows and common people' who waved Throckmorton off, amid 'tears of relations and lamentations of servants . . . as in a funeral procession'; and said farewell to his schoolmaster, Simon Hunt, when he too set out for Douai.[90] And Hunt's successor at the Grammar School was John Cottam, the brother of Campion's fellow martyr, Thomas Cottam, no less, and a recruiting-scout for the Jesuits, who spent many years 'receiving into his charge youths to be educated' for the Society.[91] But if Shakespeare wanted a model for such a vocation he needed to look no further than his Stratford contemporary, Robert Debdale, with whom he is thought to have shared a great-grandfather,[92] and whose antics as a Jesuit exorcist fascinated him long enough for them to inspire Edgar's disguise in *King Lear*. Debdale would end up on the scaffold; but in 1580 he wrote back from Rome to his family at Shottery full of optimism for his career, enclosing a crucifix and medal for his father, rosaries for his mother and sister and a coin for 'my brother John Pace' (a neighbour of the Hathaways), and 'commending my especial friend Mr Cottam, who hath been unto me the half of my life'.[93] Unfortunately, it was while carrying this letter that Thomas Cottam was arrested at Dover, with the result that the entire itinerary of Campion's mission was soon known to the torturers. Shakespeare's neighbours and teacher never did, therefore, receive news of the two 'special friends' until it was too late; but we now know enough about the route for which he was surely primed himself that the truly surprising thing is that he defied these plans, and at some point refused his cousin's invitation to take the pilgrim's staff and join the martyrs on their fatal path to Rome.

Under Throckmorton's influence, Southwell reported, 'youths flocked from all parts of the county for education' at Park Hall. He met them outside their school, according to his hagiographer, and 'used to go a great part of the way home' with them, 'urging them to piety, and exhorting them that if they were required to act against the faith, they should steadfastly refuse'. The Elizabethan crisis of allegiance evidently struck young in Warwickshire, since, according to Southwell, the Throckmorton heir 'went to neighbouring houses, asking parents to send their sons to him on feast days', and, when this was refused, 'arranged for the boy to run away from home and be educated in the same house as himself'. Considering, then, that this campaign to 'inveigle youths to fly overseas to seminaries' is so well documented;[94] and that the Jesuit college at Douai had been expressly founded as an alternative to Oxford and Cambridge for 'youths (gentlemen's son's especially)' from 'Grammar Schools in all parts of the realm',[95] it is odd that criticism makes so little of the dramatist's location on this faultline of revolt. One of the fallacies of those who assume, however, that to analyse his real historical situation is to fall into 'an historical novella' is a belief that this is to privilege Shakespeare's situation as unique. But far from 'fictive sensationalism',[96] to locate the writer in this way is to recognize just how characteristic his predicament was of the dilemma which Foucault has defined as a crossroads of modernity, when two roads diverged, 'one which led to the nation states; and the totally different movement of the Counter-Reformation'. At 'the intersection of these two tendencies', it was not, then, only the writer but his entire cohort of contemporaries that was forced to answer Hamlet's question – of whether to be true to self or state – when the oath of allegiance was imposed for university entry in 1580.[97] What bought the issue to a head in the Shakespearean Midlands, of course, was Campion's crusade, and here Simpson's work has been augmented by recent scholars, to confirm how intensely the so-called 'Campionists' dramatized the problem, in Oxford, Prague and Stratford, not least through their leader's own poetry and plays. As Alison Shell observes, it was Campion's six school plays that refined the dialogic form of Jesuit teaching to put the 'conflict between Church and heretical kings' at the core of Catholic education; while his epic poem, written, Gerard Kilroy recounts, as he was 'hesitating which way to jump', compressed Roman history (like *Titus Andronicus*) into a choice between tyranny and martyrdom.[98] Only obliviousness to recusant history prevents critics from realizing that there was nothing 'novelistic', therefore, about this intellectual formation, but that anyone born in the same time and place as Shakespeare would have been presented with the same prospects, and the same existential choice.

Shakespeare's intended future as heir to such a coercive heritage can be conjectured from the instant where Simpson's researches left off, and it points in the direction which has been reconstructed for Donne by scholars such as Arthur Marotti and Dennis Flynn, who have explored how 'the social, political and economic hierarchies of Renaissance England implied a functioning system of patronage', in which 'gentlemen of limited means . . . were especially eager, if not desperate, for success'. In a period when 'almost all literature was a literature of patronage',[99] any writer born into a devoutly recusant lineage like Donne's would have little choice, therefore, than to start out as a dependant of one of the houses of the Catholic nobility; and, in a brilliant piece of detective-work, Flynn has discovered the future Dean of St Paul's at the age of twelve listed as a page in the entourage of the then most powerful papist patron, Henry Stanley, Earl of Derby and the only man in England, apart from the monarch, entitled to call himself – by virtue of his sovereignty of the Isle of Man – a king. Donne's entrée into the household of the 'King of Lancashire', Flynn shows, was through family connections, but the climb he made was in line with the clearing system organized when the university oath, and the policy of taking boys away from recusant homes as 'School Hostages', forced Catholic nobles to smuggle children, under the cloak of livery, to the Jesuit colleges in the Ardennes. 'At a time when passage out of England was carefully scrutinized and unlicensed travel was forbidden', this ploy had the advantage, Flynn observes, that a boy such as 'young Donne did not have to crouch furtively behind barrels and parcels on a channel packet'; and so it was that in January 1585 the poet was one of fifty 'gentlemen giving their attendance' on the Earl, in a retinue of '220 avid fellow travellers . . . most of them unofficial hangers-on', who sailed with Derby on an embassy to France.[100] And when the ambassador returned in March, Donne was among those who duly travelled onwards to Antwerp with the Earl's son, William Stanley, before appearing again on the roll of Derby's servants in 1587. From then until his emergence at Court in 1591, 'Donne lived with the Earl and his family at their Lancashire estates in summer . . . and at other times was with the Earl in London', according to Flynn's discoveries.[101] Recoiling from war-torn Antwerp and the violence and ruse of the seminaries, Donne returned to Lord Derby's petty court to begin on a different trajectory; and this change of itinerary is truly intriguing, because it was as a player attached to the Stanley household that Shakespeare also surfaced in the capital in the early 1590s, a decade after his sudden departure from Stratford.[102]

'An ardent Catholic might well seek other means for the education of his son' than the two Protestant universities, surmised Dover Wilson in 1932; but, if Shakespeare 'received his education in the service of some great Catholic nobleman', it would also help 'to explain how he became an actor'.[103] The editor was responding not only to Simpson's studies of recusant Stratford but to the fact that the Chamberlain's Men, 'the first London company with which we definitely know Shakespeare to have been associated, was formed . . . around a nucleus of actors who were previously Strange's Men', sponsored by the Stanley heir, Ferdinando, Lord Strange.[104] Like Simpson, Dover Wilson was inferring, in other words, both reasons why the young dramatist was probably pushed towards a Catholic vocation and the way in which he in fact avoided one. That service with the 'Kings of Lancashire' might have been the turning-point which converted Shakespeare from a potential priest to an accredited actor is made the more plausible by the ambivalence of the patrons themselves, who, it was noted, always gave 'good countenance to religion' despite Catholic sympathies, and were proud descendants of the Stanley who won the Tudors the crown by switching sides at Bosworth.[105] Famous turn-coats, the Stanleys were ready to turn again to secure the succession for Ferdinando, as in a mirror-image, the King of tiny Navarre thought Paris (and the throne) 'worth a mass'. This was the strategy Shakespeare seems to have inscribed into *Richard III*, with its opportunistic Stanleys; and *Love's Labour's Lost*, where to succeed, King Ferdinand of Navarre learns to 'vouchsafe one change' (5.2.109–10), thus gently mocking Strange's motto, '*Sans change ma verite*'.[106] The Stanleys, we know, built a plush playhouse at Knowsley near Liverpool, where performances were given by troupes such as the Queen's Men, who in 1589 went straight from there to the King of Scotland; and tradition has it that Shakespeare's early plays were staged in this princely Court theatre.[107] In the comedy Ferdinand calls his Court 'a little academe' (1.1.13), or rival to the universities; and, with talents such as Robert Greene and Thomas Nashe in his pay, his namesake had a similar ambition. As Ernst Honigmann concludes, it was Stanley sponsorship that may therefore explain both Shakespeare's 'lost years' in the 1580s and 'the apparent suddenness of his conquest of the theatrical world'. By 1592 the writer had become 'a dominant figure in the theatre' because he 'enjoyed a very special *social* position in Lord Strange's circle', the theory runs.[108] What this begs, of course, is how the Stratford boy came to be such a favoured beneficiary of England's *de facto* crown prince.

When Campion left Stratford in October 1580 it was not chance that took him north-west to Stanley country, and that the house he made a head-quarters of his campaign was the stronghold of one of Lord Derby's most important Lancashire allies, Alexander Hoghton of Hoghton Tower, near Preston. Intermarried not only with neighbouring recusant gentry but also with a Cheshire branch of the Ardens, the Hoghtons controlled an international operation based on the mining of alum (used in John Shakespeare's business of wool-combing), with an outpost in Antwerp overseen by Thomas, head of the dynasty, who had chosen exile in 1570, after the suppression of the Catholic Northern Rising. He would be buried beside the altar at Douai, where most of his fortune had been donated to fund the college. This had actually been planned at Hoghton in 1565, during a stay by its first President, Thomas's cousin, William, later Cardinal Allen – possibly *en route* from a stint as a master at Stratford Grammar School. Whether or not the Allen paid by John Shakespeare for 'teaching the children' in 1564–65 was the same man as the principal of Douai, as is claimed,[109] some association seems to have been made between the school and Lancashire sponsors at this time, as Allen's successor was John Acton, who joined the Northern Rising, while *his* successor was a Lancastrian, Walter Roche; as was Simon Hunt, who left for Douai; John Cottam; and also his replacement, when he retired to Lancashire after Campion's arrest, Alexander Aspinall.[110] Thus, over sixty years, four (and possibly six) of Stratford's schoolmasters were from Lancashire, the only exception being Thomas Jenkins, in 1575–79. But Jenkins was also the most closely linked to Campion, having been a Fellow of St John's, Oxford, the hotbed of the 'Campionists' where the martyr was a Fellow, and where the Marian founders had taken precautions to preserve the Catholic tradition.[111] Most telling, however, are the facts that Aspinall (to whom Shakespeare gave a ribald poem with a wedding present) was from Clitheroe, close to Hoghton, and a family long employed by the Hoghtons; while the Cottams, it emerges, were from nearby Tarnacre, and Hoghton tenants. We owe this last vital piece of the jigsaw to Honigmann, whose 1985 book *Shakespeare: The 'Lost Years'* established conclusively that if Shakespeare did not go north to Hoghton Tower, to prepare for the crossing to Douai, then there was nowhere in England that his family, friends and teachers would have been more likely to send him.[112]

'Though as Ben Jonson says of him, that he had but little Latin and less Greek, he understood Latin pretty well, for he had been in his younger years a schoolmaster in the country': John Aubrey's famous anecdote about Shakespeare's 'lost years' had the authority, the antiquarian asserted, of William, son of Christopher Beeston, an actor in the dramatist's company; but it was only during the twentieth century that it came to seem corroborated by a set of independent traditions that the writer spent a period of his youth in north-west England: at Knowsley, Rufford (seat of the Hesketh family), Hoghton and even the Hoghton manor of Ashton in Cheshire.[113] The idea that Shakespeare might have lived for up to a decade attached to a series of aristocratic houses in the Duchy of Lancaster, starting at Hoghton Tower around 1580, and graduating, via Rufford, to the Earl of Derby's Players, has prompted the question, however, why 'someone whose talent was so enormous', as Peter Levi objected, 'would drift into private service in obscure Lancashire'.[114] One answer was supplied by Campion, whose time at Hoghton may have coincided exactly with Shakespeare's,[115] when he said he retreated to the Tower 'because there was more hope to find there books' to help in his battle with the Church of England.[116] The mansion was furnished with a sufficient library, in other words, for both Allen and Campion to make it an alternative college; and the possibility that Shakespeare had access to this resource was raised in 1940 by the discovery of a copy of Hall's *Chronicle*, annotated with what look like notes for his plays in the dramatist's hand, which the bookseller Alan Keen traced back to Campion's host Alexander Hoghton.[117] Keen's attribution of the marginalia to Shakespeare is unprove; but the three hundred Hoghton volumes preserved at Cartmel Priory (and now deposited at Lancaster University) are enough to justify Campion's boast that he had consulted there all the classical and Renaissance authors he required. Like many Lancashire gentry, the Hoghtons also had a tradition of maintaining players; and, though they mislaid their own Shakespeare Folio in 1639, they seem to have compiled a manuscript collection that contains a text of his second sonnet, inserted a decade before it was printed.[118] As Honigmann infers, it might be this interest in Shakespeare which explains why one of the earliest reports of his work was written by another Hoghton protégé, John Weever, in a 1599 book of *Epigrams* on the family circle, dedicated to Sir Richard Hoghton, the inheritor of the Tower who conformed and acted in court masques, where the playwright is defended as one who has likewise exchanged his religion for the devotions of the stage:

> Honey-tongued Shakespeare, when I saw thy issue
> I swore Apollo got them and none other,
> Their rosy-tainted features cloth'd in tissue,
> Some heaven-born goddess said to be their mother:
> Rose-cheek'd *Adonis* with his amber tresses;
> Fair fire-hot *Venus* charming him to love her;
> Chaste *Lucretia*, virgin-like her dresses;
> Proud lust-stung *Tarquin* seeking still to prove her;
> *Romeo*; *Richard*; more whose names I know not.
> Their sugar'd tongues and power-attractive beauty
> Say they are Saints, although that Saints they show not,
> For thousands vow to them subjective duty.
>   They burn in love: thy children, *Shakespeare*, heat them.
>   Go, woo thy Muse: more nymphish brood beget them.[119]

Weever's epigram '*Ad Gulielmum Shakespeare*' (preceding one to the actor-manager Edward Alleyn, whose mother was a Towneley relation of the family) is the best evidence we have that the playwright was not only a beneficiary of the Hoghtons but socialized with them, published as it was in a book devoted to the 'worthy name of Hoghton' and the 'gold-gilded tower', and consisting of a cycle of tributes to Hoghton connections and kin. And Honigmann points out that a tantalizing aspect of this poem is that it is the only one in Weever's book in the form of a Shakespearean sonnet, implying that 'he had seen a manuscript of the "sugared sonnets among his private friends" ... when only "private friends" could have understood the significance'.[120] This may have been the Hoghton compilation; but mention of performances of *Romeo and Juliet* and *Richard III* raises other intriguing questions. Since Weever, a poor relation of the Hoghtons from the same parish as the Cottams, came to London, by his account, only after graduating from Cambridge in 1598, it could mean that he saw these acted by Strange's Men in Lancashire. What is arresting about the poem, however, is its imagery, as this turns the theme of procreation from the Sonnets into praise of Shakespeare for begetting with his characters a new cult of 'saints', whose votaries 'burn in love', rather than sectarian flames. Weever would later record the fan-worship of *Julius Caesar*; and his analysis of the 'Shakespeare cult' is a prediction of the Simpson (and Greenblatt) thesis: that in these plays theatre took over from religion, substituting with the audiences who 'vow to them subjective duty', secular saints for martyrs. Shakespeare's creations are the icons of a post-Reformation society, according to Weever; but in slipping from Rome to Romeo, or the stake to the stage, their creator also defected, it is implied, from one idolatory to another. So, if his poems are 'said' to carry hints of the Virgin Mary – 'Some heaven-born goddess' – his dramas will live precisely because Shakespeare preferred playhouse 'heat' to the fires of faith. And the final exhortation, 'Go, woo thy muse', does read as if issued from Hoghton, where in 1617 James I would declare his *Book of Sports*, in a definitive act of political relaxation. Weever's book is witness to the quietism of his Lancastrian backers, in living down their savage fundamentalist past, and it commends 'Honey-tongued Shakespeare' among them, as a survivor who has put the Campion catastrophe behind him, by surrendering Mary for Apollo. Itself testimony to the piety which drew the Elizabethan 'saints' to Lancashire, this text is 'sworn' evidence that, if Shakespeare came north with them, the experience of their holy war was traumatic enough to convert him to the god of poetry, 'and none other'.

'I swore Apollo got them and none other': Weever's oath, sworn on the plays as if on the Bible, is proof both that the dramatist needed to be defended, in 1599, from suspicions of Catholic sympathy, and that he had in fact disavowed the faith of his father. So, coming from inside the Hoghton circle, this mock-deposition associates Shakespeare with the programme of rehabilitation that seems to be the motive of the *Epigrams*, and was so imperative for those who had welcomed the Jesuit mission. For, thanks to Simpson, we know that Campion had visited recusant homes across the Dales as far as Whitby, where the Cholmeleys controlled the port, organizing a chain of safe-houses, through which priests could pass to and from the Continent, disguised as servants or tutors. And this was the time, recalled by locals for years, when 'persons of quality spent whole nights in barns so they might be early next day to his sermon'; and when, as Evelyn Waugh enthused, 'the rich rhetoric that had stirred the lecture halls of Oxford and Douai, Rome, Prague and Rheims, rang through the summer dawn'.[121] Noting how his 'small Latin' was learned in a milieu dominated by the Jesuit, 'Shakespeare's rhetoric', opined T. W. Baldwin, 'is grandson to Campion's'; but the influence may have been yet closer, if the boy accompanied his teachers to Lancashire.[122] Echoes of 'the old hermit of Prague' (*Twelfth Night* 4.2.11) have been detected throughout the plays, as when Hermione repeats his protest on being indicted for treason, that

> Since what I am to say must be but that
> Which contradicts my accusation, and
> The testimony on my part no other
> But what comes from myself, it shall scarce boot me
> To say "Not guilty".   (*Winter's Tale* 3.2.20)

Thus, whether or not he was himself at Hoghton, the 'pastoral' mission from Bohemia clearly sank deep into Shakespeare's memory. But after nine months disaster struck, when Campion was arrested on a journey south. On 31 July 1581 the priest was racked in the Tower of London to implicate his hosts in conspiracy. On 3 August his London protector, the Earl of Southampton (father of Shakespeare's patron), therefore made his will, knowing this was his death sentence. That very day, so did Alexander Hoghton, with the same motive of fencing property and defending retainers. And on 4 August officers raided their houses, as well as Lapworth in Warwickshire, arresting everyone named by Campion. By the time that the priest was executed in December, Hoghton and the Earl had both, of course, died in detention. But Alexander's will, signed in such a dire emergency, has become one of the most quoted of all the documents that point to an interlude in a 'Bohemian' wool country for the author of *The Winter's Tale*:

> Item. It is in my mind that the said Thomas Hoghton . . . my brother shall have all my instruments belonging to the musics, and all manner of play clothes if he be minded to keep and do keep players. And if he will not keep and maintain players, then it is in my mind and will that Sir Thomas Hesketh knight shall have the same instruments and plays clothes. And I most heartily require the said Sir Thomas to be friendly unto Fulk Gillam and William Shakeshafte now dwelling with me, and either to take them into his service, or else to help them to some good master, as my trust is he will.[123]

When it was reproduced by E. K. Chambers in his survey of *The Elizabethan Stage* in 1923, Alexander Hoghton's will simply struck theatre historians as a window on to the cultural life of the northern nobility, and a glimpse of the route by which performers might be passed from one patron

Holding still

Dept of Psychology
Trinity & All Saints University College
Brownberrie Lane
Horsforth
Leeds
LS18
0113 2837484

to another.[124] But knowing now that Campion had been staying at Hoghton, we can also read this document as indicating that the theatrical perform- ances which the Jesuit had personally directed as recently as the previous summer in Bohemia continued to be a part of his curriculum. By the time of his mission, as Shell relates, Campion had developed a tragi-comedic dramaturgy involving resurrection of saints and salvage of lost fortunes that made it peculiarly apt for English Catholics. 'Comedy, in all its senses', Shell reflects, 'was perhaps easier for the first generation of Jesuits', and the endings of Campion's plays are, 'in worldly terms, brilliantly optimistic'.[125] But though written for schoolboys, these theatricals were technically ambi- tious and composed in Latin. To stage any of them at Hoghton would have required at least some of the resources Campion had exploited in the Prague of Rudolf II. So, this could be why Fulk Gillam and his father Thomas were added to the staff some time after July 1580 (when Alexander drafted an earlier list of servants that did not mention them). For the Gillams were a highly qualified firm of theatre costumiers and stage-managers, who had organized Chester civic pageants for generations, and one of whose members would become the foremost Jacobean authority on heraldry.[126] They had no reason to be at Hoghton except as masters of revels. And Campion's theatrical demands might also be why another 'servant' rewarded in Alexander's will was none other than the Stratford school- master John Cottam. His expertise would be valuable for coaching actors in dialogue; and, once again, it is hard to see why a Latin tutor would be taken on, unless for such a purpose. Perhaps he brought with him the pick of his pupils. In any case, during these months when Hoghton became home to a famous dramatist, a team of stage technicians and an ardent Catholic educator, the household furnished them with musical instruments, 'all manner of play clothes', and, Honigmann notes, 'an ideal place for the- atrical performances', in its Great Hall, with 'a minstrels' gallery for an upper stage, and an acting area below'.[127] Designed like a college, Hoghton had stood waiting for such a use since the exile of its builder a decade before; but, if it now saw the production of a 'comedy' such as Campion's *Ambrosia*, with its 'sweet rhetoric' of 'martyrdom exhumed or risked and averted',[128] the question that arises is: what part in these preparations was taken by that other house guest listed, among all the cloaks and recorders, as a companion of the players from Chester? And who was William Shakeshafte?

The realization that the William Shakeshafte said by the master of Hoghton to be 'now dwelling with me' might have been the seventeen-year- old William Shakespeare, temporarily accommodated in the household, struck Chambers, it seems, only after it had been mooted in 1937 by a Strat- ford archivist, Oliver Baker.[129] In 1944, however, he published a key essay in the evolution of the 'Lancastrian Shakespeare' theory, which plotted for the first time a possible itinerary which would have taken a young actor from Warwickshire to London, *via* the Earl of Derby's household. Since Alexander had bequeathed his brother his costumes and instruments with the proviso that 'if he will not keep and maintain players' they would pass to Sir Thomas Hesketh; and had also asked his neighbour either to take the younger Gillam and Shakeshafte into service, 'or else to help them to some good master'; and as Hesketh was known, from the Derby *Household Books*, to have brought his players to the Earl's houses, Chambers reasoned that 'If William Shakeshafte passed from the service of Alexander Hoghton into that of either Thomas Hoghton or Sir Thomas Hesketh, he might very easily have gone on into that of Lord Strange, and so later into the London theatrical world'.[130] It was with this speculation that the case for the Hoghton connection rested for forty years, until Honigmann's demonstration that John Cottam was also a Hoghton beneficiary, and long-time business associate of the family. *Shakespeare: The 'Lost Years'* failed to follow up on the Clitheroe roots and Hoghton ties of Alexander Aspinall (the one Stratford schoolmaster with whom we know the dramatist was definitely acquainted); but it did clinch Shakespeare's links with the Heskeths, showing how closely they were related to his fellow Globe trustee Thomas Savage, a native of Rufford; and mooted other associations with the Stanleys, for whom the poet may have composed epitaphs and even *The Phoenix and the Turtle*.[131] After Honigmann's exposition, it was impossible for Shakespeareans to ignore the 'Lancashire' thesis, and in the 1990s this became a talking-point of a whole series of biographies.[132] Yet in their hunt for a 'smoking gun' they all exaggerated the importance of the Hoghton will, which is an additional but inessential piece of evidence. So it was telling that not one mentioned the name of Richard Simpson. What they ignored, in other words, was the overwhelming weight of the Campion connection, and the very reasons why young Shakespeare might have travelled to Hoghton, when he is supposed to have done, to stay in the same household as the leader of the outlawed Jesuit mission.

If Shakespeare was 'Shakeshafte', he would have done what everybody committed to Campion was required to do, which was to adopt a new name as the sign of his vocation. This was no ruse, but a token of conversion. As the priest (himself called Hastings after the battle) explained, it was like Saul's change to Paul.[133] Critics who object that if Shakespeare wished to hide his identity he 'could have thought of a better alias' than 'Shakeshafte' miss the point, then, of this Jesuit ritual, which was tantamount to altering names on entering a seminary.[134] They also miss the possible significance of the slightness of the shift from a secular 'spear' to the pilgrim's 'shaft', and the sly reservation that this convert would 'shake' in his allegiance. But then, it was only ever 'a short step', as Gary Taylor contends, from Campion, Parsons, Allen and Southwell to Shakespeare;[135] and the name Shakeshafte has become a signifier of this distance. To step from Shakespeare to Shakeshafte requires a leap of faith, as it would have done for the boy from Stratford. On one side is the mass of evidence connecting almost everyone in his Warwickshire world, including his teachers and father, with the 1580 mission which ended so tragically at Hoghton; and, on the other, the fact that the first we hear of the writer is when he emerges a decade later in the theatre company from Knowsley. Tantalizing possibilities continue to emerge from Lancashire (suggesting, for example, that the Gillams had dealings with the Hathaways; and, less plausibly, that a glover named John Shakeshafte in the Preston records, whose son was called William, may be the Stratford burgess), but the gap remains unbridged. No one has worked to close it more assiduously, however, than the Jesuit Father Peter Milward, whose 1973 book *Shakespeare's Religious Background* was the first, as Honigmann acknowledges, 'to recognise how all the "Lancashire" clues in Shakespeare's biography support one another'.[136] From this structure Milward leaps across in later work to the conclusion that the plays themselves propagate Jesuit and papal doctrines, and he remains the most ardent opponent of the 'apostasy' consensus, that Shakespeare lapsed from Rome.[137] Few would jump to Milward's absolutism, and his critical isolation on the further side of faith resembles that of Ted Hughes, who also argued, in *Shakespeare and the Goddess of Complete Being*, for a 'Marian' interpretation of the plays from a position of indifference to the nuances of Elizabethan compromise.[138] However far down the route pointed by Simpson they venture, most commentators see Lancashire as, in the words of a 1958 study, 'Shakespeare's religious frontier', a virtual vanishing-point where something decisive for Shakespearean theatre might have happened, but beyond which it is impossible to go.[139]

'Exit, pursued by a bear' (*Winter's Tale* S.D. 3.3.66): considering how close Shakespeare might have come to Campion's Bohemian calamity, his most famous stage direction could be decoded as symbolic of the fate that devoured so many émigrés who followed Antigonus (the name of the mythical ferryman at Antwerp), pursued by the Earl of Leicester, the terror of Catholic exiles (whose emblem, was, of course, a bear).[140] In 1577 Campion wrote from Prague to Robert Arden, a Jesuit operating near Stratford who is thought to have been related to Mary Arden, to encourage recruits to sail for 'the pleasant and blessed shore of Bohemia'. So, if Shakespeare headed for Lancashire it may well have been as a stage towards taking the imperial road, *via* Antwerp, to 'Places remote enough' from persecution 'in Bohemia' (30).[141] As Bossy shows, that would have been one of the routes frequented by Catholics fleeing Elizabethan justice.[142] To original audiences of *The Winter's Tale*, 'fair Bohemia' (4.1.21) might, indeed, have been code for the land of Campion, and the 'barque' which travels there identifiable as the Church of Rome (3.3.8). But if so, what is striking about the play is how the rack and wreck this exit spells for the old lord are kept off-stage, when the horror as 'the bear tore out his shoulder-bone' is laughed away, along with 'the most piteous cry of the poor souls' in the sinking ship

(85–9). As Greene laments, how distant such laughter seems from the blood
and violence of the torture chamber. So remote, in fact, as to verge on hys-
teria. For as Scott Wilson remarks in a critique of Shakespearean poetics,
the torment and dismemberment of 'Catholic priests and plotters' were not,
in reality, so easily turned 'To laughter' (2.2.200), and, far from being
banished from his text by the suave ambiguous poet, 'the language of
treason, rack, torture, and confession' was constitutive of his literary personality. Thus, in the Sonnets, Wilson finds, the 'truth' of Shakespeare's
discourse is extracted from a subject position which is expressly that of
a victim of the rack, the poet's hypothetical destiny as a Catholic martyr
framing confessions ripped from him by a torturer who might otherwise
well tear out his shoulder-bone. This is, of course (as Simpson saw), a paradigm of Shakespeare's essential scenario, where an authority determined
to know how 'thy heart goes' (*King Lear* 1.1.104) confronts an equal determination that 'You cannot, if my heart were in your hand' (*Othello*
3.3.167). And Wilson connects its macabre *mise en scène*, in which 'an
amorous subject is racked as cruel chastity tears at fleshly desire', directly
to the sadistic power relations enacted by her Rackmaster on the papist
prisoners of the Queen:

> In these texts sexual, political and religious differences are collapsed into
> oppositional relations of fear ... The unconstitutional activity of torture was
> written as part of beauty's power ... [and] Shakespeare's sequence fully
> exploits the dark side of the convention. In these sonnets 'beauty herself is
> black' [Sonnet 132]; she is mendacious, immoral and foul. Dark beauty
> imprisons and tortures the hearts of subjects after they have been caught in
> snares ... This dark mistress is both the architect of crime and its jailer; she
> has the keys to the state prison and the means to adopt 'rigour' in pursuit of
> allegiance. The legal and moral ambiguity of this 'Petrarchan' heroine, who
> 'swears she is made of truth' and yet consistently lies [138], is a very dan-
> gerous notion to a Queen who wished to be written into the convention
> herself.[143]

As 'English state torture was strictly speaking illegal', and thereby 'constituted one of sovereign beauty's blacker shadows', Wilson proposes,
Shakespeare was able to construct an oppositional voice as a martyr 'racked
on a tyrant's bed', the subject of a dark monarchy that exercised its cruel
privileges in a 'twilight area' of denial. Thus, when the Rackmaster assured
victims that 'torture was so slowly begun, so unwillingly, and with so many
preparations', as to prove the Queen's mercy, the poet could do as the Jesuits
did, and turn this hypocrisy into a celebration of Elizabeth's 'gracious
clemency', even as 'limbs were extended and joints began to crack'.
Shakespeare's poetry was an exercise in political irony, on this view, which
turned state terror upon itself, by glorifying the torture chamber as a scene
of such gratifying pain.[144] This analysis, so similar to Simpson's, could be

applied to the negative dialectics of his stage, where it also seems pleasure exacts pain, and there is ironic complicity between the 'rack' that tears scenery apart (*Hamlet* 2.2.471) and the mechanics of dismemberment when the other type of 'rack dislimns' the human body piece by piece, until it cannot hold its 'visible shape' (*Antony* 4.15.10–14). Shakespeare's potential fate as a Catholic martyr haunts these dramas (if the Foucauldian reading holds) as the negative against which he could define his project to dissolve the illusions of power and 'Leave not a rack behind' (*Tempest* 4.1.156). He uses the pun, that is to say, to turn the 'rack' against itself. Certainly, the image of heavens 'separated with racking clouds' (*3 Henry VI* 2.1.27), or riven by 'ugly rack' (Sonnet 33), recurs in his work as a figure for deconstruction; as does derision for 'rackers of orthography' (*Love's* 5.2.818); compassion for 'a man new-haled from the rack' (*1 Henry VI* 2.5.3); and, above all, contempt for 'wheels, racks, fires, boiling / In leads and oils' (*Winter's Tale* 3.2.173). So, though we may never know whether he met Campion, we can guess how much he hated 'him . . . That would upon the rack of this tough world / Stretch him out longer' (*Lear* 5.3.312). Shakespeare had reason to fear to 'speak upon the rack, / Where men enforced do speak anything' (*Merchant* 3.2.32), if he was as close as appears to those who later venerated the amputated thumb of the 'pilot' of the 1580 mission, 'racked as homeward he did come' to England (*Macbeth* 1.3.26). But out of this great wreck he salvaged the rack of his own stage.

The Catholic martyrs went to their deaths, cried Southwell on the scaffold, like 'God Almighty's fools'.[145] The figure of the holy fool was Christ's own, but in the Reformation its perversity had been praised by Erasmus, and personified by his dedicatee, the foremost Tudor martyr, Thomas More, whose very name was an anagram of *Rome* and the Latin (*morus*) for fool. More's symbol was a mulberry (from *morum*), which Patricia Parker sees implicit in the fate of Thisbe, 'tarrying in mulberry shade' (*Dream* 5.1.147), and Desdemona, 'sighing by a sycamore' (*Othello* 4.3.38).[146] And since the martyr's crest was a moor, it may be that 'The Tragedy of the Moor' criticizes those who preserved his relics, such as his handkerchief, with the credulity that made Othello such a 'fool, fool, fool!' (5.2.307). Certainly, it is telling that Shakespeare associated martyrdom with this 'moron' in the one text where he speaks directly about those 'fools' who fall into the trap of 'thralled discontent / Whereto th'inviting time our fashion calls'. The disavowal in Sonnet 124 of 'the fools of time' who put their heads on the block by opposing 'fortune's bastard', when they might have lived to see 'the child of state . . . unfathered', would be as close as Shakespeare got to confessing membership of a 'fashion', or expressing a view on the 'bastard' issue of Anne Boleyn. Quoting Campion, his devotion, he insists, is beyond the kind of 'accident' that swept up saints and sinners in the Tyburn harvest, as 'Weeds among weeds or flowers or flowers with flowers gathered'. Instead, he affirms his faith as a house 'built far' from the reach of 'policy, that heretic' – unlike the mansions of those who 'suffer . . . in smiling pomp', or the ruins bequeathed by conspirators. The imagery of recusant fines and confiscation could hardly be more specific, though denial of the poet's historical situation has long obscured this text. Shakespeare may not have exactly shared the 'seigneurial quietism' which hoped to wear out 'packs and sects of great ones / That ebb and flow by th' moon' (*King Lear* 5.3.17), and that took English Catholicism (in Bossy's phrase) 'from inertia to inertia in three generations',[147] but it cannot be chance that his own spiritual testament should be made here through the metaphor of a towering house, standing 'all alone' in its secluded isolation and 'hugely politic'. Nor that the evidence that this 'repudiation of all politics' was itself deeply *politique* should be the ghostly testimony of those holy idiots whose very saintliness pushed them into the crime of treason and the limbo from which, so it seems, Shakespeare cannot quite yet release them with his prayers:

> To this I witness call the fools of time
> Which die for goodness, who have lived for crime.   (*Sonnet* 124)

The trouble with Shakespeare for modern criticism, according to Terry Eagleton, is his unstoppable loquacity, even as he gives nothing of himself away.[148] Or, as the historian Blair Worden exclaims, while the relations between art and life are always problematic, 'there can be no other writer since the invention of printing for whom we are unable to demonstrate any relationship at all'.[149] These complaints were made, however, in obliviousness of the research begun by Simpson, the point of which has been to historicize such apparent contradictions. This is not the same as inferring a mystery from Shakespeare's silence, or aligning him with Catholicism on the Jesuitical grounds that the evidence for this is hidden. To try to 'pluck out the heart' (*Hamlet* 3.2.336) of Shakespeare's identity in that way would be like the attempts made by the torturers to prise open the consciences of the condemned: prisoners such as the priest Cottam, the brother of the Stratford schoolmaster, who protested at the 'barbarous, inhumane question' put to him about his sins by the 'searchers of secrets'. As Wilson comments, 'it is a strange knowledge' which prefers to learn 'the secrets of the conscience' to the 'whereabouts of plotters, wanted Jesuits, and safe houses'.[150] For what Cottam gave the rackmen, of course, is the information we possess, thanks to his interrogation, about Campion's operations in the circles of his brother; the protection arranged for them at the Arden, Catesby, Somerville and Throckmorton houses in Warwickshire; the preparations to receive them in Lancashire; and the network that had taken so many other zealots, such as Debdale, from Shottery and Snitterfield to Italy or Bohemia. If critics remained for so long in denial about this material, that might be because, as Foucault wrote, it took Islamic revolution to remind the West that in the sixteenth century it too 'wanted to inscribe the figures of spirituality on the earth of politics'. Only now, with the return of a religious fundamentalism driven by the belief that martyrs dying in a *jihad* attain paradise, while their enemies go to eternal damnation, has it become possible, perhaps, to take seriously evidence of sectarian warfare in this author's background, or to analyse 'the labour he had to accomplish, both against these determinations and thanks to them, to produce himself as . . . the *subject* of his own creation'.[151] Shakespeare's creative autonomy is, without doubt, an evident fact, and one of the foundations of a formalist aesthetic. But only a formalist would continue to discount the equally evident fact of his religious contexts. The 'Lancastrian Shakespeare' hypothesis might be said to be the logical attempt to account for these two facts in relation to each other.

The chapters in this book were all given in sessions on 'Region and Religion' at the conference on 'Lancastrian Shakespeare' at Hoghton Tower and the University of Lancaster in July 1999. Each takes up the challenge posed when Richard Simpson first raised the issue of Shakespeare and the martyrs, and each reflects the urgency of this debate in Shakespeare studies. At no other academic gathering, Stephen Greenblatt stated in the closing lecture, had he 'experienced so much excitement and passion'. In the BBC *Newsnight* report on the event that evening he proposed that this was because 'for so long we had talked of Shakespearean England as a monolith', and what the conference marked was the belated admission that 'this was something we all knew not to be the case. This was half a century of violent spiritual upheaval.' Likewise, Katherine Duncan Jones was 'delighted to be caught up in something' that was 'generating so much debate'; and Robert Miola commented that 'though the fact of Shakespeare's stay at Hoghton remains tantalising but unproven', the conference had shown how 'we will read his plays differently if we attend to their Catholic subtexts'. The biographer Anthony Holden contended, however, that it was Shakespeare's 'Hoghton period' which was the spur to his 'life-long identification with the underdog', and that, though 'his faith failed', it was the start of a career of resistance to the Elizabethan system; while Philippa Berry argued that it was the resourcefulness of recusant women which fired the courage of Shakespeare's heroines. Above all, Gary Taylor told viewers, what the conference demonstrated was that 'Shakespeare was a European. There was no way he could be otherwise. This was a culture in constant contact with the Europe of the Counter-Reformation.'[152] In short, the Shakespeare who emerged from the 'Lancastrian' conference was spectacularly unlike the Anglocentric Bard of Protestant power despised by feminist and post-colonial critics but still celebrated at Stratford. It is true that this new 'Lancastrian Shakespeare' looked highly dramatic; yet what inspired the delegates was not some swashbuckling romance of secret masses, priest-holes and informers, but the intellectual break with the xenophobe, misogynistic and imperialist 'Royal Shakespeare' of Hollywood cliché. For though the startling idea that he was born and brought up not 'in love' but *in hate* for Elizabeth and her empire remains only a hypothesis, there can be few theories with a greater potential for transforming the way we see and study Shakespeare.

Notes

1 Richard Simpson, 'The politics of shakespeare's historical plays', *The New Shakspere Society's Transactions*, 2 (1874), pp. 396–441; Gary Taylor, 'Forms of opposition: Shakespeare and Middleton', *English Literary Renaissance*, 24:2 (1994), p. 303.

2 Richard Simpson, 'The political use of the stage in Shakespere's time', *The New Shakspere Society's Transactions*, 2 (1874), pp. 371–95, here pp. 371–2.

3 Simpson, 'Politics', p. 396.

4 Simpson, 'Political use', pp. 371–2.

5 *Ibid.*, p. 395.

6 Richard Simpson, 'The early authorship of Shakespeare', *North British Review*, 52 (1870), p. 92.

7 Pierre Bourdieu, *The Rules of Art: Genesis and Structure of the Literary Field*, trans. Susan Emmanuel (Cambridge, 1996), p. 104.

8 Simpson, 'Political use', pp. 393–4.

9 Richard Simpson, *The School of Shakespeare* (London, 1878), vol. 1, prospectus; 'Early authorship', p. 91.

10 Bourdieu, *Rules of Art*, p. 111.

11 Richard Simpson, letter to Lord Acton, 16 September 1874, in *Correspondence of Lord Acton and Richard Simpson*, ed. Josef Altholz, Damian McElrath and James Holland (Cambridge, 1975), vol. 3: 316.

12 Richard Simpson, letter to Lord Acton, 3 September 1874, *ibid.*, p. 315.

13 Simpson, 'Politics', pp. 440–1.

14 David Carroll, *Richard Simpson as Critic* (London, 1977), p. 44.

15 Simpson, 'Political use', pp. 377, 395.

16 Quoted approvingly by Samuel Schoenbaum as being a 'point made' by Arnold (in his sonnet 'Shakespeare') 'for his own age and all time', *Shakespeare's Lives* (Oxford, 1970), p. 474.

17 Simpson, 'Political use', p. 377.

18 Pierre Bourdieu, 'Intellectual field and creative project' (originally published as 'Champ intellectuel et projet createur', *Les Temps Modernes* (November 1966), pp. 865–906), trans. Sian France, in *Knowledge and Control: New Directions for the Sociology of Education*, ed. Michael Young (London, 1971), p. 162.

19 Carroll, *Richard Simpson*, p. 16. Compare the similarly daunted reaction of literary critics to the challenge of Bourdieu's historically grounded research, as discussed by Toril Moi in 'The challenge of the particular case: Bourdieu's sociology of culture and literary criticism', *Modern Language Quarterly*, 58:4 (1997), pp. 497–508.

20 Kiernan Ryan, 'Insomnia and the curse of the Bard's biographers', *Sunday Independent*, 14 November 1999.

21 Anonymous (Christopher Knight Watson), 'Was Shakespeare a Roman Catholic?', *The Edinburgh Review*, 123 (1866), pp. 146–85, esp. pp. 184–5.

22 *Ibid.*, p. 160.

23 Alexandra Walsham, *Church Papists: Catholicism, Conformity and Confessional in Early Modern England* (Woodbridge, 1993), p. 85.

24 Memorandum of Richard Davies (c.1688–1708) reproduced in E. K. Chambers, *William Shakespeare* (2 vols, Oxford, 1930), vol. 2: 255–7.

25 A recent example of the same bad faith is the Thersites-like excoriation of 'The canonisation of the Catholic Shakespeare' by Michael Davies in *Cahiers Elisabethains*, 58 (2000), pp. 31–47, which never discloses what is, in fact, revealed in the journal's notes on contributors: that the author's 'research interests currently focus on the relationship between Calvinism and English literature, particularly in the drama of William Shakespeare'.

26 Richard Simpson, 'Was Shakespeare a Catholic?', *The Rambler*, 2 (1854), p. 21; 'What was the religion of Shakespeare? I', *The Rambler*, 9 (1858), p. 179; Damian McElrath, 'Richard Simpson on Shakespeare', *Dublin Review*, 509 (1966), p. 268.

27 Simpson, 'Politics', p. 440.

28 *Ibid.*

29 Richard Simpson, letter to Lord Acton, 1 January 1874, *Correspondence*, p. 312; Samuel Gardiner quoted in Damian McElrath, *Richard Simpson, 1820–1876: A Study in XIXth Century English Liberal Catholicism* (Louvain, 1972), p. 115.

30 Simpson, 'Was Shakespeare a Catholic?', p. 21.

31 Schoenbaum, *Shakespeares's Lines*, pp. 459–60.

32 Simpson, 'Was Shakespeare a Catholic?', pp. 23–4.

33 John Carey, *John Donne: Life, Mind and Art* (London, 1981), pp. 25, 27, 35, 59.

34 Simpson, 'Was Shakespeare a Catholic?', p. 19.

35 Christopher Hill, 'Society and Andrew Marvell', in *Puritanism and Revolution: Studies in Interpretation of the English Revolution of the Seventeenth Century* (Harmondsworth, 1958), pp. 324–50.

36 Simpson, 'Was Shakespeare a Catholic?', pp. 20, 22.

37 *Ibid.*, pp. 21, 23.

38 *Calendar of State Papers Domestic, 1581–1590*, p. 126: 'Examinations of diverse persons taken before John Doyle of Merton touching certain speeches against the Queen's Majesty supposed to have been spoken by John Somerville.'

39 Simpson, 'What was the religion of Shakespeare? I', pp. 183–5.

40 *Calendar of State Papers Domestic, 1581–1590*, p. 126: 31 October 1583, 'Articles to be administered to John Somerfield touching his design for the taking away of H. M.'s life by discharging a dagg at her person . . . John Somerfield's answer to the above articles'; transcript of Somerville's confession quoted in full in Simpson, 'What was the religion of Shakespeare? I', pp. 181–2; Charlotte Carmichael Stopes, *Shakespeare's Warwickshire Contemporaries*, revised edn (Stratford-upon-Avon, 1907), pp. 76, 81.

41 *Calendar of State Papers Domestic, 1581–1590*, p. 129: 5 November 1583.

42 Simpson, 'What was the religion of Shakespeare? I', p. 186.

43 Simpson, 'What was the religion of Shakespeare? III', *The Rambler*, 9 (1858), p. 303.
44 Simpson, 'What was the religion of Shakespeare? I', p. 187.
45 *Ibid.*
46 'What was the religion of Shakespeare? II', *The Rambler*, 9 (1858), p. 236.
47 Quoted from the printed version of the 'Spiritual Testament' reproduced in Samuel Schoenbaum, *William Shakespeare: A Documentary Life* (Oxford, 1975), pp. 44–5.
48 Simpson, 'What was the religion of Shakespeare? II', p. 248.
49 Schoenbaum, *William Shakespeare*, p. 46.
50 David Ellis, 'Biography and Shakespeare: an outsider's view', *The Cambridge Quarterly*, 29:4 (2000), p. 301.
51 Simpson, 'What was the religion of Shakespeare? II', p. 247.
52 Patrick Collinson, 'William Shakespeare's religious inheritance and environment', in *Elizabethan Essays* (London, 1994), pp. 246–7; Antonia Fraser, *The Gunpowder Plot: Treason and Faith in 1605* (London, 1996), p. 114; John E. Neale, *The Elizabethan House of Commons* (Harmondsworth, 1963), p. 241.
53 Simpson, 'What was the religion of Shakespeare? I', pp. 168–74; Roger Manning, *Village Revolts: Social Protest and Popular Disturbances in England, 1509–1640* (Oxford, 1988), p. 237.
54 Anne Hughes, *Politics, Society and Civil War in Warwickshire: 1620–1660* (Cambridge, 1987), p. 63.
55 Quoted in Richard Simpson, *Edmund Campion: A Biography* (London, 1896), p. 233.
56 John Bossy, 'The social history of confession in the age of the Reformation', *Transactions of the Royal Historical Society*, 25 (1975), pp. 28–31.
57 Christopher Hill, *Intellectual Origins of the English Revolution* (Oxford, 1965), pp. 268–9; John B. Black, *The Reign of Elizabeth, 1558–1603* (Oxford, 1959), p. 377; John E. Neale, *Queen Elizabeth I* (London, 1957), p. 274; Alison Plowden, *Danger to Elizabeth: The Catholics under Elizabeth I* (New York, 1973), p. 204. For a detailed discussion of the Bond see David Cressy, 'Binding the nation: the Bonds of Association, 1584 and 1696', in Dellroyd J. Guth and John W. McKenna (eds), *Tudor Rule and Revolution* (Cambridge, 1982), pp. 218–19, 222–4.
58 Simpson, *Campion*, pp. 205, 222–3.
59 Schoenbaum, *William Shakespeare*, p. 46.
60 Herbert Thurston, 'The Spiritual Testament of John Shakespeare', *The Month* (November 1911), pp. 487–502; and 'a Controverted Shakespeare document', *The Dublin Review* (December 1923), pp. 161–76; James G. McManaway, 'John Shakespeare's "Spiritual Testament"', *Shakespeare Quarterly*, 18 (1967), pp. 197–205.
61 Stephen Greenblatt, *Hamlet in Purgatory* (Princeton, 2001), p. 249.
62 Simpson, 'What was the religion of Shakespeare? II', p. 248.
63 Jonathan Bate, 'No other purgatory but a play', *The Sunday Telegraph*, 8 April 2001.
64 Stephen Greenblatt, *Shakespearean Negotiations* (Oxford, 1990), pp. 10–11, 112–13, 119.
65 Greenblatt, *Hamlet in Purgatory*, esp. pp. 248–61.

66 John Dover Wilson, *What Happens in 'Hamlet'* (Cambridge, 1935), p. 70; James Joyce, *Ulysses*, ed. Declan Kiberd (Harmondsworth, 2000), p. 239.

67 Henry Bowden, *The Religion of Shakespeare* (London, 1899).

68 McElrath, *Richard Simpson*, p. 103; and see Carroll, *Richard Simpson as Critic*, p. 15. Simpson's Shakespeare notes are in Notebook D among his papers in the Library of Downside Abbey.

69 Simpson, 'What was the religion of Shakespeare? III', 303; 'What was the religion of Shakespeare? I', pp. 176–8; 'What was the religion of Shakespeare? II', p. 237.

70 Simpson, 'What was the religion of Shakespeare? I', pp. 170–4; 'What was the religion of Shakespeare? III', p. 319; 'What was the religion of Shakespeare? II', p. 248.

71 Simpson, 'What was the religion of Shakespeare? I', p. 172; Manning, *Village Revolts*, pp. 90–1, 238–9.

72 Simpson, 'What was the religion of Shakespeare? III', p. 303; 'What was the religion of Shakespeare? II', pp. 235–7.

73 Simpson, 'What was the religion of Shakespeare? III', p. 307.

74 Simpson, 'What was the religion of Shakespeare? II', p. 237.

75 Graham Greene, 'Introduction', *John Gerard: The Autobiography of an Elizabethan*, ed. and trans. Philip Caraman (London, 1951), pp. x–xi.

76 Francis Barker, *The Culture of Violence: Essays on Tragedy and History* (Manchester, 1993), p. 191.

77 Simpson, 'What was the religion of Shakespeare? III', p. 307, quoting Henry Chettle, *England's Mourning Garments* (London, 1603).

78 Michel Foucault, 'My body, this paper, this fire', trans. Geoffrey Bennington, in *Michel Foucault: The Essential Works: Aesthetics* (Harmondsworth, 1998), p. 416.

79 Taylor, 'Forms of opposition', p. 298.

80 Christopher Devlin, *The Life of Robert Southwell, Poet and Martyr* (London, 1956), pp. 257–73.

81 For Snitterfield and the ties between the Shakespeares and the Grants, going back three generations, see Mark Eccles, *Shakespeare in Warwickshire* (Madison, 1961), pp. 11, 21, 75.

82 James H. McDonald and Nancy Pollard Brown (eds), *The Poems of Robert Southwell, S.J.* (Oxford, 1967), p. 15.

83 For an account of these pilgrimages, 'via John Grant's house at Norbrook near Stratford, Huddington Court near Worcester, a tavern in Shrewsbury and finally into Wales itself', see Fraser, *The Gunpowder Plot*, pp. 134–9.

84 *Ibid.*, pp. 35, 90.

85 For Trussel see Clara Longworth de Chambrun, *Shakespeare: A Portrait Restored* (London, 1957), pp. 25–6.

86 Richard Simpson to Lord Acton, 21 March 1868, *Correspondence*, pp. 239–40: 'the Essex affair . . . kindled great hopes in the more patriotic Catholics from Essex's promise of toleration . . . Shakespeare was essentially of the Essex faction.' Mervyn James, *Society, Politics and Culture: Studies in Early Modern England* (Cambridge, 1986), pp. 417–18, 426–7, 435–6, 440 n. 87, 459.

87 The performance was by a troupe of actors under the patronage of Richard Cholmeley, a conspirator in the Essex Revolt and a leading Yorkshire recusant,

at Gowthwaite Hall in Nidderdale, a command-post for the 1605 conspiracy and the home of Sir John York, the godfather of the children of the Winter brothers, executed for their part in the Plot. The orphans were present during the performance. E. K. Chambers, *The Elizabethan Stage* (4 vols, Oxford, 1923), vol. 1, pp. 304–5; C. J. Sisson, 'Shakespeare quartos as prompt copies, with some account of Cholmeley's Players and a new Shakespeare allusion', *Review of English Studies*, 18 (1942), pp. 129–43.

88 Taylor, 'Forms of opposition', pp. 313–14.

89 Robert Southwell, 'Life of Brother Edward Throckmorton', ed. Henry Foley, *Records of the English Province of the Society of Jesus* (6 vols, London, 1878), vol. 4, pp. 299, 311; Devlin, *Life of Robert Southwell*, pp. 18–19, 263.

90 Quoted, *ibid.*, p. 21.

91 Historic Manuscripts Commission, Salisbury Mss., vol. 16, p. 33: 30 January 1604.

92 Edgar Fripp suggests that Debdale's great-aunt was Shakespeare's grandmother, Mrs Robert Arden, née Palmer (Debdale's priestly alias): *Shakespeare's Haunts Near Stratford* (Oxford, 1929), pp. 32, 53.

93 For Debdale and *King Lear* see F. W. Brownlow, *Shakespeare, Harsnett, and the Devils of Denham* (Newark, 1993), pp. 294–5; and Greenblatt, 'Shakespeare and the exorcists', in *Shakespearean Negotiations*, pp. 94–5. Debdale's letter is in the Public Record Office, State Papers Domestic, fol. 179, no. 4.

94 Southwell, 'Life', pp. 293–4, 299, 313–14.

95 William Allen, *An Apology and True Declaration of the Institution and Endeavours of the Two English Colleges* (Menston, 1971), pp. 12–13.

96 Davies, 'The commisation', p. 41.

97 Michel Foucault, 'Governmentality', trans. Colin Gordon, in Graham Burchell, Colin Gordon and Peter Miller (eds), *The Foucault Effect: Studies in Governmentality* (Hemel Hempstead, 1991), pp. 87–8; James McConica, 'The Catholic experience in Tudor Oxford', in Thomas M. McCoog (ed.), *The Reckoned Expense: Edmund Campion and the Early English Jesuits: Essays in Celebration of the First Centenary of Campion Hall, Oxford (1896–1996)* (Woodbridge and Rochester, 1996), p. 58.

98 Alison Shell, ' "We are made a spectacle": Campion's dramas', in McCoog, *The Reckoned Expense*, p. 118; Gerard Kilroy, 'Eternal glory: Edmund Campion's Virgilian epic', *Times Literary Supplement*, 8 March 2002, pp. 14–15.

99 Arthur Marotti, 'John Donne and the rewards patronage', in Guy Fitch Lytle and Stephen Orgel (eds), *Patronage in the Renaissance* (Princeton, 1986), pp. 207, 209.

100 Dennis Flynn, 'Donne and the ancient Catholic nobility', *English Literary Renaissance*, 19 (1989), pp. 308–14.

101 *Ibid.*, pp. 321–2.

102 The evidence for Shakespeare's association with the Stanleys, and particularly with Ferdinando, the Fifth Earl, hinges on the statement on the title-page of *Titus Andronicus* (1594) that the play was first staged by the Earl of Derby's Servants: see Chambers, *The Elizabethan Stage*, vol. 2: 122–3, 128; Schoenbaum, *William Shakespeare*, p. 124.

103 John Dover Wilson, *The Essential Shakespeare: A Biographical Adventure* (Cambridge, 1932), p. 41.

104 E. A. J. Honigmann, *Shakespeare: The "Lost Years"* (Manchester, 1985, repr. 1998), p. 59.
105 Christopher Devlin, *Hamlet's Divinity* (London, 1963), p. 82.
106 See Honigmann, 'Lost Years', pp. 64–6.
107 F. A. Bailey, 'The Elizabethan playhouse at Prescot, Lancashire', *Transactions of the Historical Society of Lancashire and Cheshire*, 103 (1951), pp. 69–81; K. P. Wentersdorf, 'The Queen's Company in Scotland in 1589', *Theatre Research International*, 6 (1980), pp. 33–6. For the implications see Richard Wilson, 'The management of mirth: Shakespeare *via* Bourdieu', in Jean Howard and Scott Shershow (eds), *Marxist Shakespeare* (London, 2000), pp. 159–77. For possible performances of *Love's Labour's Lost* and *Richard III* at Knowsley see Alan Keen and Roger Lubbock, *The Annotator* (London, 1954), pp. 80–9.
108 Honigmann, 'Lost Years', p. 71.
109 Peter Milward, *Shakespeare's Religious Background* (London, 1973), p. 41.
110 See T. W. Baldwin, *Small Latine – Shakespeare's Small Latin and Less Greek* (2 vols, Urbana, 1944), p. 460. Baldwin was the first to trace the Cottams' origins to Preston.
111 See Kilroy, 'Eternal glory', p. 15. Acton, both Cottams and Aspinall were all graduates of Brasenose, the college that produced the largest number of Catholic martyrs after St John's: see McConica, 'Catholic experience', p. 63.
112 Honigmann, 'Lost Years'. For the Cottam tenancy of Hoghton land see p. 42, reproducing information from Tom Smith, *History of the Parish of Ribchester* (1890), p. 242.
113 Honigmann, 'Lost Years', pp. 29–30, 34, John Aubrey, *Brief Lives*, ed. Oliver Lawson Dick (London, 1949), p. 276. For the tradition of Shakespeare in Lancashire see Bailey, 'Elizabethan playhouse'; and Wentersdorf, 'Queen's Company'.
114 Peter Levi, *The Life and Times of William Shakespeare* (London, 1988), p. 42.
115 See Richard Wilson, 'Shakespeare and the Jesuits: new connections supporting the theory of the lost Catholic years in Lancashire', *Times Literary Supplement*, 19 December 1997, pp. 11–13.
116 Edmund Campion quoted in Simpson, *Edmund Campion*, p. 233.
117 Keen, *The Annotator*.
118 See Gary Taylor, 'Some manuscripts of Shakespeare's sonnets', *Bulletin of the John Rylands Library* (1985–86), pp. 210–46. Taylor attributes the compilation to Mary Hoghton, sister of Sir Richard Hoghton (1570–1630).
119 Modernized from the text printed in Ernst Honigmann, *John Weever: A Biography of a Literary Associate of Shakespeare and Jonson, together with a photographic facsimile of Weever's "Epigrammes" (1599)* (Manchester, 1987), p. 108.
120 Honigmann, 'Lost Years', pp. 54–6.
121 Simpson, *Edmund Campion*, p. 266; Evelyn Waugh, *Edmund Campion* (Oxford, 1935), p. 127.
122 Baldwin, *Small Latine*, p. 460.
123 Quoted, Honigmann, 'Lost Years', p. 136.
124 Chambers, *The Elizabethan Stage*, vol. 1, p. 280.
125 Shell, ' "We are made a spectacle" ', p. 112.

126 *DNB*; 'Records of the Chester Midsummer Day pageant', in J. H. E. Bennett, *The Rolls of the Freemen of the City of Chester* (Chester, 1906); Eccles, *Shakespeare in Warwickshire*, p. 74; Alan Keen, correspondence, *Times Literary Supplement*, 18 November 1955, p. 689.

127 Honigmann, 'Lost Years', p. 27.

128 Shell, ' "We are made a spectacle" ', p. 114.

129 Oliver Baker, *In Shakespeare's Warwickshire, and the Unknown Years* (London, 1937), pp. 297–319.

130 E. K. Chambers, *Shakespearean Gleanings* (Oxford, 1944), pp. 52–6.

131 Honigmann, 'Lost Years', chaps 7–9.

132 In chronological order: Gary O'Connor, *William Shakespeare: A Life* (London, 1991); Ted Hughes, *Shakespeare and the Goddess of Complete Being* (London, 1992); Ian Wilson, *Shakespeare: The Evidence* (London, 1993); Eric Sams, *The Real Shakespeare* (New Haven, 1995); Park Honan, *Shakespeare: A Life* (Oxford, 1998); and Anthony Holden, *William Shakespeare: His Life and Work* (London, 1999).

133 Quoted in Simpson, *Edmund Campion*, p. 414.

134 Peter Holmes, *Resistance and Compromise: The Political Thought of the Elizabethan Catholics* (Cambridge, 1982), p. 118.

135 Taylor, 'Forms of opposition', p. 306.

136 Honigmann, 'Lost Years', p. xi; Peter Milward, *Shakespeare's Religious Background*.

137 Peter Milward, *The Catholicism of Shakespeare's Plays* (Tokyo, 1997); 'Was Shakespeare a Catholic?' and 'Holden's Shakespeare', *The Renaissance Bulletin of Sophia University Renaissance Institute*, 26 (1999), pp. 8–22.

138 Hughes, *Shakespeare and the Goddess*.

139 Robert Stevenson, *Shakespeare's Religious Frontier* (London, 1958).

140 For the ferryman Antigonus as legendary founder and protector of Antwerp see Jervis Wegg, *Antwerp, 1477–1559* (London, 1916), p. 1. Leicester's emblem of a bear remains the symbol of Warwickshire.

141 Edmund Campion to Robert Arden, 6 August 1577, quoted in Simpson, *Edmund Campion*, pp. 120–1.

142 John Bossy, 'Rome and the Elizabethan Catholics: a question of geography', *The Historical Journal*, 7:1 (1964), pp. 135–42.

143 Scott Wilson, 'Racked on the tyrant's bed: the politics of pleasure and pain and the Elizabethan sonnet sequences', *Textual Practice*, 3:2 (1989), pp. 234–49, esp. 235, 242.

144 *Ibid.*, p. 238. Wilson points out (pp. 235–6) that the metaphor of verse as 'like that Tyrant's bed, where some who were too short were racked, others too long cut short', was first used in English by the Catholic Ben Jonson: see C. H. Herford and Percy Simpson (eds), *Ben Jonson: The Man and His Work* (Oxford, 1925), p. 133.

145 Quoted in Milward, *Shakespeare's Religions Background*, p. 60.

146 Patricia Parker, 'Sound government: morals, murals and mulberries', unpublished paper, Sixth World Shakespeare Congress, Valencia, 2001.

147 John Bossy, 'The character of Elizabethan Catholicism', *Past and Present*, 21 (1962), p. 57.

148 Terry Eagleton, *William Shakespeare* (Oxford, 1986), p. 1.

149 Blair Worden, 'Shakespeare and politics', *Shakespeare Survey*, 44 (1992), p. 2.
150 Wilson, 'Racked', p. 246.
151 Michel Foucault, 'Is it useless to revolt?', originally published as 'Inutile de se souveler?', *Le Monde*, 11 May 1979, trans. James Bernauer, in Jeremy Carette (ed.), *Religion and Culture by Michel Foucault* (Manchester, 2000), p. 132; Bourdieu, *Rules of Art*, p. 104.
152 Transcript, BBC2, *Newsnight*, 24 July 1999.

Bare ruined choirs: remembering Catholicism in Shakespeare's England

Till fairly recently most scholars of late Tudor England thought of it as essentially a Protestant place in which Catholicism was a problematic dimension: the Roman Catholic clerical presence in Elizabethan and Jacobean England was a 'mission', and Catholicism was one of the alien elements against which early modern English identity was defined.

This is true no longer. As contemporary English life has increasingly divested itself of its Protestant character, we have come to look with fresh eyes at the religious complexities – one is tempted to say pluralism – of even so explicitly confessional a state as early modern England, and the continuing and pervasive influence of Catholicism as a political, religious and cultural force in the England of Elizabeth and James – the England of Shakespeare – has become more visible.

One aspect of this process of reassessment has been the recovery of the Catholic dimension of early modern English culture, most obvious in music and architecture, represented by William Byrd and Inigo Jones, but more recently and sensationally focused on the reappraisal of Shakespeare's religion – of which not the least significant aspect may be the perception that he might actually have had a religion. What follows is an essay in literary history, intended to further in a modest and tentative sort of way the reappraisal of the religious significance – or at any rate the religious context – of the work of England's national bard. And it focuses on a discussion of the language of a single line in Sonnet 73.

> That time of yeare thou maist in me behold
> When yellow leaves, or none, or few doe hange
> Upon those boughes which shake against the could,
> *Bare ruin'd quiers, where late the sweet birds sang.*

Few human enterprises are more certainly doomed than the attempt to provide precise historical expositions of Shakespeare's Sonnets: these most elusive of poems defeat and will no doubt continue to defeat all attempts to decipher the story or stories they tell, or to identify the contemporary allusions they might be held to make, and Sonnet 73 is no exception. But its fourth line deploys an image which, whatever its precise reference, could hardly have been written at any time before the late Elizabethan age, and one which represents Shakespeare's appropriation of a highly charged contemporary historical trope, laden with contentious social and religious significance. Shakespeare's one-line evocation of the ruins of England's monastic past, the ruins of England's Catholicism, can hardly have been casual or unselfconscious, for in Elizabethan England these walls had, if not ears, then mouths, and, in the mode in which Shakespeare chose to evoke them, cried out against the cultural revolution which had shaped the Elizabethan religious settlement.

It is well recognized that the Henrician dissolution of the monasteries was crucial for the emergence in Tudor England of an acute sense of the *mutability* of even the most apparently permanent institutions: ruins, as Margaret Aston has demonstrated, make historians. The overthrow of monasticism brought not just the destruction and pillage of some of England's greatest buildings but a massive transfer of land and influence, a drastic shift from clerical to lay patronage within the church, and a fundamental reorientation of English society. Early modern English men and women were intensely conscious of all these elements of tranformation: as Antonio in *The Duchess of Malfi* declared,

> all things have their end
> Churches and cities (which have diseases like to men)
> must have like death that we have.[1]

Protestant conviction complicated these feelings: scholarly reformers such as John Bale might loath monasticism, and its 'superstitious mansyons' harbouring 'lasy lubbers and poppysh bellygoddes', and yet lament the destruction of venerable monastic buildings and great monastic libraries, 'those noble and precyouse monumentes' of the past. The first great county chorographer of Elizabethan England was William Lambarde, and his *Perambulation of Kent*, published in 1576, was a seminal influence on the development of Elizabethan antiquarianism and chorography. He was also an ardent Protestant, who reflected thus on the monastic ruins at Canterbury:

> And therefore, no marvaile, if wealth withdrawn, and opynion of holynesse remooved, the places tumble headlong to ruine and decay.
> In which part, as I cannot on the one side, but in respect of the places themselves pitie and lament this generall decay . . . So on the other side, considering the maine Seas of sinne and iniquitie, wherein the worlde (at those daies) was almost wholy drenched, I must needes take cause, highly to praise God that hath thus mercifully in our age delivered us, disclosed Satan,

unmasked these Idoles, dissolved their Synagogs, and raced to the grounde all monuments of building erected to superstition and ungodlynesse.

And therefore, let every godly man ceasse with me from henceforth to marvaile, why Canterbury, Walsingham, and sundry such like, are now in these our daies becom in maner waste, since God in times past was in them blasphemed moste: and let the souldiers of Satan and superstitious mawmetrie, howle and cry out with the heathen poet . . .

The Gods each one, by whose good ayde this empire stoode upright
Are flowne: their entries and their altars eke, abandoned quight.[2]

For Lambarde, bare ruined choirs, therefore, might be poignant reminders of vanished greatness, but they evoked no fond memories of sweet monastic birdsong: the monastic past was an abomination, the monks and their houses 'harborowes of the Devil and the Pope . . . which in horrible crimes contended with Sodome, in unbeliefe matched Ierusalem, and in follie of superstition exceeded all Gentilitie'. By the just judgement of God, therefore, Canterbury and places like it 'came suddenly from great wealth, multitude of inhabitants and beautiful buildings, to extreme poverty, nakedness and decay'.

Few Elizabethan or Jacobean antiquaries shared Lambarde's doctrinaire hostility to the religious past whose visible remains increasingly fascinated them and their readers. Notoriously, John Stow's *Survey of London*, one of the highwater marks of Elizabethan antiquarianism, published in 1598 and vastly expanded in 1603, is saturated through and through with nostalgia for the medieval golden age which had shaped the London townscape and its social and religious institutions. At one level, Stow's work is a sustained lament for the decay of sociability and old decency which he believed was one of the major consequences of the Reformation shattering of ancient buildings and the monuments they contained. The destruction of the Catholic past had been motivated by greed, not goodness, typified in the covetousness which had led men to pluck up the very funeral brasses from the 'defaced tombes and prints of plates torn up and carried away', bringing oblivion to the honourable dead and their good works, 'a great injurie to the living and the dead . . . but not forborne by many, that eyther of a preposterous zeal or of a greedy minde spare not to satisfy themselves by so wicked a meanes'.[3]

Stow's *Survey*, therefore, did more than lovingly map the bare ruin'd choirs of Shakespeare's London. It offered a benign account of the antique world, when 'service sweat for duty not for meed' (*As You Like It* 2.4.19), a world which had been lost in the dismantling of the early Tudor religious system. His famous description of midsummer religious celebrations such as the St John's fires, with its idealised evocation of 'every man's doore being shadowed with green birch, long fennel, St John's wort, Orphin, white lillies and such like', of hospitable houses hung about with lamps in honour of the saints, is notorious for its social romanticism:

In the moneths of June and July, on the Vigiles of festivall days ... in the evening after the sunne setting, there were usually made Bonefiers in the streetes, every man bestowing wood or labour towards them: the wealthier sort also before their doores neare to the saide Bonefiers, would set out tables ... furnished with sweete breade and goode drinke ... whereunto they would invite their neighbours and passengers also to sit, and bee merry with them in great familiaritie, praysing God for his benefites bestowed on them. These were called Bonefiers aswell of good amitie amongst neighbours that, being before at controversie, were there by the labour of others reconciled, and made of bitter enemies, loving friendes, as also for the vertue that a great fire hath to purge infection of the ayre.

Stow's private papers from the 1560s reveal his hostility to successive manifestations of Protestant zeal in the city, and his memoranda are openly sympathetic to the Catholic clergy rabbled by the London crowds. Unsurprisingly, he was vehemently and probably correctly suspected of being 'a great favourer of papistry', and his house and books were raided and ransacked for incriminating material in 1569. Stow was gradually to come to accept and endorse the Elizabethan settlement and its leaders such as Parker and Whitgift, but the whole drift of his published work was towards a positive reappraisal of the Catholic past, worlds away from the Reformation polemic of Bale or Lambarde. Nostalgia for the visible remains of Catholicism, and a backward and approving look at the religion which had produced them, were therefore hard to separate. The ruins of the monasteries were only the most striking example of the general destruction of the forms of the old religion. From the outset of the Elizabethan settlement, the fate of religious buildings in general, from monasteries to chantries, from cathedrals to parish churches, were intimately intertwined with the ideological systems they represented. That interconnection had been revealed at the start of Elizabeth's reign in a London event in which Stow took an intense interest, the furore surrounding the burning of St Paul's after the steeple was struck by lightning on Wednesday 4 June 1561.

St Paul's Cathedral was very much the symbolic focus of Reformation in London: in Edward's and Mary's reigns ritual change there had become for conservative commentators a barometer of the progress of Protestantism more generally, and this remained true as the main features of the Elizabethan settlement were set in place. The burning of the Cathedral in a freak storm, on the feast of Corpus Christi of all days, therefore, was certain to elicit pointed confessional commentary, and so the Elizabethan regime moved swiftly to forestall such comment. James Pilkington, Bishop of Durham, preached on the fire at Paul's Cross the following Sunday, declaring that the fire was a sign of the wrath of God against the sins of the time, in particular the decay of obedience to properly constituted authority – he called his hearers to 'humble obedience to the lawes and superior powers, whiche vertue is much decayed in our days', and he announced the tight-

ening up of the laws 'agaynst persons disobedyent aswell in causes of
religion, as civil – to the great rejoicing of his auditours'. He added that the
profanation of the cathedral by walking, jangling, brawling and bargaining
in service time was a particularly heinous offence before God: the nub of
his sermon, however, was an answer to the evil-tongued persons who were
already spreading it abroad that this 'token of God's deserved ire' was a
direct response to the 'alteration or rather Reformation' of religion. The
sermon therefore concluded with a lengthy review of great church fires
of history, designed to show that St Paul's and other famous churches
'both nigh to this realm and far off, where the church of Rome hath most
authority', had frequently been the targets of similar acts of God. He
concluded that 'every man should judge, examine and amend himself, and
embrace, believe, and truly follow the word of God' lest worse calamities
follow.[4]

Pilkington's sermon was a sign of the seriousness of the early Elizabethan
regime's anxiety about the capital which conservative critics of the religious
settlement had already made of the fire four days after its outbreak. It was
rapidly answered in a pamphlet called *An Addicion, with an Apologie to
the Causes of the Brinnynge of Paule's Church*, attributed to John Morwen,
Bishop Bonner's chaplain. This short pamphlet was a highly effective piece
of polemic, brief, forceful and telling. It began with a resume of biblical
examples of judgements by burning, from Sodom and Gomorrah through
the idolators Dathon and Abiron the prophets of Baal, and the destruction
of Jerusalem itself because of the apostosy of Israel. The fire at St Paul's
was a judgement not on sin in general but on London's infidelity and
apostasy in particular. St Paul's had been burned because it had first been
profaned by a false religion. Talking, buying and selling in church were
bad, but

> there be worse abuses, as blaspheming God in lying sermons, polluting the
> temple with schismatical service, destroying and pulling down holy altars, that
> were set up by good blessed men . . . yea, where the altar stood of the Holy
> Ghost, the new bishops have made a place to set their tails upon, and there
> sit in judgement on such as be Catholic and live in the fear of God.

The new religion was a mushroom growth, 'never heard tell of before
Luther's time, which is not forty years old': therefore we must obey
Jeremiah the prophet: 'Stand upon the way of the blessed fathers, and consider and ask of the old paths and high-ways, which is the good way, and
walk therein, and ye shall find refreshing to your souls.' And Pilkington's
portrayal of the Middle Ages as a time of superstition and error was dismissed as a lie – for then

> God was served devoutly night and day, the people lived in fear of God, every
> one in his vocation, without reasoning and contention of matters of religion,
> but referred all such things to learned men in general councils and universi-

ties . . . then was the commandments of God and virtue expressed in living, now all is talk and nothing in living: then was prayer, now is prating, then was virtue, now is vice; then was the building up of churches, houses of religion and hospitals, where prayer was had night and day, hospitality kept and the poor relieved: now is pulling down and destroying of such houses . . . by means whereof God's glory is destroyed and the commonwealth impoverished; then was plenty of all things, now is scarceness of all things: therefore *operibus credite*; the fruit will show whether then was superstition and ignorance, or now in these days.[5]

The *Addition* is a short work – it runs to only six pages of print in the Parker Society edition of Pilkington's works – but it is an accomplished and damaging piece of conservative propaganda, and stung Pilkington into an elaborate *Confutation* more than twenty times as long. Several of its themes had a long future ahead of them as staples of recusant polemic against the Reformation, not least the appeal to walk in the old ways.

In the early years of the settlement this was a voice which enraged and alarmed the advocates of Protestantism, who paid it the compliment of mocking it. In 1562 Pilkington, in his commentary on Haggeus, conplained bitterly of the widespread murmuring against the cleansing of the churches, such 'lewd sayings' as

'What shall I do at Church? I may not have my beads; the church is like a waste barn: there is no images nor saints to worship and make curtsey to: little God in the box is gone: there is nothing but a little reading or preaching, that I cannot tell what it means: I had as lief keep me at home:' This is a woeful saying.

Jewel took up the same woeful sayings for attack in the *Second Book of Homilies*, in the following year, when he makes two ignorant wives lament: 'Alas Gossip, what shall we do at church, since all the saints were taken away, since all the goodly sights we were wont to have are gone, since we cannot hear the like piping, singing, chanting and playing upon the organs that we could before'.[6]

It is in the light of this popular complaint against the official imposition of 'bare ruin'd quiers', not only in the monasteries but in the parishes, that we should understand the early Elizabethan regime's preoccupation with plaster and whitewash, and against which we should read John Shakespeare's involvement in the defacing and whitewashing of images in Stratford. The Elizabethan injunctions of 1559 recognized that the very stones of the parish churches remembered their Catholic past, and attempted to bulldoze away that material memory: the clergy were enjoined to

take away, utterly extinct and destroy all shrines, covering of shrines, all tables and candlesticks, trundles or rolls of ware, pictures, paintings and all other monuments of feigned miracles, pilgrimages, idolatry and superstition, *so that there remain no memory of the same* in walls, glasses, windows or elsewhere within their churches or houses. And they shall exhort all their parishioners to do the like within their several houses.[7]

The trouble was, in many communities this purging of the memory just did not happen. Stratford, like other conservative towns, was slow to implement the injunction, and, notoriously, John Shakespeare was chamberlain when, three years into the settlement, the corporation eventually got round to the removal of the rood-loft and other images. He was chief alderman in October 1571, and therefore deputy to the Protestant bailiff Adrien Quiney, when the latter secured the corporation's agreement to sell off the parish's Catholic vestments.[8]

In the late 1920s the editors of the Stratford corporation accounts took these activities as a sign of John Shakespeare's ardent Puritanism. Nowadays we know better, and it is the tardiness of this action which strikes us, together with the fact that the Stratford purges of 1562 and 1571 were almost certainly a response to external prodding rather than spontaneous zeal. Sales of illegally retained Catholic vestments and books were being forced on the localities by the ecclesiastical authorities all over England in the late 1560s and early 1570s, as their subversive potential as focuses of vestigial loyalty to the old religion was increasingly felt. This perception had been given frightening particularity in the Northern Rebellion on 1569, when concealed altarstones and holy-water vats were resurrected from the dunghills and gardens where they had been buried and became the focus for resistance to the Elizabethan settlement.

In 1571, indeed, Stratford had acquired a new bishop, Nicholas Bullingham, recently arrived as Bishop of Worcester. While still Bishop of Lincoln, Bullingham had presided in 1566 over a systematic purge of 'monuments of superstition' from the churches of Lincolnshire, and in the same years had been invoked as visitor against a Provost of King's College, Cambridge, suspected of being popishly inclined: at King's too Bullingham presided over the destruction of a 'great deal of popish stuff' from the chapel. It is no surprise therefore to find the disposal of the remaining relics of popery taking place at Stratford soon after the arrival of this Protestant new broom.

The attitudes of the man and woman in the pew towards all this are hard to assess, and must often have been ambivalent. In the late 1560s a Yorkshire yeoman who had been part of the syndicate which had bought up the timber and bells from the steeple of Roche Abbey was asked by his son 'whether he thought well of the religious persons and the religion that was then used'. When he replied that he had indeed thought well of the monks, having had no occasion to think otherwise, his son asked 'then how came it to pass you was so ready to distroy and spoil the thing you thought well of? What could I do, said He: might I not as well as others have some profit of the Spoil of the Abbey? For I did see all would away: and therefore I did as others did'.[9] Consciences continued to stir uneasily about all such spoil. Nicholas Roscarrock told the story of Jane Burlace, a farmer's wife from Rejarra in Cornwall who took up one of the four great stones used as a rest for relics and crosses on the annual Rogationtide procession to the parochial chapel of St Neghton, and used it to make a cheese press. When Mistress Burlace died in November 1582, however, her spirit could not rest till this sacrilege had been put right: accordingly, the stone 'was in the night tyme carryed back by one willed so by her after her death or by some thinge assuminge her personage and remaineth, I think, still where it did'. Roscarrock, a recusant antiquary, was hardly a neutral reporter, but he claimed to have had this story 'from report of such as were of her kins-folkes and friends who had cause to know it', and the ambivalences revealed in the episode must have been common enough.[10]

Shakespeare grew up, therefore, in a world where attitudes towards the material remains of the Catholic past were more often than not a touch-stone of loyalty to or disatisfaction with the Elizabethan settlement. Con-sider, for example, the most universal of all these reminders of the Catholic past, stained glass.

The English Reformation was unusual in the extent of its hostility towards pictures in glass, which were virtually never the object of cult. The Edwardian and Elizabethan injunctions had called for the removal of all Catholic stories and images 'so that there remain no memory of the same in walls, glass windows or elsewhere within their churches'. The Elizabethan injunctions had added the practical qualification that windows were not to be destroyed if this meant the wind and weather would be let in. Zealous Protestant bemoaned this pragmatism, which left intact so many 'monuments of superstition', but even William Harrison, the ardent Protes-tant polemicist whose *Description of England* celebrated and justified the removal of screens, images and all the other furniture of the old religion from the parish churches as 'altogether needless' in a reformed church, noted phlegmatically:

> only the stories in glass windows excepted, which, for want of sufficient store of new stuff and by reason of extreme charge that should grow by the altera-tion of the same into white glass throughout the realm, are not altogether abolished in most places at once but by little and little suffered to decay, that white glass may be provided and set up in their rooms.[11]

Stained glass remained everywhere, therefore, and was a potential focus of intense ideological feeling. The recusant antiquary and chorographer of Worcestershire, Thomas Habington, in whose house Henry Garnet was arrested after the Gunpowder Plot, left a lavish and detailed account of the great narrative and doctrinal series of windows in Malvern Priory, 'the glasse whereof is a mirror wherein we may see how to beleeve, how to live, how to dye, how to pass through temporality to eternity'.[12]

Consider, by contrast, the attitude of the Cheshire Puritan John Bruen
to the glass in his own parish church in the late 1580s, where on succeed-
ing to the lordship of the manor he found still

> many superstitious images and idolotraous pictures in the painted windowes,
> and they so thicke and dark that there was . . . scarce the breadth of a groat
> of white glass amongst them: he knowing the truth of God, that though the
> Papists will have images to bee lay mens bookes, yet they teach no other
> lessons but of lyes, nor any doctrines but of vanities to them that professe to
> learne by them: and considering that the dumbe and darke images by their
> painted coates and colours, did both darken the light of the Church, and
> obscure the brightness of the Gospell, hee presently tooke order, to pull downe
> all those painted puppets and popish idols, in a warrantable and peaceful
> manner, and of his own coste and charge, repaired the breaches, and beauti-
> fied the windows with white and bright glasse again.[13]

These contested and contending views were not merely current in the
1590s, when Shakespeare's Sonnets were being written, but had been built
into the heart of recusant complaint literature and apologetic. As government pressure on the recusant community mounted, the material ruins of
the monastic and Catholic past became emblematic not only of the condition of the Catholic community but of the calamities which the Reformation had brought on England itself, not only in the destruction of right
doctrine and religious practice but in the overthrow of charity, social
deference and the roots of community. This is the lament for the shrine at
Walsingham usually attributed to St Philip Howard:

> Bitter, bitter, o to behold
> The grass to grow
> Where the walls of Walsingham
> So stately did show.
> Such were the works of Walsingham
> While she did stand;
> such are the wracks as now do show
> Of that holy land.
> Level, level with the ground
> The towers do lie,
> which with their golden glittering tops
> Pierced once to the sky.
> Where were gates no gates are now
> The ways unknown
> Where the press of peers did pass
> While her fame far was blown.
> Owls do shriek where the sweetest hymns
> Lately were sung;
> Toads and serpents hold their dens
> Where the palmers did throng.
> Weep, weep, O Walsingham,

whose days are nights,
Blessings turned to blasphenmies,
Holy deeds to despites.
Sin is where our Lady sat,
Heaven turned is to hell.
Satan sits where our Lord did sway:
Walsingham, O, farewell.[14]

The lament for Walsingham, however, is only one example of a whole genre current in the 1590s, like this ballad, for possession of which Thomas Hale of Walthamstow was indicted before the Essex assizes in 1594:

Weepe, weepe, and still I weepe,
For who can chuse but weepe,
To thyncke how England styll,
In synne and heresy doth sleepe.

The Christian faythe and catholick,
Is everywhere detested,
In holy servyce, and such like,
Of all degrees neglected.

The sacramentes are taken awaye,
The holy order all,
Religious men do begg astraye,
To ground their houses fall.

The Bushppes and our pastors gone,
Our Abbottes all be deade,
Deade (alas) alyve not one,
Nor other in their steede.

The Churches gaye defaced be,
our altars are thrown downe,
The walles left bare, a greefe to see,
That once coste maney a Crowne.

The monumentes and lefe of Sayntes
Are Brent and torne by vyolence,
Some shedd the holy Sacramentes,
O Christe they wondrous pacyence.[15]

There was far more at stake in all this than the fate of buildings or even a change of doctrine. In this complaint literature the decay of the externals of Catholicism reflected and indeed had caused the collapse of the moral fibre of society: grief for the bare ruined choirs was the objective correlative for despair over the collapse of social value. Reformation meant ruin, in more senses than one. William Blundell, Catholic squire of Little Crosby in Lancashire in the early 1590s, expressed the matter thus:

The tyme hath been wee hadd one faith,
And strode aright one ancient path,
The tyme is now that each man may
See newe Religions coynd each day.
Sweet Jesu, with thy mother mylde,
Sweete Virgine mother, wth thy chylde,
Angells and Saints of each degree,
Redresse our contrees miserie.

The tyme hath beene the prelate's dore
Was seldome shott against the pore,

The tyme is now, so wives goe fine,
They take not thought the beggar kyne.

The tyme hath been feare made us quake
To sinn, least god should us forsake,
The tyme is now the lewdest knave
Is sure (hee'l say) God will him save.

The tyme hath been, with in this land
One's woord as good as was his band;
The tyme is now, all men may see,
New faithes have kild old honestie.

Sweet Jesu, with thy mother mylde,
Sweete Virgine mother, with thy chylde,
Angells and Saints of each degree,
Redresse our contrees miserie.[16]

These poetic products of the 1580s and 1590s were matched by the emergence about the same time of a number of prose texts which similarly constructed an idealized Catholic past, keyed to the contemplation of its physical ruins in both the parish and the monastery. The best-known and most elaborate of these texts is the anonymous *Rites of Durham* of 1593, which lovingly reconstructed not only the layout of every altar, tomb and painted window in the Abbey church but also the monastic liturgy for which they provided the setting. *The Rites of Durham* is written in language deliberately charged with the sweetness of nostalgia, like the description of the altarpiece of the Jesus altar:

> All of the hole Passion of our Lord Jesus Christ most richlye & curiously sett furth in most lyvelie colours all like the burninge gold, as he was tormented and as he honge on the cross which was a most lamentable sight to behold.

The monastic liturgy is depicted throughout as beautiful and affecting, 'all singinge reioycing and praysing God most devoutly', and the humility of the monks and their charity to the poor is stressed. The villains of the *Rites of Durham* are those who defaced and threw down the monuments of the church, 'lewde disposed personns, who despised antiquities and worthiness of monuments after the suppression of Abbeys', above all the first Elizabethan Dean, the Genevan minister Dean Whittingham and his wife, who took holy stones to make door steps and salting blocks, and who made a washing house for laundresses out of the century garth where the Priors were buried, 'for he could not abyde anye auncyent monument, nor nothing that appertayned to any godlie Religiousness or monasticall liffe'. And in the same mode as Roscarrock's story of Mistress Burlace's ghost and the cheese press, the *Rites* includes the story of a mysterious aand comely old beggarman who warned a Durham householder whose courtyard was paved with gravestones from the Cathedral 'that whilest those stones were theire nothinge wolde prosper aboute the house and after divers of his children and others died so he caused them to be removed into the Abbey yard where now they are'.[17]

The *Rites of Durham* was probably compiled by William Claxton, squire of Wynyard, who died in 1597. Claxton, a dedicated antiquary and a cor-respondent of Stow's, to whom he loaned many books and manuscripts, was not, it should be noted, a recusant, though he had close relatives who were. He may have had the assistance of George Clyff, the last monk of Durham, who effectively conformed to the new church in 1559, even though he never signed the Elizabethan articles (despite which he held a series of livings in the diocese of Durham and even retained his stall in the Cathedral till his death in 1595). It is worth remininding ourselves that so blatantly papistical a text, and so positive an assessment of the monastic past, could survive and articulate itself in literary form down to the 1590s among men who outwardly conformed to the Protestant establishment.[18]

A close parochial equivalent to the *Rites of Durham* is the now famous and familiar account written by the unquestionably recusant gentleman Roger Martin of the last days of the old religion in the Suffolk parish of Long Melford. In Martin's oft-quoted account the same saturated sweet-ness of descriptive language is in evidence, for example in the description of the image of our Lady of Pity, 'a fair image of our Blessed Lady, having the afflicted body of her dear son, as he was taken down, off from the Cross, lying along in her lapp, the tears, as it were, running down pittyfully upon her beautiful cheeks, bedewing the said sweet body of her son'. Martin wrote not merely to record the glory which had once filled the bare ruin'd choir of Long Melford, but as a gesture of resistance and of hope for the future: he lovingly details the *disjecta membra* of the pre-Reformation orna-ments of the church, some of which were 'in my house much decayed, and the same I hope my heires will repaire, and restore again, one day'. And he offers an implicit criticism of the Protestant present by projecting an ide-alized account of the ritual life of Henrician Long Melford, in which gor-geous ceremonial and the sacred calendar cemented the bonds of deference and patronage between rich and poor. In a passage on bonfires uncannily reminiscent of Stow's more famous account, on which indeed it may be modelled, Martin presents the same picture of flower-bedecked plenty, shared in neighbourly charity, 'and in all these bonefires, some of the honest and more civil poor neighbours were called in, & sat at the board, with my grandfather'.[19]

This was a recusant document, which inevitably emphasized the superiority of the old religion and its benign effects on society. But as we have seen such perceptions were not confined to Catholics. Protestant polemicists denounced the conservative folk-culture of conformist parishioners for their backward glances at the fleshpots of Egypt, revealed in proverbial saws such as 'It was merry world when the Mass was, for all things then were cheap'. In 1581 George Gifford's fictional Essex countryman, Atheos, was loud in repudiation of the Pope and all idolatry, but looked back to England's Catholic past as a time of communal harmony and good fellowship.

> I will follow our forefathers: now there is no love: then they lived in friendship, and made merrie together, now there is no neighbourhood, now every man for himelfe, and are ready to pull one another by the throate.

His Protestant interlocutor, Zelotes, foamed with indignation at such perverse romanticism:

> Ye follow your owne fond and doting opinion that ye imagine a thing which never was: for the world hath ever bene like it selfe, full of debate and strife, a very few in all ages which have had true love.[20]

Nor was it Catholics alone who applied this romanticism specifically to the monasteries. We have seen that the compiler of the *Rites of Durham*, of all texts, was probably a conformist. He was far from being alone. Michael Sherbrook, Elizabethan rector of Wickersley in the East Riding of Yorkshire, completed a treatise on the *Fall of Religious Houses* in 1591. It is an extraordinary work from the pen of an Anglican incumbent, for it was a sustained defence of the monasteries as good landlords and benign employers, centres of charity and industry. Sherbrook had no doubt that England had been in steep moral decline since the Reformation,

> for the estate of the realm hath come to more Misery since King Henry 8 his time, than ever it did in all the time before: If it be a Misery to have more theives, whores, extortioners, usurers and contentious persons striving the one against another in suits of law, and to be short, far more Beggars than ever was before.

The history of Reformation England was one long sequence of 'the going away, or rather driving away of godly devotion, and the bringing in of Carnall liberty, making small Concience, or rather none at all, of most things'. Anyone who compared pre- and post-Reformation England must agree, Sherbrook thought, that the 'Builders and Maintayners of monasteries' 'were far wiser in building of them, than we in destroying them, and the governors of the Common Weale then far better'.[21]

Sherbrooke is an extreme case, though in the light of Ian Doyle's identification of the conformist Anglican authorship of the *Rites of Durham* he looks a little less isolated than he once seemed: at any rate, some of his views were evidently common enough. In 1589 Francis Trigge, a Lincolnshire cleric, published a defence of the Reformation entitled 'An apologie or Defence of our dayes against the vaine murmurings and complaints of many', in which he admitted that 'many do lament the pulling downe of the abbayes, they say it was never merrie world since: they highly commend their liberalitie to the poore, their curtesie to their tenants, their commoditie to the commonwealth'. Trigge flatly rejected all this as so much moonshine: in fact, he thought, the monasteries had been full of

> pryde, idlenesse, fullnesse of breade and unmercifulnesse. In so much that the fatnesse and haughtiness and idleness of monkes, came into a proverbe amongst all men: in so much, that idle persons were called abbey lubbers: fatt men were said to have abbotts faces.[22]

We have travelled a roundabout route, but I hope by now it will be evident where we are going. Sonnet 73 was probably written in the late 1590s. Religion is neither its subject matter nor the primary source of its poetic energy. Its allusion to the Reformation, and the monasteries, is certainly oblique and perhaps unconscious. Yet in the fraught religious atmosphere of the last decade of the old Queen's life, its phrasing decisively aligns Shakespeare against the Reformation: line 4's evocation of monastic ruins and the 'sweet birds' who had once sung there must have sent to its first reader's a clear and unambiguouslly *un*Protestant message. It is not of course a line which need only have been written by a Catholic: as we have seen, there were conforming Anglicans, such as Stow and Sherbrook, whose writings reveal just as positive an attitude to the Catholic past as is implicit in the phrase 'where late the sweet birds sang'.

But we can and should press Shakespeare's words for further nuances of meaning. Consider the significance here, for example, of the word 'late'.

Where *late* the sweet birds sang:

The word 'late' there has in fact been taken by some commentators to rule out the application of the image to the monasteries at all, for in the 1590s the dissolution of the monasteries was two generations back, and so could hardly be described as 'late'.[23] On the contrary, however, I believe the tell-tale word 'late' once again aligns Shakespeare with a dangerously positive reading of the religious past. Delight in and reverence for the ruins of the old religion made the antiquarian movement as a whole a Trojan horse within the embattled Protestantism of Tudor and early Stuart England – as we have seen, there were many recusants and fellow travellers among the ranks of the antiquaries. But open assertions of the virtues of the last stages of monasticism were rare: antiquarian indignation at the depradations of the iconoclasts operated at a fair degree of generality – what such attacks represented was barbarism, the decay of reverence, lack of respect for traditional pieties. But we can see the carefully demarcated confessional limits of this attitude at work in one of the clasic antiquarian products of the early Stuart period, *Ancient Funeral Monuments*, by Shakespeare's admirer, the Hoghton protégé John Weever, published in 1631 but in preparation for two decades before that.

Weever's work, based on his own perambulations of the diocese of Canterbury, Rochester, London and Norwich, and on the collections of Sir Robert Cotton, is a celebration of the value and importance of funeral inscriptions, and as such it shares the general antiquarian hostility to iconoclasm. Weever quotes 'a late nameless versifier' to this effect:

> What sacred structures did our elders build
> Wherein Religion gorgeousaly sat deckt?
> Now all thrown downe, Religion exil'd
> Made Brothel-houses, had in base respect,
> Or ruin'd so that to the viewers eye
> In their own ruins they intombed lie:
> The marble urnes of their so zealous founders
> Are digged up, and turn'd to sordid uses;
> Their bodies are quite cast out of their bounders
> Lie un-interr'd. O greater what abuse is?
> Yet in this later age we now live in,
> This barbarous act is neither shame nor sinne.[24]

These were the sentiments used by Laud and his associates to justify their campaign to recover the beauty of holiness, and Weever's book, which is dedicated to Charles I, contains many asides which show that he supported the recovery of architectural and ritual dignity within the Church of England's worship. He also displays a regard for the religious customs of his home county of Lancashire which demonstrate an unmistakable animosity to advanced Protestantism and the campaign for a godly England, as in his remark that

> in the country where I was borne, the vulgar sort especially, doe most commonly swear by the cross of their own parish kirke, as they call it: and in ancient times, children used to sweare by the Sepulchres of their parents . . . But, with us in these dayes, I see no such reverence that sonnes have to their fathers hands or to their Sepulchres. I heare no swearing by Kirkes, Crosses or Sepulchres. I heare sometimes, i must confesse, forswearing to build Churches; swearing to pull downe crosses, or to deface and quite demolish all Funerall Monuments; swearing and protesting that all these are the remaines of AntiChriste, papisticall and damnable.[25]

Weever, then, is unmistakably friendly to much in the Catholic past, and to the idea of monasticism – he remarked in the dedicatory epistle that 'it may seeme, peradventure, unpleasing to some, for that I do speake so much of, and extoll the ardent pietie of our forefathers in the erecting of Abbeyes, priories, and such like sacred Foundations'. His account of the early Anglo-Saxon monastic movement, based on Bede and Capgrave, is glowing and laudatory: unlike Bale and other Reformation polemical historians, he thinks well of Augustine of Canterbury and appears to credit his miracles. He is also deeply sceptical of the motivation of the Henrician dissolutions, which he seen as driven by greed and santimonious hypocrisy.

It is all the more striking, therefore, that Weever adopts an unreconstructedly Protestant account of the *later* history of monasticism, as one long tale of decline and lapse from primitive virtue. He draws heavily on Lambarde in his treatment of the diocese of Canterbury, and retells and adds to many of Lambarde's scandalous anecdotes about popish superstition and gullibility in the later Middle Ages. He also reiterates the usual Reformation catalogue of the vices of the monks – 'pride, covetousnesse, insatiable luxurie, hypocrisie, blinde ignorance, and variable discord amongst the Church-men and all other our English votaries'. Despite the bad faith of the Henrician reformers, therefore, the 'fatal and finall period of the Abbeyes, Priories and such like religious structuires: with the casting out to the wide world of all their religious Votaries' was 'chiefly occasioned by their owne abhominable crying sinnes, more than by any other secondarie meanes'.[26]

Weever's ambivalence about England's monastic past reveals the inconsistencies and unresolved contradicitions within the thinking of the antiquarian movement about the past. For our purposes, however, it is of interest chiefly in highlighting the radically contrasting reading of the monastic past implicit in Shakespeare's phrase 'where *late* the sweet birds sang'. For Weever, monasticism had its glories: it was born in zeal and sanctity, it wrote a golden page in England's history, and its ruins, choice pieces of antiquity, were for that reason noble and to be treasured. But its *final* phase was sordid and disreputable: for Weever at any rate, of *late*, no sweet birds sang in England's quires, but only the carrion fowl of a corrupt system which had bred its own decay. By contrast, Shakespeare's 'where late the sweet birds sang' implies a reading of the last stages of monasticism, and of the roots of the Reformation, far more favourable to Catholicism.

Let me by way of conclusion make it clear what I have *not* been arguing. I do not think Sonnet 73 constitutes evidence that Shakespeare was a Catholic: as we have seen, its rhetoric, and the historical and religious attitudes implicit in that rhetoric, closely resemble the ideologically and theologically charged antiquarian and nostalgic writing about the religious past which seems to have been a special feature of the 1590s. That sort of writing would continue well into the Jacobean and Caroline periods, and it had a future in the mid- and late Stuart tradition of writing about sacrilege which we associate with Sir Henry Spelman. Some of these Elizabethan and early Stuart texts were indeed produced by recusants, but others by conformist fellow travellers such as Stow and Sherbrook and Claxton. As far as the evidence of Sonnet 73 takes us, Shakespeare might just as well be placed among the fellow travellers as among the Catholics. But if we cannot quite be sure that Shakespeare was a Catholic, it becomes clearer and clearer that he must have struck alert contemporaries as a most unsatisfactory Protestant.

Notes

1 Cited by Margaret Aston in her essay 'The dissolution of the monasteries and the sense of the past', *in Lollards and Reformers: Images and Literacy in Late Medieval Religion* (London, 1984), p. 315.

2 William Lambarde, *A Perambulation of Kent* (facsimile ed., Trowbridge, 1970), pp. 267–8.

3 For this and the quotation that follows, John Stow, *A Survey of London*, ed. C. L. Kingsford (Oxford, 1908), vol. 1:229; vol. 2:75; and see Ian Archer, 'The nostalgia of John Stow', in D. L. Smith, R. Strier and D. Bevington (eds), *The Theatrical City: Culture, Theatre and Politics in London 1576–1649* (Cambridge, 1995), pp. 17–34.

4 Official accounts of the burning by the regime in *A true report of the burninyng of the steple and churche of Poules in London* (1561) (*STC* 19930), and in W. Sparrow Simpson (ed.) *Documents Illustrating the History of St Paul's Cathedral*, Camden Society, ns 26 (1880), pp. 113–19. See also Alexandra Walsham, *Providence in Early Modern England* (Oxford, 2000), pp. 232–3.

5 Morwen's tract was included with a refutation in *The burnynge of Paules Church in London in the yeare of oure Lord 1561* (1563), reprinted, in *The Works of James Pilkington, BD, Lord Bishop of Durham*, ed. James Schofield (Parker Society, 1842), pp. 481–6.

6 *Sermons or Homelies Appointed to be Read in Churches in the Time of Queen Elizabeth of Famous memory* (London, 1833), p. 381.

7 W. H. Frere (ed.), *Visitation Articles and Injunctions of the Period of the Reformation, vol. III 1559–1575* (Alcuin Club, vol. XVI, 1910), p. 16. Injunction 23, my emphasis.

8 R. Savage and Edgar Fripp (eds), *Minutes and Accounts of the Corporation of Stratford upon Avon* (Publications of the Dugdale Society, Oxford, 1921–30), vol. 1:137–41; vol. 2:54.

9 A. G. Dickens (ed.), *Tudor Treatises* (Yorkshire Archaeological Society, 1959), p. 125.

10 Nicholas Orme (ed.), *Nicholas Roscarrock's Lives of the Saints: Cornwall and Devon* (Devon and Cornwall Record Society, 1992), pp. 94, 160.

11 William Harrison, *The Description of England*, ed. G. Edelen (Washington, 1994), pp. 35–6: Richard Marks, *Stained Glass in England During the Middle Ages* (London, 1993), pp. 231–2.

12 J. Amphlett (ed.), *A Survey of Worcestershire by Thomas Habington* (Worcester Historical Society, Oxford, 1895), vol. 2, pp. 177–8.

13 William Hinde, *A Faithfull Remonstrance of the Holy Life and Happy Death of John Bruen* (London, 1641), p. 78.

14 *The New Oxford Book of Sixteenth Century Verse*, ed. E. Jones (Oxford, 1991), pp. 550–1.

15 F. G. Emmison, *Elizabethan Life: Disorder* (Chelmsford, 1970), pp. 59–61.

16 T. E. Gibson (ed.), *Crosby Records* (Chetham Society, 1887), pp. 28–31.

17 J. T. Fowler (ed.), *Rites of Durham: being a description or brief declaration of all the ancient monuments, rites, and customs belonging or being within the monastical church of Durham before the suppression, written 1593* (Surtees Society, vol. 103, 1903 repr. 1964), pp 33, 61–2.

18 A. I. Doyle, 'William Claxton and the Durham Chronicles', in James P. Carley and Colin G. C. Tite, *Books and Collectors 1200–1700* (London, 1997), pp. 335–55, esp. 347–9.

19 Martin's account is edited in David Dymond and Clive Payne, *The Spoil of Melford Church* (Salient Press, 1992), pp. 1–9.

20 George Gifford, *A Briefe Discourse of certaine points of religion, which is among the common sorts of Christians, which may be termed the Countrie Divinitie* (London, 1601).

21 Dickens, *Tudor Treatises*, pp. 90–1.

22 *Ibid.*, p. 38.

23 For example, S. Greenblatt *et al.* (eds), *The Norton Shakespeare* (New York, 1997), note 1 to Sonnet 73, p. 1947.

24 John Weever, *Ancient Funerall Monuments With In the United Monarchie of Greate Britaine and the Islands adiacent, with the dissolved Monasteries therein contained* (London, 1631), p. 4.

25 *Ibid.*, pp. 37–8.

26 *Ibid.*, pp. 73, 115.

Shakespeare's Jesuit schoolmasters

Shakespeare's links with both the county of Lancashire and the Society of Jesus may be traced back to his early childhood in Stratford-upon-Avon. They are both various and far-reaching. They also converge on the persons of the schoolmaster at Stratford Grammar School during that period. Of these schoolmasters no fewer than three are known to have come from Lancashire (*via* the University of Oxford): Walter Roche (1569–71), John Cottam (1579–82) and Alexander Aspinall (1582–1624). As for William's own schooling, we may assume it took place in between the periods of office of Roche and Cottam. Yet another Lancastrian, who subsequently founded the English seminaries at Douai (Rheims after 1578) and Rome, William Allen of Rossall, seems to have been staying in the neighbourhood of Stratford about the very year of Shakespeare's birth in the capacity of tutor or usher. He also stayed at the newly built residence of the wealthy Thomas Hoghton, Hoghton Tower, to rally the gentry of Lancashire to the cause of Catholic recusancy.[1]

As for the young Shakespeare's links around this time with the newly founded Society of Jesus (in 1540), they may be seen in the three schoolmasters in between Roche and Aspinall who were more directly responsible (it is assumed) for his schooling: Simon Hunt (1571–75), Thomas Jenkins (1575–79) and the abovementioned John Cottam.

First, it was in 1575 that Simon Hunt decided to quit his position at Stratford and repair to the Catholic Continent, first to the English seminary (or college) at Douai and then on to Rome, where he entered the Society of Jesus, remaining in Italy without ever returning to his native country. He became penitentiary at St Peter's in Rome in succession to Fr Robert Parsons in 1580 and died there in 1585.[2] He did not travel alone but took with him one of his pupils, Robert Debdale of Shottery. After completing his seminary studies Debdale returned to England as a priest in 1580 and was almost immediately arrested and imprisoned till September 1582. Then he may have visited his family before being caught up in the exorcizing activities at Denham and elsewhere chiefly connected with the name of the Jesuit

Fr William Weston (alias Edmonds). He was arrested and executed in 1586 on the combined charges of treason and magic. The exorcisms in which he was involved found their way into two of Shakespeare's plays, *The Comedy of Errors* and *King Lear*.[3] The suggestion has even been made that Hunt also took the young Shakespeare with him to both Douai and Rome, but without any reliable evidence.[4]

Second, turning to Jenkins who followed Hunt at Stratford, we note a contrast between the one whose footsteps led him from Stratford to Douai and Rome and the other who left Stratford for the Anglican ministry – though where his sympathies lay during his period as schoolmaster is unknown. What is significant about him for our purpose is that before he came to Stratford he had been a fellow of St John's College, Oxford, graduating B.A. in 1566 and M.A. in 1570. There he must have known the future Jesuit and martyr Edmund Campion, who was the star of St John's and all Oxford till 1569, when for reasons of conscience he left Oxford for Dublin and then Rome. How friendly Jenkins had been with Campion is not known; but Campion's influence was great within his small college, and it is not unlikely that the young Shakespeare would have heard much about Campion, as well as the Society of Jesus, from Jenkins.

Third, by the time Jenkins had completed his period of office in 1579, the young Shakespeare would probably have finished his time of schooling at the Grammar School; and he and his parents may have been looking round for some means of employment, not forgetting his taste for the theatre. This was the time that Jenkins's friend from Oxford days, John Cottam, of Dilworth near Preston, took over as schoolmaster. His parents seem to have conformed at least outwardly to the Anglican Church, but he and his brother Thomas returned to Catholicism at Oxford, owing to the influence of a cousin to the Earl of Southampton, Thomas Pounde of Belmont. As for his brother, after graduating from Oxford Thomas went overseas to the seminary at Douai, before going on, like Hunt, to join the Jesuit noviceship in Rome, only to be dismissed for reasons of health. After completing his studies for the priesthood back at Douai, he came over to England in the same year as Campion, 1580, but was soon arrested by the English authorities in London, where he was found with a letter for Debdale's family at Shottery. The letter was never delivered, but for that very reason it was survived in the state papers. After his arraignment with Campion and others in 1581, he had his execution deferred till the following year; and while in prison he was readmitted into the Society of Jesus.[5] The date of his death significantly coincides with that of the termination of John Cottam's brief period of office as schoolmaster at Stratford.

Now the home of the Cottams in Lancashire was not far from one of the many properties of the abovementioned Thomas Hoghton, who had not only given hospitality to William Allen but also followed him into exile for conscience's sake. From the time of his exile till his death in 1580 the administration of these properties fell into the hands of his younger brother Alexander, who seems to have temporized in matters of religion (like so many male Catholics of the time), though his household remained recusant. He himself died in the late autumn of 1581, after having drawn up a will dated 3 August of that year, including a bequest of musical instruments and play clothes to his half-brother also named Thomas. But, he adds, if Thomas does not wish to keep players, 'it is in my mind and will that Sir Thomas Hesketh Knight shall have the same instruments and plays clothes. And I most heartily require the said Sir Thomas to be friendly unto Fulk Guillam and William Shakeshafte now dwelling with me, and either to take them into his service or else to help them to some good master'. The discovery of this will in the 1930s has led to the now widely accepted 'Shakeshafte theory' of what are called the 'lost years' of Shakespeare.[6]

Many reasons come together in support of this theory, making it more than just an idle conjecture. First, there is the old saying concerning the dramatist's early years, attributed to William Beeston, actor son of one of Shakespeare's actor colleagues Christopher Beeston, that he had once been 'a schoolmaster in the country'. The saying, recorded by John Aubrey in his *Brief Lives*, is mentioned as explaining that Shakespeare 'understood Latin pretty well', in refutation of Ben Jonson's more famous assertion that his rival had 'little Latin and less Greek'.[7] But, it may be asked, how could the young Shakespeare have taught as a schoolmaster even in the country without a university degree, unlike all his masters at Stratford, and contrary to the law? This could only have been the case if he had served as a private tutor for children in a gentleman's household, such as that of Alexander Hoghton of Lea Hall near Preston, whom we know to have been keeping such a tutor already.

But then, it may further be asked, why should William Shakespeare of Stratford-upon-Avon have gone to the remote countryside of Lancashire? There was the abovementioned presence of the new schoolmaster, John Cottam of Dilworth near Preston, at Stratford in the critical year 1579; and he may have acted as go-between for Alexander Hoghton and John Shakespeare, the poet's father. What the former would have needed was a promising young tutor for the children of his household, while for the latter here was a safe Catholic retreat and a convenient way of fostering dramatic tastes, since part of a tutor's task would have been to present plays for the entertainment of the household in times of festivity, such as Christmas.

This concern on the part of John Shakespeare for his son's Catholic formation presupposes Catholic sympathies in the poet's family at Stratford. On his mother's side, William could claim descent from the noble Warwickshire family of Arden, going back beyond the Conquest even to Saxon times. This family largely held firm to the 'old faith' in the early years of Elizabeth's reign; and they suffered for that faith as a result of the so-called Somerville Plot (really a plot by the powerful upstart Earl of Leicester against the Ardens) in 1583. The 'plotter', John Somerville, had married the daughter of Edward Arden, the head of the family who resided at Park Hall near Birmingham; and not only he but also Edward Arden were put to death that year as traitors. The magistrate appointed to examine the 'plot' in all its real and imaginary ramifications was none other than Shakespeare's legendary enemy, the Puritan Sir Thomas Lucy of Charlecote Park, a former pupil of the martyrologist John Foxe. Of him it was said by Richard Davies and Nicholas Rowe in the late seventeenth and early eighteenth centuries that in various ways he was pilloried by Shakespeare, in revenge for a deer-poaching incident, in 2 *Henry IV* and *The Merry Wives of Windsor* (as Justice Shallow).[8]

On his father's side, there is more precise proof of John Shakespeare's Catholic recusancy. Not only do we find his name mentioned in the recusancy returns of 1592, at a time when the victims sought were Catholic (not Puritan) recusants. We also have the document known as the 'Spiritual Testament' drawn up in John's name and hidden in the rafters of the Shakespeare house in Henley Street – discovered there in the mid eighteenth century when the house was undergoing repairs. The genuineness of this document, at first doubted by the great scholar Edmund Malone, has been critically established in the present century by Fr Herbert Thurston and is generally accepted by scholars.[9]

Still, it may be asked, how did John Shakespeare acquire his copy of this 'Testament'? And what kind of document was it? It was composed about 1580 by the saintly archbishop of Milan Carto Borromeo, specially for the benefit of persecuted English Catholics prevented from making outward profession of their faith or even receiving the last sacraments before death owing to what Shakespeare calls (in *The Merchant of Venice* 3.2.18) 'these naughty times'. That same year, on their way from Rome to England, Campion and Parsons stayed for a time at Milan, where they were welcomed by Borromeo and presumably given copies of the 'Testament' for distribution among the Catholics. It soon proved to be so popular that they had to write back for more copies. On their arrival in England, the two Jesuits took their several ways from London through the provinces; and Campion's route may be traced, from the confessions he subsequently made under torture in the Tower of London (and kept among the Burghley papers), through the Midlands into Yorkshire and then Lancashire.[10] Among the hosts named on this journey was Sir William Catesby, a relative of the Ardens and father of the conspirator Robert Catesby, whether at Lapworth in Warwickshire to the north of Stratford or at Ashby St Leger across the border in Northamtonshire. Either place would have been a comfortable riding distance from Stratford, whether for the father John or for his teenage son William or for them both together.

Then, while the father remained at home to fill in the gaps of the 'Testament' applying them to himself, we may imagine the son riding north to the Catholic county of Lancashire and the household of Alexander Hoghton whether at Lea Hall or at Hoghton Tower. Campion for his part had a more arduous journey to make, to visit the houses mentioned in his confessions, both in Yorkshire and in Lancashire – though whether he actually visited them all or not may be doubted, as being a ruse of the wily Cecil to implicate as many Catholic recusant households as possible, while implying that Campion had betrayed his hosts under torture. Among the houses in Lancashire specific mention is made of Park Hall, Charnock Richard, the residence of Richard Hoghton, and Rufford Hall, the residence of Bartholomew Hesketh, a cousin of Sir Thomas. It was in the spring of 1581, between the feasts of Easter and Whitsun, that Campion resided in Lancashire at the houses of the Catholic gentry; and it was then that the young William Shakespeare/Shakeshafte would have had easy access to him from Lea Hall.

A final query often raised concerning the validity of the 'Shakeshafte theory' is how to explain the apparent discrepancy in the use of the surname.[11] The name of Shakespeare appears here and there in Warwickshire, especially in the area of Rowington and Wroxhall; but it was not so fixed in form but that it might not take on such variants as 'Shaxberd' and 'Shakeshafte', not to mention the mocking 'Shakescene' devised by Robert Greene for his rival in *A Groatsworth of Wit* in 1592.[12] On the other hand, the name of Shakeshafte occasionally appears in Lancashire, even in the area of Preston. It may have been that the young Shakespeare purposely chose this form of his name to make his presence in the county less obtrusive.[13]

Now I come to the climax of my argument, which is admittedly more conjectural, less factual than what has preceded. Up to this point I have been dwelling on those three Stratford schoolmasters who may be said to have had Jesuit connections, if tenuously so in the case of Jenkins. But now I come to the time when Shakespeare himself became 'a school-master in the country' of Lancashire, and when he may have enjoyed the instruction of the great Jesuit martyr Edmund Campion, if only for a couple of months. If then we may assume that the two men met each other with some frequency during this period, especially considering that the young Shakespeare may already have been known to the Jesuit, to what extent, it may be asked, did the one influence the other? in particular, to what extent may it be said that Campion influenced the subsequent dramatic career of Shakespeare? In general, it may be conjectured, this influence took two basic forms, one in the realm of ideas, the other in that of dramaturgy.

To begin with the realm of ideas, one of the main tasks of Jesuit priests such as Campion both in England and elsewhere, as well as the secret of their success, was the individual direction of the faithful in certain 'spiritual exercises' according to a book composed by their founder St Ignatius Loyola soon after his conversion to Christ in the north of Spain in 1521. This book was intended not for the reading of the person making the exercises, or 'exercitant', but for the guidance of the person giving the exercises. So it was rarely printed at this time, let along translated into English. The aim of these exercises was to impart to the exercitant, first, a self-knowledge leading to repentance and, second, an understanding of the life and teaching of Christ with a constant personal application to the individual. From the viewpoint of Campion, so soon after his arrival in England, a meeting with the young Shakespeare whether at Lapworth or in Lancashire must have impressed him with the rich promise evident in him; and he may well have given him the full exercises during his stay in Lancashire.

This is more than idle speculation. In the plays of Shakespeare I have long since, as a Jesuit familiar with the exercises of St Ignatius, noticed not a few echoes of the one in the other which can hardly be dismissed as merely fortuitous.[14] At least, let me mention some of these echoes in the order they appear in the *Spiritual Exercises*.

First, the meditation on personal sin in the First Week, with its 'cry of wonder' at the reaction of 'all the creatures', seems to be echoed in Ariel's words to the 'three men of sin' in *The Tempest* 3.3.73–5: 'The powers delaying, not forgetting, have / Incens'd the seas and shores, yea all the creatures, / Against your peace.'

Second, the ideal response of the exercitant after meditating on the Kingdom of Christ at the beginning of the Second Week is aptly reflected in the words of the loyal old Adam to his young master Orlando in *As You Like It* 2.3.69–70: 'Master, go on, and I will follow thee / To the last gasp with truth and loyalty.'

Third, the global view of the world seen through the eyes of the divine persons at the beginning of the contemplation on the Incarnation in the Second Week may be found echoed in the words of the young soldier Michael Willams on the eve of Agincourt in *Henry V* 4.1.145–9: 'Some swearing, some crying for a surgeon, some upon their wives left poor behind them, some upon the debts they owe, some upon their children rawly left.'

Fouth, the distinction drawn by St Ignatius between the two standards of Christ and Satan in one of the basic contemplations of the Second Week is twice paralleled in the plays of Shakespeare: once in the words of Friar Laurence in *Romeo and Juliet* 2.3.27–8: 'Two such opposed foes encamp them still / In man as well as herbs, grace and rude will'; and again in the words of Belarius in *Cymbeline* 4.2.27: 'Nature hath meal and bran, contempt and grace'.

Fifth, the further consideration of three classes of men, particularly those of the second class who 'want to rid themselves of their attachment, but wish to do so in such a way that they retain what they have acquired', is aptly illustrated by Claudius in his soliloquy of repentance in *Hamlet* 3.3.56: 'May one be pardon'd and retain the offence?'

Sixth, the central theme of the exercises, that of election or resolution or reformation, is echoed in play after play at the height of Shakespeare's dramatic career: in *Henry V* 1.1.28–34: 'Consideration like an angel came . . . / Never came reformation in a flood, / With such a heady currance, scouring faults'; in *Hamlet* 3.2.68–70: 'Since my dear soul was mistress of her choice / And could of men distinguish, her election / Hath seal'd thee for herself'; in *Troilus and Cressida* 1.3.348–9: 'Choice, being mutual act of all our souls, / Makes merit her election'; and in *King Lear* 1.2.111: 'I would unstate myself to be in a due resolution.'

Seventh, in *King Lear* Cordelia stands for the ideal of true love, as expressed rather in deeds than in words, and as emphasized by St Ignatius in a note to his concluding contemplation on Divine Love. So she declares to her father in the opening scene: 'My love's more richer than my tongue . . . What I well intend, I'll do't before I speak' (1.1.79–80, 228–9). The same love of giving appears in Juliet, when she tells Romeo: 'My bounty is as boundless as the sea, My love as deep; the more I give to thee, The more I have, for both are infinite' (2.2.133–5).

As for the field of dramaturgy, it was another important task for the Jesuits from their earliest days after the founding of their Society in 1540 to engage in the formation of Catholic youth, till they came to earn the title of 'educators of Europe'. In this formation they laid emphasis not only on religious and moral instruction but also on a humanistic education based on the classics of Greece and Rome, including dramatic productions. Indeed, by the mid-seventeenth century the Jesuit drama had become famous throughout Europe, with Jesuit masters composing their own plays, usually on sacred subjects, for their students to enact, if in Latin, for the entertainment of the local people and dignitaries. Campion himself, before being chosen to go on the English mission, had been teaching boys at the Jesuit college of Prague in Bohemia, and he had composed his own Latin plays for them to perform, some of which have even come down to us.

In view of this, one may well imagine Campion directing the young Shakespeare not only in ways of spiritual life but also in practical methods of dramaturgy, while allowing for the use of English rather than Latin with the boys of Lancashire, and for their tutor's lack of a university education. Then, what William Shakeshafte may have done in a groping way for the boys of the Hoghton household, he may have gone on to do with more confidence for the players of Sir Thomas Hesketh at Rufford Hall, till through that knight's introduction to the Earl of Derby he came to be accepted as a member of Lord Strange's Men. And then eventually, on the mysterious death of Lord Strange, now Earl of Derby, in 1594, the way was open for him to emerge as principal dramatist for the newly formed Chamberlain's Men.

Meanwhile, events were happening in the outside world of the 1580s to modify and reshape the transition of Shakespeare from the young 'schoolmaster in the country' to the budding dramatist challenged by Robert Greene in London. The first was the arrest of Campion at Lyford Grange in Berkshire on 17 July 1581, as a result of which he was taken to the Tower of London and examined under torture. We still have the abovementioned list of names of those who gave him hospitality, especially in the counties of Yorkshire and Lancashire, though the list was no doubt drawn up beforehand by Lord Burghley as a basis for questioning him. Anyhow, at his trial he particularly asked for the forgiveness of those whose names had been wrung from him by the excruciating pain of the rack. Consequently, the Catholics of those areas in the north must have been fearful of further examination of themselves and their families; and such fear may well have hastened the death of Alexander Hoghton within a few months of the will he had made on receipt of the news of Campion's arrest. It might also have been the occasion, even before the prosecution of the Arden family in 1583, for John Shakespeare to hide his copy of Borromeo's 'Spiritual Testament' in the rafters of his house.

As for the young William Shakespeare, when he found his employer dead and his Jesuit teacher tortured and executed before the year was out, he must have found it more prudent, instead of joining Hesketh's players at Rufford Hall, to return to the greater safety of his home, far from the impending examination of Catholic recusant houses in Lancashire. So it was during the following year that he wooed and won his bride, Anne Hathaway of Shottery. Their marriage licence is dated 28 November 1582, at least that is the date they applied for it. But we have no record of the marriage itself, which may have already taken place at the bride's church in the village of Temple Grafton. There the priest was one of the old Marian priests, one John Frith, who is mentioned in the Puritan *Survey of the Ministry* for Warwickshire in 1586 as noted for his skill in curing hawks.[15] Then in the following May Anne gave birth to Shakespeare's first and favourite daughter Susanna, who went on to follow the example of her grandfather John in having her name included in the recusancy returns for 1606, the year after the Gunpowder Plot. Subsequently, in 1585 Anne gave birth to the twins Hamnet and Judith, named after their Catholic godparents Hamnet and Judith Sadler.[16] The years from then onwards, till Greene's mention of 'Shakescene' in 1592, are customarily regarded as the 'lost years' of Shakespeare.

Only, in view of what has been said about Shakespeare and his connections with the Society of Jesus, both through his Stratford schoolmasters and through Campion, it may not be difficult to entertain some degree of enlightened conjecture. After the birth of his twins, Anne seems to have given him no more children. His own relationship with her, his senior by some eight years, seems to have grown cold, if we may judge both from what is said about such a marriage by the Duke to Viola in *Twelfth Night* (2.4.29–31) and from the odd omission of Anne by name in his will.

So we may retrace his steps back to Lancashire, once the storm had blown over, so as to avail himself of Hoghton's recommendation and to join Hesketh's players. They are in turn recorded as visiting the country house of the Earl of Derby in 1587; and when the following year Sir Thomas Hesketh died, it would have been only natural for Shakespeare to take his place with Strange's Men, who were now augmented by Leicester's Men on the death of their patron in 1588. From now on the way for William Shakespeare/Shakeshafte/Shakescene lay southwards *via* Stratford and Oxford to London.

At last, let us turn to the all-important question as to the extent which all this schooling under Jesuit influence, whether direct or indirect, had on the subsequent drama of Shakespeare. For this we may well begin with the example of Thomas Hoghton, who had built Hoghton Tower and then gone into voluntary exile for conscience's sake and for the assistance of William Allen in his project of a Catholic seminary at Douai. We may even compare him to those 'loving lords' who follow the banished Duke to the Forest of Arden in *As You Like It* (1.1.108). Hoghton's example also extolled in the words of his extolled memorable poem 'The Blessed Conscience', which may have first come to the attention of the young Shakespeare soon after his arrival in Lancashire in the year of the poet's death:[17]

> At Hoghton High, which is a bower
> Of sports and lordly pleasure,
> I wept and left that lofty tower
> Which was my chiefest treasure.
> To save my soul and lose the rest
> It was my true pretence;
> Like frighted bird I left my nest
> To keep my conscience.

The refrain of this poem recurs in the last line of each stanza, 'To keep my conscience'; and we find it interestingly echoed in one of Shakespeare's earliest plays for the Strange's Men, *Titus Andronicus*. Here we find words put into the mouth of the villain Aaron the Moor, and addressed to the upright Lucius Andronicus, which strangely and uniquely (for Shakespeare) combine the noun 'conscience' with the adjective 'popish':

> Yet, for I know thou art religious,
> And hast a thing within thee called conscience,
> With twenty popish tricks and ceremonies,
> Which I have seen thee careful to observe,
> Therefore I urge thy oath.   (5.1.74–8)

In other plays, it seems, the dramatist instinctively avoids this Protestant-sounding adjective; though on another occasion, in *All's Well That Ends Well* (1.3.57–62), he puts the no less Protestant-sounding noun 'papist' into the mouth of the clown Lavache, who is immediately chided by the Countess for being 'a foul-mouthed and calumnious knave'.

As for the reality implicit in the purpose, 'To keep my conscience', it is everywhere present in the plays of Shakespeare, who seem to be ever brooding as well in his comedies as in his tragedies on the sad plight of the disinherited whether by enforced banishment or by voluntary exile. The play which deals most explicitly with this theme is the abovementioned *As You Like It*, where the parallel with Elizabethan Catholics such as William Allen and Thomas Hoghton is specially noticeable, placed as it is by the dramatist in the (for him) familiar setting of the Forest of Arden, which is further associated with the Ardennes to the north-east of France, close to the seminary of Douai. Yet another important keyword in the play is that put into the mouth of Celia as together with Rosalind and Touchstone she makes her way into the forest: 'Now go we in content / To liberty and not to banishment' (1.3.140–1).

From the forest of *As You Like It* there is, moreover, a significant line of connection with the open heath of *King Lear*, for all the seeming difference between a happy comedy and a sad tragedy. To begin with, the words of Celia to Rosalind are interestingly echoed by Kent as he casts in his lot with the banished Cordelia: 'Freedom lives hence, and banishment is here' (1.1.184). Not that he makes his way at once to the heath; but he returns to the side of Lear in the disguise of a servant, and so he follows Lear and the Fool on to the heath, which now comes to serve as the destination, like the Forest of Arden, of all the good characters in the play: Edgar and Cordelia, Kent and the Fool, as well as the repentant old men, Lear and Gloucester. Edgar in particular is characterized (on his own initiative, for the sake of disguise) as possessed by the devil in terms derived by the dramatist from Samuel Harsnet's satirical exposure of the exorcising activities of William Weston and Robert Debdale, in his *Declaration of Egregious Popish Impostures* (1604). Before that he appears also as one of the hunted priests in terms recalling Campion's self-description in a letter to the Jesuit general superior in Rome: 'I am in apparel to myself very ridiculous; I often change my name also . . . Threatening edicts come forth against us daily' (17 November 1580).[18]

Yet another play, the early historical 'tragedy' of *Richard II*, looks forward both to the comedy of *As You Like It* and to the tragedy of *King Lear*, not least for its impressive presentation of the theme of exile and the plight of the disinherited. Here the vow of the loyal Kent, to 'shape his old course in a country new' (*King Lear* 1.1.190), is anticipated by the deposed Richard on his way to imprisonment (as he thinks) in the Tower, when he passes his sorrowing queen Isabella and gives her the same sad advice:

> Hie thee to France,
> And cloister thee in some religious house:

Our holy lives must win a new world's crown,
Which our profane hours here have stricken down. (5.1.22–5)

These are words that might well have been uttered by Sir Thomas More on the way from his trial in Westminster Hall to the Tower, when he met his sorrowing daughter Margaret. She indeed accompanied her husband William Roper to Canterbury; but the advice was followed by not a few daughters of Catholic recusant families, including some descendants of More himself, as they went to fill convents founded to receive them in the Low Countries.

What is more, the same advice is echoed and rechoed in other plays of Shakespeare, where a choice is proposed between married love and devoted chastity. Most famous is the advice given by Friar Laurence to Juliet when they enter the tomb only to find Romeo dead. 'Come,' he urges her, 'I'll dispose of thee / Among a sisterhood of holy nuns' (5.3.156–7). No less famous is the alternative proposed by Theseus to Hermia at the beginning of *A Midsummer Night's Dream*:

Either to die the death, or to abjure
Forever the society of men . . .
For aye to be in shady cloister mew'd,
To live a barren sister all your life,
Chanting faint hymns to the cold fruitless moon. (1.1.65–73)

These three plays, history, tragedy and comedy, all belong to the same year 1595. After them we find the dramatist recurring to the same advice in *Much Ado About Nothing*, where it is offered by yet another friar for the poor heroine Hero, in case his plan for her fails:

And if it sort not well, you may conceal her –
As best befits her wounded reputation –
In some reclusive and religious life,
Out of all eyes, tongues, minds and injuries. (4.1.239–42)

Finally, there is the advice given by Hamlet to poor Ophelia, to be gone 'to a nunnery' (3.1.124).

This may all serve to show how Shakespeare's mind, so far from turning abruptly from his years of Jesuit-influenced formation, was deeply affected by it throughout his dramatic career, if at a level hidden from the eyes both of contemporary audiences and of modern scholars. It may also serve to suggest an answer to the question why he took so many of his plots either from beyond the seas or from medieval England, but rarely if ever from his own age or nation. Yet, like so many English Jesuits and seminary priests, Campion and Cottam, Hunt and Debdale, he is always returning to his native country, if (like the faithful Kent) in disguise. We may, for instance, recall the riddling conversation between Bassanio and Portia in *The Merchant of Venice* preceding the former's choice among the three caskets, turning as it does on the torture of the rack, 'where men enforced do speak anything' (3.2.33). We may also point to the not infrequent allusion, as in *Romeo and Juliet* (3.5.156) and *King John* (2.1.503–8), to the subsequent punishment of being dragged on a hurdle to the place of execution at Tyburn, which is in turn recalled by Berowne in *Love's Labour's Lost* as 'the shape of love's Tyburn, that hangs up simplicity' (4.3.54). And then there is the culminating torture when the poor victim is drawn from the gallows and cut into quarters and his palpitating heart is pulled out and held up by the executioner to the frenzied crowd.

No wonder Shakespeare, in view of all this, came to compose the tragedies he did, culminating in such a bitter portrayal of sorrow as at the end of *King Lear*, with its evident appeal to recusant audiences in Yorkshire during the winter of 1609–10.[19] No wonder he had previously composed such serious, even tragic comedies as *The Merchant of Venice* and *As You Like It*, whose happy endings are brought about only by an implausible *tour de force*. No wonder if his plays of English history are summarized in the lament of John of Gaunt over 'this England', a lament that applied no less to the reign of Elizabeth I than to that of Richard II. This is what the Queen herself is said to have recognized in her historic remark to the antiquarian William Lambarde, 'I am Richard II, know ye not that?'[20] Only in his last plays does the dramatist turn from these sad thoughts of England's past to a new conceived hope for the future under King James I, as when he puts into the mouth of the British king Cymbeline the concluding resolve, 'Let / A Roman and a British ensign wave / Friendly together' (5.5.480–2).

Such a consistent portrayal of the plight of English Catholics under Elizabeth and the early James, following on the dramatist's presumed Jesuit schooling, may lend probability to the seemingly odd remark that slipped from the pen of the seventeenth-century Anglican clergyman Richard Davies, that Shakespeare 'died a papist'.[21] All too often this remark has been dismissed as insufficiently justified by the plays themselves. Yet such a dismissal is based on a superficial reading of those plays and a failure to realize how much the dramatist had to hide. On the other hand, a careful reading of the plays from a Catholic perspective, such as I have suggested in outline, is more than sufficient to prove that Shakespeare not only died a papist but also lived as one to the best of his limited ability, so far as the conditions of what Portia calls 'these naughty times', allowed him. Here, if anywhere, is the deep reason not only for what is commonly called the Shakespearean enigma (even by those who are loudest in their opposition to the Catholic interpretation), but also for his unique inspiration and his universal (literally, Catholic) appeal from the narrow confines of Elizabethan England to men of all ages and all nations.

Notes

1 Cf. entry under Allen, William, by Thompson Cooper, in *DNB*, vol. 1 (Oxford, 1917), pp. 314–22. Allen's visit to Lancashire is called 'a most important event in the history of Lancashire'.

2 Cf. H. Mutschmann and K. Wentersdorf, *Shakespeare and Catholicism* (New York, 1952), pp. 76–80: 'The Stratford Schoolmasters'; H. A. Shield, 'A Stratford schoolmaster', *The Month* (August 1961), pp. 109–11.

3 Cf. P. Caraman, *The Autobiography of an Elizabethan* (London, 1955); K. Muir, Arden ed. *King Lear* (London, 1952), pp. 253–6: 'Samuel Harsnett and *King Lear*', and *Shakespeare's Sources* (London, 1957), pp. 148–61.

4 A. Keen and R. Lubbock, *The Annotator* (London, 1954), p. 102.

5 In the official prison list of 'Papists, and the Places where they are committed', we find the name of 'Thomas Cottam now in the Tower', in the year 1581; cf. *Catholic Record Society*, vol. 2 (London, 1960), p. 219.

6 Cf. E. A. J. Honigmann, *Shakespeare: 'The Lost Years'* (Manchester, 1985, new edn 1998). The main proponents of the theory are: o. Baker, *In Shakespeare's Warwickshire and the Unknown Years* (London, 1937), E. K. Chambers, *Shakespearean Gleanings* (Oxford, 1944), L. Hotson, *Shakespeare's Sonnets Dated* (London, 1949), Keen and Lubbock, *The Annotator*, p. Milward, *Shakespeare's Religious Background* (London, 1973).

7 Cf. E. K. Chambers, *William Shakespeare*, vol. 2 (Oxford, 1930), pp. 254–4, on Aubrey.

8 Cf. Chambers, *Shakespeare*, vol. 2, pp. 255–7, on Davies, pp. 264–9 on Rowe.

9 The evidence was fully presented by H. Thurston, 'A controverted Shakespeare document', *The Dublin Review* (October–December 1923); cf. J. H. de Groot, *The Shakespeares and 'The Old Faith'* (New York, 1946).

10 Lansdowne 30 (Burghley Papers 1580), no. 78.

11 S. Schoenbaum, *William Shakespeare: A Compact Documentary Life* (Oxford, 1977), pp. 114–5, criticizes the 'Shakeshafte theory' and my defence of it in particular, referring to the article of D. Hamer, 'Was William Shakespeare William Shakeshafte?', *RES*, 21 (1970), pp. 41–8; but he and Hamer are in turn refuted by E. A. J. Honigmann.

12 Cf. Chambers, Shakespeare, vor. 2: 188, on R. Greene.

13 This is the suggestion of Keen and Lubbock, *Annotator*, p. 75.

14 I published an article on this subject in Japanese, 'Zen-sekai wa hitotsu no butai' (All the world's a stage), in *Shiho kara no ibuki* (*Inspiration from Four Winds*) (Tokyo, 1991), pp. 157–73.

15 *Survey of the State of the Ministry in Warwickshire* (1586), published in *A Parte of a Register* under Puritan auspices (1593); cf. Mutschmann and Wentersdorf, *Shakespeare and Catholicism*.

16 Cf. *ibid.* on the Sadlers.

17 Cf. Bede Camm, *Forgotten Shrines* (London, 1910), pp. 185–6, 'The blessed conscience'.

18 Cf. P. Caraman, *The Other Face* (London, 1960), pp. 114–15.

19 The first account of these players goes back to C. J. Sisson, 'Cholmeley's players', *RES*, 18 (1942); but the fullest presentation is by M. Takenaka, 'The Cholmeley players and the performance of *King Lear* in Yorkshire', *Renaissance Bulletin*, 27 (2000).

20 Cf. Chambers, *Shakespeare*, vol. 2, p. 326, on W. Lambarde.

21 Cf. *ibid.*, pp. 255–7, on R. Davies.

Jesuit drama in early modern England

Introduction

The story of Jesuit drama is inseparable from the story of Jesuit schools.[1] Within a decade of its inception in 1540, Ignatius Loyola's small company, the Society of Jesus, established colleges in Messina, Palermo, Padua, Bologna, Tivoli, Alcalá, Valencia, Barcelona, Valladolid, Saragossa, Salamanca, Gandia, Coimbra, Cologne, Ingolstadt, Louvain, and India (three schools). By the mid seventeenth century about five hundred Jesuit schools served students of virtually every major European city and town. Humanistic in curriculum and moral in purpose, the Jesuit school periodically staged original Latin plays, usually on prize days or special occasions. William H. McCabe, S.J., estimates that at least a hundred thousand of these dramas, usually tragedies drawn from the Old Testament or antiquity as well as comedies, played during the seventeenth century. Only a fraction of these reached publication and an even smaller number appeared in European vernaculars. But the cumulative effect of Jesuit drama was anything but local and provincial. Many plays moved outside academic precincts to become grand civic spectacles with dignitaries in attendance. The Munich *Constantinus* (1574) played in the central square and involved over a thousand players. Avancini staged *Pietas victrix* (1659) with tremendous pomp and a full panoply of Baroque effects to three thousand Viennese nobles and Emperor Leopold. Jesuit drama left its mark on many major European writers: Lope de Vega, Calderón, Molina, Maffei, Goldoni, Tasso, the brothers Corneille, Molière, and Voltaire. Jesuit theatre stretched the boundaries of dramatic genre, staging Senecanized sacred tragedies, tragicomedies that ended in repentance and salvation, and, as we shall see below, comico-tragedies. Its adoption of music and dance on stage had important consequences for the development of French ballet and German music. And its aesthetic, manifest in visual and minor arts as well, contributed formatively to the achievements of the Baroque.[2]

The idea of theatre was particularly well suited to Ignatian educational principles and methods, though the Jesuits did not invent college drama. Lutheran schools in Germany and Protestant schools in England had utilized the academic stage well before boys at Messina began reciting dialogues in 1551. But Ignatius himself had recommended the practice of oration and recitation of dialogues (1556) to 'make things more interesting' for the students, to give pleasure to them and their parents, and to add prestige to the school.[3] These schools, famous for their rigorous discipline, trained the intellects of their students and bent their wills to the service of Christ. But with equal fervor Jesuits teachers sought to win the hearts of their students as well. Not a diversion but a considered strategy, theatrical activity aimed to stir the passions in order to foster authentic commitment, in other words, to educate by arousing delight, pity and fear. The first draft for the *Ratio studiorum* (1586), the plan and charter document for Jesuit education, puts the matter succinctly:

> Adolescentes tandem, eorumque parentes mirifice exhilarantur atque accenduntur, Nostrae etiam deuinciuntur Societati, cum nostra opera possunt in Theatro pueri aliquod sui studii, actionis, memoriae specimen exhibere. Agendae itaque videntur Comoediae ac tragoediae, ea tamen moderatione, quae Regula 58 Prouincialis praescribitur.

> Young boys, however, and their parents become marvellously excited and inflamed, and also very much attached to our Society, when the boys are able to display on stage our labours, some results of their study, their acting ability, and a sample of their powers of memory. Hence, we recommend that comedies and tragedies be performed, with the moderation, however, which is prescribed by the Provincial's Rule 58.

The key terms here, *mirifice exhilarantur atque accenduntur*, 'marvellously delighted and inflamed', reveal much about the purpose of playing in Jesuit schools. Then, as now, the Jesuits sought to inflame their students with zeal for virtue, a hatred of sin and a love of God. Presenting on stage concrete embodiments of virtue and vice, the Jesuits promoted an active, affective, personal encounter with abstract principles, one which would effect conversion and transformation.

The Jesuits adoption of theatre came naturally for reasons spiritual and material. At the centre of Ignatian spirituality lies the imagination. Ignatius's *Exercises* continually requires exercitants to use their imagination in order to reform and rise to love of God.[5] Throughout the four weeks, the exercitant must practise the composition of place, imaginatively reconstructing scenes from the Bible in all their detail and colour, supplying the sensory experiences of smell, touch, taste, hearing and sight. Daily devotion includes the Colloquy, or conversation with the persons of the Trinity or Mary. Meditations direct the retreatant to visualize specific scenes. Celebrating the imagination, Ignatius revered its capacity to enkindle the spirit and prepare the soul to receive the indwelling Word. There were also mundane motivations and practical advantages. Rhetorical and theatrical skill characterized Jesuit disputation and preaching. And, working in dangerous places such as England, Jesuit missionaries practised impersonation to survive. As the autobiographies of John Gerard and William Weston amply illustrate, Jesuits frequently changed horses, clothing, names and identity. Edmund Campion, S.J., for another example, entered England as a jewel merchant. So doing, he and his disguised companions were following the instructions of their superiors, who had dispatched them to the hostile country with this instruction, *nemini aperiant se sacerdotes esse, multo minus de Societate*, 'let them reveal to no one that they are priests, much less members of the Society [of Jesus]'.[6] There were allowable exceptions to the general rule of secrecy, of course, but the Jesuit way of proceeding necessarily required exercise of the theatrical imagination.

Jakob Bidermann's *Cenodoxus*

Perhaps the most important Jesuit dramatist, Jakob Bidermann, staged *Cenodoxus* on 3 July 1602 at the Jesuit college in Augsburg.[7] The play enjoyed a civic revival in Munich (1609) before a distinguished and appreciative audience. *Cenodoxus* dramatizes the legend of a learned and well-esteemed Doctor of Paris. After death, his corpse rose up on three successive days, proclaiming that he was accused, sentenced and finally damned. A shocked onlooker, Bruno, thereupon retreated to the wilderness to found the Carthusian monks. Bidermann calls the doctor Cenodoxus, 'Vainglory', and his play reveals that the apparently good doctor actually falls prey to the sin of pride. Though outwardly virtuous, Self-love rather than charity motivates him; Hypocrisy guides all his choices and actions. When others are near, Cenodoxus pretends to virtue; when alone or with the spirits, he acts solely for himself. Panurgus and his fellow demons win the battle for his soul against Conscientia and Cenodoxphylax, his guardian angel.

As befits a school play, *Cenodoxus* has a large cast – forty speaking parts and three choruses. Bidermann writes a robust and slangy Latin, filled with technical terms and echoes of Plautus and Terence. A parasite from New Comedy, Mariscus, begins the play in laughter; this continues through some brightly funny scenes (those featuring the shipwrecked Navigerus, the Rusticus). Soon Senecan rhetoric, spoken by tenebrous visitors from hell, darkens and deepens the action; the gathering gloom culminates in the chilling triumph of the demons and the frightening damnation of Cenodoxus. The last scenes alternate between the heavenly court, where a stern Christ weighs the evidence and gives judgement, and the earthly scene, where amazed mourners hear of Cenodoxus's fate.

As a Jesuit, Bidermann drew on Ignatian traditions to endow hell and the devils with frightening reality. The Fifth Exercise of the First Week is a meditation on hell: exercitants must 'see in imagination the great fires, and the souls enveloped, as it were, in bodies of fire'; they must hear 'the wailing, the screaming, cries, and blasphemies'; they must smell the 'smoke, the brimstone, the corruption, and rottenness'; they must 'taste bitter things, as tears, sadness, and remorse of conscience'; they must feel 'how the flames surround and burn souls' (59). (Such imagery inspired the Jesuit's famous hellfire sermon in Joyce's *Portrait*.) The Meditation on Two Standards like-wise requires the exercitant to envision Lucifer 'seated in the centre of the vast plain of Babylon, on a great throne of fire and smoke' (76). The Rules for the Discernment of Spirits portray Satan as a relentless and cunning adversary; if a person facing temptation loses courage and takes flight, 'no wild beast on earth is more fierce than the enemy of our human nature as he pursues his evil intention with ever increasing malice' (132). The devo-tions of the Jesuit inspired the dramatist. Panurgus soliloquizes on hell with vivid immediacy, remarking the great gorge that 'Devours continually without satiety'. 'Whatever we feed into it inflames / Its fearful hunger. Everywhere my comrades / Seek, hunt, seize, snatch and harry all human-kind' (408 ff.). In the premonitory dream, one devil commands Cenodoxus, 'Spew up your soul, guilt-laden with vast crimes' (987). The devils threaten various forms of torture: Panurgus sneers: 'You're ours, for good; seize, rend him, bear him off' (993). Another cries: 'Still muttering? Put red-hot irons and torches / Against his side' (1005–6). Hell appears as a night-marish locality, full of specific sights, smells and pains: 'Hell's door yawns open. / I feel the oven's fires and sulphurous flames. / Dispatch the beast' (1016–18). After Cenodoxus's death, Panurgus mocks his reputation for learning: 'Why, then, we'll make him Dean of Liberal Studies / In fiery hell' (2121–2, a witty translation for *Antistes litteris Phlegethontcis*). Ignatian meditations on the tortures of hell and the malice of the devil lend concrete reality to the dramatist's evocations.

The real hero of the play turns out to be the uncomprehending Bruno, shocked and miserable at the revelation of the Cenodoxus's damnation:

> From eating, culture, leisure,
> Discussion, reading, talking, Cenodoxus
> Prevents me: sleeping, he wakes me; when awake,
> He haunts me, present even in his absence.
> What's left? He kills my life; makes me dread death.   (2147–51)

After imagining the torments of hell, Bruno and his followers decide to renounce the world:

> Pleasure, farewell; farewell, all lust for glory;
> Farewell, soft garments for my pampered body;
> And farewell, rings – no, rather call them shackles,
> Not rings. Farewell, all honours . . .   (2208–11)

In order to save his soul, Bruno resolves to don sackcloth and a hairshirt, to mortify his flesh with fasting and flagellation:

> I'll ruin it, lest it should ruin me.
> I am resolved to seek the harshest wilderness
> And thus set free my soul, now I have seen
> How Cenodoxus lost his. (2227–30)

The comico-tragedy thus ends on a felicitous note, with the reformation of sinners and the establishment of the Carthusian order. Cenodoxus and Bruno act as paired opposites, the one life warning against pride, the other commending humble sacrifice and service to God.

Bidermann's Catholic *Cenodoxus* furnishes interesting comparisons with Marlowe's Protestant *Doctor Faustus*.[8] Both employ comedy to set up the central figure's tragedy; both show evil spirits battling good ones; both end in terrifying scenes of damnation. But Bidermann minimizes the individuality of the central figure, focusing instead on the relentless operation of divine laws – inflexible, clear, universal and just. Blinded by self – love, Cenodoxus plays Doctor Faustus only to discover after death that he is Everyman, a weak and vain sinner who persisted in folly despite the stings of conscience, the admonitions of the angel and the warning dream. The published version of the play (Munich, 1666) advertised it as a 'Comico-tragoedia', in other words as a play which featured the falls and calamities of common and ordinary people (*personarum vulgarium, humiliumque casus & calamitates*).[8] Marlowe's Faustus, on the contrary, is an extraordinary hero in every way, achieving bad eminence by living an inverted saint's life with all the passion and thrill of humanist aspiration. Marlowe's verse gives Faustus a voice that eloquently registers his brilliance, terror, remorse and hopelessness. The play embodies the traditional orthodox framework, descended from medieval and morality plays, but Faustus lives and dies alone in a reformed universe. As Bevington and Rasmussen have observed:

> Certainly Doctor Faustus faces a Protestant dilemma. The stunning mood of alienation and loss that we experience in the play owes much of its force to a new sense of the isolated human soul in Luther's and Calvin's views of salvation.[10]

Deprived of the miraculous as well as of the reassuring company of saints, the superbly characterized and compelling Faustus struggles alone with his God and his devil. He falls uniquely and tragically. Bidermann's proud, hypocritical and vainglorious sinner, like all the sinners in the audience, perversely chooses ephemeral pleasure over heavenly reward. His story is our own.

Furthermore, the structure of Bidermann's play, its pairing of the sinning Cenodoxus and the saintly Bruno, illustrates Catholic doctrine regarding the freedom of the will. Cenodoxus chooses to spend his life serving sinful Pride; watching his fall, Bruno chooses to abandon worldly comfort and serve the Lord. The play thus dramatizes the workings of conscience, the dynamics of individual volition and our terrible freedom of choice. A different, more restrictive theology operates in Marlowe's play, informed by the debates on Calvinist predestination in English culture generally and at Cambridge. According to this doctrine, no mortal can choose damnation or salvation, but each, to a greater or lesser extent, must obey the ordinances of an omniscient and inscrutable God. This God chose his elect and his reprobate before the beginning of time. A reprobate such as Doctor Faustus manifests his iniquity in his despair and in his inability to shed tears of repentance (A-text, 5.2.15, 30–1). The spectacle of his fall excites pity and terror but not repentance, which must be inefficacious, nor conversion, which must be meaningless. It can merely, in the words of the Choral Epilogue, 'exhort the wise / Only to wonder at unlawful things' (A-text, 5–6).

Bidermann's portrait of damnation, by contrast, stunned contemporary audiences and moved them to repentance and reformation. The *Praemonitio ad lectorem* to the published edition in *Ludi theatrales* (1666) recalls the effect of the 1606 performance in Munich.[11] The jokes and hilarity were most rich in fruit (*fructu . . . uberrimas*), accomplishing more good in a few hours than one hundred sermons (*centenae conciones*). The spectators witnessed the final trial in numbed silence and fear, as if the lightning bolt of just damnation threatened their own heads, not less than the wretched head of Cenodoxus (*justaeque damnationis fulmen non minus suo, quam Cenodoxi miserabilis capiti jamjam impenderet*). After the performance fourteen men, now changed, in a most healthy fear of God (*saluberrimo Dei timore*), asked to make an Ignatian retreat. The actor who played the title role joined the Society and for many years lived a holy and innocent life (*pluribus annis adeo innocenter ac sancte vixit*).

Edmund Campion's *Ambrosia*

In 1566 Queen Elizabeth visited Oxford and was so impressed with a student's disputation there that she recommended him to Leicester and Burghley. About ten years later that student, Edmund Campion, then a Jesuit in Prague, wrote *Ambrosia*, a school play which disputed regnant Protestant orthodoxies, challenging the sovereignty of the Queen herself in religious matters.[12]

Ambrosia relates some important events in the life of St Ambrose, who confronts and defeats the Empress Justina, defender of the Arian heresy. Ambrose celebrates the discovery of holy relics, the remains of two martyrs, Gervasius and Protasius. Miraculously he performs an exorcism on stage and returns a blind man to sight. After Emperor Theodosius falls prey to infernal forces and massacres seven thousand at Thessalonica, Ambrose denies him entrance to the church. The Emperor makes a confession, performs appropriate penance and receives absolution. The action also portrays St Augustine's reformation and Arsenius's imprisonment and release.

Ambrosia reflects and anticipates three theological controversies important to the Reformation and the English mission, namely, the dispute over saints and relics, the disagreement over the sacraments, especially penance; the conflict concerning the powers of church and state.[13] Article 22, of course, had pointedly prohibited the invocation of saints and the adoration of images such as relics. Thomas Rogers scorned such practices:

> They have canonized for a saint the chains which bound St Peter; to say nothing of the adoration they give unto the hair, milk, smock of the blessed Virgin; unto the head, hair, thumb, coat of St John Baptist; unto the breeches of Joseph, the sword and handkerchief of St Paul, the keys of St Peter and unto many other things which of modesty I will not mention.[14]

In his Convocation sermon (1536) Hugh Latimer likewise warned against 'juggling deceits', the veneration of saints' relics that are actually pig bones, the vain pilgrimages to St Blaise's heart at Malvern and to St Algar's bones.[15] Cranmer's chaplain, Thomas Becon, contrasted the Biblical prohibition against images (Exodus 20) with the encouragement of Antichrist, i.e., the Pope:

> Antichrist saith it is lawful not only to have images, and to set them up in temples, chapels, oratories, &c., but also to worship them, to kneel before them, to kiss them, to pray before them, yea, and to them, to kneel before them, to set candles before them, to deck and trim them, to offer unto them, to cense them, to put off our caps unto them, and at the last what not? Antichrist also diggeth out of the ground the old rotten bones or reliques of saints, translateth them, incloseth them in gold, keepeth them in precious shrines and costly clausures, and setteth them forth to the people to be kissed and worshipped.[16]

In a letter dated 2 November 1559 John Jewel lamented the 'wilderness of superstition' which had arisen 'in the darkness of the Marian times. We found in all places votive relics of saints, nails with which the infatuated people dreamed that Christ had been pierced, and I know not what small fragments of the sacred cross.'[17] It remained for James Pilkington to expose the intrinsic folly of reliquary proliferation: 'If the relics, as arms, head, legs, scalp, hair, teeth, &c., were together in one place, that are said to be worshipped in many, some should have two or three heads, more legs and arms than a horse would carry.'[18]

The veneration of saints and relics, however, long flourished as a vital tradition in the Middle Ages and Tudor period. The Council of Trent

(Session 25) urged the reform of abuses but ratified the practice. Images and relics possess no 'divinity, or virtue' in themselves, the Council explained, but they refer believers to the 'prototypes', thus confirming them in the 'habit of remembering'.[19] In his *History of Ireland*, Edmund Campion included a chapter on Irish saints, 'being loath to neglect the memory of God's friends, more glorious to a realm than all the victories and triumphs of the world'. In his *Decem rationes*, he confronted the iconoclasts directly: how can relic-burners 'possibly be reconciled to Augustine', who wrote a book on care for the dead, 'besides sundry sermons and a long chapter in a noble work on the miracles wrought at the Basilicas and Monuments of the Martyrs?' Campion goes on to cite Prudentius, Jerome and, finally, Ambrose, who 'honoured his patron saints Gervase and Protase' and who was honoured 'with more than one miracle'.[20]

In *Ambrosia* 1.3 Ambrose and a choir of clerics enter singing praises of Christ's martyrs, Gervasius and Protasius, whose remains they have just discovered.[21] As the play continues, God affirms the power of the saints and their relics with two miraculous cures. A possessed man, Energumen, enters to destroy the relics; Ambrose exorcizes his demon. The blind Severus then appears, begging Gervasius and Protasius for a cure; he regains his sight. His miraculous cure converts Justina's hostile soldier: 'May the Catholic faith flourish, farewell to all heresy, may Arius rot, may the faith of martyrs reign' (247–8). These miracles affirm the Catholic cultivation of saints and their practice of venerating relics; such practices, the play demonstrates, rout the devil, confound heresy and bear witness to the faith here on earth.

The exorcism in *Ambrosia* (1.5–6) dramatizes a Catholic practice particularly repellant to reformers. Samuel Harsnet's anti-Catholic diatribe, *A Declaration of Egregious Popish Impostures* (1603), presents exorcisms as impostures, as staged performances by clever Jesuits and their minions for gullible spectators.[22] Campion himself makes several posthumous appearances in the *Declaration*, as Harsnet mocks reports of his relics discomfiting and expelling demons (265–70, 295–7). Harsnet's *Declaration*, of course, inspired the language and action of *King Lear*, particularly the storm sequence and the scenes involving Edgar as Tom. At first glance, Shakespeare seems to re-present Harsnet's denial of possession and miracle, and thus to endorse the Protestant position against that of *Ambrosia*. Edgar feigns madness and possession, even naming the phony devils Obidicut, Hobbididence, Mahu, Modo, and Flibbertigibbet (Q 4.1.62–6) of 'chambermaids and waiting-women', Harsnet's confessed liars, Sara and Fid Williams. He also stages a fake miracle, the survival of his father after a supposed fall from a high cliff (4.6), and reports a kind of exorcism. As his blinded, dazed father regains consciousness, Edgar tells him of the figure he saw accompanying him, a 'fiend' with eyes like 'two full moons . . . a thousand noses, / Horns whelked and waved like the enraged sea' (69–72).

Gloucester's companion on top of the non-existent cliff, all spectators know, was Edgar himself.

But Shakespeare transforms Harsnett's monotonous argument into a polyphonous discourse. Edgar may not experience demonic possession but he does suffer real evil, Edmund's deception and malice. The supernatural metamorphoses here into the unnatural as humanity, in the persons of Edmund and the evil sisters, preys on itself like 'monsters of the deep' (Q 4.2.51). Edgar's disguise as Mad Tom, furthermore, occurs in the context of his many other impostures and culminates in his appearance as the masked knight who fights for justice. Such theatrical impersonation functions not as a cheap trick but as means of survival in the world ruled by the wicked. (More than one commentator, in fact, has noted the parallels between Edgar's situation and that of the priests, especially Jesuits, in England, disguised, maligned and hunted like prey.) Furthermore, Edgar's staging of Gloucester's fall cures a corrosive despair and prevents suicide, a desperate remedy especially encouraged by the devil (cf. 3.4.53–4 n.), according to popular belief. Edgar's theatrical fiction saves Gloucester's body and the soul. 'Thy life's a miracle' (4.6.55), he says to his awakening father, and so it is. Theatrical impersonation may look like trickery but it also looks like religious ritual, a salvific action performed with costume, script and props. Weak and erring mortals in this cruel world, the play suggests, require illusions; the truth told to Gloucester, Edgar reports later, proves fatal. Neither overtly Protestant nor Catholic in its outlook, *King Lear* transforms Harsnet's rant into a compelling meditation on evil, suffering, sacrament and miracle in the fallen world.

Campion's *Ambrosia* engages other Reformation controversies, affirming emphatically the Catholic view of penance as a sacrament. Campion directly expressed his outrage at the Protestant devaluation of sacraments in *Decem rationes*: 'I hasten to pass on to the Sacraments. None, none, not two, not one, O holy Christ, have they left' (127). In fighting Counter-Reformation spirit, the play features sacramental baptism, the Eucharist, and, most fully, penance. This last sacrament inspired indignation and controversy on both sides. Luther 'deprived the once-tripartite act [contrition, confession, satisfaction] of any distinctively priestly authority to absolve', restricting that power to 'Christ himself as the only High Priest and Mediator, his plenary merit rendered directly accessible to the sinner through predestined faith, itself a gift of God'.[23] Luther, Melanchthon and Calvin dissected and dismantled the three traditional components: contrition was simply the usual state of mortification for the regenerate believer; confession could be useful if individuals wished to confess to each other or a pastor, this latter simply to be reminded of God's grace; satisfaction was merely an indulgent fiction. No priest could grant an absolution; no sinner could atone for their sin. The devaluation continued, albeit differently, in England:

Thomas Cranmer, leader of the Anglican reform, retained the practice of
private confession and absolution in the ritual for the Visitation of the Sick
in the Prayer Book of 1549 and 1552; but he denied that Penance was a Sacrament of dominical institution, a denial found in article 25 of the *XXXIX
Articles of Religion* of 1563.

In 1581 Parsons notes that new legislation made it high treason to be
absolved and reconciled by a priest in the sacrament of penance.[24]

In response to reformist attacks, the Council of Trent affirmed and
defended the sacramentality of Catholic penance in nine doctrinal chapters
and fifteen canons.[25] One year after Campion's death, Robert Parsons,
in *An Epistle of the Persecution of Catholics in England* (1582), noted
reformist discrepancies on the subject: 'if they were demanded of particular sacraments, as of penance: one would hold it no sacrament with Calvin,
another a sacrament with Melanchthon, another only a sacramental sign
with Luther in one place, and in another, a very true sacrament, having
annexed to it the promise of grace' (7). Parsons affirmed the importance of
the three traditional parts of the sacrament (contrition, confession, satisfaction) (22); in contrast, he noted, the adversaries required 'only to believe,
which is a very easy point' (23).

Ambrosia dramatizes Catholic doctrine concerning sin and the sacrament
of penance. Campion begins by exploring the origins of sin in infernal
temptation: Julian the Apostate, along with Furies, Alecto (Vengeance) and
Mastix (Whip), and assorted demons plan to ensnare Theodosius by arrang-
ing the murder of his emissaries. Enraged, Theodosius then sins in retalia-
tion. Theodosius has free will, of course, the Fury asserts, in a moment of
Counter-Reformation angst: *Arbitria quamvis libera adigi non queant, /
Illecta poterunt vincier malo tamen*, 'Although the free will cannot be
forced, when it is attracted it will possibly be overcome by evil' (657–8).
In 4.1 Ambrose dissuades Theodosius from reprisal after the murder, but
soon after others arouse his wrath: 'The city shall be given to the sword',
he declares; 'Thousands shall pay' (823). His soldiers fall on Thessalonica
and massacre seven thousand people.

Ambrose sternly denies Theodosius entrance to the basilica and the
Emperor immediately repents his sin. Regretting the 'savage and wild
impulse of hasty anger' (1031–2), he feels the full weight of his crimes and
unworthiness: 'With what face shall I look upon Heaven?' 'I confess that I
deserve hell' (1032, 1038). Having heard this confession of sin and consulted with other clerics (1039ff.), Ambrose decides on an appropriate
poena, 'penalty or satisfaction'. He decides on a public confession to the
people (1181ff.), a stay among penitents, special attention to the sin of
wrath and a granting of reprieves to the condemned. Ambrose dutifully
submits to the disciplines of penance.

Campion's play vindicates each of the three parts of the Catholic sacrament. The contrition expresses specific sorrow and betokens a change of

heart; the confession takes two forms, private and public; the satisfaction cleanses the sinner of the specific sin. Throughout the process *Ambrosia* ratifies the authority and power of the priest administering the sacrament, a point of strenuous debate between Catholics and Protestants. Matthew Harding, for example, recalled Ambrose's ministrations to Theodosius precisely to prove that a priest possessed an invested power to bind and loose sins. His adversary, John Jewel, insisted that God alone forgave sins and that a priest could function only as a judge and a dispenser of spiritual medicine.[26] Campion, contrarily, presents the Bishop as the material agent of God's grace, His representative on earth, clearly empowered to bind and loose sins. 'When I summon you again, I shall undo your chain; then you will be sufficiently cleansed and proved', Ambrose says, thus promising forgiveness and deliverance from guilt, fear and sin. When Theodosius completes his penance, Ambrose gives absolution: *Vinclis exuo*, 'I liberate you from your shackles' (1255). An angelic chorus rejoices at the return of the soul to grace.

Ambrosia also articulates a Catholic view regarding the respective powers of church and state. Ambrose's rebuke and Theodosius's humble submission figured importantly in English discourse, causing considerable embarrassment to reformers who had appointed their King head of the church. Patrick Collinson surveys various Protestant reactions:[27] Bilson and Nowell profess to find the story unobjectionable; Hooker dismisses it an extraordinary case with no implications for the exercise of ordinary ecclesiastical jurisdiction. Others attempt recuperation. Pilkington praises Theodosius for good and humble behaviour before a minister of God; two manuscript orations to Elizabeth cite Ambrose to defend the temerity of offering reproof or admonition to the ruler. Campion, however, as Alison Shell has noted, structures his play to emphasize the subordination of state to church, beginning with Ambrose's defiance of the heretical empress Justina, and continuing in the stories of Gervasius and Protasius, who died rather than assent to Nero's absurd rituals (*Insanos ritus*, 100) and vain dreams of gods (*vana deorum / Somnia*, 100–1).[28] These incidents culminate in Ambrose's rebuke of the penitent Theodosius for trespassing in the sanctuary; abashed, Theodosius humbly retreats and waits to receive the Eucharist with the other laity. Ambrose thus teaches the difference between an Emperor and a priest.

The political struggle between church and state here depicted had prophetic importance for Campion and for England. Two years after *Ambrosia* opened, Campion arrived in England as a missionary. The next year, 1581, he was arrested for treason, hanged, drawn and quartered at Tyburn. Like Gervasius and Protasius in the play, Campion became a martyr to those who remained on earth to combat heresy. Throughout his career he distinguished himself as a champion in disputation, an art central to the English mission.[29] This genius for argument, evident in his student days at

Oxford as well as in his famous 'brag', polemical writing, and debates in the Tower before his death, appeared also in the playhouses of Prague where *Ambrosia* instructed and delighted its audiences.

Joseph Simons's *Mercia*

Joseph Simons, S.J., an English exile at the college of St Omers, wrote tragedies that circulated widely throughout Europe in the early seventeenth century. His *Mercia* tells the story of the seventh-century English king Ulferus, persecutor of Christians, his two sons, and Ceadda (St Chad).[30] Ceadda converts the princes, Ulfadus and Ruffinus, who renounce pagan gods and serve Christ. Enraged, their father executes them, suffers remorse, experiences divine forgiveness and finally converts to Christianity himself.

Like Campion's *Ambrosia*, Simons's *Mercia* reflects the struggles of Catholic subjects and Protestant rulers in England. The princes suffer exile, imprisonment and execution in their native land. They meet priests and receive sacraments in secret; they suffer betrayal by infiltrators and false accusations. Several times they play the role of Protestant iconoclasts, destroying a temple and statue of Jove and attacking a statue of Phoebus Apollo (120, 190). Like the other Christians in the play, who burn down the temple of Apollo, *Ille marmore aeterno tholus / Arx illa superum, vertice feriens Polum* (137), 'that temple of eternal marble, that citadel of the gods above, striking the heavens with its peak', the princes appropriate to themselves the characteristic Protestant gesture and expression of power. Even Ceadda must act in the familiar, fallen world of England, where priests had to resort to theatrical impersonation: *Ceadda . . . sacerdotes mittit, qui dissimulata persona in Aulam penetrent, Principesque baptizent* (175), 'Ceadda sends priests [to the prisoners], who disguise themselves to get into the court and baptize the princes'. The priests carry holy water in a staff and sword-hilt. In the last lines of the play Ulferus summons straying subjects, *quo vocat Christus*, 'whither Christ calls', and declares religious peace and unity in Britain, surely expressing the hope of its exiled author: *Unus orbe dominatur Deus. / Unus Britanum Chritus Imperium regit* (235), 'One God rules the world. One Christ rules the British empire'.

Like Simons's *Vitus*, which tells of Diocletian the emperor torturing a Christian youth, *Mercia* is a martyr tragedy. Beginning perhaps with Stefonio's *Sancta symphorosa* (Rome, 1591), 'Jesuit playwrights of every generation all over Europe' wrote martyr tragedies, presenting 'an unfailing file of heroes' to their audiences.[31] Simons defines these heroes as Christian by opposing them to classical paganism as represented by Senecan dramatic conventions. A Senecan phantasm, *Genius Furoris*, the Prologue to *Mercia*, invokes *Lamenta, Lacrymae, Gemitus* ('laments, tears, groans'), and envisions houses swimming in blood (*sanguine natatantes domus*), throats cut (*Iugula recisa*) and limbs torn from limbs (*avulsa membris membra*)

(110–11). At one point the disguised priest Tityrus vows that nothing can separate him from Christ, even if Furor, the weapons of the Furies, and the whole marsh of Acheron rage against him (181). Characters burn with insatiable, Senecan rage. And Senecan demons seem to prevail at the climax of the play when the father kills his own sons; *Furor intus ardet*, 'Furor burns within' (228), he says, recapitulating the archetypal filicides of Seneca's *Hercules Furens* and *Medea*. But the sons die calling on their Heavenly Father, not Ulferus; and, reappearing with Christ, they beg mercy and forgiveness for their father. Ulferus repents and reforms: *O quis me deus / Transformat intus*, 'Oh, what god transforms me deep within?' (233). He becomes a Christian: *Christi potens / Agnosco numen* (234), 'I recognize the powerful divinity of Christ'; *Abiuro deos* (235), 'I abjure the gods'. The Christian God and his martyrs turn Senecan tragedy to spiritual triumph.

Simons's *Mercia* has a precise, structural counterpart in English drama, Philip Massinger and Thomas Dekker's *The Virgin Martyr*.[32] This play (licensed in 1620, published in 1622) tells the tale of St Dorothea, wooed by Antoninus, whom she turns to love of God, and confronted by Christeta and Caliste, whom she converts to Christianity. Dorothea suffers torture but remains miraculously unharmed, and finally is martyred and translated to glory. Massinger and Dekker domesticate the Senecan phantasm to a morality-play devil, Harpax, who opposes an angel, Angelo. The converts, like Simons's princes, declare allegiance to Christianity in a dramatic desecration of Jupiter's image: *They* [Christeta and Calista] *both spit at the image, throw it down, and spurn it* (3.2.53 S.D.). Like Ulferus, Theophilus, the enraged father of these new Christians, has his children killed for their apostasy. Villainous accomplices in both plays, Verebodus in *Mercia* and Harpax in *The Virgin Martyr*, incite the fathers to the murder, thus deflecting some of the blame and allowing for paternal reformation. Like Ulferus, Theophilus witnesses a miraculous apparition, repents and finally converts to Christianity.

The compelling formal parallels between Simons's *Mercia* and Massinger's and Dekker's *The Virgin Martyr* support Louise George Clubb's identification of the English play as a *tragedia sacra*.[33] This Counter-Reformation genre, popular in Europe in the latter half of the sixteenth century, often featured beautiful, inviolable virgins, who endured torments, worked miracles and conversion, and enjoyed, finally, heavenly rewards. The English play imitates the form and content, though not necessarily the confessional doctrine, of the popular, Continental Catholic genre.[34] Dorothea might as easily be a Protestant as a Catholic martyr.

Conclusion

Aut prodesse aut delectare (Horace, *Ars Poetica* 333) – either to benefit or to delight. Continental commentators on Horace and Aristotle and their

English descendants, including Sidney, Nashe, Webbe and Puttenham, all affirm these twin ends of poetry. More specifically Sidney argues that comedy gives examples to avoid and tragedy 'maketh kings fear to be tyrants, and tyrants manifest their tyrannical humours; that, with stirring the affects of admiration and commiseration, teacheth the uncertainty of this world and upon how weak foundations gilded roofs are builded'.[35] The Jesuit plays here noticed variously work to these moral ends. But, unlike contemporary secular drama, Jesuit plays operated out of clearly defined Catholic traditions. Enormously popular in their own time, such plays reflect convictions about the moral purpose of literature largely absent in our critical discourse, despite the incessant posturing of writers and literary critics. Jesuit drama played as Baroque spectacle in Europe but also as an aid to the serious business of living and dying morally in this world. The stakes of the endeavour were high: the salvation of individual souls, the promotion of order and justice in the state, service to the kingdom of God. The achievement, certainly open to debate, remains worthy of consideration.

Notes

1 I draw this paragraph from Edna Purdie, 'Jesuit drama', in *The Oxford Companion to the Theatre*, ed. Phyllis Hartknoll, 3rd edn (London, 1967), pp. 508–15; W. Grenzmann, 'Jesuit drama', in *New Catholic Encyclopedia* (New York, 1967), vol. 7:893–7; William H. McCabe, S.J., *An Introduction to the Jesuit Theater*, ed. Louis J. Oldani, S.J. (St Louis, 1983); John W. O'Malley, *The First Jesuits* (Cambridge, Mass., 1993), pp. 223–5. See also Nigel Griffin, *Jesuit School Drama: A Checklist of Critical Literature* (London, 1976); also his *Jesuit School Drama: A Checklist of Critical Literature, Supplement No. 1* (London, 1986).

2 On this last point see Rudolf Wittkower and Irma B. Jaffe, eds, *Baroque Art: The Jesuit Contribution* (New York, 1972).

3 McCabe, *Introduction*, pp. 11–12.

4 G. M. Pachtler, S.J., *Ratio studiorum et institutiones scholasticae Societatis Iesu*, 4 vols (Berlin, 1887–94), vol. 2:176. Subsequent versions of the *Ratio* show nervousness about an increasing vital theatrical tradition; see McCabe, *Introduction*, pp. 13ff.

5 *The Spiritual Exercises of Saint Ignatius*, trans. Anthony Mottola (New York, 1989). See also Ernest C. Ferlita, S.J., 'The road to Bethlehem – is it level or winding? The use of the imagination in the *Spiritual Exercises*', *Studies in the Spirituality of Jesuits*, 29.5 (1997), pp. 1–23; Pedro Arrupe, S.J., 'Art and the spirit of the Society of Jesus', *Studies in the Spirituality of Jesuits*, 5.3 (1973), pp. 83–92; Clement J. McNaspy, 'Art in Jesuit life', *ibid.*, pp. 93–111.

6 John Gerard, *The Autobiography of an Elizabethan*, trans. Philip Caraman (London, 1951); William Weston, *The Autobiography of an Elizabethan*, trans. Philip Caraman (London, 1955); *Letters and Memorials of Father Robert Persons, S.J.*, ed. L. Hicks, S.J. (London, 1942), p. 318.

7 Jakob Bidermann, *Cenodoxus*, ed. and trans. D. G. Dyer and Cecily Longrigg (Austin, 1974).

8 Christopher Marlowe, and his collaborators and revisers, *Doctor Faustus: A- and B- texts (1604, 1616)*, ed. David Bevington and Eric Rasmussen (Manchester, 1993).

9 I quote from Bidermann's great teacher Jacob Pontanus, *Poeticarum institutionum libri tres* (Ingolstadt, 1594), p. 89.

10 Bevington and Rasmussen, ed., *Doctor Fanstus*, p. 12.

11 Jakob Bidermann, *Ludi theatrales* (1666), ed. Rolf Tarot, facs. rpt, 2 vols (Tübingen, 1967), 1: +8 v—++1. Loyola College of Maryland delighted audiences with the first production in English, 1940, replete with balletic interludes, musical selections from Bach, Stravinsky, and others, carefully chosen costumes and set design, and two professional actors. On the Loyola production see Nicholas Varga, *Baltimore's Loyola / Loyola's Baltimore* (Baltimore, 1990), pp. 299–300. The College Archives contain the script and ancillary materials, including reflections by Father Grady, the translator and producer, and a review from *Time*, 11 March 1940.

12 I quote from *Ambrosia: A Neo-Latin Drama by Edmund Campion, S.J.*, ed. and trans. Jos. Simons (Assen, 1969).

13 There are other issues as well. The controversy over the Arian heresy, which denied the full divinity of Christ to be incarnate in human flesh, has relevance to the debates on transubstantiation, as apologists on both sides recognized; see, for example, Thomas More, *A Letter against Frith*, in *Complete Works*, vol. 7 (New Haven, 1990), pp. 238–9.

14 *The Catholic Doctrine of the Church of England: An Exposition of the Thirty-nine Articles by Thomas Rogers*, ed. J. J. S. Perowne (Cambridge, 1854), p. 225.

15 *Selected Sermons of Hugh Latimer*, ed. Allan G. Chester (Charlottesville, 1968), pp. 23–5.

16 *The Works of Thomas Becon, STP*, ed. John Ayre, 3 vols (Cambridge, 1843–44), vol. 43:521.

17 John Jewel as reprinted in *The Zurich Letters, Comprising the Correspondence of Several English Bishops and Others*, trans. and ed. Hastings Robinson, 2 vols (Cambridge, 1842–45), vol. 1:44.

18 *The Works of James Pilkington*, ed. James Scholefield (Cambridge, 1842), p. 147.

19 *The Canons and Decrees of the Sacred and Oecumenical Council of Trent*, trans. J. Waterworth (London, 1848), pp. 234–5. See also Eamon Duffy, *The Stripping of the Altars: Traditional Religion in England c.1400–c.1580* (New Haven, 1992).

20 Edmund Campion, *A Historie of Ireland (1571)*, intro. Rudolph B. Gottfried (New York, 1940), p. 42; also his *Ten Reasons* (London, 1914), pp. 112, 113–14.

21 Ambrose explains that he originally received instructions from a vision of St Paul, whom he recognized from his image, *ab imagine* (161). This recognition, suggesting the currency of icons, became a point of contention in the Harding Jewel controversy. John Jewel, *Works*, ed. John Ayre, 4 vols (Cambridge, 1845–50), vol. 2:654–5.

22 F. W. Brownlow reprints Harsnett's text with a substantial introduction, *Shakespeare, Harsnett, and the Devils of Denham* (Newark, 1993); for the parallels with *King Lear* see Kenneth Muir's Arden edition (1955), Appendix 7; for the text of *Lear* I have used R. A. Foakes's Arden Three edition (1997).

23 George Huntston Williams, *The Radical Reformation*, 3rd edn (Kirksville, 1992), p. 88; see also Euan Cameron, *The European Reformation* (Oxford, 1991), pp. 132–5.

24 *New Catholic Encyclopedia*, vol. 11:77; for Parsons's note see *Miscellanea IV* (London, 1907), p. 3; on earlier prohibitions, Nicholas Sander, *The Rise and Growth of the Anglican Schism* (1585), trans. and ed. David Lewis (London, 1877), p. 307.

25 See A. Nampon, S.J., *Catholic Doctrine as defined by the Council of Trent* (Philadelphia, 1869), pp. 472–519.

26 Jewel, *Works*, vol. 3:366–79 (p. 374).

27 Patrick Collinson, 'If Constantine, then also Theodosius: St Ambrose and the integrity of the Elizabethan *Ecclesia Anglia*', in *Godly People: Essays on English Protestantism and Puritanism* (London, 1983), pp. 109–33.

28 Alison Shell, ' "We are made a spectacle": Campion's dramas', in *The Reckoned Expense: Edmund Campion and the Early English Jesuits: Essays in Celebration of the First Centenary of Campion Hall, Oxford (1896–1996)*, ed. Thomas M. McCoog, S.J. (Woodbridge and Rochester, 1996), pp. 103–18.

29 See Thomas M. McCoog, S.J., ' "Playing the champion": the role of disputation in the Jesuit mission', in *The Reckoned Expense*, pp. 119–39; James V. Holleran (ed.), *A Jesuit Challenge: Edmund Campion's Debates at the Tower of London in 1581* (New York, 1999).

30 Joseph Simons, *Mercia* (Rome, 1648) (bound with *Zeno*); see also *Jesuit Theater Englished: The Five Tragedies of Joseph Simons*, ed. Louis J. Oldani, S.J., and Philip Fischer, S.J. (St Louis, 1989).

31 McCabe, *Introduction*, p. 171. One Jesuit playwright, Nicolaus Caussinus, S.J., *Tragoediae sacrae* (Paris, 1620), says of the agonies of Christian martyrs, *quos ignorare, flagitium est, contemnere piaculum*, 'to ignore them is a sin, to condemn them, an expiation' (*Hermenigildus*, p. 93v).

32 *The Virgin Martyr*, ed. Fredson Bowers, in *The Dramatic Works of Thomas Dekker*, vol. 3 (Cambridge, 1958); Cyrus Hoy, *Introduction, Notes, and Commentaries* to Bowers's edition, vol. 3 (Cambridge, 1980).

33 Louise George Clubb, '*The Virgin Martyr* and the Tragedia Sacra', in *Italian Drama in Shakespeare's Time* (New Haven, 1989), pp. 205–29 (revised from her earlier article in *Renaissance Drama*, 7 (1964), pp. 103–26).

34 This distinction is lost on Julia Gasper, *The Dragon and the Dove: The Plays of Thomas Dekker* (Oxford, 1990), pp. 136–65, who strenuously denies the formal parallels with the *tragedia sacra* on doctrinal (and other) grounds and who reads the play as militant Protestant hagiography.

35 Philip Sidney, 'An apology for poetry', in *Elizabethan Critical Essays*, ed. G. Gregory Smith, 2 vols (Oxford, 1904, rpt 1971), vol. 1:177.

Richard Verstegan and Catholic resistance: the encoding of antiquarianism and love

In 1582 Richard Verstegan printed John Alfield's reply to Anthony Munday's report on the trial and execution of Edmund Campion and then fled to the Continent. Living in exile, Verstegan worked as a printer and engraver, as a martyrologist, as an intelligencer for William Allen, Robert Parsons and Henry Garnet. He wrote political tracts and translated devotional works. In 1605 he wrote an antiquarian history, *A Restitution of Decayed Intelligence*, which was dedicated to King James, printed in Antwerp, and entered in the Stationers' Register to be sold in London by John Bill. In 1608 he provided English translations for Otto Vaenius's multilingual *Amorum emblemata*, printed in Antwerp, with a dedication in this version to the Earl of Pembroke and the Earl of Montgomery.[1]

Daniel Woolf has described *Restitution* as the first work 'to glorify the Saxons above all other English peoples'; Glenn Burgess has credited it with the 'destruction of the myth of British origins'.[2] Despite these acknowledgements Verstegan's place within early modern antiquarianism has not been defined in any detail. Scholarly interest has focused almost exclusively on the Protestant monarchical and republican interests with which sixteenth- and seventeenth-century antiquarian movements were inflected; Whigs and Tories, king and Parliament have been at issue, not Protestants and Catholics.[3] And there has been little effort to resolve the seeming contradiction between the Verstegan who wrote such harsh denunciation of the Tudors and the seemingly disinterested antiquarian to whom Woolf, Burgess and others refer.[4] Similarly, although Vaenius has been credited with creating in *Amorum emblemata* a book attractive to the market for love poetry, Verstegan's contribution has been barely noticed. It is the purpose of this chapter to discuss both of these books briefly in order to fill out some aspects of Verstegan's writing on behalf of English Catholics during the early years of the reign of James.

Far from being disinterested, Verstegan deployed in *Restitution* an antiquarian discourse in order to present early in the reign of James a non-inflammatory but none the less comprehensive reiteration of the key positions on English religious-political policy that the English Catholic leadership had disseminated during the 1580s and 1590s. In part, the difficulty in identifying these arguments is attributable to Verstegan's having cast *Restitution* not as a work of controversy but as description, definition and compilation. Posing as the disinterested scholar committed to getting the facts right about English antiquities, Verstegan claimed that he wished only to correct some errors in the work of others who were also interested in British antiquity, a project he carried out for 338 pages – approximately one half of which is historical narrative, the other half an Anglo-Saxon glossary. In this material Verstegan provided, if not the Catholic arguments themselves, certainly the documentation that supported three interlocking English Catholic arguments of this period: first, that the Tudor Protestant rule was based on myth, lies and pretension; second, that the mainstay of English political traditions rested in the notion of elected and popularly supported kings who could be removed from power; and third, that kings were not to be the head of the church.

In the preliminaries to *A Restitution*, Verstegan stated that the purpose of his book was to offer correction to those authors who had erred in their 'lack of due distinction' between the British and the English, with the result that 'our true originall ... antiquitie lieth ... obscured'. He referred to three authors whose errors were most at issue: Jean Bodin (known for his defence of absolute monarchy) and two architects of Tudor propaganda – John Foxe and Thomas Cooper – although, depersonalizing the attack on the English, Verstegan referred to Foxe and Cooper not by name but by citing the titles of the books at issue. The title of Cooper's Latin/English *Thesaurus* appears in the text; the title *Acts and Monuments* is inserted in the margin.

In choosing Anglo-Saxon antiquities, and specifically the difference between British and English, as the grid on which to mount his project, Verstegan returned to the antiquarian project that had been initiated by John Leland and Matthew Parker, and supported by Burghley at the beginning of the reign of Elizabeth,[5] while at the same time positioning himself against the rhetoric of 'difference' that Foxe had deployed for defining 'the antichristian nature of the papal church'.[6] The religious-political goals of Tudor Protestant rule had required complex arguments, ranging from myths of Trojan origin to arguments regarding the origins and nature of royal authority, ecclesiastical institutions, and legal and constitutional precedents. These arguments involved the privileging of British origins, a castigation of the Saxons as the brutal pagan intruders and an emphasis on the British King Arthur as descendant of Constantine and source of the Tudor line. As Glenn Burgess has emphasized, antiquarian constitutionalism 'looked like a glorification of the ancient past, but it was in fact a glorification (and a justification) of the present'. Burgess continues:

> English ancient constitutionalism took shape during the late sixteenth century when the paramount political need was for a defence of the *status quo* in church and state. Thus it developed, in sharp contrast to most other parts of Western Europe, into a form of political conformism . . . It was thus an antidote to Calvinist resistance theory, not a form of it.[7]

And we may add, it was also an antidote to Catholic resistance theory.

As a master of such antiquarian argument, Foxe had described the period of Roman invasion, from the reign of Lucius to the reign of Vortigern, as one during which the land was Christian under British dominance and infidel under Roman. His narration of the pagan Saxons in Britain – the sequence that is especially a target of Verstegan's revisionism – began with the reign of the British king Vortigern, who first invited the Saxons to come to Britain, and concluded with the Saxons having driven the British into Wales. While Foxe granted that there were interludes of good rule under the Saxons, including that of the revered Ethelbert, for the most part Foxe defined Saxon dominance as cruel and tyrannical, a central story being that of Vortigern, who, having usurped the throne and needing assistance, sent for the Saxons, who in turn sent him Hengist. Subsequently Hengist was established as King of Kent, with other Saxons in control of the six other kingdoms. Although the reign of Arthur brought peace and victory, in 568 the land fell again to the Saxons, 'by whom all the clergy and Christian ministers of the Britaines were then utterly driven out'. These 'idolatrous Saxons prevailed in number and strengths', 'wasting Christianity . . . throught the whole realm' (*Acts and Monuments*, 1583, sig. K3r).

Cooper's *Thesaurus* (1565) carried the same perspective on Arthur and the Saxons by way of the glosses for 'Arthur' and 'Britain', where Arthur is represented as the vanquisher of the barbaric Saxons.[8] In the *Britannia*, William Camden, who had entered Magdalen College under Cooper's patronage and had dedicated the first editions of the *Britannia* to Burghley, repeated much of the Foxian thesis regarding the importance of early British history, with the exception that he expressed doubts about the Brutus and Trojans myths and placed a higher value on the Roman contribution. Later, in the *Remaines* (1605) and virtually at the same time as Verstegan's *Restitution*, Camden would cast the Saxons in more positive light, a revision he articulated within a Protestant framework; there, in the opening section on 'Britaine', Camden declared Britain's 'precedence' in 'true Christian Religion' and that Britain acknowledged 'no vassalage to emperour or Pope. The power of the Kings [being] more absolute, than in most other kingdomes' (7).

Catholic polemicists were highly visible as these antiquarian battles waged on. In 1565, the same year as Cooper's *Thesaurus*, the exiled Thomas Stapleton had published his translation of Bede's *Ecclesiastical Historie of England*, accompanied by an introductory essay summarizing the errors 'of

Bale, of Fox, of Beacon'. And later there was Robert Parsons, who disseminated his views most controversially in *The Conference about the Next
Succession*, which Verstegan had seen through the Antwerp press in mid-
1595, and in which Parsons had analysed six claims to succession, privileging the Infanta of Philip II over James VI. Drawing support for his
arguments regarding the principles of succession and elected kingship often
from Anglo-Saxon history, Parsons treated the elevation of the British as a
self-serving tool of the Tudors and the Cecils. On the eve of the death of
Elizabeth, Parsons was reiterating similar arguments in *A Treatise of Three
Conversions*. Dated 1 March 1603, Parsons's 'Epistle Dedicatorie to the
Catholiques of England' was followed by 'An addition . . . upon the newes
of the Queens death' in which Parsons's, calling Elizabeth 'your old
persecutor', expressed the hope that soon King James would be converted. Parsons's next major book would be his reply, in 1606, to Edward
Coke's *The Fift Part of the Reports*, which had come out in 1605.

Dissociating himself from Parsons's and his own earlier controversialist
styles, Verstegan cast *Restitution* as a set of facts about the English-Saxons.
He explained that British antiquities were irrelevant to his particular topic
– 'as yf they properly appertayned unto Englishmen'. Anyone who argued
otherwise was simply in error, for 'their ofsprings and descents are wholy
different' (+3v). He dispensed as well with both Trojan and Roman traditions. Mocking the use in Britain and in Europe of the tradition of Trojan
descent, Verstegan asserted that Brute had most likely come from Gallia,
and thus that the Britons were descendants of the Gauls, actually, he
suggested, a far better ancestry than being known as deriving from 'the
miserable fugitives of a destroyed city' (M4r).

Replacing the Britons and Romans with the centrality of the Saxons
required erasure of two traditions, rehabilitation of another. Drawing on
the authority of Tacitus, Johannes Baumgarten (Pomarius) and Justus
Lipsius, Verstegan replaced the Foxian version of Saxon cruelty with a
version of the Saxons that emphasized their continency, purity (they 'kept
themselves unmixed with forrain people', F2v), courage and learning – they
excelled, he tells us, in rhetoric, logic, arithmetic, artillery and printing (F3r–G2v). In these examples and others, Verstegan's revisionism
replaced the Britain-Roman-Constantine tradition with an English-Saxon-
Charlemagne-Habsburg tradition. In *Britannia*, Camden had ended his
account of the Britons with a sudden turn to Henry VII and Henry VIII;
Verstegan's account of the Saxons deferred to a different tradition. What,
asked Verstegan, would Tacitus say were he 'to see the seat of the Roman
Emperor placed in Germanie, and the Emperor himself to bee a German,
yea the Emperial dignitie (the greatest temporall state of the world) to
have continued in that nation & race, thease 800. Yeares, Charles the
great that first thereunto brought it, beeing a German by birth & descent'
(G3r)?

Whatever reasons other antiquaries had for becoming invested in Saxon history, for Verstegan the advantage included the opportunity it afforded for making a Catholic argument against absolute monarchy – and by implication, against royal supremacy in matters ecclesiastical. Verstegan's chief target, in other words, is that linchpin – royal supremacy – that had made the suppression of Catholicism possible, and that had called forth from Foxe and others a version of history that would authorize it. Thus Verstegan's goal was slightly different from that of Parsons in *Conference about the Next Succession*, which had emphasized 'the popular basis of the tenure of the Crown' in order 'to prove that . . . the one rightful claim to the throne of England at Elizabeth's death was that of the Spanish Infanta'.[9] Arguing that 'nearnes by blood' is not enough on which to base a title (B4r), and that people of different nations had chosen different forms of government depending on their preferences (C2r–C3v), Parsons had reviewed the means by which a commonwealth had traditionally limited the monarch's authority, including law, councils, parliaments, courts, diets, and had singled out for special praise the method by which the German electors had chosen the emperor. And he had argued that 'Kings lawfully possessed may be deprived if they fulfil not the lawes and condicions' (D5v), for the people as a whole are superior to the king. In *Trew Law of Free Monarchies* (1598) James had answered such arguments when he declared kings 'the authors and makers of the Lawes, and not the Lawes of the kings' (p. 62). In his first speech to Parliament, March 1604, he had reconfirmed his 'descent lineally out of the loynes of *Henry* the seventh' (271), and decried the false claims of the Pope, who 'claimes to bee Spirituall head of all Christians' and 'to have an Imperiall civill power over all Kings and Emperors' (275). At the same time as Verstegan's *Restitution*, Coke had repeated James's position in his chapter 'Of the Kings Ecclesiasticall Lawe' in *The Fift Part of the Reports*, where he justified once more the English execution of priests and recusants by repeating that England was an absolute monarchy and the king supreme over ecclesiastical and temporal persons and causes, an argument Parsons would answer the following year. But, as we see, Parsons was not alone in keeping up the resistance.

Following certain sections of Parsons's *Conference* often point-by-point, narrative by narrative, but without polemical embellishments, Verstegan matter-of-factly tells how the Britons, 'abandoned' by the Romans and 'being unable to defend themselves' from the barbarian Scots and Picts, 'elected' Vortigern as king, who in turn asked assistance from the Saxons, whose response was the arrival of the 'most valiant Saxon Princes' Hengist and Horsa. Unlike Foxe and Camden, who had described this arrival as portending the 'destruction of Britain', Verstegan declared that, 'because these noble gentlemen were the very first bringers & conductors of the ancesters of Englishmen into *Britaine*', he was honouring that contribution by including in his book a picture of their arrival (P2v). He also emphasized that these men had been brought up in the service of the Emperor Valentinian, an emperor Persons had singled out as famous for having obeyed the laws. Verstegan next moved swiftly through a set of allusions – which included Richard Cordelion, Henry the Lion, Duke of Saxony and Charles Emanuel, 'the now duke of Savoy' (P4v) – that privileged the line of Charles V, and, by implication, recalled the claim to the English throne of the Infanta of Spain but also suggested the significance to England of ongoing Catholic European alliances.

Verstegan's emphasis on elected kingship continued with his explaining that the Britons, wishing to be 'subjects of a better king', had deposed Vortigern and elected Vortimer (Q4v–R1r). Giving brief mention to 'the famous king Arthur', Verstegan, citing Bede, told how Saxon rule was honored by King Ethelbert, the first Saxon king to receive the Christian faith. He then inserted a picture of St Augustine, attended by other monks, 'bringing . . . the Christian faith unto Ethelbert' (S4v).

The coming of William the Conqueror is the next milestone in Verstegan's story, an event Foxe had decried as a foreign usurpation but praised as an instance when the king dominated the church. To King James, William's rule exemplified the notion that the laws came from the king: William of Normandy, James had explained, 'made himselfe king . . . by force, and with a mighty army . . . gave the Law, and tooke none, [and] changed the Lawes . . . Whereof the like was also done by all them that conquested them before' (*Trew Law of Free Monarchies*, 63). In contrast Verstegan, like Parsons before him, used the sequence from Edmund Ironside through Hardicanute to illustrate how it often occurred that, when the succession was interrupted, as after the death of Hardicanute, it fell to noblemen to decree how the succession would be delimited. As for William himself, Verstegan represented him as inept, unable to govern his own country and thinking absurdly that he could secure a title merely by force. With sly humour Verstegan reported that, when William got out of his boat, he slipped and fell, a bad omen, he quipped (Y4v). In another acknowledgement of elected kingship, he recalled that, upon the overthrow of Harold, 'the citizens of London would have set up . . . Edgar Etheling' who instead was forced to flee with his sisters Margaret and Christian to Scotland. If Verstegan was taking issue with James's version of William, he was also foregrounding the king's Saxon roots, the alternative to his Tudor roots that Verstegan hoped James would more fully embrace.

The political and religious argument implicit in Verstegan's historical narrative is present also in his extensive glossary of Anglo-Saxon words, where he selected words, shaped definitions and provided illustrations which further support his Catholic position. Not recognizing this agenda, previous scholars have routinely praised Verstegan for producing this early list of Anglo-Saxon words and for the accuracy of many of his etymological explanations. Reading no other significance in it, and being baffled by

Verstegan's selection of words, they have typically moved on to discuss other Anglo-Saxon lexicons, including those of John Leland, Matthew Parker, Laurence Nowell, John Jocelyn, Thomas Cooper and Camden – all of whose lexicons they have understood to have been inflected with Protestant politics. In the long version of this chapter I treat this glossary in considerable detail. I suggest that Verstegan coded some sections so as to represent the attack on Cecil that had been a feature of his 1592 tracts. Verstegan also used a section on titles and honours to emphasize the power that resided in offices other than that of king, including those offices held by the Howards, whose family member, Henry Howard, Earl of Northampton, was, in 1605, the prominent Catholic on James's Privy Council, and himself engaged in research into the authority of the office of Earl Marshal. But, for the purposes of this shorter chapter, it may be more appropriate to refer to some of the most basic features of the glossary.

Verstegan divided his representation of 'our ancient English toung' into four sections: a list of 'a number of our moste ancient English woords' (Cc3v), followed by chapters on proper names, on surnames and, finally, the section on ancient English titles and offices. Praising his list 'of nearly 700 words' as 'the first such list in, print', Philip Goepp identified a feature that characterizes the glossary's seeming peculiarity, namely 'the basis of selection . . . is baffling'.[10] Careful study of the glossary suggests that this peculiarity of selection characterizes nearly every aspect of it: the categories into which material is divided, details in the etymologies and the names chosen to illustrate words and etymologies. But here, as in the first half of *Restitution*, clarity replaces at least some of the confusion once one begins to surmise that Catholic interests have at least at certain points guided Verstegan's selection and discussion.

For example, in his first list of English words, where he includes words and simple definitions – for words that mean planted, number, gift, tribe, snow – he also includes a reference to the name Campion: the word he lists is '*Cemp* or *kemp*', which he then defines as 'one that fighteth hand to hand . . . whereof is deryved our name of *Campion*, which after the French ortography some pronounce Champion' (Dd3r). Our knowing Verstegan's connection to a particular Campion, Edmund Campion, and our knowing as well the chivalric language of Ignatius of Loyola, who had instructed his followers to be champions for Christ, makes it possible for us to feel quite certain that here Verstegan is referring to his martyred friend. It is, of course, the nature of codes to be devious and riddling. For example, in this first section, Verstegan makes a reference to his own name and to the despair that exile has brought him. Using typographical and orthographical puns and playing off the interchangeability of black letter 'U' and 'V', Verstegan prints a word twice – 'Upstigan or Vpstegan' – with a 'V' replacing the 'U'. Recognizing Verstegan's name hidden in this spelling gives significance to the selection of words that follow and which are glossed as 'departure', 'outcast', 'lac', 'infirm', 'despair', and 'distrust'. In the midst of that list, there is another orthographical pun; the entry 'Ut awurpen' provides a muffled reference to 'Antwerp' (Gg2r).

As we continue through the glossary, we find that Verstegan has represented in a variety of ways his political and religious concerns. For example, an important feature of the next section, on 'the ancient Saxon proper names of men and women', is the inclusion of several names of people prominent in church history. Listing Bede, Verstegan describes him as 'our first famous English wryter', a remark relevant to any who preferred Bede's accounts to those of John Bale or John Foxe. He lists several people whose place in history Bede had defined as their having privileged the power and authority of church over that of secular rulers, including Dunstan, Willebrord, Wilfrid and Winfrid. Similarly, the devout women in Verstegan's list include Winifrid the dedicated young woman of Holywell, whose head was cut off when she resisted the prince; at the spot where it fell, a spring gushed forth. Her name would be used as the code name for the Gunpowder Plot. This list also includes the name 'Allin or Allen', glossed as 'Sunne-bright' in *Remains* (56), but which Verstegan glosses as meaning 'Beloved-of all' – surely a reference to William Allen, who had died in 1594.

The third section of the glossary is dedicated to 'the surnames of our ancient families'. This section comprises an alphabetized list not of names but of the 'terminations of surnames', that is, their final syllable – among others, the terminations 'den', 'dish', 'field', 'hurst', 'legh', 'pool', 'by', 'spear' and 'tun'. If this list had no examples or many examples, it would be hard to generalize about Verstegan's principles of selection, and, even as it is, there are many details in which I see no particular significance. But I do see significance when for the termination 'dish' he lists Cavendish, for 'field' 'Bedingfield', for 'hurst' both Stanihurst and Stonihurst, for 'by' 'Holtby', and for 'pool' Walpole, all names of prominent Catholics in the later sixteenth century. Once we see names such as these in the glossary, of people and families and places known for their recusancy, exile and martyrdom, or association with it, we begin, justifiably I believe, to look to see who and what else might be here. Having said that, I must virtually take it back and acknowledge that, no matter how clear an allusion may seem, the significance depends always and entirely on what the reader brings to the reading, not on what Verstegan says.

Thus, under 'land' and in the word 'Leyland' – which we know to be a town in Lancashire – there is also what I take to be an insulting allusion to John Leland, whose Protestant antiquarian programme is what Verstegan aims to undermine; in that entry, Verstegan gives the example: '*Leyland* of the lying legh or empty thereof, to wit uncultyved' (Oo2v). Immediately following, under 'Legh', Verstegan lists 'Leslie'. I assume that Verstegan uses this entry in order to include an allusion to John Leslie, Bishop of Ross, the defender of Mary, Queen of Scots.

Under 'ton', which he declares to be 'one of the greatest terminations wee have' (Oo4r), his definition of 'tun' as a 'strong hedge' built around a house to defend it from enemies calls to mind the fenced houses pictured in Burghley's map of the northern Catholic homes, and perhaps first of the home of the Hoghtons as it is pictured there. But Verstegan does not list what we have now come to expect. For the termination 'ton', he does not list 'Hoghton' nor does he list 'Middleton', the family name of Margaret Clitherow, who had been pressed to death for having used her house to harbor priests and to whom Verstegan had referred as Margaret Middleton in his 1587 martyrology. Instead, he gives as his examples, '*Cote-tun* now *Cotton*, . . . *North-tun* now *Norton*, . . . [and] *South-tun*, now *Sutton*' (Oo4r). From one perspective the emphasis on 'north' and 'south' smacks of the perfunctory. On the other hand, if a Catholic context is to be brought to bear, then it would be appropriate to note that, in addition to Margaret Clitherow, there had been eight other people martyred whose names ended in 'ton', including two Suttons and one Norton. But we are the ones who bring these readings to this entry; and one worries, alternately, about finding too much and about missing too much.

Not all the names in the glossary have an obvious Catholic match. Under 'ey', for example, Verstegan lists Sidney. True, the Sidney family were friends to Campion; still, the presence of this name of a prominent Protestant family puts us on our guard. Verstegan lists 'Kenelmeworth' – which we may know as the home of Leicester – and glosses it with the generalization, 'such nooks of ground having of old tyme bin chosen out for places of saftie' (Pp1r), perhaps a reference to John of Gaunt, who had lived at Kenilworth and whose claim to the throne was important in Persons's repudiation of the Tudors.

Whatever we make of this entry, the overall importance of Verstegan's glossary lies in its representation of Catholic people and places as constitutive parts of English identity. For Verstegan, what originated as the purity of the Anglo-Saxon had come down through the ages, represented in Campion, Holtby, Sutton, Norton, Walpole and others whom the Elizabethans had determined to erase, but whom Verstegan had, in his record of the origins of the English, now restored. Verstegan memorialized them in *Restitution* even as Foxe had created a book to serve as a monument for Protestant martyrs. But most importantly, Verstegan offered *Restitution* as a defence against a continuation of Tudor versions of history and policy; looking to the future, *Restitution* represents the profound connection that existed historically between England and the European Catholic community. Acknowledging the possibility that King James also understood that connection, Verstegan had praised the King in the dedication for the peace he had made with Spain and France. In *Amorum emblemata* he would again deal with the matter of peace and unity from an international perspective.

Printed at the beginning of 1605, *Restitution* preceded the Gunpowder Plot
by some months. In its aftermath the situation for Catholics in England
greatly worsened, with two new penal laws passed by Parliament in May
1606. Catholics were now required to participate in the Eucharist once a
year or be subject to a schedule of annual and increasing fines of £20, £40
and £60. The fine for refusing to attend church was £20 per month or
possible loss of two-thirds of their property. As W. B. Patterson has emphasized, 'These measures were intended to sap the strength of the Roman
Catholic community, even at the expense of making the eucharist, the sacrament of unity, into a weapon of coercion.'[11] The penal laws also introduced
an Oath of Allegiance, whereby James sought to make it possible for his
recusant subjects to swear allegiance to him only as their temporal ruler.[12]
Motivated by the desire to secure Catholic loyalty and assuming that, in
the context of England's treaty with Spain, the Oath might find broad
acceptance on the Continent, including the approval of the Pope, James was
unprepared for the torrent of Catholic polemics that he had unleashed –
with Cardinal Bellarmine in the forefront of the attack and King James
himself the prompt answerer in *Triplici nodo, triplex cuneus: or, An Apologie for the Oath of Allegiance* (1607). Even as Verstegan's *Restitution*
deserves a place among other books by Catholic antiquarians, so does his
contribution to Otto Vaenius (van Veen)'s *Amorum emblemata* belong on
bibliographies that deal with the aftermath of the Gunpowder Plot.

In the midst of the scores of books of controversy pouring from English
and international presses during this time there also appeared this unusu-
ally beautiful book of emblems. Printed in Antwerp in 1608, *Amorum
emblemata* was designed so that the engravings featuring Cupid stood alone
on the recto page, with the accompanying verses on the verso page. Prepared for an international market, all editions of the book were polyglot,
with three different combinations of languages, (1) Latin, Dutch and
French, (2) Latin, Italian and French, and (3) Latin, English and Italian.[13]
The translator of the poems into English for the edition prepared for the
English market was Verstegan, whose 'contribution consists of the English
verses, 616 lines in all', comprising 'a commendatory poem, signed R. V.,
on the verso of the fourth leaf; "Cupid's epistle"; introductory sonnet: and
the 124 quatrains in the text'.[14] Whereas Vaenius dedicated all other editions to William of Bavaria ('kinsman of Ferdinand of Bavaria . . . the
Prince-Bishop of Liège and the Archbishop of Cologne'),[15] the edition with
Verstegan's English translations, dated 20 August 1608, was dedicated 'To
the moste honorable, and woorthie brothers, William Earle of Penbroke,
and Philip Earle of Mountgomerie, patrons of learning and chevalrie'.
Noting that the fame of these brothers had come to 'our spatious continent', Vaenius remarked that he hereby invited their attention 'by dedicat-
ing unto your honors . . . these my invented emblems, that subjecteth
princes no less then subjects'.

Amorum emblemata has been categorized as belonging to the seven-teenth-century vogue of love emblem books, produced for aristocratic and bourgeois consumption. That the interests of Vaenius ran also to other subject matter, however, is clear from the fact that just prior to *Amorum emblemata* he had published *Q. Horatii Flacci emblemata* (1607), which 'voices a stoically inspired aristocratic philosophy, clearly parallel to the writings of Justus Lipsius', by means of quotations from Horace ... sys-tematically made into emblems'.[16] In 1610 he published *Vita D. Thomae Aquinatis*. And, at the request of the Archduchess Isabella, Vaenius would later rework *Amorum emblemata* as *Amoris divini emblemata* (1615), a book which is explicit in its religious orientation and now regularly placed in a category with other books of religious emblems, such as the Jesuit Herman Hugo's *Pia desideria* (Antwerp, 1624) and the Calvinist Francis Quarles's *Emblemes* (1635).[17] As for Verstegan, a skillful engraver and poet, as well as polemicist, he had produced, in addition to political tracts and the later antiquarian history, *Primer, or Office of the Blessed Virgin Marie* (1599) and the emblematic verse in *Odes in Imitation of the Seaven Peni-tential Psalmes, With Sundry other Poems and ditties tending to devotion and pietie* (1601).

Although *Amorum emblemata* appears to be only a book of courtship and seduction, the other interests of the artists, the method of the work, and its historical context, suggest that its deeper affinity lies with the reli-gious and political works these artists produced. Only ostensibly a book of seduction and courtship, *Amorum emblemata* may better be understood as an encoded book of poems and emblems representing spiritual experience, longing and devotion. Moreover, the encoding of *Amorum emblemata* is directed so that the emblems also have the capacity to represent the Catholic commitment to remaining true to the faith even in the midst of persecution, as well as to suggest an internationalized social and political ideal of broth-erly love and union. Although we may assume that the book was intended for the English Catholic reader, this book, like Parsons's *Christian Exer-cises*, could have found appreciative readers among Protestants. Perhaps of more importance, however, the dedication to the brothers Pembroke and Montgomery may constitute not only a solicitation of their favour to the arts but a solicitation for charity on behalf of the persecuted English Catholic subjects.

Karel Porteman, a distinguished scholar of the emblem, has produced significant work both on *Amorum emblemata* and on Jesuit emblems, though without finding a religious significance in the former. Reading *Amorum emblemata* as poems encouraging the young to marry, Porteman notes that, although Vaenius's emblems have occasionally been described as representing passages from Ovid, in fact the texts that accompany the emblems are from a wide variety of authors, including Seneca, Plutarch, Cicero, Virgil, Horace, Plautus, Tacitus, Plato, Aristotle, Lucretius, Boethius and others.[18] Summarizing the themes of the emblems, he notes the presence of commonplaces of love; love is overruling, is eternal, knows no limits, vanquishes its enemies, cannot be escaped or outrun, is beyond measure, is the source of virtú, lacks reticence, and is incurable.[19] He also mentions the unusual focus on Cupid, who is 'not only *constantly* present, but . . . pictorially dominant in all respects'.[20] In many emblems Cupid is the only figure; in others the representation includes him as well as another *putto*, a woman, a man or an animal. Reading these emblems within the conventions of amorous love, Porteman pursues quite different criteria when he examines the Jesuit emblem tradition.

Among Porteman's other projects has been the study of a branch of Jesuit emblematics that flourished in Antwerp at the beginning of the seventeenth century. Describing the theology and cult of images that lay behind Jesuit emblem rhetoric, as well as its roots in the *Spiritual Exercises* and meditative tradition of Ignatius of Loyola, Porteman emphasizes the persuasive aspect of the emblem tradition ('emblems are images intended to persuade and thus are particularly suited to the transfer of values'), the wit and erudition constitutive of the genre which provides 'the mind-provoking game of hiding and revealing', the belief in the 'affective power of illustrations' and the spiritual goal of promoting the praise and 'honour of God *in* the world'.[21] Porteman also describes the theory and method of the Jesuit religious emblem:

> The Jesuits "rhetoricised" the emblem genre. They made it part of the rhetorical doctrine of tropes . . . In rhetoric tropes are words which are used in a meaning they do not truly possess, but onto which that meaning is transferred whenever they take the place of words which do have that meaning. In the emblem it is the "images" or "picturae" which receive the figurative meanings. (22)

The task of ' "emblematising" a set subject . . . was not the *decoding* of emblems, but the *encoding*', of 'expressing subjects in emblems' (23).[22] It is my contention that the artistic and intellectual resources of *Amorum emblemata* are closely associated with this branch of Jesuit emblematics that Porteman has described.

If we apply Porteman's understanding of the religious emblem to a reading of *Amorum emblemata*, the small shift that is required is to understand that the love that is being represented is the spiritual experience of knowing divine love – of being loved by God, of being someone who loves God and of having one's actions in the world affected by these experiences. Cupid represents the unbounded, unqualified love of God for which one will sacrifice all, in emulation of the sacrifice God made for humankind. Read in this manner, *Amorum emblemata* may be understood as offering a devotional and meditative experience, as well as representation both of the ability to remain true to one's faith despite suffering and of the ability to extend charity to those in need.

The first seven emblems invite this combination of readings. In the engraving for the first, a sky filled with billowing clouds forms the background for a Cupid seated in a structure suspended from the heavens. The accompanying verse, 'Love is everlasting' ('Amor aeternus'), supports the notion that the engraving represents love for God and God's love: 'No tyme can ruin love'. The second verse, titled 'Only one' ('No number els but one in Cupids right is claymed, / All numbers els besydes he sets his foot upon'), calls attention to the number which is the object of Cupid's keen focus in the accompanying engraving, the perfect number one or, again, God. In the engravings for the next five emblems, a pair of *putti* are shown in one or another relationship, subject matter that again redirects the reader from the idea of amorous love, while suggesting as well the possibility of also a social and political register. In the third and fourth emblems, the relationship is one of contention, each figure striving for dominance, as they shoot arrows at each other and engage in a tug-of-war. In the next three, however, the relationship is expressed as mutual dependence; Fortune pours for them into only one cup, one *putto* carries the lame companion on his back, and finally they embrace, 'Union is loves wish' (16). Presented in a polyglot book distributed in different versions internationally, these emblems thus speak to a range of subjects, including the union of Christendom and international peace.

With these spiritual and political ideas represented from the outset, the emblems which follow may be read within any or all of those contexts. To generalize, many of the emblems emphasize the strength and value of this love. In 'Nothing hindreth love', Cupid dashes a pedestal to the ground while the verse declares, 'None els but Cupid can put back the terms of love ... Save only love it self which force may not remove' (18). Love requires loyalty: 'For in the law of love hath loyaltie decreed' (6). In 'Love is the cause of virtue', the subject of the engraving is a man struck with Cupid's arrow who has defeated a dragon (33). True love survives trial (44), and is best known by deeds (46).

Admittedly, in some cases, the verses and engravings explicitly suggest amorous love. In 'No love without warre', the helmeted Cupid recalls Petrarch's sonnet 21,[23] but suggests as well the religious valency of being a soldier for God: 'Love hath his formed camp, his soldiers lovers are' (48–9). Lust expressed with fire is a topic of 'Love inwardly consumeth' (96, cf. 218), 'For one pleasure a thowsand paynes' (102) and 'Loves miserie' (114). While most of the sonnets do not refer to a lady, some do – as when Cupid laments 'Not to enjoy the sight of my faire ladies face' (122) – and for certain readers may also be porous enough to suggest the Virgin Mary, as well as the notion fundamental to the Petrarchan tradition that all yearning for another, all desire, is ultimately fulfilled in union with God.

Further, some of the emblems seem to invite readings that consider the implications of outward conformity and equivocation. In contrast to love poems that complain about the changeable lover or beloved, *Amorum emblemata* states the necessity of being able to be 'as the camelion' to 'change' one's 'colour' (62), and warns that by 'speech of love often is betrayd' (68). Similarly, silence is recommended, for 'silence us'd in love doth make it unespyed' (70). The challenge of exile may be broached in 'Love fyndeth meanes', where Cupid uses his quiver as a boat; here love will use all means for its expression, even if it means crossing the seas (92). It may be then, that *Amorum emblemata* ultilizes the full range of a double- or triple-voiced system in which sometimes one or another voice or frame of reference is more present. Surely, 'Love excuses from perjurie' recalls situations of equivocation: 'the lover freedome hath to take a lovers oth, / which if it prove untrue hee is to bee excused, / For Venus doth dispence in lovers othes abused, / And love no fault comitts in swearing more then troth' (140). In the engraving for this verse, Cupid rests his hand on a book as if swearing, Venus stands by, while above God looks down.

As these examples suggest, many aspects of the book merit the closest attention if one is to locate the possibilities of meaning. While the ubiquitous presence of the Cupid figure throughout would seem to limit the book to the subject of amorous love, the actions of Cupid often complicate that assignment of meaning; it is not Cupid's dominant presence but his dominant actions that refer the reader to religion and politics. In 'Love will appeer', we are told that love cannot be hidden; in the accompanying engraving, *putti* are tilting a large container as light pours from the bottom and out the side, reminiscent of the instruction not to hide one's candle under a bushel (Matthew 5:15). In 'Love in enduring death', the engraving represents Cupid burning at the stake (184). On the next page, the verse, 'The greater love, the greater feare', refers to the caution that fear prompts; those who value their love do all they can to protect it, are 'carelesse never found' (186); the accompanying engraving features one *putto* holding another up. In 'Without ceasing', where the engraving depicts a man whose chest is shot full of arrows (not unlike St Sebastian), the verse comments, 'Yet all this, and yet more, will constant love abyde' (214). Those who take pleasure in killing others are represented in an engraving of a man being attacked by a smiling crocodile; the accompanying verse moralizes, 'the laghing serpent moste the loving harte annoyes' (226). The book concludes with two emblems on death, one emphasizing the 'Love is not kild by death, that after death doth last', the other, in death 'it onlie must bee known'.

Understood as having implications beyond amorous love, *Amorum emblemata* suggests that books of controversy were not the only means to plead on behalf of Catholics in the aftermath of the Gunpowder Plot. In *Restitution*, dedicated to King James, Verstegan had made an implicit appeal to Northampton by way of the attention he gave the Howard family in the section on 'offices'. The dedication of *Amorous emblemata* to the brothers Pembroke and Montgomery sought attention not only from a family known as patrons of poetry and art but from a powerful Protestant family whose family members had influence with the king. Twenty-four years old in 1608, Philip had married Susan Vere, daughter of the Earl of Oxford, just four years earlier. A favorite of King James, he had held the post of Gentleman of the Bedchamber beginning in 1605, the same year that 'James created the peerage of Montgomery for him'; in 1608, he was named Knight of the Garter.[24] Twenty-eight years old in 1608, William was already a patron of the arts, connected to Inigo Jones, Ben Jonson, John Donne and George Chapman. In prison in 1605 over *Eastward Ho!*, the then-Catholic Jonson had written to both Pembroke and Montgomery for assistance.[25] As the years passed, Pembroke especially would become associated with the militant branch of the Protestant party in Parliament, opposing a Catholic marriage for Prince Charles. For Vaenius and Verstegan to offer this book of love to Pembroke and Montgomery was to appeal directly to the Protestants, to those who could influence the decision, for a change in policy.

Although scholars have described Verstegan's *Restitution* and contribution to *Amorum emblemata* as signalling his withdrawal from politics, this chapter suggests that Verstegan remained closely aligned with Robert Persons early in James's reign. Parsons too had written extensively during these and in response to the Gunpowder Plot and the Oath of Allegiance. At the same time as *Amorum emblemata*, Parsons had objected in *The Judgment of Catholike English-man living in banishment for his religion* (1608) that King James had given public distribution to his *Apologie for the Oath of Allegiance*, a move that had exacerbated the situation of Catholics. In his conclusion he expressed the hope that the king who had so recently prompted a union of 'Great Kingdomes' might encourage those kingdoms in 'sweet and temperate proceeding toward all, as despayre, the mother of headlong precipitation, enter not . . . Some reasonable toleration, and friendly treatie would bynd up woundes from bleeding on all sydes' (p. 128). In *Restitution*, Verstegan chose a discourse that Persons had also used but presented it in a nonconfrontational voice. In *Amorous emblemata*, Verstegan made another attempt, this time, in the company of Vaenius, using a language quite different from the language of controversy or chronicle, but again expressing thoughts that Parsons and he shared. Verstegan kept his hand in English politics; in the 1620s he wrote political tracts on behalf of the proposed Spanish match. But from that point on, he wrote only in and on behalf of the Dutch.

Notes

1 The section of this chapter on *Restitution* has appeared in a longer and more extensively documented version as 'Richard Verstegan's *A Restitution of Decayed Intelligence*: a Catholic antiquarian replies to John Foxe, Thomas Cooper, and Jean Bodin', *Prose Studies*, 22 (1999), pp. 1–39. For biography of Verstegan see Anthony G. Petti, ed., *Letters and Dispatches of Richard Verstegan*, Catholic Record Society, 52 (London, 1959). The section on *Amorum emblemata* has not been previously published.

2 D. R. Woolf, *The Idea of History in Early Stuart England: Erudition, Ideology, and the 'Light of Truth' from the Accession of James I to the Civil War* (Toronto, 1990), p. 202; Glenn Burgess, *The Politics of the Ancient Constitution: An Introduction to English Political Thought, 1602–1642* (Houndsmills, 1992), p. 101.

3 The seminal study is J. G. A. Pocock, *Ancient Constitution and the Feudal Law: A Study of English Historical Thought in the Seventeenth Century. A Reissue with a Retrospect* (Cambridge, 1987); I am grateful to John Pocock for his comments on an early version of the paper, read at the Folger Institute Seminar, 'Stuart Catholicism', November 1998. See also William Klein, 'The ancient constitution revisited', in *Political Discourse in Early Modern Britain* (Cambridge, 1993), pp. 23–44; Janelle Greenberg, 'The confessor's laws and the radical face of the ancient constitution', *English Historical Review*, pp. 104 (1989), 611–37; Christopher Hill, 'The Norman yoke', in *Puritanism and Revolution* (London, 1958), pp. 50–122; Johann P. Sommerville, 'History and theory: the Norman Conquest in early Stuart political thought', *Political Studies*, 34 (1986), pp. 249–61.

4 For example see R. F. Jones, *The Triumph of the English Language* (London, 1953), pp. 220–1, 224–8. Directed towards Protestant republican antiquarianism and assuming Verstegan's disinterestedness, Graham Parry, *The Trophies of Time: English Antiquarians of the Seventeenth Century* (Oxford, 1995), asserts, 'There is no need to pursue Verstegan's synopsis of English history in any detail' (p. 62); 'He himself did not intend to make any political point, but by drawing attention to a system of rule that had once prevailed in England, Verstegan was providing material that future supporters of Parliament would find very useful' (p. 67). Samuel Kliger, *The Goths in England: A Study in Seventeenth and Eighteenth Century Thought* (Cambridge, Mass., 1952), noted that seventeenth-century defenders of Parliament drew on Verstegan (pp. 115–222, 142, 201); Woolf, *Idea of History*, noted that Verstegan referred to Tacitus, Justus Lipsius and Bodin (pp. 202–3).

5 For Parker's letters to Burghley on the antiquarian project see John Bruce and Thomas Thomason Perowne, ed., *Correspondence of Matthew Parker*, Parker Society Publications, vol. 33 (Cambridge, 1853), pp. 253, 424–6. See also Eleanor N. Adams, *Old English Scholarship in England from 1566–1800* (New Haven, 1917); Hugh Trevor-Roper, *Queen Elizabeth's First Historian: William Camden and the Beginnings of English 'Civic History'* (London, 1971).

6 Anthony Kemp, *Estrangement of the Past: A Study in the Origins of Modern Historical Consciousness* (Oxford, 1971), pp. 84, 85.

7 Burgess, *Politics of the Ancient Constitution*, pp. 17, 18; see also Kevin Sharpe, *Sir Robert Cotton, 1586–1631* (Oxford, 1979), pp. 25–40.

8 See J. W. Binns, *Intellectual Culture in Elizabethan and Jacobean England: The Latin Writings of the Age* (Leeds, 1990), pp. 293–4.

9 C. H. McIlwain, ed., *Political Works of James I* (1918; rpt New York, 1965), pp. l–li.

10 Philip H. Goepp, II, 'Verstegan's "Most Ancient Saxon Words"', in *Philologica: The Malone Anniversary Studies*, ed., Thomas A. Kirby and Henry Bosley Woolf (Baltimore, 1949), pp. 249, 249–55. Scholarly assessments of the relative merits of Verstegan's and Camden's glossaries differ and are affected by their assumptions about each compiler's goals; see Adams, *Old English Scholarship*, p. 43; Woolf, *Idea of History*, p. 204; Parry, *Trophies of Time*, p. 68.

11 W. B. Patterson, *James VI and I and the Reunion of Christendom* (Cambridge, 1997), p. 77; for an excellent discussion of the Gunpowder Plot and the Oath of Allegiance controversy that followed see pp. 75–123.

12 For the details of the oath see *ibid.*, pp. 77–80.

13 For details on the different editions see Karel Porteman, 'Introduction', in Otto Vaenius, *Amorum emblemata* (Aldershot, 1996), pp. 4–7; Stephen Rawles, 'The bibliographical context of Glasgow University Library SMAdd.392: a preliminary analysis', in *Emblems and the Manuscript Tradition*, ed., Laurence Grove (Glasgow, 1997), pp. 105–17. Facsimiles of the edition with English translation include: Vaenius, *Amorum emblemata*, intro. Porteman; Peter M. Daly *et al.*, ed., *The English Emblem Tradition* 4 (Toronto, 1998); and Otto van Veen, *Amorum emblemata*, intro. notes by Stephen Orgel (New York, 1979). Of these the only version that preserves the beautiful proportions and formatting of the original, with emblem alone on the recto side, is the Orgel/Garland edition.

14 A. G. Petti, 'A bibliography of the writings of Richard Verstegan (c. 1550–1641)', *Recusant History*, 7 (1963) p. 97.

15 Porteman, intro., *Amorum emblemata*, p. 5.

16 Karel Porteman, *Emblematic Exhibitions (affixiones) at the Brussels Jesuit College (1630–1685)* (Brussels, 1996), p. 17.

17 For these emblematists and the traditions associated with them see also Daly *et al.*, ed., *The English Emblem Tradition* 4; Porteman, 'Introduction', pp. 1–20; Karl Josef Holtgen and John Horden, 'Introduction', in Francis Quarles, *Emblemes (1635)* (Hildesheim, 1993), pp. 1–26; William A. McQueen, 'Introduction', *A Selection of Emblems from Herman Hugo . . . Francis Quarles . . . and Edmund Arwaker* (Los Angeles, 1972), pp. 1–7; and Mario Praz, *Studies in Seventeenth-century Imagery* (Rom, 1964–74), pp. 134–68.

18 Porteman, *Emblematic Exhibitions*, p. 12.

19 *Ibid.*, p. 17.

20 *Ibid.*, p. 12.

21 *Ibid.*, p. 20.

22 *Ibid.*, pp. 22–3.

23 The version by Henry Howard, Earl of Surrey, reads, 'Love that liveth and reigneth in my thought, / That built his seat within my captive breast, / Clad in the arms wherein with me he fought'.

24 Richard L. Greaves and Robert Zaller, ed., *Biographical Dictionary of British Radicals in the Seventeenth Century*, 3 vols (Brighton, 1983), vol. 2:78–9.

25 See *DNB*; David Riggs, *Ben Jonson: A Life* (Cambridge, Mass., 1989), pp. 124–5, 176–9. Jonson had converted to Catholicism in 1598, although the fallout from the Oath of Allegiance controversy would lead him to distance himself from it in 1610.

Catilines and Machiavels: reading Catholic resistance in *3 Henry VI*

Speculation about Shakespeare's religious attitudes has always been limited by the sparsity of recognized topical allusions to confessional or polemical works,[1] while many of his acknowledged sources have not, until recently, been extensively explored from Catholic perspectives. A work falling into both these categories which may shed light on Shakespeare's Catholic connections in Lancashire is *A Treatise of Treasons Against Queen Elizabeth and the Crown of England*. This pamphlet was published anonymously in January 1572 in Louvain, but is now thought, on strong internal evidence, to have been written by John Leslie (1527–96), Bishop of Ross, distinguished Scottish jurist and historian, Catholic polemicist and ambassador of Mary Queen of Scots to the English Court.[2] Shakespeare's familiarity with Leslie's other writings has been inferred previously from *Macbeth*.[3] In *3 Henry VI* he alludes to Leslie's *Treatise* in Richard of Gloucester's first soliloquy in 3.2. In the Folio text towards the end of his speech, Richard vows:

> Ile play the Orator as well as *Nestor*,
> Deceiue more slyly then *Vlisses* could,
> And like a *Synon*, take another Troy,
> I can adde Colours to the Camelion,
> Change shapes with *Proteus*, for aduantages,
> And set the murtherous *Macheuill* to Schoole.   (1712–17[4])

In the related octavo version of the play, *The True Tragedy of Richard Duke of York* (1595) the allusions to Nestor, Ulysses and Sinon are absent, and the final line reads 'And set the aspiring *Catalin* to schoole' (C8v). This reference to Catiline has eluded modern editors. But in 1947 Lily B. Campbell identified it as deriving from Leslie's *Treatise of Treasons*, in which the terms 'Catiline' and 'Machiavel' occur interchangeably as terms of abuse for two of Elizabeth's most powerful ministers: Sir Nicholas Bacon, Lord Keeper, and William Cecil, later Lord Burghley, and Lord Treasurer.[5] Leslie attacks Bacon and Burghley as ambitious upstarts who have manipulated the young and inexperienced Queen, destroyed the old religion, and undermined the nobility – chiefly the Duke of Norfolk – in order to set up a protestant 'Machiavellian State'.[6] *A Treatise* also establishes a Catholic oppositional discourse directed against gradually centralizing state power under Burghley's control.[7] Leslie elaborates his charges through the use of two historical analogies. One compares the current political 'tragedy' to the fall of Troy, in which the Elizabethan 'Catiline' and 'Machiavel' correspond to the Greeks Ulysses and Sinon. Like Shakespeare's Richard, the latter has 'a smooth tongue, an aspiring mind, a shamelesse face, no honour, litle honestie, and lesse conscience, and was a slie and suttle shifter to compasse whatsoeuer he would' (4v). Leslie's second more telling analogy compares Bacon and Burghley's treatment of Mary, Queen of Scots, with the tyrannical persecutions of Richard III. In a sixteen-point sequence, which continues to use the terms 'Catiline' and 'Machiavel' frequently, Leslie parallels Richard's duplicitous rise to power with the careers of Bacon and Burghley. The two ministers skilfully deploy a bureaucratic smokescreen of letters, strategic leaks and official pronouncements, spinning them to political advantage in series of public shows, like actors 'comme to the Stage to play bloody partes', '[dazzling] the dimme sighted eies, [clawing] the itching eares, and [filling] ye hungry mouthes of the babling multitude' (R3r–v). Just as Richard's ultimate goal was the 'rooting out [of] the Masculine Rase of King Edward the fourth' (Q5r), Leslie concludes that Bacon and Burghley have 'wrought and seduced' Elizabeth to keep her unmarried (O4r), 'to the rooting out of all Heires of [the] blood Roiall' (Q6r). These passages recall Richard's variant line in *True Tragedy*, when he departs to dispatch the last direct male survivor of the house of Lancaster, Henry VI, after participating in the murder of his son Prince Edward:

> Glo. *Clarence*, excuse me to the king my brother,
>   *I* must to London on a serious matter . . .
> Cla. About what, prethe tell me?
> Glo. The Tower man, the Tower, Ile root them out (E5r)

The fact that both versions of *3 Henry VI* allude to Leslie's *Treatise of Treasons*, yet in different ways, strongly suggests that Shakespeare himself wrote both passages, especially the variant lines in Richard's soliloquy. In that case he must be at least partly responsible for the underlying text of *True Tragedy*, a play which has been regarded for much of the past century as a non-authorial, memorially derived version of *3 Henry VI*. The otherwise unusual comparison to 'Catiline' also suggests that this more obscure but distinctive label came first, and that Shakespeare later distanced himself from its topical associations by substituting the popular stereotype 'Machiavel' in the Folio text. Part Three's additional references to Sinon and Ulysses might continue to remind some spectators of the context of

Leslie's defamatory analogies, but they could also be understood more simply as conventional classical comparisons.

Bishop Leslie's attack quickly became notorious, and the circumstances of its reception may shed light on Shakespeare's possible connections with Hoghton Tower. A government inquiry was set up to discover the authorship of *A Treatise* by tracing connections with its printer.[8] A royal proclamation defending Bacon and Burghley and calling for all copies of the pamphlet to be destroyed followed on 28 September 1573. This proclamation was probably written or directly ordered by Burghley himself.[9] While it speaks only of seditious books in general, there is no question it has Leslie's *Treatise* uppermost in mind, for, midway through, the proclamation summarises and refutes Leslie's accusations of a '*regnum Cecilianum*'. It is important to get a full sense of the intensity of the government's response:

> they haue lately caused to be compiled, and printed in diuers languages cer-
> tayne seditious bookes and libelles . . . condemnying generally the whole pol-
> licie of the present estate, as hauing no religion, nor pietie, nor iustice, nor
> order, no good ministers at al, either for diuine or humane causes: & yet to
> abuse such as are strangers to the state, they haue glosed some of theyr late
> libelled bookes with argumentes of discoueries of treasons, intended, as they
> do craftily alleage, by some special persons beyng counsaylers, agaynst her
> Maiestie, and the state of this crowne and Realme, with reprocheful tearmes
> of most notorious false assertions and allegations: bendyng their mallice moste
> specially agaynst two, who be certaynely knowen to haue alwayes ben moste
> studiously and faythfully careful of her Maiesties prosperous estate, and ver-
> tuous gouernment . . . These cheefly, besyde theyr general reproouing of al
> other, hauyng charge in this gouernment, they studie by theyr venemous and
> lying bookes, to haue specially myslyked of her Maiestie, contrary to theyr
> manyfolde desertes, so approoued by long and manifest experience, whiche
> both her Maiestie, and al the rest of her good counsaylours and nobilitie, with
> other the states of the Realme, haue had, and dayly haue of the very same
> counsaylours, who also are the more to be allowed of her Maiestie, in that
> she seeth, and of her owne meere knowledge truely vnderstandeth, that al the
> perticuler matters wherewith the sayde libellers labour to charge the sayd
> counsaylours, as offences, be vtterly improbable & false[10]. (fol. 151)

The proclamation concludes by charging 'al manner of persons, to despise, reiect, and destroy suche bookes and libelles, whensoeuer they shal come to theyr handes, for the malitious slaunders and vntruethes conteyned in them, and that no man wyllyngly do bryng into this Realme, dispearse, dispose, or delyuer to any other, or keepe any of the sayde bookes or libelles without destroying [them]' (fol. 152). Contemporary manuscript annota-tions in the Huntington Library and Harvard Library copies of the procla-mation identify *A Treatise of Treasons* as the book particularly intended to be suppressed.[11] And in the Landsdowne collection of Burghley's papers in the British Library a list of 'Traytorous and popish bookes intercepted [in 1584]' is headed by Leslie's *Treatise*, and twenty copies are itemised.[12] Clearly his pamphlet continued to be regarded as exceptionally seditious, particularly in the context of the Jesuit missions and new government measures against recusants in the early 1580s. At the time it was officially banned, Shakespeare was only nine, and he undoubtedly read it some time later. Where did he do so? And why did he do so?

Given its outlawed status, he could not read *A Treatise of Treasons* freely, and presumably he did not own his own copy but read someone else's. Only determined Catholics and ones who felt themselves relatively secure would bother taking such a risk. It is theoretically possible that he encountered the book through his schoolmaster, Simon Hunt, who left England in 1575 for the Catholic seminary at Douai and eventually became a Jesuit. But circulating such a work amongst pupils would have been very dangerous, and seems unlikely. It is more plausible to imagine Shakespeare reading Leslie in the private library of a Catholic family, such as the renowned collection at Hoghton Tower, if Shakespeare was in Lancashire during the early 1580s. This speculation rests partly on identifying Shakespeare with the 'William Shakeshafte' who is commended by Alexander Hoghton of Lea Hall in his will of 3 August 1581.[13] That was also the year of Edmund Campion's mission to Lancashire. Having arrived in England from Rome in 1580 and gone on a first circuit during that summer without visiting Lancashire, Campion planned to stay there on his second circuit in the autumn. We know he was at Hoghton over Easter and Whitsun 1581, and probably for some months before. During his time there, Campion wrote *Decem rationes* (*Ten Reasons*), his learned refutation of Protestant doctrine.[14] One of his express purposes for going to Hoghton was to research and document *Decem rationes*, and he later praised its library's large holdings of 'Epistles, Homilies, Volumes, and Disputations'. The likelihood that Bishop Leslie's clandestine *Treatise of Treasons* was amongst these seems very strong. Leslie had written other works of political controversy such as *A Defence of the Honour of Marie Quene of Scotlande* in 1569, and *A Copie of a Letter Writen out of Scotland* around 1572.[15] The latter partly provided a model in 1584 for its better-known namesake, later called *Leicester's Commonwealth*, which characterized the militantly Protestant Earl of Leicester, among other things, as a Machiavel.[16] While Campion was at Hoghton, the first Jesuits were being tortured in London for information about their English mission. As Richard Wilson has noted, one of the questions prepared by government ministers was about their contacts with Bishop Leslie, who had gone into exile in France and written *A Treatise* from the Continent.[17] After Campion himself was captured in the summer of 1581, and during his subsequent trial, queen's counsel charged him with having conferences with Leslie. Campion denied the charge, challenging prosecutors to produce proof, but none was forthcoming.[18] On 2 August the Privy Council ordered Campion to be tortured to extract information from him about his lodgings in Lancashire and the whereabouts of his books. Richard Hoghton was arrested at the same time for harbouring Campion. Two days later the Council instructed Sir Walter Mildmay to search the house of a Master Price in Huntingtonshire,[19] where 'Edmund Campion . . . confessed that he appointed his man Ralph Emerson to bring certain books and papers which he left at the house of one Richard Hoghton of Lancashire.'[20] This search proved fruitless, however, because by that time Campion's library had been dispersed.[21] Richard Wilson speculates that it 'would be strange if some of these tomes were not carted away by the boy named Shakeshafte'. I do not think we have to go this far in the case of *3 Henry VI*, however, to speculate about Shakespeare's use of the Hoghton library *in situ*. The certain but unextensive allusions to *A Treatise of Treasons* in both *True Tragedy* and *3 Henry VI* suggest a distant memory of Leslie's book, rather than its being immediately at hand at the time Shakespeare was composing or revising his play. A contrasting situation exists in *3 Henry VI*'s use of another minor source, Arthur Brookes's *The Tragicall Historye of Romeus and Juliet* (1562). When Shakespeare re-read Brookes for the sea and shipwreck imagery in Queen Margaret's oration to her troops before the battle of Tewkesbury in 5.4, the echoes are developed at length in considerable verbal detail.

But this is not the end of Campion's and perhaps Leslie's connections with *3 Henry VI*. For a second possible allusion with even stronger topical and Catholic associations seems to occur in the unusual passage that opens 5.1. The scene takes places on the walls of Coventry, where Warwick is awaiting reinforcements prior to the battle of Barnet. Two messengers inform him that Oxford is marching from Dunsmore, south-east of Coventry, and that Montague is on his way from Daintry (i.e. Daventry), further to the south-east. A figure identified in the Folio text only as 'Someruille' (2680) then enters to report that Clarence is two hours away at Southam, also south and a little east of Coventry but closer to Stratford-upon-Avon. Warwick hears an off-stage drum and concludes prematurely that Clarence has already arrived:

> *War.* Then *Clarence* is at hand, I heare his Drumme.
> *Someru.* It is not his, my Lord, here Southam lyes.
>   The Drum your Honor heares, marcheth from *Warwicke.*
> *War.* Who should that be? belike vnlook'd for friends.
> *Someru.* They are at hand, and you shall quickly know. (2685–9)[22]

It is not Clarence who enters, however, but King Edward and his supporters. The point of this invented episode seems to be that Warwick's over-confidence and muddled sense of local geography foreshadow his imminent loss of authority and tactical misjudgement in the forthcoming battle.

Somerville's pointed correction also anticipates Warwick's complete surprise at Clarence's defection later in the scene, when he switches loyalties back to the Yorkists. The whole moment's little excursion into Warwickshire place-names around Coventry and Stratford-upon-Avon unmistakably bears Shakespeare's personal signature. We can be certain about this because 3 *Henry VI* is otherwise a play in which specific topographic references and particularized spaces are relatively rare. The cluster which occurs here delineates a zone of activity for events outside the historical narrative, and hints at an absent figure to be connected with the underdetermined 'Someruille'. And because this area was the playwright's home, the moment seems to function as a personal memory-site, inviting us to identify Somerville with Shakespeare's time and story, rather than with those of the Wars of the Roses.

Somerville's name was first expanded to 'Sir John' by Edward Capell, and virtually all modern editors have followed suit. But the historical Sir John Somerville lived a century before 1471 and is too early to be connected with the events at Barnet; and, in any case, no Somerville is mentioned by Hall or Holinshed.[23] Dramatically there is no need to name the character, any more than the two anonymous messengers who precede him. If any historical figure seems likely to be represented by this scene, it is Thomas Somerville of Warwickshire.[24] He settled at Edston near Bearley north-east of Stratford in the reign of Henry VII, and died there in 1516. His direct descendant was John Somerville,[25] who gained national notoriety in 1583. The Somervilles were Catholics. John had married Margaret, daughter of Edward Arden of Park Hall, whose family was also Catholic. They may have been Shakespeare's relations, if Mary Arden's father, Robert of Wilmcote, was descended from one of the younger sons of the Park Hall Ardens.[26] In 1583 John Somerville became mentally unstable, and he set off for London after declaring his plans to assassinate Elizabeth. He is alleged to have become impassioned after reading a book given to him by his sister Elizabeth, *Of Prayer, and Meditation* by Luis de Granada, translated into English by Richard Hopkins (1582 and many reissues). The dying Warwick's monologue in 3 *Henry VI* 5.2.23–8 seems to echo passages in de Granada's chapter 'How filthie and lothsome the bodie is after it is dead: And of the buryinge of it in the graue' (fol. 201v–205r, CcIv–5r). Shakespeare later recalled this same chapter in the Gravediggers' scene (5.1) in *Hamlet*.[27] Somerville was arrested on 25 October, and under torture he implicated his wife, his parents-in-law Edward and Mary Arden, and a local Catholic priest named Hugh Hall who went in disguise as the Ardens' gardener. Since Somerville had openly discussed his intentions with them and other neighbours prior to departing for London, the Privy Council employed Thomas Wilkes, Sir Thomas Lucy and their agents to search for incriminating books and writings that would uncover the whole 'plot'.[28] The Somervilles, Ardens and Hall were indicted on 2 December, with many people serving at the trial who were known to Shakespeare's family. But only John Somerville and Edward Arden were condemned on 16 December. Their execution was set for the 20th, and the day before they were transferred to Newgate. But within two hours of arriving, John Somerville was found strangled in his prison cell. He may have been mercifully killed by Catholic friends to escape the much more grisly horrors which awaited condemned traitors, and which Edward Arden suffered the next day. Both Arden's and Somerville's heads were cut off and placed on London Bridge.[29]

The vicious methods used to extract information from the suspects and the flimsy legal grounds for trying Somerville and Arden caused a outcry, and not just among Catholics. Somerville had very clearly been insane and not responsible for his actions, while all the government's extensive searches and interrogations had failed to produce any evidence of Edward Arden's culpable involvement. The government felt pressured into defending its actions, the main upshot of which was the publication of Burghley's *The Execution of Iustice in England . . . against certeine stirrers of sedition.* Burghley had actually begun writing this pamphlet to defend the government's position in the trial of Campion two years earlier, which like Somerville's was based on dubious legal process and had elicited a stream of attacks. But when he published the book, Burghley dated its title-page with unusual precision: 17 December 1583 – the day after Somerville's and Edward Arden's indictment. He thus apparently intended the pamphlet to do double duty, restating the case against Campion and the Jesuits but also rationalizing the trials of Somerville and Arden.[30] In a passage denouncing the 'forged catalogue' of martyred Catholics, Burghley explicitly refers to:

> a furious yong man of Warwickeshire, by name *Someruile*, to increase their Kalender of y[e] *popes* martyrs, who of late was discouered and taken in his way, comming w[t] a ful intent to haue killed her Maiestie . . . The attempt not denied by y[e] traitor himselfe, but confessed, and that he was moued thereto . . . by often reading of sundry seditious vile books lately published against her Maiestie.[31]

Given what we know of the proclamation banning *A Treatise of Treasons*, as well as its presence in the list of raided books preserved in Burghley's papers, it is reasonable to assume that one of these 'seditious vile books lately published against her Maiestie' which inspired Somerville was Leslie's. Burghley's *Execution of Justice* was widely circulated and had an official government profile.[32] It was answered by Cardinal Allen's *A True, Sincere, and Modest Defense of English Catholics* in 1584. Allen points out that Somerville was not in his right mind at the time of his actions, as Burghley himself implicitly admits. He also alleges that Somerville was murdered in his cell to prevent discovery of the deliberate entrapment of 'the worshipful, valiant, and innocent gentleman Mr Arden'.[33] In same year responsibility for the trials of Somerville and Arden was also laid at the feet of the reviled Earl of Leicester in *The Copie of a Leter, Wryten by a Master of Arte of Cambrige* (i.e. *Leicester's Commonwealth*), which is traditionally ascribed to Campion's fellow Jesuit Robert Persons.[34]

In the context of the considerable notoriety and vigorous exchanges surrounding the deaths of Somerville, Arden and Campion, it seems certain that Elizabethan audiences watching *3 Henry VI* could have connected the unhistorical and somewhat gratuitous appearance of the locally well-informed Somerville with his later descendant, as well as his fellow victim Edward Arden, both of whom were likely connected to the playwright's family. Shakespeare portrays Somerville in a surprisingly positive light, boldly correcting the mildly confused Warwick, yet clearly loyal to the Lancastrian cause.[35] His superior perception pointedly demonstrates he is not what Burghley calls a 'furious' man. It is Warwick who in fact appears distracted. Given that Somerville plays no further role in this scene and is never referred to again, his underlying purpose seems to be to present a coded portrait challenging the official verdict on his contemporary namesake. And, if that is the case, Somerville represents a riposte to the government's unjust treatment of Shakespeare's recently disgraced Catholic relations, and perhaps to Burghley himself, with the playwright joining the ideological company of Campion, Allen and Persons.[36] Such a claim would not be unprecedented, since Shakespeare has been thought previously to have satirized Burghley and his policies. Curtis C. Breight has recently restated older arguments that the civil wars dramatized in *Henry IV* were meant to recall the Northern Rebellion of 1569. In particular Breight argues that Bolingbroke's usurpation parallels that of the 'Protestant new men led by Burghley who had no pedigrees to justify their power, only cunning and ruthlessness'.[37] In a different context Jonathan Bate suggests that Sonnets 1–3 may poke fun at Burghley's failure to persuade the Earl of Southampton to marry his granddaughter Bridget Vere in 1597 – if Southampton is identified with 'Mr W.H.'.[38]

Somerville's links with Campion, implied by Burghley and other government apologists, and possibly with Leslie's *A Treatise of Treasons*, likewise resonate with Richard's 'Catiline' and 'Machiavel' references earlier in *3 Henry VI*. Together these allusions draw our attention to Shakespeare's use of, and participation in, a range of Catholic oppositional discourses. In the past such encoded meanings have been depreciated or suppressed. This has had the effect of reinforcing traditional assumptions that Shakespeare routinely censored confessional controversy in his plays, thereby preserving the playwright's association with emergent and ultimately dominant national values. The allusions to John Leslie and John Somerville in *3 Henry VI*, however, problematize such assumptions.

Notes

1 Those which have been traced have seemed overall, even to pro-Catholic critics, to represent more of a rejection or an erasure of Shakespeare's religion. Peter Milward S. J., *Shakespeare's Religious Background* (London, 1973), pp. 68–78; *The Catholicism of Shakespeare's Plays* (Tokyo, 1997), pp. 116, 137.

2 *DNB*, vol. 11, pp. 972–8. A. C. Southern, *Elizabethan Recusant Prose 1559–1582* (London and Glasgow, c.1950), p. 447.

3 Henry N. Paul argues that Shakespeare read and used Leslie's *De origine, moribus, et rebus gestis Scotorum* (1578) for the image of Banquo's family tree which depicts a direct succession of Stuart kings. *The Royal Play of Macbeth* (New York, 1950), pp. 171–6. Excerpts from Leslie's *De origine* and the family tree are reproduced in Geoffrey Bullough, ed., *Narrative and Dramatic Sources of Shakespeare*, vol. 7 (London, 1973), pp. 517–20.

4 Folio text quotations and through-line numbers are taken from *The Norton Facsimile: The First Folio of Shakespeare*, ed. Charlton Hinman (New York, 1968).

5 *Shakespeare's Histories: Mirrors of Elizabethan Policy* (San Marino, 1947), p. 322.

6 Burghley had deemed Leslie 'the principal instrument' of the Northern Rebellion several years before. His opinion was shared by Lord Hunsdon: 'al this rebellion and practice with foreign nations proceeds from him.' *Calendar of State Papers, Foreign, 1569–171*, pp. 171, 176, quoted in Campbell, *Shakespeare's Histories*, p. 232.

7 Curtis C. Breight, *Surveillance, Militarism and Drama in the Elizabethan Era* (London, 1996), p. 2.

8 Southern, *Elizabethan Recusant Prose*, p. 33.

9 Frederic A. Youngs remarks that 'Nowhere is the personal involvement of Cecil . . . more clearly demonstrated than in his activities leading to the issue of the proclamation of 28 September 1573' (*The Proclamations of the Tudor Queens* (Cambridge, 1976), pp. 222–3).

10 *A Booke Containing all svch Proclamations, As were Pvblished Dvring the Raigne of the late Queene Elizabeth, Collected together by . . . Humfrey Dyson, of the City of London Publique Notary* (London, 1618) [England, Queen Elizabeth, BL 6364], fol. 152.

11 The Harvard annotation is noted by Youngs, *Proclamations*, p. 223, n. 103.

12 BL Landsdowne vol. 42, ch. 78, fol. 174. The entire list (without numbers of copies and somewhat altered) is reproduced in Charlotte Carmichael Stopes, *Shakespeare's Warwickshire Contemporaries* (Stratford-upon-Avon, 1907), p. 88.

13 Oliver Baker, *In Shakespeare's Warwickshire and the Unknown Years* (London, 1937), pp. 297–319; E. K. Chambers, *Shakespearean Gleanings* (Oxford, 1944), pp. 52–6; E. A. J. Honigmann, *Shakespeare: The 'Lost Years'* (Manchester, 1985), pp. 3–4 and *passim*.

14 Richard Simpson, *Edmund Campion: A Biography* (London, 1867), pp. 179–88.

15 *A Defence* refutes arguments against female rule set forth in John Knox's *First Blast of the Trumpet against the Monstrous Regiment of Women* (Geneva, 1558). The same issues, including references to the *First Blast*, are rehearsed

again in *A Treatise of Treasons*. Shakespeare apparently echoes a phrase from the *First Blast* in *3 Henry VI* at 1.4.141. See introduction in my edition (Oxford University Press, 2001).

16 Edited by D. M. Rogers, English Recusant Literature vol. 192 (Ilkley and London, 1974), p. 103 and *passim*. It also described three previous reigns in which excessive favouritism of wicked counsellors had led to the king's downfall: Edward II, Richard II and Henry VI (pp. 197–8). Milward, *Shakespeare's Religious Background*, pp. 186–90, discusses Leslie's *Treatise of Treasons* but connects it unconvincingly to *Richard II* and *Troilus and Cressida*.

17 Richard Wilson, 'Shakespeare and the Jesuits', *Times Literary Supplement*, 19 December 1997, pp. 11–13. E. E. Reynolds, *Campion and Parsons: The Jesuit Mission of 1580–1* (London, 1981), p. 177.

18 Simpson, *Edmund Campion*, p. 291.

19 Stanford E. Lehmberg, *Sir Walter Mildmay and Tudor Government* (Austin, 1964), p. 194.

20 Simpson, *Edmund Campion*, p. 243.

21 George C. Miller, *Hoghton Tower: The History of the Manor, the Hereditary Lords and the ancient Manor-House of Hoghton in Lancashire* (Preston, 1948), pp. 11–12, 78.

22 This exchange does not appear in *True Tragedy*. Warwick instead says 'Then Oxford is at hand, I heare his drum' (E1r), which does not contradict 'Summerfield'.

23 Stopes, *Shakespeare's Warwickshire's Contemporaries*, p. 83. *The Third Part of King Henry VI*, ed. Michael Hattaway (Cambridge, 1993), p. 68.

24 He did not directly participate in the Wars of the Roses. W. H. Thomson identified him as Sir Thomas Somerville (d. 1500) of Aston-Somerville, Gloucestershire, a different branch of the same family, but this is also an unconvincing guess (*Shakespeare's Characters: A Historical Dictionary* (New York, 1951), p. 275).

25 Stopes, *Shakespeare's Warwickshire Contemporaries*, pp. 68–9.

26 S. Schoenbaum, *William Shakespeare: A Documentary Life* (Oxford, 1975), pp. 15–16. Mark Eccles, *Shakespeare in Warwickshire* (Madison, 1961), pp. 12, 79.

27 See Harold Jenkins's Arden edition (London and New York, 1982), V.i.74–110, pp. 550–1.

28 E.g. a warrant to Henry Rogers dated 20 November 1583 to search 'sondrie houses and places for bookes and writinges dangerous to her Maiestie and the state' (Stopes, *Shakespeare's Warwickshire Contemporaries*, p. 96). Eccles, *Shakespeare in Warwickshire*, p. 75.

29 Stopes, *Shakespeare's Warwickshire Contemporaries*, pp. 79–81. *DNB*, vol. 18, pp. 660–1. E. K. Chambers, *William Shakespeare: A Study of Facts and Problems*, 2 vols (Oxford, 1930), vol. 2:300.

30 Stopes, *Shakespeare's Warwickshire Contemporaries*, p. 106. Arden is not actually named, probably because there was no evidence or legal grounds against him. But he is clearly implied by Burghley's remarks about Somerville (see above).

31 *The Execution of Iustice in England ... against certeine stirrers of sedition* (London, 1583), Diiiv. A printed note reading 'Iohn Someruile' appears in the margin.

32 Introduction, *The Execution of Justice in England by William Cecil and A True, Sincere, and Modest Defense of English Catholics by William Allen*, ed. Robert M. Kingdon (Ithaca, 1965), pp. xvii–xviii. Copies of *The Execution* in English and translation were sent to English diplomats for presentation to foreign courts. Kingdon's edition is based on the second edition of Burghley's work published in January 1584 – the one used by Allen. Earlier in *The Execution of Justice* a marginal note states 'A conclusion that all the infamous bookes against the Queene & the Realme are false' (Ciiv).

33 Kingdon, Introduction, *The Execution of Justice*, pp. 108–9. In 1585 Nicolas Sanders similarly charged that Arden had been executed 'shamefully' (*Rise and Growth of the Anglican Schism*, trans. David Lewis (London, 1877), p. 322).

34 Ed. Rogers, p. 166.

35 For Shakespeare's connections with and sympathies to this house and county see Richard Dutton, 'Shakespeare and Lancaster', *Shakespeare Quarterly*, 49 (1998): 1–21.

36 Gary Taylor argues that 'it is a short step from Persons, Allen, Southwell and Farin to Shakespeare' ('Forms of opposition: Shakespeare and Middleton', *English Literary Renaissance*, 24:2 (1994): 283–314, especially 306).

37 Breight, *Surveillance*, p. 173, and *passim* pp. 171–220. See also Donna B. Hamilton's admiring but sceptical review of Breight's book in *Medieval and Renaissance Drama in England*, 12 (1999): 334–8.

38 *The Genius of Shakespeare* (London and Basingstoke, 1997), p. 49.

'This Papist and his Poet': Shakespeare's Lancastrian kings and Robert Parsons's *Conference about the Next Succession*

John Speed's scornful and indignant comments linking the Jesuit Robert Parsons and the playwright William Shakespeare are at once well known and strangely thought-provoking. In the 1611 edition of *The Theatre of the Empire of Great Britain*, Speed denounces Parsons's (alias Nicolas Doleman, or 'N. D.') unwarranted accusations against the proto-Protestant martyr Sir John Oldcastle, these being 'taken from the *Stage-plaiers*'. Parsons and Shakespeare – 'this Papist and his Poet' – had in fact a lot in common, according to the historian; they were 'of like conscience for lies, the one euer faining, and the other euer falsifying the truth'. The marginalia sum up these statements laconically; one reads: 'Papists and Poets of like conscience for fictions'.[1] Already one is aware of how easily religion, politics and poetic truth can become intertwined in ways which may require some exploration.

As head of the English mission of 1580–81, and later as an exiled defender of the cause of English Catholicism, Robert Parsons was not only a very active member of the Society of Jesus – he was also a very prolific author. A glance at Pollard and Redgrave's *Short-title Catalogue of Books* reveals no fewer than ninety-two works of various natures – editions and re-editions – that can be ascribed to Parsons. Among those is *A Treatise of the Three Conversions of England* (1603–4), which contains a less well-known reference to Shakespeare's Sir John Oldcastle (later changed to Falstaff), whom Parsons calls 'a ruffian knight, as all England knoweth, and commonly brought in by comedians on their stages'.[2] Speed's scorn was no doubt partly prompted also by the Jesuit's use of the stage to bolster his historical argumentation. The author of *The Theatre of the Empire* had paradoxically no sympathy for one who resorted to drama to prove his point. Parsons – whose life reads like an adventure story – had in fact to invent a style of writing which combined careful religious argumentation and fictional devices: in the context of religious warfare and persecution the Jesuit often wrote under another identity, creating other geographical circumstances, staging situations, using strategies of evasion. In the works he more clearly destined to be read in England, he purported to inform only, he denied sedition, appealed to the notion of freedom of expression (or 'Libertye of pen', as he called it in a 1581 clandestine pamphlet)[3] while at the same time using propaganda; he claimed allegiance, denied responsibility and constantly sought to work from inside to act on and change situations.

Parsons was also someone who was evidently aware of the existence and importance of theatre. He had first been reminded of its importance when, at Oxford, fellows of Balliol College had conspired against him, accusing him of having taken one of the boys he tutored to the theatre in London. This is an episode which Parsons recalls in a tone of amusement in his memoirs through the use of theatrical allusions. Indeed, wrote the Jesuit father, 'This boy supplied the argument for the comedy' ('*Hic argumentum dedit comediæ*').[4] During the English mission a letter he addressed to Pope Gregory XIII proves that his knowledge of the ideological climate was quite considerable and that it extended to the theatre: 'They are publishing most threatening proclamations against us, as well as books, sermons, ballads, libels, fables, comedies'.[5] Even when he had left England, his knowledge of home events remained fairly precise and very often connected to a familiar network. In a letter to his superior in 1584 Parsons mentions the ravings of a madman named Somerville who 'accused his father-in-law – Arden by name, who is of good birth and a courageous man – along with his wife, who is of the Throckmorton family'. A little later in the same letter, he holds the Earl of Leicester responsible for the unjust persecutions that ensued, adding: 'he has always pursued Arden and Throckmorton with a peculiar enmity'.[6] We are here suddenly very close to Shakespeare's native roots in the Midlands, as the Ardens were relatives of Shakespeare on his mother's side, while the Throckmortons were, of course, the famous recusant family which lived some eight miles from Stratford.

In the light of some of the connections brought forward by E. A. J. Honigmann and, more recently, by Richard Dutton and Richard Wilson, there is in fact cause to reconsider the ideological and artistic context of Shakespeare's earlier work in particular, and, more specifically, of his history plays. Whether or not Shakespeare was 'Shakeshafte', a player kept by the Hoghton family of Hoghton Tower in Lancashire, Parsons's polemic input within the context of the Counter-Reformation certainly adds complexity to the political and religious debate surrounding the production of Shakespeare's history plays. Moreover, the Jesuit's 1594 *Conference about the Next Succession to the Crowne of Ingland* – a truly seminal work that enables one to grasp the scope and complexities of the religious and political debates in late sixteenth-century England – seems to favour the Catholic descendants of the House of Lancaster.[7] In this case also, we are taken back to the network of Catholic households – both in the Midlands and in the north of England – with which Shakespeare was at least acquainted.

The Jesuit mission of 1580–81 – from religious ideal to temporal politics

Overshadowed by Edmund Campion in the eyes of Catholic historians and vilified by his Protestant opponents, Robert Parsons is in fact a much misconstrued figure of the Elizabethan ideological scene and an unrecognized source of inspiration of both devotional and literary works in the latter part of the sixteenth century. His network is one which, as I have already suggested, has connections with the theatre, while his own personal journey, I shall contend, is at the heart of the political and religious controversies of his time. Someone whose political and personal itinerary was as ambiguous as Parsons's was no doubt in some way telling and exemplary for those who knew him or knew of him in the English Catholic community. A recent commentator, in an attempt to do justice to Parsons's contribution to Elizabethan politics, has spoken too mildly, it seems, of 'his single-minded devotion to the restoration of Catholicism in England'.[8] J. H. Pollen's 1908 introduction to the Jesuit's memoirs paints a less flawless and more humane portrait of Parsons speaking of his involvement in politics, of 'his loss of temper' and concluding: 'But for all that the trial was one which might well "make a saint swear"'.[9]

It is precisely this tension between the pastoral and missionary ideal of Parsons and the realities of his involvement in the temporal world which I would like to explore, with a view that Parsons's unique destiny may have informed Shakespeare's own perception of the links between religion and politics. 'Yes Parsons was no angel', writes John Bossy, 'he got his hands dirty, he was touched with the sin of the world; but if he had kept himself as clean as Campion perhaps nothing would have got done at all'.[10] But just how, and why did Robert Parsons get his hands dirty, one may ask.

Indeed, the official instructions given to Parsons and Campion in 1580, prior to their entry into England, were particularly clear on the aims of the mission and on the type of behaviour required of the missionaries. If the language is warlike, the contents seek to define adequate ethical grounds: 'it behoves our men to be armed with two weapons especially: firstly, with virtue and piety out of the ordinary; and, secondly, with prudence'.[11] Caution and secrecy were advocated, but the divide between the Jesuit mission and the field of English politics was clearly stated: 'They [the missionaries] are not to mix themselves in the affairs of States, nor should they recount news about political matters in their letters to this place [Rome], or to that [England].[12] The intent of not meddling with political matters is again repeated on arrival in England in a document directly addressed to the powers that were, i.e. in what is now known as 'Parsons's Confession of Faith for the London Magistrates' (19 July 1580).

The tone adopted is meant to be reassuring as the missionaries are supposed to be politically neutral:

For we have been sent by men who have practically no knowledge of your secular conditions here ... not even the Catholic Princes, though they pressed them very strongly in the matter, were able to induce them to mix themselves in any way in their secular government. Not only therefore is this the end for which they have now sent us, but they have banned all conversation about your politics and have been unwilling to listen to any who made mention of them.'[13]

A year later, however, Parsons had crossed the Rubicon. The Jesuit reported back to his general, Claudio Aquaviva, with a newlyfound sense of purpose: 'for there is nothing which helps and has helped and will protect in the future and spread our cause so much as the printing of Catholic books, whether of controversy or of devotion'.[14] The equal standing given to the words 'controversy' and 'devotion' is telling. The persecutions had increased and the ideological warfare was raging; Parsons saw to it that some of the books printed had a political, or a temporal edge to them, at all events. In 1582, in a letter to Agazzari, the Rector of the English College in Rome, Parsons was to report the unfortunate and all too easy capture of the unguarded Father Bishop in terms which again brought to the fore the painful choice to make between *actio* and *contemplatio* – a choice that was also to haunt Shakespeare's Lancastrian monarchs, as we shall see later. Parsons wrote: 'To many people, however, such simplicity in the face of these very cunning wolves does not commend itself. But what shall we say? ... Bishop was warned about this at the time when he was about to go on board, but he seemed so absorbed in meditating on heavenly things as to be quite oblivious of human affairs'.[15]

For Parsons the balance between the 'heavenly' and 'the human' had, it seems, quite radically tilted towards the world of human affairs. New evidence, put forward by John Bossy in a recent article even suggests that the Jesuit father may have been directly involved in a plot to assassinate Queen Elizabeth.[16] Bossy notes Parsons's embarrassment when writing to Aquaviva about his activities. Central to these schemings was Tolemeo Galli, Cardinal of Como and Pope Gregory XIII's secretary of state. It is thus somewhat unsettling to find in the body of a letter written in cipher by the Nuncio in France and addressed to the Cardinal of Como a memorial by Parsons about a projected military invasion of England through Scotland. Dated 22 May 1582, this letter (which Bossy does not quote) describes Parsons as 'a man of great discretion', while the Jesuit father himself writes that 'the soul of the whole affair is secrecy', openly recommending that written propaganda be used and that men be employed 'for the writing and secret printing of some books which we may write for the occasion to render the English people compliant'.[17]

Parsons's decizion to follow the path of a politicized Catholicism was going to have more general consequences as far as the fate of 'the Old Religion' was concerned. But his more activist interpretation of Ignatius

Loyola's doctrine about finding God in all things was later to be challenged by Parsons's own general, Claudio Aquaviva, who favoured more contemplative modes.[18] Parsons's choice was an uneasy option that, almost certainly, forced him to go through some kind of personal crisis. In a letter of 10 September 1584 he seemed to regret the fact that he now bore the mark of sin – not only in the eyes of his enemies but also in those of his superiors. His involvement in politics had not allowed him to reach martyrdom: 'For my sins having prevented, as I have said, my sharing in the most fruitful conflict undergone by my holy companion, Campion, who is now my patron'.[19] But the secular world of politics was to bring an equally bitter disappointment. In 1581 the Duke of Alençon's ambassador, Jean Bodin, had come over to begin marriage negotiations with the Queen. Parsons, as he recalled later in his memoirs, had tried to plead the cause of those English Catholics who were imprisoned and pending execution (including Campion himself). But this had had no effect on Bodin, who, writes Parsons, 'answered perversely, as he was a politike, and as some thinke worse, saying that he came to treate matters of marriage, and not of Religion'.[20] What became apparent to Parsons was that the weight and influence of priests in the realm of politics was no longer self-evident in a world where the *politiques* were setting their own rules, those of the new science of politics to which Bodin contributed so famously through his writings. Later, as he looked back, it would seem that Parsons-the-'politike'-father had himself been betrayed by politics; but, looking even further back to the period when he was about to join the Society of Jesus, he found a measure of reassurance. In a passage of his memoirs which reads like a confession he writes that he had indeed aspired to a contemplative life, so as to 'putt myself into some remote and solitary monastery or celle never to converse more with men; some other times [I] purposed to live a secular life, but yet retyred and gyven to studdy'.[21]

Robert Parsons and the plight of Shakespeare's first Lancastrian king

> O God! Methinks it were a happy life
> To be no better than a homely swain.
> To sit upon a hill, as I do now;
> To carve out dials quaintly, point by point,
> Thereby to see the minutes how they run.   (*3 Henry VI* 2.5.21–5)[22]

These are the words of Shakespeare's first Lancastrian king, Henry VI, in a play which was described, on the title-page of its 1595 publication, as *The True Tragedy of Richard, Duke of York, and the Death of Good King Henry the Sixth*. Applied to a ruler who, quite clearly in the play, is a political disaster, the adjective 'good' stands out in a puzzling way. Shakespeare's weak and contemplative monarch has indeed been often a source of embarrassment for critics. This, I would argue, stems from the fact that the vein of ethical and spiritual debate which runs from Henry VI to Henry V, Shakespeare's last Lancastrian monarch (if one takes the plays in the order they were probably composed) has been insufficiently acknowledged. As a character Henry VI seems to embody Shakespeare's image of an ideal of virtue – albeit one which is painfully ill-adapted to the temporal world and one which condemns him to martyrdom. In fact Shakespeare lends to this king many of the defining traits of the Catholic faithful:

> But all his mind is bent to holiness,
> To number Ave-Maries on his beads,
> His champions are the prophets and apostles,
> His weapons holy saws of sacred writ,
> His study is his tilt-yard, and his loves
> Are brazen images of canonizèd saints.   (2 Henry VI 1.3.58–63)

The difficult choice between *actio* and *contemplatio* is nowhere considered lightly or taken for granted in Shakespeare's history plays – it is repeatedly dramatized in terms which no doubt rang somewhat truthfully to the ears of English Catholics. Even behind the Duke of York's bravado in *3 Henry VI* there lurks a question that many Catholic subjects of Queen Elisabeth had considered to be a burning one:

> But in this troublous time what's to be done?
> Shall we go throw away our coats of steel,
> And wrap our bodies in black morning gowns,
> Numb'ring our Ave-Maries with our beads?
> Or shall we on the helmets of our foes
> Tell our devotion with revengeful arms?   (3 Henry VI 2.1.159–64)

York's martyrdom at the hands of Queen Margaret remains, however, a cruel parody of the death of those Catholics who were executed for their beliefs. In *An Epistle of the Persecution of Catholickes in England* (1582?) Parsons describes the martyrdom of Edmund Campion and depicts a scene of humiliation, which may well have played on the imagination of the young Shakespeare. He writes: 'This good man ... was by oure aduersarie slaundered as a sediciouse persone, and to that end and effect, a large paper was most spitefullie written with greate letters, which they forced hym to beare vppon his heade in this triumphe'.[23] This mock 'triumphe' is one which Shakespeare's Richard Duke of York is submitted to by the wife of the 'good' King Henry VI before his execution:

> York cannot speak unless he wear a crown.
> (*To her men*) A crown for York, and, lords, bow low to him.
> Hold you his hands whilst I do set it on.
> *She puts a paper crown on York's head.*
> Ay, marry, sir, now looks he like a king.   (3 Henry VI 1.4.94–7)

The paper hat is the one worn by mock-kings and Christ-like martyrs, but here Shakespeare's staging of martyrdom is distorted and ironic. Even York's last words, 'Open thy gate of mercy, gracious God – / My soul flies through these wounds to seek out thee' (1.4.178–9), do not allow us to forget that York is a false martyr, one who – ultimately – died for the cause of political scheming and ambition, who rejected *otium* to embrace *negotium*.

Parsons's *Conference about the Next Succession* and Shakespeare's later Lancastrian monarchs

On a more general level it appears that Shakespeare's repeated probing into the past – into the *English* past in particular – coincided with the emergence of a genre which was gaining an unprecedented measure of importance. Chronicle history had always been the place where the nation could be reunited to its 'valiant dead', but it was now giving poets and antiquarians the opportunity to begin exploring the nature of political events. But dramatists and chroniclers still shared a largely *instrumental* view of history. For the poet, as for the amateur antiquarian, history was closely tied to the art of persuasion.

For missionaries such as Robert Parsons and Edmund Campion history possessed evangelical powers, and it is slight wonder to find references to it as a central part of the methods they used during the 1580–81 mission. A 1583 document, written by George Gilbert, who was a close friend of Parsons, gives confirmation of this. *A Way to Deal with Persons of All Sorts so as to Convert them and Bring Them Back to a Better Way of Life – Based on the System and Methods Used by Fr. Robert Persons and Fr. Edmund Campion* recommends that when in the house of a heretic the opportunity should be created 'for conversation suited to the occasion, when they are seated at table or when there are a number of people assembled, on the subject of history'.[24] History became – as so often in Shakespeare – a quiet means of entering the all too controversial field of religion.

It is precisely under the guise of an informative historical document of analysis that a 1594 work mainly ascribed to Robert Parsons – *A Conference about the Next Succession to the Crowne of Ingland* – presents itself to the reader. In the preface to the second part of the *Conference* this pretence of neutrality and impartiality is reaffirmed strongly, as the facts, says the writer, will be set down 'playnly and indifferently without hatred or partial affection' (Preface). Father Leo Hicks, in one of the few modern articles devoted to the *Conference*, was to underplay the controversial aspects of the work, insisting on its 'impartiality' which some of Parsons's contemporaries were supposed to have considered 'quite exceptional'.[25] The work, none the less, was born out of a context, which we have started to highlight through Parsons's correspondence, and which was certainly far from being neutral.

Even before the news of the execution of Mary, Queen of Scots, reached Rome in March 1587, Parsons had begun researching the descent of the House of Lancaster with the intent of supporting Philip II's claim to the English throne. As early as 1582 Parsons had expressed ideas which contrast powerfully with the view still held today by some that the Elizabethan period was marked by an overall consensus of opinion. No doubt as an incentive to military action he had written in a letter to the Pope and the King of Spain that the English were 'naturally somewhat inclined to revolutions and big changes, especially when they are displeased with government of their prince and there is some initiative and aid from without'. Characteristically, he sought a proof of that in chronicle history: 'This we see from experience, for our history tells of thirteen attacks made on us in England by intruders'.[26]

In a 1587 document revealingly entitled *Considerations Indicating That It Would be in No Wise Advisable That the Special Interest of His Majesty* [i.e., Philip II of Spain] *in the English Succession Should be Made Known to His Holiness in Advance of the Enterprise*, the author places the Lancastrian claim to the throne at the heart of the matter, in ways which we would call cynical – but ones which seem to find an echo in a later Shakespearean history play, *Henry V*. He writes, imagining the happy outcome of Philip II's invasion plans, that: 'His Majesty would be in a much better position to put forward such matters as his descent from the House of Lancaster, the inadmissibility of other claimants, the will and testament of the Queen of Scotland, the bull of Pope Pius V, the fact that conquest in a just war and for a just cause is usually considered to give a very valid right to a kingdom'.[27]

Henry V, Shakespeare's last Lancastrian king, is one who believes in a just war. Yet, again, Shakespeare's view of the collusion between temporal power and a politicized clergy leaves theatre audiences uneasy. The same pretence of neutrality is evoked by Henry in his address to the Archbishop of Canterbury, who has turned historian, and is also about to deliver his Salic Law speech: 'And God forbid, my dear and faithful lord, / That you should fashion, wrest, or bow your reading' (1.2.13–14). The audience, of course, are not allowed to forget that in the preceding scene they have witnessed the Bishop of Ely and Canterbury himself agree well in advance to support the king in order to preserve the 'temporal lands' given to the Church (1.19). With the Salic Law speech, the Archbishop of Canterbury furnishes Henry with a genealogy that will enable him to serve his political purposes under the pretence of law and religion.

History and genealogy had long been a concern of the most active of English Catholics, but with the invasion plans and later, in the mid-1590s, with the problem of succession it had become an ideological terrain that had to be occupied at all costs. Another 1587 document entitled *Some Points On Which His Majesty's Decision Is Desired At The Earliest Moment, The Matters Themselves Demanding This Urgency* declares most explicitly the need for a book on the succession to the Crown of England defending Philip II's rights to the English throne: 'A book on this subject can be written secretly, if his majesty wishes, and after the victory is won this could be immediately published and distributed throughout England'.[28]

After the successive failure of invasion plans – including that of the invincible Armada – the blueprint for what was to become the *Conference* was no doubt seriously revised. These altered circumstances probably explain why Part 1 of the *Conference* revolves so much around political theory. Published in 1595,[29] the *Conference* coincides with the probable date of Shakespeare's *Richard II*. Without arguing that Shakespeare actually used the *Conference* to write this play or the two parts of *Henry IV*, I would like to suggest that the coincidence of dates is not entirely fortuitous. Dedicated to the Earl of Essex, the work begins with an open attack against the divine right of kings, stating that 'propinquity of birth or blood alone, without other circumstances, is not sufficient to be preferred to a crowne'.[30] Among other sulphurous statements, Parsons reminded his readers that political power was given to the prince by the community, and, furthermore, that a body politic is not bound to one head: 'a body ciuil may haue diuers heades, by succession, and is not bound euer to one, as a body natural is'. Therefore, if the head is sick, like any other member of the body politic it can and must be severed. Having established these points, Parsons then goes on to say that Richard II was rightly deposed because this was the will of the commonwealth: 'the best of al their titles after the deposition of king Richard the second, depended of this authority of the common wealth'.[31]

The dedication of the *Conference* to the Earl of Essex was a source of embarrassment for the Earl himself – and there is reason to believe that this was intended. Be that as it may, Shakespeare, Parsons and Essex were again to be closely associated as a result of this publication. Indeed, after Essex's failed coup, which involved the famous subversive staging of Shakespeare's *Richard II*, Essex was put on trial. During this time Devereux sought to blacken Robert Cecil's name by mentioning his alleged support of the Archduchess Isabella, who, as we shall see, was said to hold rights to the Crown from her Lancastrian ancestors. Sir William Knollys was brought in to testify and he confirmed that Parsons's *Conference* had been discussed but that Cecil had dismissed Parsons's genealogical claim as 'a strange impudence'.[32]

Parsons, in truth, had gone to great lengths to produce a suitable heir to the throne who could also be agreeably matched in marriage. He thus established the rights of Isabella, the Infanta of Spain, writing that 'from the dukedomes of Britanie, Aquitaine, and the like, that came to the crowne of France by women, and are inheritable by women, she cannot be in right debarred, as neyther from any succession or pretence in Ingland'.[33] Added to this, the second part of the *Conference* discredits Henry VII and his descendants; indeed, according to Parsons, Henry VII's own claim to be descended from the House of Lancaster was extremely tenuous.[34] That Shakespeare never wrote a play called *Henry VII* may be a matter of circumstances, but that he only afforded him a minor – albeit conclusive – role in *Richard III* may not have been entirely a coincidence.

The second part of Parsons's *Conference* gradually lifts the veil over the writer's intentions. As the treatise unfolds, the tone gets increasingly more serious. The allusions to the War of the Roses had been instrumental in forming his readers' opinions about the whole question of royal succession. But the civil wars he had described could well become a reality again. This is the warning that seems to emerge from the last pages of the *Conference*, as the tone becomes more prophetic. Here is what Parsons's temporal lawyer says: 'These are my reasons and coniectures why it is like that armes wilbe taken at the beginning in Ingland, before this controuersie can be decided'.[35] Along with some isolated allusions to Ferdinando, Lord Strange – Shakespeare's theatrical patron – the lineage of his mother the Catholic Countess of Derby is also mentioned repeatedly. This was no doubt because Parsons wished to favour a potential match between a male heir of the Countess and the Infanta of Spain.[36]

But the bulk of the second part of the *Conference* is in fact devoted to a defence of the Lancastrian title to the Crown of England. To consolidate this defence both Henry VI and Henry IV are seized as icons of the rights that Parsons would like to see vindicated. For Parsons, as to an extent for Shakespeare, the truly sacred monarch is Henry VI not Richard II. The Jesuit has words for Henry VI which are rarely met in the historical prose of the period: 'king Henry the sixt put downe by the house of Yorke, was a good and holy king, and had reigned peaceably 40 yeares, and neuer committed any act, vvorthy of deposition' – contrary, one is tempted to add, to Richard II.[37]

For Parsons, at all events, John of Gaunt should have reigned in Richard's place; it was thus normal that Henry, Duke of Lancaster, son of John of Gaunt, succeeded Richard II, whose claim to the throne was weaker.[38] In an emotionally charged scene which is now famous (*Richard II* 2.1) Shakespeare endows Gaunt – as he had done for Henry VI – with a prophetic and spiritual aura. What is more, Richard's so-called holiness and sacredness are severely put in question by his own delusions: 'God for his Richard hath in heavenly pay / A glorious angel' (3.2.56–7). But perhaps – I would suggest – where Shakespeare may be seen to take his distance from Parsons's arguments is in his own complex staging of Henry IV.

For Shakespeare, Bolingbroke's belief in a smooth political transition is a fallacy. Shakespeare's Richard II has perfected the role of the saintly king so well that Henry has no other choice but to bear the accusation of having deposed a holy monarch. When Exton murders Richard he puts an end to Bolingbroke's wishful thinking – this is Richard's legacy. Despite his evident good will and qualities as a ruler, Shakespeare's Henry IV is a man who does not manage to keep his hands clean, and who, as a consequence, will be tormented by his choice. Henry IV is not, by far, a contemplative king, so the sinful *action* that made him king can be redeemed only by a religious and spiritual *act*. Henry will henceforth live tormented by this desire and become obsessed by the idea of a crusade to the Holy Land: 'I'll make a voyage to the Holy Land / To wash his blood off from my guilty hand', he promises in the last scene of *Richard II* (5.6.49–50). In 2 *Henry IV* the King again reminds himself of his holy mission: 'We will our youth lead on to higher fields, / And draw no swords but what are sanctified' (4.3.3–4). His lot, however, will be endless civil war and strife. Like Parsons, his involvement in the temporal world will prevent him from reaching a much desired martyrdom. He ironically falls short of that Jerusalem:

> It hath been prophesied to me many years
> I should not die but in Jerusalem,
> Which vainly I supposed the Holy Land;
> But bear me to that chamber; there I'll lie;
> In that Jerusalem shall Harry die. (2 *Henry IV* 4.3.365–9)

Significantly, Shakespeare's last Lancastrian king, Henry V, is clearly less spiritually tormented as a ruler. For him religion is something that the crafty politician may use – another weapon to defend an endangered legitimacy: 'We are no tyrant, but a Christian king, / Unto whose grace our passion is as subject', proclaims Henry IV's formerly rebellious son (*Henry V* 1.2.241–2). Henry V does have a few contemplative moments in the midst of his so-called holy war against France, but – contrary to Henry VI – they are not, for him, an escapist means of eschewing the reality of temporal politics. Henry V describes the happy state of the slave who, contrary to the king, can sleep:

> The slave, a member of the country's peace,
> Enjoys it, but in gross brain little wots
> What watch the King keeps to maintain the peace,
> Whose hours the peasant best advantages. (4.1.278–81)

But Henry V has no aspirations to live like a slave – *otium* is a spiritual option Henry discards. How telling, indeed, that in *Henry V* it is now left to the King's subjects to remind the monarch of his 'conscience' – as the English Catholics would have perhaps wished to remind the powers that were that politics ought to involve conscience. Or, in the words of private

Williams, 'if the cause be not good, the King himself hath a heavy reckoning to make' (*Henry V* 4.1.133–4).

To conclude, I would argue that Robert Parsons's journey as a Jesuit activist and as a writer is of definite importance.

First, one should bear in mind that Parsons's work repeatedly crossed ideological barriers and that the circulation of his ideas and writings was quite extraordinary. His devotional work, *The Christian Directory*, was not only a kind of 'best-seller' at the time, but it was also reprinted and adapted for English Protestant uses. Furthermore, Parsons's *Conference* not only caused considerable stir – judging by the number of responses it prompted – but it was also to be plagiarized and to reappear unexpectedly in 1648 in pirated version under the pen of Oliver Cromwell's own publicist, the Puritan Henry Walker.[39] Militancy will be militancy and oppositinal groups – in this case the English Catholics and the Puritans – have often many similarities. Such a reappearance can be explained also because of Parsons's initial insistence on the powers of Parliament.

If Papists and Puritans sometimes led the same clandestine lives in early modern England, what about Papists and Poets? Were they really of 'like conscience for fictions', as John Speed would have it in 1611? Both Parsons and Shakespeare were actors in their own different ways: Parsons in his writings, and in the whole range of his disguises (his arrival at Dover in 1580 dressed like an army captain returning from Flanders testifies notoriously to this fact). As for Shakespeare, in view of his Catholic associations and even of his Jesuit connections, it is difficult to continue to speak of his neutrality and aloofness from political and religious matters. But if Shakespeare the actor and playwright did have Catholic leanings, was he then hiding 'his serious meaning' from a largely Protestant audience?[40]

This question poses again the whole problem of the relationship between ideology and discourse. If one wants to regard Shakespeare's plays as masks, I would contend that the so-called 'real Shakespeare' is not in hiding behind the mask – he is found in the mask itself. Whereas for Parsons the mask was *instrumental*, for Shakespeare it formed an *essential* part of an art that was necessarily built on illusion.

Parsons's implicit aim in writing the *Conference* was to oppose the idea of a possible separation between matters of religion and matters of state. If such a divide was accepted, it would render all he had fought for redundant. He thus denounced 'the absurd opinions of diuers atheistes of our tyme, that will seeme to be great politiques, who affirme that religion ought not to be so greatly respected in a prince, or by a prince'.[41] But, as Shakespeare could well have pointed out, even Machiavelli – the archetypal atheist for Elizabethans – had written that religion was a worthy means of maintaining the stability of states for princes and politicians. Thus, the 'mutual conspiracy of silence' between Parsons and Shakespeare, which

Peter Milward speaks of, may, in fact, have been partly broken in the theatre
by Shakespeare's disturbing and somewhat critical staging of the collusion
between a politicized form of Catholicism and the government of men.[42]

Notes

1 John Speed, *The Theatre of the Empire of Great Britain, Presenting an exact
geography of England, Scotland, Ireland* (n.p., 1611) (*STC* 23041), p. 637.

2 Peter Milward, *The Catholicism of Shakespeare's Plays* (Southampton, 1997),
p. 103.

3 The pamphlet in question was probably printed by Stephen Brinkley at
Greenstreet House, East Ham, and not at Douai, as the title-page fictitiously
affirms (Robert Parsons, *A Briefe Censure uppon Two Bookes Written in
Answere to M. Edmonde Campions offer of disputation* (Douai, 1581) (*STC*
19393).

4 J. H. Pollen (ed.), *Memoirs of Father Robert Persons*, vol. 2 (London, 1906),
p. 21.

5 Parsons to Gregory XIII, London, 14 June 1581, (L. Hicks (ed.), *Letters and
Memorials of Father Robert Persons, S.J.* (London, 1942), vol. 1:66.

6 Parsons to Aquavia, 12 June 1584, (L. Hicks (ed.), *Letters and Memorials*,
vol. 1:193.

7 This work was printed in 1594 and published the following year only as Parsons
had to wait for the Pope's official approval (Peter Holmes, 'The authorship and
early reception of *A Conference About the Next Succession to the Crown of
England*', *Historical Journal*, 23 (1980), pp. 415–29).

8 Michael L. Carrafiello, *Robert Parsons and English Catholicism, 1580–1610*
(Selinsgrove and London, 1998), leaf cover.

9 Pollen (ed.), *Memoirs*, vol. 4 (London, 1908), pp. 202–3.

10 John Bossy, 'The heart of Robert Persons', in Thomas M. McCoog, S.J (ed.),
*The Reckoned Expense: Edmund Campion and the Early English Jesuits. Essays
in Celebration of the First Centenary of Campion Hall, Oxford (1896–1996)*
(Woodbridge, 1996), pp. 141–58 (141).

11 Hicks (ed.), *Letters and Memorials*, vol. 1:319.

12 *Ibid.*, p. 321.

13 *Ibid.*, p. 38.

14 Parsons to the General, 21 October 1581 (*ibid.*, p. 107).

15 Parsons to the Rector of the English College, Rome, London, 1 March 1582
(*ibid.*, p. 133).

16 Bossy, 'The heart of Roberts Persons'.

17 The Nuncio in France to the Cardinal of Como. Containing Copy of Parsons's
memorial to the Nuncio, 22 May 1582 (Hicks (ed.), *Letters and Memorials*, vol.
1:146–7).

18 Bossy, 'The heart of Roberts Persons', p. 158.

19 Parsons to Ribadenaira, 10 September 1584 (Hicks (ed.), *Letters and
Memorials*, vol. 1:235.

20 Pollen (ed.), *Memoirs*, vol. 2:183.

21 *Ibid.*, p. 24.

22 All references to Shakespeare are taken from the Stanley Wells and Gary Taylor edition of the *Complete Works* (Oxford, 1986).

23 Robert Parsons, *An Epistle of the Persecvtion of Catholickes in England* (Douai, 1582) (*STC* 19406).

24 Hicks (ed.), *Letters and Memorials*, vol. 1:334.

25 L. Hicks, 'Father Robert Persons S.J. and *The Book of Succession*', *Recusant History*, 4:3 (1957), pp. 114–37 (109).

26 Parsons's Memorial to the Pope and King of Spain, Paaris, 22 May 1582 (Hicks (ed.), *Letters and Memorials*, vol. 1:162).

27 Hicks (ed.), *Letters and Memorials*, vol. 1:24.

28 Circa June 1587 (*ibid.*, p. 308).

29 See note 7.

30 Robert Parsons, *A Conference abovt the next Svccession to the Crowne of Ingland* (Antwerp, 1594) (*STC* 19398), part 1:1.

31 *Ibid.*, p. 195.

32 Antonia Fraser, *The Gunpowder Plot: Terror and Faith in 1605* (London, 1997), p. 13.

33 Parsons, *A Conference*, part 2:150.

34 'vvherin riseth the question vvhether those men, I meane king henry the seuenth, & his discendents, may properlie be said to be of the true house of Lancaster or no' (*ibid.*, part 2:163).

35 *Ibid.*, part 2:261.

36 *Ibid.*, part 2:263; 266.

37 *Ibid.*, part 2:96.

38 *Ibid.*, part 2:94.

39 Hicks, 'Father Robert Persons', note 56.

40 This is, largely, what Peter Milward seems to put forward: 'the dramatist may not have wished his serious meaning (from a secretly Catholic point of view) to be readily apparent to a largely Protestant audience' (*Catholicism*, p. 117).

41 Parsons, *A Conference*, part 2:94.

42 Milward, *Catholicism*, p. 110.

Catholic exiles in Flanders and *As You Like It*; or, what if you don't like it at all?

Two of the major themes of Shakespeare's *As You Like It* are the contrast between Court and pastoral life and the Cain theme of one brother's wronging another. The locale of the play is envisioned either as the forests of Arden near Stratford or the Ardennes in France. The introduction to the Arden edition of the play notes: 'Scholars have learnedly argued that the setting is clearly in some French duchy and it must be in the Ardennes near the Flanders border.'[1] It is interesting to note that William Allen's college was located at Douai which is near the Ardennes. Many Catholic exiles from Queen Elizabeth's Court would have passed through and been sheltered at Douai in the late 1570s and early 1580s when Shakespeare could have been a student there. The play depicts a seeming first-hand knowledge about the life of the exiles that a student at Allen's school would have seen frequently. The plot has some parallels with the story of the exiled Thomas Hoghton I, who left the country for 'conscience's sake' and placed his property in the hands of a brother. Whether the setting Shakespeare had in mind was the Forest of Arden in Warwickshire or the Forest of Ardennes in Flanders, he set the play in a sheltering and comforting forest where those who have been wronged in various ways at the sophisticated, deceptive, and ruthless court find peace, honesty and brotherly love. There is a strong suggestion, although it is not specifically stated, that those who fled the Court actually left the country.

During the long reign of Queen Elizabeth the majority of Catholics remained in England and survived as best they could, employing the evasive devices John Shakespeare used to safeguard his property. Some could not, for conscience's sake (their terminology), remain in the country and consequently sought refuge abroad, living on the meagre incomes they were able to salvage, although a few were granted sinecure offices of small pensions by the King of Spain. Some went to Rome, some to Paris, but the favourite place of refuge was Flanders, where the exiles could find shelter in the well-established network of seminaries: the Catholic University at Louvain (1425), Douai (1568), Rheims (1568–93), Anchin (1569), Eu (1582) and

St Omers (1593).[2] In addition to the schools, English convents and monasteries were scattered about the north of France and Belgium where refugees could seek help.

Aside from sympathy with the misfortune of exiles he knew, what else might have motivated Shakespeare to depict on the London stage an idealized and unquestionably unrealistic picture of the life of the exiles abroad? Was the play a kind of travel or vacation brochure intended to attract other disaffected Catholics to join their brethren? To combat the exodus of wealthy Catholic citizens from the country, the English government had begun publishing accounts of the destitute lives of the exiles, some of whom had been promised relief by Spain only to find that the promises were empty ones. Whether or not it was Shakespeare's intention, *As You Like It* portrays an apt rebuttal to the government's propaganda, picturing life in exile as an idyllic, Christian antithesis to the duplicitous and dangerous life at Court.

By 1585 the government was waging a campaign to dissuade potential exiles from leaving the country. A part of that campaign was a book published in 1585 supporting Don Antonio's claim to Portugal in opposition to Philip of Spain, who was moving to pre-empt the Portuguese throne. The purpose of the book was to enlist support for Don Antonio's cause, which started with the premise that Philip was automatically a villain. One of the arguments was intended to dissuade English Catholics from resorting to exile abroad under the protection of Spain by drawing a bleak picture of the conditions under which the exiles in Spain and Flanders were living. The substance of the argument came from a private letter written by a man who had served under Philip. The letter was addressed to a Catholic relative who was contemplating going into exile. John Strype quotes from the letter:

> That himself being five or six years past in these parts of Flanders subject to the Spanish king, he saw a miserable troop of his unhappy countrymen; some, gentlemen of good houses in England, wandering in poor habits and afflicted gestures, heavily groaning under the burden of extreme and calamitous necessity; on the one side, by their heedless demeanour there, debarred from return into their country; and on the other, overlooked by the proud eyes of disdainful Spaniards; and for want of due regard in that comfortless service, perishing without either pity or relief.[3]

Strype's assessment of this propaganda is interesting: 'As the Roman Catholics of this nation made great complaints, and publicly clamoured against the severity used towards them, so it was necessary the state should as publicly be vindicated.'[4] Verstegan, the chief agent of the Catholics in Antwerp, 'had to admit that our miseries are such in truthe as that our Catholique friends in England may thereat be much agreaved.' It was fifteen months, he wrote, since any money had come from Spain, in spite of 'lies and deluding promises . . . God comfort us and send us meanes to live withoute depending upon any forraine friends'.[5] Men once well-to-do and now too old to work were forced to beg for bread; some actually died of starvation. Yet another example of how their misfortunes were used as propaganda by the English government was a pamphlet published in 1595 in London on the 'Usage of the English fugitives by the Spaniard'.[6] Perhaps Shakespeare's play was a kind of rebuttal to the government propaganda.

As there are no quarto editions of *as you like it* to help in the dating of it, we must rely on the facts that it was not mentioned by Francis Meres in 1598, but there was an entry in the Stationers' Register for 4 August, 1600 of a play by that name.[7] Therefore the date of composition probably lies between 1598 and 1600, well beyond the Portuguese problem, but the exodus of exiles from England was still a problem for the English government in 1600, prompting arguments to dissuade more from leaving.

The plot of the play was probably not intended to parallel a specific real-life story but rather was a way of exploring contemporary problems and parallel themes. However, the main action does bear some resemblance to a story about a member of the Hoghton family Shakespeare might have known. One of the conscientious objectors who went into exile was Thomas Hoghton I of Hoghton Tower and Lea Hall. If Shakespeare lived with the Hoghtons during the 1580s, he would have known the unhappy story of Thomas Hoghton and the difficulties he had with his brothers. These brothers appear to have taken advantage of his estrangement from England to 'play upon him', as he phrased it in his letters to the only relative who remained loyal to him, his half-brother, Richard Hoghton of Park Hall, Charnock Richard. If, on the other hand, Shakespeare's only connection with Lancashire was as a member of Ferdinando Stanley's acting group, Shakespeare perhaps could have heard the story anyway, for the Stanleys and the Hoghtons were close friends.

If Shakespeare actually had in mind the Hoghton family when he wrote the play, he obviously changed the ages of the characters, but the major change is that the characters in the play are not protesting on religious grounds. The play would never have made it to the boards with religious exile as the overt basis of the conflict between the brothers. Instead, the younger brother Orlando (of the play) protests that his older brother Oliver has denied him the means by which he can advance in society. That, too, pointed to a contemporary problem of many young Englishmen.

Primogeniture provided for the eldest, but the other brothers had to fend for themselves, in many cases going into the priesthood. However, young Catholic men no longer had that option, and the materialism of the Court society shut the door to those who lacked wealth and lands, one of Orlando's problems in the play. Sometimes the rifts between brothers were the result of one brother's religious exile and another's conformance to the

English Church; sometimes the motivation was simply greed and power. The disagreement between the Hoghton brothers seemed to a combination of the two. The story of the Hoghton brothers and Queen Elizabeth's intervention in their lives would have been en excellent model for Duke Frederick's treatment of his brother and his usurpation of Oliver's property.

Two possible routes by which Shakespeare could have become acquainted with the Hoghton story have been mentioned. There is yet another possibility. The Hoghton saga occurred exactly when Shakespeare could have been a student in a school abroad in the Ardennes, which might have placed him near the old exile, Thomas Hoghton I. Thomas Hoghton's tribulations ended with his death in June 1580, just at the time Shakespeare would have been ready to return to England to join the Hoghton family as a tutor, perhaps first going as Campion's guide to Lancashire and then remaining as a schoolmaster and eventually becoming part of the group of actors in the household. Shakespeare would probably have left grammar school to go abroad somewhere between 1576 to 1578 and would have finished his course of study by the age of sixteen in 1580, so his time abroad could have coincided with part of Thomas Hoghton's time there.

Thomas Hoghton I (1518–80) left England without permission in 1569 to go into exile at Antwerp and Liège because he was a Roman Catholic recusant. Before he left he replaced 'the old manor house at Houghton Bottoms' with Hoghton Tower on a ridge six miles south-east of Preston.[8] He was a friend of William Allen, who attended the opening of the rebuilt Hoghton Tower, and, additionally, Hoghton assisted William Allen in the founding of Douai College. Note the timing of Hoghton's departure in connection with the founding of William Allen's seminaries, which began in 1568. Thomas Hoghton I's son, Thomas, was debarred from the succession to the property because he had gone into exile with his father, and, shortly after becoming a priest at Douai, he was sent back to England as a missionary. Thomas I's 'bad' brothers back in England crossed him and offered a thousand marks 'to hinder my licence / That I should not come home again'.[9] Hoghton died on 4 June 1580 and was buried at Liège.

The manuscript letters between Thomas Hoghton I and Richard Hoghton of Park Hall from 1576 to 1580 (in the John Rylands Library of the University of Manchester)[10] attest to the financial and legal difficulties that arose between Thomas Hoghton I and the brothers who remained at Hoghton Tower and Lea Hall, the family seats. One of these brothers was Alexander Hoghton, who inherited the Hoghton estate on the death of Thomas Hoghton I. Alexander died the following year, and it is his 1581 will that gave birth to the speculation that William Shakespeare served in the Hoghton home.

The nephew of Thomas I, Sir Richard Hoghton (1570–1630), exemplified Elizabeth's technique of wresting sons away from Catholic families to mould them into zealous Protestants. Richard was placed in wardship with Sir Gilbert Gerard, the Master of the Rolls, to be brought up a Protestant. The result was that Richard married Sir Gilbert's daughter, Katherine, and became an active pursuivant of Catholic recusants and High Sheriff of Lancashire in 1598. As his reward for service to the government, he was knighted on 28 June 1599 and was named a baron in 1611. This Richard was connected with John Davies, who dedicated *Epigrammes* to him, to Peter Legh of Lyme, and to some of the Lancashire Ardens, an important considerations in looking for links between Shakespeare and Lancashire, for John Davies also dedicated to Shakespeare.

If Shakespeare was in the Hoghton household, he would have known the other Richard Hoghton (of Park Hall in Charnock Richard). This Mr Hoghton, who was the illegitimate son of the old grandfather, Sir Richard, and half-brother to Thomas I and Alexander, managed the business affairs during the exile of Thomas Hoghton I, his eldest brother. Alexander Hoghton and Thomas II later divided their time between Lea Hall and the Tower, as did the younger Sir Richard Hoghton, who was to live there along with his widowed mother. On 17 March 1576 Mr. Richard Hoghton, who remained loyal to Thomas I, obtained a licence from Queen Elizabeth to visit the exile in Antwerp to persuade him to obey the Queen. 'Hoghton was anxious to return, but could not make terms with the Court to retain his religion' and so he remained abroad and died at Liège on 2 June, 1580, aged 63.[11]

Roger Anderton, Hoghton's butler, who went into exile with his master, seems very like old Adam of the play, who contributes his life savings to finance Orlando's escape from the dangerous Court. Roger Anderton's loyalty to his master led him to praise Thomas Hoghton and to tell his sad story in verse, which records Thomas's dying words:

> At Hoghton, where I used to rest
>   Of men I had great store,
> Full twenty gentlemen at least,
>   Of yeomen good three score!
> And of them all, I brought but two
>   With me, when I came thence.
> I left them all ye world knows how
>   To keep my conscience! . . .
> When to my brethren I had sent
>   Ye welcome that they made
> Was false reports me to present,
>   Which made my conscience sad.
> My brethren all did thus me cross
>   And little regard my fall,
> Save only one, that rued my loss,
>   This is Richard, of Park Hall,

He was ye comfort that I had;
   I proved his diligence;
He was as just as they were bad,
   Which cheered my conscience.[12]

Ernst Honigmann speculates that the brothers were afraid they would be incriminated by the presence of their recusant relative and blocked his return by withholding documents he needed.

To obstruct Thomas's return was also to obstruct the will of the Queen, who wanted him back in England enough to send his half-brother to Europe to retrieve him. In 1576, the same year the correspondence between Thomas and Richard began, the Queen signed a licence allowing Richard to go to Antwerp 'to the intent to advise, persuade and counsel Thomas Hoghton, late of Hoghton, . . . to return unto this our realm'.[13] Hoghton was declared an outlaw, and possession was taken of his estates.[14] Her insecurity about Richard's return is very similar to Duke Frederick's concern about Oliver's trustworthiness when Frederick sends Oliver to find and return with his brother Orlando. In addition to taking possession of his estates, Queen Elizabeth required two sureties to be bound with Richard if he failed to return to England within two months. The men posting the money would each lose £200 if Richard did not return. How similar the situation is to Duke Frederick's command to Oliver:

Find out thy brother, whereso'er he is;
Seek him with candle; bring him dead or living
Within this twelvemonth, or turn thou no more
To seek a living in our territory.
Thy lands, and all things that thou dost call thine
Worth seizure, do we seize into our hands
Till thou canst quit thee by thy Brother's mouth
Of what we think against thee. (3.1.5–12)

The evil brother, Duke Frederick and Oliver are redeemed in the play in an almost 'wishful thinking', fairytale type of resolution that the real Thomas Hoghton I would have welcomed. Oliver is redeemed through love, and Duke Frederick is redeemed through a change of religion. In the play Oliver is willing to forfeit all of his wealth, his evil having been overpowered by the goodness of his brother, Orlando, and his love for Celia. The religious goodness of the new society in the wholesome, pastoral setting of the play seems to provide a remedy for each evil of the old society. Orlando exemplifies Christ's teaching to turn the other cheek, shown when he saves the life of Oliver who had so wronged him earlier. The power of this religion is great enough to transform so obstinate and vengeful a man as Duke Frederick into a religious monk:

Duke Frederick, hearing how that every day
Men of great worth resorted to this forest,

Addressed a mighty power, which were on foot
In his own conduct, purposely to take
His brother here and put him to the sword;
And to the skirts of this wild wood he came,
Where, meeting with an old religious man,
After some question with him, was converted
Both from his enterprise and from the world,
His crown bequeathing to his banished brother,
And all their lands restored to them again
That were with him exiles.   (5.4.159–70)

The persuasive, old religious man is very like many exiled Catholic priests who roamed northern Europe performing such miracles.[15] Frederick's redemption might have suggested that, if enough 'Men of great worth resorted to this forest' (5.4.160) of Ardennes, the Queen might be so convinced of the sincerity of their convictions and their religion that she would call the exiles home to their restored lands.

There were other exiles whom Shakespeare might have known whether or not he lived with the Hoghtons or the Heskeths, because by 1592 Shakespeare is believed to have been a member of Ferdinando Stanley's group of actors, and there were interesting and dangerous connections between Ferdinando and some of the exiled Catholics. A fragile link between the play and Ferdinando may be the name Shakespeare assigned Rosalind as her alias, 'Ganymede'. Might there have been an obscure connection between Rosalind and Chapman's praise of Ferdinando as 'Ganymede' in the second hymn of 'Shadow of Night' (1595)? Perhaps Ferdinando took the role of Rosalind in an early performance of the play. It is an androgynous role suiting a slightly more mature young man than usually played the women's roles. If the play were written to reflect Ferdinando's sympathies, as well as Shakespeare's, this would help explain the positive religious overtones in the forest of Arden (Ardennes) where Touchstone points out, 'Here we have no temple but the wood' (3.3), literally true of the exiles, for they had had to leave their temples behind in England. Lord Strange was a Catholic who was connected by family members and friends to Catholic exiles abroad, some of whom backed him as a successor to Queen Elizabeth because of his mother's descent from the sister of Henry VIIII.

Shakespeare's Forest of Arden is not tainted with the intrigue of the true picture of the exiles' relationship with the Court, yet he surely would have been aware of some of the intrigue if he lived with Thomas Hesketh of Rufford. Richard Hesketh, third son of Thomas, became intangled in a complicated and questionable scheme to put Ferdinando Stanley on the English throne. Through this Richard and a cousin of Ferdinando, Sir William Stanley (author of the plot), both related to as well as visitors of the Heskeths of Rufford and the Stanleys of Derby, Shakespeare might have encountered a shady character named Jaques who hovered around the wings of much of the subversive activity of the exiled Catholics.

Jaques of the play has some traits in common with the real-life Jaques of the dark side of life in exile. The real Jaques served under Sir William Stanley twice: he was Stanley's lieutenant in Ireland in 1585 and later served under Stanley in the Netherlands.[16] Sir William Stanley is notorious for his surrender of the city of Deventer to the Spanish as part of his Catholic protest against Queen Elizabeth's effort to Protestantize the Dutch. Stanley also played instrumental roles in both the Babington Plot and the Richard Hesketh Plot to put Ferdinando Stanley on the English throne.[17] In addition Stanley was a personal friend of Robert Parsons.[18] Stanley was later associated with Robert Catesby, a relative of Shakespeare, in the Gunpowder Plot.[19] William Stanley was related to Ferdinando Stanley, and 'the heirs of the two great Stanley houses of Hooton and Lathom were on terms of great and suspicious intimacy'.[20] Shakespeare could very well have been acquainted with the man Jaques through the Stanleys.

A brief biographical sketch of the real Jaques reveals personality traits which perhaps inspired Shakespeare to inject a version of the personality in the utopian world of Arden. Jaques (Jacomo Francisci), commonly called Captain Jaques, was a soldier of fortune, born in Antwerp of a Venetian father. He was described as 'a dangerous and violent man', and the English spies constantly reported his 'injurious words, and malevolent, nay treasonable, persuasions and acts'.[21] He dressed in black satin, had a black beard and always had a man attending him.[22] His personality comes alive in an account of the interrogation of Edward Windsor, one of the conspirators in the Babington Plot, who complained to Hatton that the government seemed to be strangely lenient toward Captain Jaques. He contended that Jaques had been one of 'the chief workers of this conspiracy and to be wholly employed by Ballard to be ready in anything they could do for the assistance of the invasion, the one in the North, the other in Ireland'.[23] Windsor asked to see Jaques face to face and was surprised that he was allowed to do so. Jaques swore his innocence, 'laughing at me, and saying I was drunk, and that I had a devil within me, and how I was a dead man'.[24]

The real-life Jaques had affinities with Duke Senior's melancholy Jaques in the play. There is a darkness surrounding Shakespeare's Jaques that is discordant with the loving and Christian world around him. Shakespeare's Jaques in some ways seems to be an addition to the play, for he is not essential to the plot or any relationship and seems out of tune with the almost naive goodness of the exiles. He seems haughtily disdainful without cause when he begs Amiens to sing to gratify his own desires but is not really grateful for his service: 'Well then, if ever I thank any man, I'll thank you. But that they call compliment is like the encounter of two dog-apes; and when a man thanks me heartily, methinks I have given him a penny, and he renders me the beggarly thanks. Come, sing! and you that will not, hold your tongues' (2.5.23–8). He seems not to like anyone in the play, not even his master, Duke Senior, of whom he says: 'And I have been all this day to avoid him. He is too disputable for my company. I think of as many matters as he; but I give heaven thanks and make no boast of them' (2.5.32–45). He is a loner and prefers his own company to that of so likeable a person as Orlando, for he says with little provocation, except his intolerance of Orlando's verses: 'I thank you for your company; but, good faith, I had as lief have been myself alone' (3.2.252–3). Shakespeare's Jaques, self-consciously aware of the aloof, disdainful, and melancholy personality he has cultivated, could very suitably have dressed in black satin and worn a black beard as the real Jaques did. In a like manner the real Jaques could have said of himself:

> I have neither the scholar's melancholy, which is emulation; not the musician's, which is fantastical; not the courtier's, which is proud; nor the soldier's, which is ambitious; nor the lawyer's, which is politic; nor the lady's, which is nice; nor the lover's, which is all these: but it is a melancholy of mine own, compounded of many simples, extracted from many objects, and indeed the sundry contemplation of my travels, in which my often rumination wraps me in a most humorous sadness. (4.1.10–19)

He seems almost to sneer at Amiens's simple song, a song which could have been an invitation to other disaffected to come join the exiles:

> Who doth ambition shun
> And love to live i' the sun,
> Seeking the food he eats,
> And pleased with what he gets,
> Come hither; come hither, come hither!
> Here shall he see
> No enemy
> But winter and rough weather.   (2.5.36–43)

Jaques makes up his own version of the life the exiles are living and scoffs at their foolish stubbornness:

> If it do come to pass
> That any man turn ass,
> Leaving his wealth and ease
> A stubborn will to please,
> Ducdame, ducdame, ducdame!
> Here shall he see
> Gross fools as he,
> An if he will come to me.   (2.5.48–55)

The picture of the real Jaques is of a man who is disdainful of all, committed to his own interests, haughty and aloof. This same description applies to Shakespeare's Jaques. His assessment of all of mankind is a reflection of his own duplicitous nature:

Why, who cries out on pride,
That can therein tax any private party?
Doth it not flow as hugely as the sea
Till that the wearer's very means do ebb?
What woman in the city do I name
When that I say the city woman bears
The cost of princes on unworthy shoulders?
Who can come in and say that I mean her,
When such a one as she, such is her neighbour?
Or what is he of basest function
That says his bravery is not on my cost,
Thinking that I mean him, but therein suits
His folly to the mettle of my speech? (2.7.73–85)

The ironic picture of Jaques at the end of the play, abandoning the world to join the convertites, from whom there was much to be learned (5.4.190), and acknowledging the worth of each of the other characters before his departure, is another fairytale ending that would have been humorous to those who knew the real Jaques.

The conviviality of Rosalind and Celia is in marked contrast to Jaques's jaded, lone demeanour. In some respects their sudden decision to disguise themselves and flee from the Court seems unrealistic. This is not very different, however, from the story of two young ladies who actually lived such an adventure. Richard Simpson tells of Anne Dimocke, a maid of honour to the Queen, who had learned from the Court preachers that there was no hell, 'but only a certain remorse of conscience for him that did evil, which was to be understood for hell, and that all the rest were but bugbears to fright children'.[25] Obviously this was a reference to the Protestant ban on references to purgatory. Simpson recounts her attempts to find out the truth about hell by going to Robert Parsons, 'under whose instructions she at once became Catholic, and afterwards left the court and the world'.[26] She and one of Lord Vaux's daughters followed Parsons to Rouen where Anne entered a convent.

In England, legally, these two girls were traitors, just as Rosalind and Celia become traitors in the play: 'If she [Rosalind] be a traitor, / Why, so am I [Celia]!' (1.3.75–6). Rosalind has done nothing to merit the accusation that she is a traitor, and the very fact that Shakespeare used the term and then had the girls disguise themselves for their departure must have suggested to the audience instances of just such flights by friends and relatives. The plan of the girls could also have served as a 'how to' guide for those who were contemplating leaving but needed direction in how to accomplish as escape. Peter Milward observed that 'The unjust accusation of treason commonly made against Catholics in Elizabethan England, and

particularly against all priests since the harsh penal laws of 1585, is interestingly reflected in quite a number of plays'.[27] In particular Milward sees
a reference to Lord Burghley in Duke Frederick's response to Rosalind's
protestations of innocence: 'Thus do all traitors; If their purgation did
consist in words, They are as innocent as grace itself' (1.3.54–6). Milward
suggests that his words seem to echo those of Lord Burghley himself in his
self-justifying pamphlet on *The Execution of Justice in England* (1583): 'It
hath been in all ages and in all countries a common usage of all offenders
for the most part, both great and small, to make defence of their lewd
and unlawful facts by untruths and by colouring and covering their deeds
(were they never so vile) with pretences of some other causes of contrary
operations or effects.'[28] Milward then contrasts this to the contemporary
complaint of a Catholic against Elizabethan judges: 'It is ordinary with them
to call Catholics traitors, and to proceed against them in their
judgements as on cases of treason, notwithstanding that the case be directly
conscience.'[29]

For those like Anne Dimocke, the Vaux daughter and Thomas Hoghton
I, to be called traitors must have been particularly puzzling. Certainly not
all exiles belonged in one category, so not all treason laws should have
applied to all exiles. There is little question that Sir William Stanley, and
perhaps Richard Hesketh, were engaged in treasonous plots that were a
great danger to the Queen. There were enough like Stanley to make it
imperative for the government to take action against them. The majority,
however, left the country for genuine religious beliefs – a move that required
courage and steadfastness in the face of great misery and deprivation. The
play softens the hardship of life in exile to make it seem bearable in a
manner parallel to Edmund Campion's attitude about life in exile. Campion
glorified the simple life and contrasted it with Court life in a letter he wrote
to novices at Brno, after he had taken his vows and had returned to the
college at Prague:

> Believe me, my dearest brethren, that your dust, your brooms, your chaff,
> your loads, are beheld by angels with joy, and that through them they obtain
> more for you from God than if they saw in your hands sceptres, jewels, and
> purses of gold. Would that I knew not what I say; but yet, as I do know it, I
> will say it; in the wealth, honours, pleasures, pomps of the world, there is
> nothing but thorns and dirt. The poverty of Christ has less pinching parsi-
> mony, less meanness, than the emperor's palace.[30]

And again he wrote from Prague (1575):

> Which of us would have believed, unless He had called him and instructed
> him in this school, that such thorns, such filth, such misery, such tragedies,
> were concealed in the world under the feigned names of goods and pleasures?
> Which of us would have thought your kitchen better than a royal palace: your
> crusts better than any banquet? your troubles than others' contentment?

. . . . One sigh of your for heaven is better than all their clamours for this dirt; one colloquy of yours, where the angels are present, is better than all their parties and debauched drinking-bouts, where the devils fill the bowls. One day of yours consecrated to God is worth more than all their life, which they spend in luxury.[31]

The sad truth is many exiles died of starvation and in great penury. Some, like Thomas Hoghton I, were replaced by men like his nephew, Richard Hoghton, who turned Protestant and inherited all the wealth and property Thomas Hoghton had renounced for his conscience's sake. Richard Hoghton made doubly sure he was secure in his position by becoming a renowned hunter of Catholic recusants. A few, it is true, were a real threat to the English government because of their subversive activity. The contrast Shakespeare drew between life at the English Court and the pastoral life of the exile is persuasive although heavily slanted. It would have beckoned to Catholics to live their religion abroad for their consciences' sake. On a larger scale, the play was a plea to English Christians, Protestants and Catholics alike, to reconcile their differences in Christian forgiveness and love.

Notes

1 William Shakespeare, *As You Like It*, eds Louis B. Wright and Virginia A. LaMar (New York, 1959), p. vii.
2 'The ancient English hospice in Rome became a seminary somewhat casually and no date can be assigned. Students were sent there from Douai as early as aug 76 (D. 109)', Godfrey Anstruther, O.P., *The Seminary Priests* (ware, 1968), p. xi.
3 John Strype, *Annals of the Reformation and Ecclesiastical Memorials* vol. III, pt 1 (Oxford, 1820), vol. 1, p. 513.
4 *Ibid.*
5 M. D. R. Leys, *Catholics in England, 1559-1829 A Social History* (New York, 1961), p. 53.
6 *Ibid.*
7 Shakespeare, *As You Like It*, eds Wright and LaMar, preface, p. xiv.
8 Joseph Gillow, 'Thomas Hoghton', in *Bibliographic Dictionary of English Catholics* (London, 1885–1902).
9 E. A. J. Honigmann, *Shakespeare: The 'Lost Years'* (Manchester, 1985), p. 11.
10 John Hoghton, 'Letters.' English Ms. 213. The John Rylands University Library, University of Manchester.
11 Gillow, 'Thomas Hoghton'.
12 Honigmann, *'lost years'*, p. 10.
13 *Ibid.*, p. 11.
14 Gillow, 'Thomas Hoghton'.
15 The Jesuits, having won Deventer, immediately wrote to the Pope, Philip, Parma, and Allen, magnifying the importance of the service, and claiming reward, and

countenance for Stanley and his regiment. 'Down came priests thick, and three-fold, from France and Italy, catechising the new soldiers with many masses and continual sermons, and generally men that, for their conscience, lay dispersed in other parts, all drew down thither, in hopes of the great payment and golden world that was there talked of' (Strype, *Annalsrd*, vol. II: 428). (Deventer was surrendered to the Spanish by Sir William Stanley 28 January 1586–7, Cardinal Allen, *Defence of Sir William Stanley's Surrender of Deventer*, ed. Thomas Heywood, Esq., F.S.A., Chetham Society, vol. 25, 1851–52, p. xxvi. Allen wrote a defence of Stanley's surrender, first published in 1587. A second edition was printed in 1588, and a third in 1588.)

16 Eric Saint John Brooks, *The Life of Hatton* (London, 1947), p. 260.

17 Heywood, *Cardinal Allen's Defence*, pp. xiii, xlii.

18 *Ibid.*, p. xxx.

19 *Ibid.*, p. liv.

20 *Ibid.*, p. xlii. Sir William Stanley, who married Alice of Timperley in 1375, had an eldest son, also Sir William Stanley; the latter married Margery of Hooton (Wirral, Cheshire) and founded a co-lateral branch of the family, the Stanleys of Hooton, in which an unbroken line of seven successive Sir William Stanleys led to Sir Rowland Stanley in Queen Elizabeth's time; and his son, Sir William Stanley (1548–1630), contemporary with his namesake William Stanley, Sixth Earl of Derby, eventually deserted to Spain. Arthur Walsh Titherley, *Shakespeare's Identity* (Winchester, 1952), p. 7, footnote.

21 Fr J. H. Pollen, *Mary Queen of Scots and the Babington Plot* (Edinburgh, 1922), p. 95.

22 Saint John Brooks, *Life of Hatton*, p. 276.

23 *Ibid.*, pp. 278, 279.

24 *Ibid.*, p. 279.

25 Richard Simpson, *Edmund Campion: A Biography* (London, 1896), p. 241.

26 *Ibid.*

27 Peter Milward, S. J., *Shakespeare's Religious Background* (Bloomington, 1973), p. 71.

28 *Ibid.*

29 *Ibid.*, pp. 71, 72.

30 Simpson, *Edmund Campion*, p. 97.

31 *Ibid.*, p. 100.

Requiem for a prince:
rites of memory in *Hamlet*

'Denmark's a prison.' Hamlet's words seem a statement of the obvious, but they also express the reality of the Catholic community at this time. 'On my return to England', wrote John Pibush in November 1600, 'I found that it was one huge prison for all who, like us, profess the true faith.'[1] It is a central plank of Robert Southwell's *An Humble Supplication to Her Majestie*, written in 1591: 'And if this saying be true, that none are troubled for religion, what keepeth at this hower at London, Yorke, Wisbeche and other places, great numbers of Catholiques in prison.'[2] John Gerard's moving account of Mass being said in the Clink makes clear how prisons became the focus of life for Catholics in this period:

> Though I was locked up, I looked on this change to the Clink as a translation from Purgatory to Paradise. I no longer heard obscene and bawdy songs, but, instead, I had Catholics praying in the next cell. They came to my door and comforted me, and then they showed me how I could have freer dealings with them through a hole made in the wall, which they covered over and concealed with a picture. Through this hole they handed me, the next day, letters from some of my friends, and at the same time gave me paper, pen and ink, so that I could write back.[3]

As early as 1583 it was said, 'The prisons are so full of catholics that there is no room for thieves.'[4] Even worse than the fines and imprisonment was the atmosphere of secrecy, disguise, deception and betrayal so movingly described by John Gerard. 'As we were preparing everything for mass before daybreak we heard, suddenly, a great noise of galloping hooves . . . I was hardly tucked away when the pursuivants broke down the door and burst in.'[5] Every priest who was captured put the whole Catholic community in peril as he was racked for information on his protectors, as Campion was at least three times in July and August 1581.[6]

This world of disguise, spying, fear, of forked tongues, of landing like a foreigner in one's own country, *is* the world of *Hamlet*. Just as Anne Bellamy was used in 1592 to trap Robert Southwell, who supposed she wanted to go to confession, so Ophelia is made to seem engaged in 'devotion', while supervised by Polonius, the living embodiment of the whole apparatus of spying operated by Burghley and Walsingham.[7] Just as Reynaldo is dispatched to Paris to watch over Laertes, John Gerard passes through Paris in 1588, thinking he has gone undetected, but is spotted by one of Walsingham's spies.[8] As the Spanish Ambassador noted as early as 1564, 'the evil lies in the universal distrust, for a father dares not trust his own son'[9]. To be held a virtual prisoner at Court, spied on, with every word and letter being scrutinized: this is Hamlet's lot: and it was an exact emblem of the recusant community of the time.

Campion arrived at the Tower on Saturday 22 July 1581, with a paper stuck in his hat 'inscribed "CAMPION THE SEDITIOUS JESUIT"'.[10] For Shakespeare, whose cousin Southwell had been tortured there by Topcliffe, and who may have spent some time with Edmund Campion in Lancashire,[11] the Tower must have been a symbol of all that was worst in the regime's repression. What was always at issue was sedition; the questions put to priests under torture were intended to prove treason. The question was universally known as the 'bloody question', devised by Burghley in 1583, in which recusants were asked what they would do if the Pope were to send over an army. 'Whose side would you be on – the Pope's or the Queen's?'[12] By the late 1590s the mood of the Catholic community was increasingly desperate.

It is no wonder that Hamlet's struggle with his conscience, overheard by the King and the spymaster, reads like the reflections of a whole community on whether this was any kind of life at all: 'To be or not to be, *that* is the question . . .' (3.1.55).

The 'bloody question' is, under these conditions, an irrelevance, but the phrase has found its way into the play: 'But since so jump upon this *bloody question* . . .' (5.2.375). Horatio's words at the end of the play must have had a terrifying resonance for all recusants, and yet they extend the meaning of the often-used phrase: the carnage at the end of the play is an image of the tragic destruction of a whole kingdom as a result of this politico-religious conflict of loyalties.

The most striking feature of *Hamlet* is its concern with the passage from life to death, with the rites of memory associated with that transition, and with being dead. Indeed, to understand the play's concern with memory and remembrance is to penetrate into the heart of the greatest controversy in sixteenth-century England: how are the dead to be remembered? Were Masses for them still to be said? 'Wherever one turns in the sources for the period one encounters the overwhelming preoccupation of clergy and laity alike, from peasant to prince and from parish clerk to pontiff, with the safe transition from this world to the next, above all with the shortening and easing of their stay in Purgatory.'[13]

Hamlet's own passage from this world is marked by the last of many goodnights in the play:

Good night sweet prince,
And flights of angels sing thee to thy rest. (5.2.538–9)

Translated into Latin, this verbal anointing by Horatio, ending with the
word *requiem*, is only a minor alteration of the *In paradisum*, the antiphon
of the burial service following the Latin Requiem Mass: '*In paradisum ded-
ucant te angel i . . . Chorus angelorum te suscipiat, et cum Lazaro quondam
paupere aeternam habeas requiem.*' Hamlet's own dying words focus on the
same word: 'The *rest* is silence' (5.2.538). Rest is clearly both 'cetera' and
'requies'.

Not only were all Masses specifically outlawed – indeed a treasonable
offence since 1581 – but, as Christopher Haigh has pointed out, 'Catholic
funerals were more difficult, for there was a conflict between the desire to
have the traditional ceremonies and the desire to be buried in consecrated
ground.'[14] Prayers for the dead, as Eamon Duffy has made clear, remained
one of the most profound causes of doctrinal unease among the population
at large. The prayer-book service offered no such prayers, since it was 'in
many ways a starkly reformed service, speaking much of predestination': it
implied that all had died 'in sure and certain hope of salvation'.[15] But ministers found it hard to declare that the notorious sinner or the obviously
unrepentant were so sure of salvation; suicide, where there was no time for
repentance, made vividly apparent the disadvantages of abandoning belief
in purgatory, since one could not even pray for the soul of the desperately
dead.

The truth is that belief in purgatory was slow to die away, particularly
as prayers and Masses for the dead formed such an important part of the
devotional practice of English families. Pre-Reformation wills nearly always
made provision for Masses to be said, and Eamon Duffy has shown that
this practice continued long after the Reformation, and not just among
recusant families: 'Insistence on due performance of this and the other rites
of passage became a frequent bone of contention between traditionally
minded parishioners and Protestant clergy.'[16] Laertes's concern that there
should be adequate ceremonies for his sister's funeral seems to echo a
central concern not just of this play but of the whole period: 'Must there
no more be done?'

The priest's reply about the state of Ophelia's soul echoes the Ghost's
anxiety about the way he has passed to the next life, and takes a very conformist line:

We should profine *the service of the dead*
To sing sage *requiem* and such rest to her
As to peace-parted souls. (5.1.236–8)

The priest seems to contrast a Catholic requiem with the 'service of the
dead' in the *Book of Common Prayer*, even if he justifies his attitude with

a canonical judgement on Ophelia's possible death. As James V. Holleran has argued, whatever the legal justification for the priest's position, 'we feel that the denial of full burial rites for Ophelia is unfair'.[17]

The Ghost has suffered a far worse fate. He may have been buried 'according to customary funeral practices', as Holleran says,[18] but he has been cut off 'even in the blossoms of my sin' and not been given the last rites, which include the three Catholic sacraments of confession, communion and extreme unction: 'unhouseled, disappointed, unaneled'. The result is that he is now clearly in a pre-Reformation purgatory:

Doomed for a certain term to walk the night
And for the day confined to fast in fires
Till the foul crimes done in my days of nature
Are burned and purged away. (1.5.10–13)

The Ghost, then, gives a very Catholic version of the next life, and it is not a peripheral part of the play's meaning, since Hamlet himself is later much concerned with what may come in 'the undiscovered country' and refuses to dispatch Claudius 'in the purging of his soul / When he is fit and seasoned for his passage' (3.3.86).

It cannot be an accident that this Ghost suffering in a very Catholic purgatory should encounter a son who is a student at Luther's university of Wittenberg where he would have been taught *not* to believe in such notion.[19] Hamlet is forced not just to come home from Wittenberg by the death of his father but to spend much of the play conversing with souls beyond the grave; he who is compelled by circumstances to play the fool spends the interim before his death conversing with the skull of an earlier fool. This graveyard colloquy seems almost an emblem of Robert Southwell's portrait of Catholics in this period: 'And we like God Almighties fooles (as some scornefully call us) lay our shoulders under every loade, and are contented to make patience the onely salve for all sores.'[20] For Catholics were not only treated as fools and madmen but seem to have accepted the self-mocking epithet of 'fools' with a fiercely proud humility. Shakespeare may be referring to the martyrs as 'fools of Time' in Sonnet 124, and Edgar's assumed disguise as a mad beggar in *King Lear* includes a deliberate adoption of the language of Samuel Harsnett's anti-papist pamphlet.[21]

This may explain one of the most enigmatic statements in the play: 'I am but mad north-north-west.' (2.2.378). If being mad was a codeword for recusancy, Lancashire was most certainly the centre of the recusant world. As Christopher Haigh argues, 'Lancashire, then, was at the end of Elizabeth's reign by far the most recusant Catholic county in England.'[22]

This might seem merely fanciful if it were not for the fact that Hamlet follows this as cryptically with: 'I know a hawk from a handsaw.' The Jesuit John Gerard landed in England in 1588, the most dangerous time possible, and used his knowledge of hawking as a cover: 'I had only gone a short

distance when I saw some country folk coming towards me. Walking up
to them I asked whether they knew anything about a stray hawk . . .
Whenever I saw anybody in the fields I went up to him and asked my usual
questions about the falcon.'[23] Again with Lady Digby, the wife of the
Gunpowder conspirator Sir Everard Digby, his disguise is so convincing that
she cannot believe him to be a priest: 'And he's been out hunting with my
husband, and I've heard him myself talking about hunting and about
hawking, and he never trips in his terms.'[24] Even more significantly he
instructed Robert Southwell in the terms of falconry: 'Frequently, as he was
travelling about with me later, he would ask me to tell him the correct terms
and worried because he could not remember and use them when need
arose.'[25] Is Hamlet's apparently wild comment a cryptic tribute to a fellow-
poet, Southwell, who had been executed only five years before the play
was written, and whom Gerard describes as 'wise and good, gentle and
loveable'?[26] The most probable site for Shakespeare's marriage, according
to Park Honan, is Temple Grafton, where the priest John Frith was 'old
and Unsound in religion': that is, Catholic. He too seems to have used
hawks as a cover: 'His chiefest trade is to cure hawkes yt are hurt or dis-
eased, for which purpose manie doe usuallie repaire to him.'[27] One wonders
how many of these were actually going to confession. The most likely date
for the marriage is 1 December 1582, the first anniversary of Campion's
execution.[28]

There are times when Hamlet seems close to being Death itself, the ultimate fool, mocking the pretensions of the living, as in *Richard II*:

> For within the hollow crown
> That rounds the mortal temples of a king
> Keeps Death his court, and there the antick sits,
> Scoffing his state and grinning at his pomp. (3.2.160–3)

A. D. Nuttall has suggested that Hamlet's journey to England has all the
elements of a journey to his death.[29] He is intended to die there, and returns
with all the mysterious quality of a revenant. Like Orestes, he is thought
to be dead, and re-enters the play in the shadow of the graveyard: almost
out of the grave itself. His first action is to converse with gravediggers, to
stare at his own reflection in the skull of Yorick. Hamlet, who has been
playing the fool at the Court, gazes at the skull of the former fool, in the
presence of the stage fool. 'This is I, / Hamlet the Dane.' (5.1.257–8).
Hamlet's remarkable proclamation by the side of the grave (casting a
shadow over it in Olivier's film version of this scene) not only lays claim to
the kingdom. It marks his arrival at the same point as his dead, ghostly
father. For when Hamlet searches for the appropriate mode of address in
his first encounter with the Ghost he cries: 'I'll call thee Hamlet / King,
father, royal Dane.' (1.4.44–5). Hamlet has now become the 'royal Dane'.
For he too is a ghost come back mysteriously from the dead. It is no acci-

dent that the 'young Hamlet' (1.1.170) should, in emphatic parallel, so emphasize the name he gives to his father and so solemnly announce his own name. For in both halves of the play Hamlet, the visitant from the dead, comes to remind us of the transience of all human power, and of the need for remembrance. As Nuttall has argued, Hamlet twice proclaims himself *dead*, not just dying:

> I am dead, Horatio . . .
> But let it be. Horatio, I am dead.[30]   (5.2.332–3)

Of course, this can be taken as merely proleptic, but it does seem to point to a deeper reality of Hamlet's status as a revenant, a soul come back from the dead. Hamlet has grown up only to grow dead, as Barbara Everett has argued;[31] he has reached the age widely regarded in medieval and Renaissance thought as the age of maturity at the point at which he passes from this world to the next. He too has become a voice from beyond the grave.

This language seems, in any case, curiously close to Campion's description of himself in his famous challenge to the Privy Council 'as a *dead* man to this world',[32] and his boast at his trial that the missionaries were '*dead men to the world*': echoed the Queen's Counsel's retort on Campion's clothes: 'Are they weeds for *dead* men?'[33] In Hamlet's first conversation with the Ghost he endlessly implores him to speak, but the roles are reversed in their second and final encounter. The Ghost's last words are a summons to speak. He now implores Hamlet to speak to his mother: 'Speak to her, Hamlet.' (3.4.115). It is as if the Ghost is handing over his role to his son, the role of speaking from the dead. Hamlet's next address to his mother is less that of angry son than of ghostly confessor:

> Confess yourself to heaven,
> Repent what's past, avoid what is to come.   (3.4.150)

The Ghost's primary concern was with his unconfessed sins – 'Unhouseled, disappointed, unaneled' (1.5.77). – And Hamlet seems almost literally to have taken this over from *his* Ghostly father; he has become his mother's *ghostly father*. His concern is now with the state of his mother's soul.

Confession was one of the most controversial issues in Elizabethan England, partly because it became an offence after 1570 in an Act providing that 'if any person after the same 1 July should take upon him to absolve or reconcile any person . . . or if any shall willingly receive and take any such absolution or reconciliation' he was guilty of high treason.[34] It became one of the main tasks of the missionary priests, as in this account of Campion himself: 'I ride about some piece of the country every day . . . Then I talk with such as come to speak with me or hear their confessions.'[35] It was a particularly important task of the priest at the time of death. As Duffy points out, 'But comfort was not the exclusive task of the priest, or

the only deathbed priority.' His task was to take them through the commandments, to establish 'whether they recognized and repented their own
sinfulness'.[36] It is difficult to avoid the impression that Hamlet is adopting
the role of a priest in this scene, a role beautifully illustrated in the emblematic print of 1594 by the Dutch artist Jan van Straton, which is called *The
Frailty of Human Life, or Presenting the Mirror of Life*. Roland Frye
describes it as follows:

> Set in a chamber replete with luxury, the print shows a seated lady of inde-
> terminate age, with withered flowers in her lap. She is addressed by a robed
> counsellor, completely hooded, who holds up the two tablets of the Mosaic
> law, and below these a double mirror. The larger glass reflects the lady's face,
> while a smaller panel extended out to the right reveals a death's head.[37]

Hamlet follows his explicit command to repent with a series of five goodnights. But who is going to sleep? On a literal level, his mother is in her
closet, preparing for bed. On a more important metaphysical level Hamlet
is preparing to depart for almost certain death. His five goodnights seem a
curious echo of the cult of *The Five Wounds of Christ* – a devotion that
came to symbolize the Pilgrimage of Grace and formed a central part of
the devotional practice enjoined by the *Ars moriendi*, 'the standard late
medieval handbook on how to die a Christian death'.[38] Hamlet is departing for sleep and death, and bidding goodnight to his mother, just as
Ophelia bids goodnight to the ladies of the Court as she walks out to her
muddy death. The moment of transition is marked in Hamlet's case with
ritualistic intensity, echoed by the 'snatches of old lauds' (4.7.177) which
Ophelia sings as *she* drifts melodiously into the next world. 'Lauds' is an
unusual word, rarely found outside its liturgical context: the canonical hour
sung at dawn. It was so unusual that the Folio and Q1 both changed it to
'tunes'. But 'lauds' is more appropriate because Ophelia's death is liturgical in every aspect: she passes baptismally through water, singing 'lauds',
liturgical hymns of praise, and is then carried in solemn procession, and:
'the bringing home of bell and burial' (5.1.234). Bells and processions had
both been banned in 1547, but Ophelia, like Hamlet, is given as near to a
full *requiem* as was possible in 1601.[39] Both Hamlet and Ophelia are sung
to their rest and angels invoked for their passing.

The whole play seems dominated by the notion of *passage*. In its very
structure it shows a concern with the passage of generations. Beginning with
the Ghost of Hamlet's father, it ends with the corpse of Hamlet being carried
in solemn procession, and his soul being sung to rest. The Ghost himself
passes across the stage twice in the first scene. He passes across the stage
again later in the first Act when Hamlet follows it. But it is not simply the
transit, which might be explained as a theatrical device, but the emphasis
put on the brief term the Ghost has in this world, between midnight and
the crowing of the cock.

But soft, methinks I scent the morning air;
Brief let me be.   (1.5.58–9)

The Ghost's shadowy appearance is almost an emblem of our brief journey through this world. Indeed, even his more substantial, earthy brother gives us a vivid sermon on the passage of the generations when he is trying to persuade Hamlet to cut short the 'rites of memory':

Fie, tis a fault to heaven
A fault against the dead, a fault to nature,
To reason most absurd, whose common theme
Is death of fathers.   (1.2.101–4).

If we are not persuaded by Claudius's rhetoric the argument of the play itself shows us a swift succession of four kings in one kingdom: Hamlet, Claudius, Prince Hamlet and Fortinbras: 'A man's life no more than to say one'. The only permanence is death, the worm 'your only emperor for diet' (4.3.21).

This must surely help explain the very odd transition of Fortinbras across the kingdom. A prince of this world, honourable in his way, he appears criss-crossing Hamlet's journeys. As Hamlet leaves for England (or death) and as Hamlet is carried out dead, Fortinbras makes his fortuitous appearances. For all the play's sense of Denmark as a prison, it is full of journeys: the return of Hamlet and Horatio from Wittenberg, Hamlet's departure to and return from England. Laertes returns to Paris and comes back again on his father's death. The Ghost comes back from the dead on three separate occasions. This world, the play seems to emphasize, is a world of transition; the only place we can 'lie' is in the grave.

Even loyalty is transient. Gertrude's grief is so soon changed to new love 'within a month' (1.2.153). Hamlet's love for Ophelia is changed to manic rejection. Will no man be remembered? In contrast to the way in which Hamlet's father is 'cut off even in the blossoms of his sin' and the memory of his death, green as it is, so quickly neglected, the deaths of the three young people at the end of the play have a ritualistic formality that ensures their safe passage.

Ophelia, whose madness becomes the focus of sympathy of both Court and audience, is given the dignity of the only formal eulogy in the play. Gertrude's speech, so full of liquid sounds, reminiscent of both a messenger speech in Greek tragedy and a liturgical *In Paradisum*, conducts Ophelia on her long baptismal transition. She is laid to rest in the most contemplative scene in the play: a scene in which we hold death in general before our eyes and watch Ophelia in particular laid to rest. Allowed her 'virgin crants, / Her maiden strewments and the bringing home / Of bell and burial' she is sung to her rest. The rest denied to the perturbed spirit of Hamlet's father at the stage of the play is given to Ophelia at the end.

Laertes may be the instrument of the King's unworthy purpose but he is allowed to be the herald of truth, to speak aloud his guilt, to acknowledge his part in the poisonous plot, and to cry dramatically: 'The king, the king's to blame' (5.2.320). Even more important than this open confession of guilt is his asking for *absolution* at the hands of Hamlet, and absolving Hamlet in his own father's death:

> Exchange of forgiveness with me, noble Hamlet.
> Mine and my father's death come not upon thee
> Nor thine on me. (5.2.329–31)

Hamlet's response is swift and significant, absolving Laertes and identifying himself with this mirror-image of his own cause on a shared journey: 'Heaven make thee free of it! I follow thee' (5.2.332). Both Laertes and Hamlet die absolved of their sins, each by the other.

In 1577 Sir Philip Sidney met Edmund Campion in Prague, and Campion was afterwards moved to pray for the 'poor wavering soul' of this 'glass of fashion'. Robert Parsons described their meetings:

> Sir Philip was afraid of so many spies set and sent about him by the English Council; but he managed to have divers large and secret conferences with his old friend. After much argument he professed himself convinced, but said that it was necessary for him to hold on the course which he had hitherto followed: yet he promised never to hurt or injure any Catholic, which for the most part he performed[40]

Katherine Duncan-Jones takes a more positive view than earlier biographers of Campion's own interpretation of these meetings, and goes so far as to suggest that Sidney's description of himself 'to the Catholic Lady Kytson' as 'Your Ladyship's fellow and friend' in March 1581 is significant.[41] It is hard not to see the conflict between Laertes and Hamlet as in some way reflecting the tragic way in which the intellectual flower of England was divided by the religious and political conflict of these decades. As Meyer writes: '*Tragic* is the only word which describes such a conflict as this.'[42]

The allegorical element becomes most marked in the extraordinary last scene. Holleran has pointed to the many suggestions in this scene of a desecrated Mass: 'A warped eucharistic requiem in which all the principal characters die is a fit ending for a drama so preoccupied with death and so full of maimed funeral rites.'[43] What Claudius organizes is not just a reverse of Hamlet's *Mousetrap* but a massive parody of the *eucharistic ceremony*. This is particularly evident when he drinks from the cup into which he has thrown 'an union'; this 'pearl' of great price, 'Richer than that which four successive kings' (5.2.273) have worn in their crown. The moment of consecration becomes a *desecration*, the words uttered over the chalice of wine no longer a transubstantiation but a calculated sacrilege. The moment at which the wine becomes the blood of Christ had, until 1547, been marked by the ringing of bells, internal and external. Claudius's sounding of drum, trumpets and shot seems like a secular travesty of this sacred moment; still worse, it marks the poisoning of the kingdom itself. Claudius's betrayal of the kingdom to *policy*, so vividly embodied in his servile following of all Polonius's schemes (just as Queen Elizabeth was said by some to be inferior in power to 'King Cecil'), puts poison in the cup of life itself. The attempt to trap the son who returns to the kingdom from abroad, as so many loyal subjects had done, actually destroys 'the effects' for which he did the murder.

It is wholly appropriate that Gertrude, who may be seen, at one level, to represent the kingdom itself, is the first victim of this poison. The Ghost of the old religion complained that she has declined 'Upon a wretch whose natural gifts were poor / To those of mine'. His main concern is with remembrance, memory, as is that of the Eucharistic ceremony. Christ's words are recited just after the consecration: 'Haec quotienscumque feceritis, in mei *memoriam* facietis.' (As often as you do this do it in *memory* of me.) This is a play dominated, as was the canon of the Mass, by the notion of memory:

> Remember thee?
> Ay thou poor ghost, whiles memory holds a seat
> In this distracted globe. Remember thee?   (1.5.95–7)

Remembering the dead, as the Mass specifically did, and as the beleaguered community of recusants vividly did for Campion and every one of the martyrs, is very much what this play does throughout its unusual length. The ghost of the original Hamlet cried, 'like an oyster-wife, Hamlet, revenge!' Is it not really surprising that *this* Ghost asks, at the end of his long discourse to Hamlet, simply to be *remembered*?

Hamlet's graveyard remembrances of Yorick seem to combine endless personal acts of remembrance. Muriel Bradbrook reminded us all that Hamlet, played by Burbage, may be remembering the clown Dick Tarlton.[44] A more important clue to the emotional intensity of this moment, I suggest, may lie in the name Yorick, which no editor has been able to explain. Given the strikingly specific quality of the '23 years' of the Second Quarto, normally dated as 1604, it is possible that there is a cryptic reference to an actual person who died in 1581. YORICK is an anagram of the Greek word KURIOS, used throughout the New Testament for Christ, and entirely suitable for Edmund Campion, the master and lord who had followed his Master to martyrdom on 1 December 1581. The intensity of 'I knew him, Horatio' (5.1.184) could be explained as a private testament, the testimony of someone who at the age of sixteen had encountered one of the most charismatic figures of the late sixteenth century, as he moved through Warwickshire to Lancashire. 'I knew him, Horatio' is the opposite of Peter's denials of knowing Christ, and very much in line with John Shakespeare's testament, placed secretly, around 1581, under a roof tile.[45]

If this speech is a personal, but cryptic, tribute of affectionate memory to Campion, its conclusion makes far more sense. 'Now get you to my lady's chamber and tell her, let her paint her face an inch thick, to this favour she must come' (5.1.194). After Hamlet's rapprochement with his mother at the end of the closet, scene, it is surprising to find him so virulent towards her; but, if these lines refer to Elizabeth I, they would be entirely appropriate. Her face-painting was notorious for its density, and she was deeply involved in the interrogation and torture of Campion, even if she was not personally present at his first interrogation in York House by the Earl of Leicester, on 26 July 1581.[46] Campion's *Brag*, and even more the later provocative distribution of the *Decem rationes* on 27 June at Commencement in Oxford, had clearly caused her as much annoyance as Hamlet's letter causes Claudius when he arrives back 'naked in [his] kingdom' (4.7.44).[47]

There may be an echo of another Jesuit scholar in the meditation on the transitory nature of two of the greatest leaders of the Greek and Roman world: Alexander and Julius Caesar. Robert Southwell in 'Upon the Image of Death' had specifically linked these two:

> Though all the East did quake to hear
>   Of Alexander's dreadfull name,
> And all the West did likewise feare
>   To heare of Julius Caesar's fame
> Yet both by Death in dust now lie;
>   Who then can scape, but he must die?[48]

Is Shakespeare paying his own graveside homage to his fellow-poet Southwell?

Hamlet not only dies in a worthy cause, slaying the source of the play's injustice, but has time to reconcile himself to dying on his return from England. His acceptance of his likely fate seems so close to the attitude of the seminary priests as they faced daily the threat of capture and death. 'There is a special providence in the fall of a sparrow. If it be now, 'tis not to come; if it be not to come; if it be not now, yet it will come – the readiness is all' (5.2.221–2). Campion had written, 'I cannot escape the hands of the heretics; the enemy have so many eyes, so many tongues, so many scouts and crafts. I am in apparel to myself very ridiculous; I often change my name also. I read letters sometimes myself that in the first front tell news that Campion is taken.'[49]

The play may be seen as a meditation on death: a very traditional *contemptus mundi* view of the kingdom of this world as worthless, corrupt and transient, a brief passage between darkness and death. It is not surprising that so much of the play seems to take place in the darkness of death, or in the interior darkness of the soul. By the end of the play this other world has become more real than the shadowy existence of Claudius and his Court. Plato's cave myth does not seem far away from Hamlet's reflection 'Then are our beggars bodies and our monarchs and outstretched heroes the beggars' shadows' (2.2.263–4). Hamlet's riddling speech and the mirror images of the play allow us to look at ourselves 'in a glass darkly'. The famous image from St Paul's Letter to the Corinthians seems to lie behind much of the imagery of the mirrors of the play, but it is surely the Greek original, and not the new translation, which lies behind Hamlet's riddles. '*Blepomen gar arti di'esopterou en ainigmati*: now we see through a glass in a *riddle*.'[50]

So preoccupied have we been in the last one hundred and fifty years with the psychological readings of Hamlet's mysterious lack of action in this world that we have ignored the central concern of the play with the other world: specifically the world of the soul and the dead. The catalogue of brilliant young men who went willingly to be tortured by Topcliffe in the Tower, and to be publicly butchered alive reminds us that in no other period of English history has a *contemptus mundi* been more vividly and chivalrously cultivated. Robert Southwell, suspended by his hands for seven hours at a stretch, could be induced to say only, 'My God and my all'.[51] Edmund Campion's final words before sentence capture the spirit of these men:

> It was not our death that ever we feared. But we knew that we were not lords of our own lives, and therefore for want of answer would not be guilty of our deaths. The only thing we have now to say is, that if our religion do make us traitors, we are worthy to be condemned; but otherwise are, and have been, as good subjects as ever the Queen had.
>
> In condemning us you condemn all your own ancestors – all the ancient priests, bishops and kings – all that was once the glory of England, the island of saints, and the most devoted child of the see of Peter.[52]

Henry Walpole, who had been present during the conferences of Campion in the Tower, was splashed by Campion's blood as he was quartered. He resolved then to follow Campion's path.[53] Before he went abroad to study for the priesthood, and his own martyrdom, Walpole composed a thirty-stanza poem, six pentameters each, on Campion.[54] Despite all the government's attempts to suppress this poem, it became one of the best-known poems of the decade, and was set to music by Wiliam Byrd.[55] It starts by immortalizing the phrase from the exchange with Fulke in the third conference:

> Why do I use my paper, inke and penne
> And call my wits to counsel what to say?

And goes on defiantly in stanza 19:

You thought perhaps, when lerned Campion dyes,
His pen must cease, his sugred tong be still?
But you forgot how lowde his death it cryes,
How farre beyond the sound of tongue and quill!
You did not know how rare and great a good
It was to write his precious giftes in blood.[56]

This poem was still being transcribed at the end of the 1590s, and was only one of a flood of ballads and pamphlets and engravings which appeared between 1581 and 1585. The intensity of the battle fought after his death over the memory of Campion between Catholic pamphleteers and the government is attested by the letter of the Oxford Regius Professor of Divinity to the Earl of Leicester:

> This can I say with truth that the ghost of the dead Campion has given me more trouble than the *Rationes* of the living – not only because he has left his prison behind him, like the fabled Bonasus which in its flight burns up its pursuers with its droppings, but much more because his friends dig him up from his grave, defend his cause, and write his epitaph in English, French and Latin . . . and in place of the single Campion, champions upon champions have swarmed to keep us engaged.[57]

The Preface to *A True Report of the Disputation*, published by the Queen's own printer in January 1583/84, anxiously refers to 'reports and pamphlets every where so framed and dispersed, as though Campion like some great beare or lyon rather (as they would have him seeme) had shaken us all off like cowardly curres one after another', and fears 'they will cavill at this, as our biting of a dead man, whom being alive, they will say, we could not all matche'.[58] The *True Report* was clearly intended to discredit Campion in the area of his greatest strength – his learning – and ludicrously tried to show that Campion could not read Greek. Burghley was sufficiently worried by the picture of England being spread abroad that he published, twice in 1583, *The Execution of Justice in England for maintenance of publique and Christian peace against certeine stirrers of sedition, and adherents to the traytors and enemies of the Realme, without any persecution of them for questions of religion as is falsely reported and published by the fautors and fosterers of their treason xvii December 1583*.[59]

Hamlet itself seems to contain its own personal, 'encrypted' tribute of memory to Edmund Campion, to Robert Southwell, and to all these 'God Almighties fooles'. The Folio is surely right, therefore, to focus at the end of the play on 'rites of memory', as Fortinbras, like some accidental Hermes, embraces his fortune:

> I have some *rites of memory* in this kingdom
> Which are to claim. My vantage doth invite me.   (5.2.388–9)

The play seems to honour the dead, to provide them with the rituals of remembrance and laying to rest denied the people of Elizabethan England; it contains its own tributes to that charismatic inspiration of all English martyrs after 1581; and it is a reminder of the place of honour and affection which Edmund Campion seems to have held in the mind of Shakespeare himself.

The play's central concern with memory, with remembrance, with rites of passage, with the ritual of *requiem*, with conducting souls to rest, must be fully honoured if we are not to cut off the play in the blossom of its early life, if we are not to 'profane the service of the dead' (5.1.236). In this play where words are so important, it is not only the Ghost who must speak. Words must be said over the dead, goodbyes must be uttered, goodnights liturgically chanted. In facing death and the dishonour of forgetting the dead, the play lays to rest its ghosts. Words of ritual forgiveness are uttered, graves are sprinkled, chants are sung. The rites of memory, so shockingly ignored at the start of the play, are honoured in full ceremonial fashion at the end. 'Cum Lazaro quondam paupere aeternam habeas *requiem*.'

Notes

1 John Pibush to Henry Garnet, 26 November 1600, enclosed in a letter to Claudio Aquaviva, 11 March 1601 after the execution of John Pibush: *Records of the English Province of the Society of Jesus* by Henry Foley, S.J. (London, 1877–83), vol. 7, p. 1351.

2 Robert Southwell, *An Humble Supplication to Her Majestie*, ed. R. C. Bald (Cambridge, 1953), p. 9.

3 John Gerard, *Autobiography*, trans. Philip Caraman (London, 1951), p. 78.

4 Quoted by Arnold Oskar Meyer, *England and the Catholic Church under Queen Elizabeth* (London, 1415), p. 166.

5 Gerard, *Autobiography*, p. 59.

6 Richard Simpson, *Edmund Campion: A Biography*, revised edition (London, 1896), pp. 341–3. Evelyn Waugh, *Edmund Campion* (London, 1935), pp. 174–5.

7 For a full account of the arrest see Christopher Devlin, *The Life of Robert Southwell, Poet and Martyr* (London, 1956), pp. 279ff.

8 Gerard, *Autobiography*, p. 8.

9 Meyer, *England and the Catholic Church under Queen Elizabeth*, p. 170. Christopher Devlin, *Hamlet's Divinity* (London, 1963), p. 65, gives a vivid picture of how the young Fitzherbert in 1588 'entered into bonds to give three thousand pounds unto Topcliffe if he would persecute his father and uncle to death'.

10 Simpson, *Edmund Campion*, p. 322, and Katherine Duncan-Jones, *Sir Philip Sidney: Courtier Poet* (London, 1991), p. 213. The scene quickly became legendary, as attested by its portrayal in the engraved plate which appears in the 1582 publication by Robert Parsons, a copy of which is at Downside: *De persecutione anglicana libellus quo explicantur afflictiones, calamitates, cruciatus,*

& acerbissima martyria, quae Angli Catholici nunc ob fidem patiuntur. Quae omnia in hac postrema editione aeneis typis ad vivum expressa sunt.

11 Richard Wilson, 'Shakespeare and the Jesuits', *Times Literary Supplement*, 19 December 1997, pp. 11–13, for a convincing development of the assertion earlier argued in great detail by Ernst Honigmann in *Shakespeare: The 'Lost Years'* (Manchester, 1985), pp. 15–30.

12 Gerard, *Autobiography*, pp. 98–9.

13 Eamon Duffy, *The Stripping of the Altars* (London, 1992), p. 301.

14 Christopher Haigh, *Reformation and Resistance in Tudor Lancashire* (Cambridge, 1975), p. 258. See also Eamon Duffy, *The Stripping of the Altars*, pp. 577ff.: 'Episcopal visitations frequently singled out funeral ritual as one of the most recalcitrant areas of continuing Catholic practice, particularly the use of candles and Crosses about corpses, and the ringing of peals both before funerals and on All Souls' Eve, to elicit prayers for the dead.' John Bossy, *The English Catholic Community 1570–1850* (London, 1975), pp. 140–3, records the intense controversy over burial. The 'usual response . . . was for Catholics to bury their dead at night'. At Sefton, in response to the rector who refused burial to recusants, the Blundell family created its own burial ground in 1611. 'During the next eighteen years over a hundred people were buried in Blundell's graveyard, "and amongst them some had stones on their graves with crosses, according to the Catholic manner, which had been put there by their relations." '

15 Duffy, *The Stripping of the Altars*, p. 590.

16 *Ibid.*, p. 590. See also Bossy, *The English Catholic Community*, p. 140: 'If the dead person had been a recusant, he or she had in principle died excommunicate, and so was not entitled to parish burial; in any event Catholics were not very willing to let the parson read the Anglican burial service over their dead.'

17 In 'Maimed funeral rites in *Hamlet*', *English Literary Renaissance*, 19:1 (Winter 1989), pp. 65–93. Holleran focuses on the issue of suicide, but the refusal of full burial rites to Ophelia would have had other implications for the recusant community.

18 *Ibid.*, p. 78.

19 Philip Edwards discussed the full significance of the theology of Wittenberg in 'Tragic balance in *Hamlet*', reprinted from *Shakespeare Survey*, 36, pp. 43–52, in *Hamlet: New Casebook*, ed. Martin Coyle (London, 1992), p. 32.

20 Christobel M. Hood, *The Book of Robert Southwell* (Oxford, 1926), p. 68.

21 See Wilson, 'Shakespeare and the Jesuits', p. 12, for a full discussion of the significance of using Harsnett's 'sneering Protestant polemic'.

22 Haigh, *Reformation and Resistance in Tudor Lancashire*, p. 278. See also Bossy, *The English Catholic Community*, for a detailed discussion on pp. 91–4 of Lancashire. Lancashire remains dominant in the map of recusant concentrations in 1641, p. 404.

23 Gerard, *Autobiography*, pp. 10–11.

24 *Ibid.*, p. 165.

25 *Ibid.*, p. 15.

26 *Ibid.*, p. 17.

27 Park Honan, *Shakespeare: A Life* (Oxford, 1998), p. 85.

28 *Ibid.*, p. 85.

29 In '*Hamlet:* conversations with the dead' (1988), *Proceedings of the British Academy, 1989–89*, ed. E. A. J. Honigmann, pp. 226–7.

30 In '*Hamlet:* conversations with the dead', p. 226, Nuttall compares these lines to those of Orestes which must have had such resonance for the returning seminary priests: 'I do not live for the wicked: I see the light.'

31 Barbara Everett, *Young Hamlet* (Oxford, 1989), p. 33.

32 *The Letter to the Privy Council*, which became known as Campion's *Brag*, is quoted in full by Simpson, *Edmund Campion*, pp. 225–8; by Waugh, *Edmund Campion*, pp. 219–23; and by E. E. Reynolds in *Campion and Parsons: The Jesuit Mission of 1580–1* (London, 1980), pp. 78–81. This sentence reads: 'I would be loath to speak of anything that might sound of any insolent brag or challenge, especially being now a dead man to this world and willing to put my head under every man's foot, and to kiss the ground they tread upon.' See Dom Hilary Steuart in *Review of English Studies*, 20:80 (October 1944), pp. 272–85, for an assessment of the style of this remarkable piece in 'The place of Allen, Campion and Parsons in the development of English prose.'

33 Simpson, *Edmund Campion*, pp. 405–13; and E. E. Reynolds, *Campion and Parsons*, pp. 178–9, for a full transcript of this exchange.

34 Waugh, *Edmund Campion*, p. 45.

35 Meyer, *England and the Catholic Church under Elizabeth*, p. 194.

36 Duffy, *The Stripping of the Altars*, p. 315.

37 Roland Mushat Frye, *The Renaissance Hamlet* (Princeton, 1984), p. 164, who notes that 'the Prince "smites" his mother in ways that might be expected of one who was educated at Wittenberg'.

38 Duffy, *The Stripping of the Altars*, pp. 242–8: 'The Cult of the Five Wounds was, therefore, one of the most important and far-reaching in late medieval England.' Duffy goes on to show how 'The fivefold symbolism of the wounds was ubiquitous, even when that link with them was not made explicit, as in the Somerset will of 1471 which instructed the executors to give "to five poore men 5 gownes, and also every Friday by an hoole yere next ensuying my decease 5d."' (p. 246).

39 Duffy, *The Stripping of the Altars*, pp. 451–2. See Bossy, *The English Catholic Community*, p. 141: 'At Allensmore in Herefordshire, in May 1605, the body of a yeoman's wife was brought to the churchyard at five o'clock in the morning with cross, bell and candles, and fifty armed men stood round while she was buried, fending off the parson, who had woken up in the meantime, and sparking off a general commotion in the region.' A list of those present is given in *Catholic Record Society*, II. (1906), p. 291: 'Philip Giles bares the crosse . . . William Marshe apprehended . . . Richard Smith bare ye Bell.'

40 Simpson, *Edmund Campion*, pp. 115–16.

41 Katherine Duncan-Jones, *Sir Philip Sidney*, pp. 125–7, for a discussion of this letter to John Bavand. The draft of the letter in Campion's own hand is preserved in the library of Stonyhurst, *Anglia* I/4a, and translated in full in Simpson, *Edmund Campion*, p. 123: 'A few months ago Philip Sidney came from England to Prague, magnificently provided. He had much conversation with me – I hope not in vain, for to all appearances he was most eager. I commend him to your sacrifices, for he asked the prayers of all good men, and at the same time put into my hands some alms to be distributed to the poor for him, which I have

done. Tell this to Dr Nicholas Sanders, because if any of the labourers sent into the vineyard from the Douai seminary has an opportunity of watering this plant he may watch the occasion for helping a poor wavering soul. If this young man, so wonderfully beloved and admired by his countrymen, chances to be converted, he will astonish his noble father, the Deputy of Ireland, his uncles the Dudleys, and all the young courtiers and Cecil himself. Let it be kept secret.' See also Waugh, *Edmund Campion*, p. 71, and John Buxton, *Sir Philip Sidney and the English Renaissance* (London, 1964), p. 88, who offers a sceptical interpretation. For a far-reaching discussion of the influence of Campion on Sidney see Katherine Duncan-Jones, 'Sir Philip Sidney's debt to Edmund Campion', in *The Reckoned Expense*, ed. Thomas McCoog, S.J. (Woodbridge, 1996), pp. 85–102, an article that also analyses the similarities between Sidney's Philanax and Edmund Anderson, Q.C., 'who prosecuted Campion' (p. 100).

42 Meyer, *England and the Catholic Church under Elizabeth*, p. 163.

43 Holleran, 'Maimed rites in *Hamlet*' p. 92, who gives a full account of the symbolism of the pearl. Especially useful are the references to the scriptural pearl of great price in Matthew 13, and to Campion's disguise as a jewel merchant. It would not be surprising to feel that the soul of the kingdom has been poisoned and placed in the cup of life itself in the England described by Robert Southwell to Richard Verstegan, December 1591, *Anglia* I, no. 70, fol. 122, reprinted in Catholic Record Society, 52 (London, 1959), pp. 1ff.

44 Muriel Bradbrook, *Shakespeare the Craftsman* (London, 1969), p. 135.

45 Wilson, 'Shakespeare and the Jesuits', p. 11, where he points out that the deposition was handwritten, locating it firmly as coming from the first Jesuit mission of 1580.

46 Simpson, *Edmund Campion*, p. 338. Waugh, *Edmund Campion*, p. 171, embellishes the scene. Marion Colthorpe in 'Edmund Campion's alleged interview with Queen Elizabeth in 1581', *Recusant History*, 17 (1985), pp. 197–200, examines the evidence for this interview, correcting the place to York House, the date to 26 July, and arguing that the Queen was not present. Leicester seems to have been trying to save Campion, who had been something of a protégé, and whom he had selected to give the funeral oration for Amy Robsart: see Katherine Duncan-Jones, 'Sir Philip Sidney's debt to Edmund Campion', p. 87.

47 Described in full by Duncan-Jones in *Sir Philip Sidney*, pp. 212–13.

48 *The Poems of Robert Southwell, S.J.* ed. James H. McDonald and Nancy Pollard Brown (Oxford, 1967), p. 74. Of course, as Harold Jenkins makes clear in the New Arden *Hamlet* (London, 1982), p. 551, the theme was a familiar *topos*, and the reflections on Alexander occur in a similar passage by Luis de Granada, translated into English in 1582: 'Then do they make a hole in the earth of seven or eight foot and no longer though it be for Alexander the great whom the whole world could not hold.'

49 Waugh, *Edmund Campion*, p. 137.

50 1 Corinthians 13:12.

51 Hood, *The Book of Robert Southwell*, p. 51.

52 Waugh, *Edmund Campion*, pp. 205–6.

53 Augustus Jessop, *One Generation of a Norfolk House* (Norwich, 1878), p. 92, and note on p. 96 for sources in Walpole's own account.

54 Jessop, *One Generation of a Norfolk House*, prints a full version of this, pp. 97–102, copied, he asserts, from the only surviving manuscript then contained in the Bodleian Library. The four most interesting manuscript texts are: Ms. Laud Misc. 755, a beautiful codex from the end of the sixteenth century; Ms. Rawl. Poet 148 dating from around 1599 and containing much material connected with St John's College, Oxford; and Ms. Eng poet b.5, 111, a 1950s acquisition dating from around 1650, and the Arundel Harington Manuscript, where the poem is in Sir John Harington's own hand. J. H. Pollen, S.J., in his edition of a *A Briefe Historie of the Glorious Martyrdom of Twelve Reverend Priests Father Edmund Campion and His Companions by William Cardinal Allen* (London, 1908), pp. 26–31, follows the only printed version available in the British Library (*STC* 4537). Jessop explains, on p. 96, the reasons for the paucity of texts: the government's successful and prolonged campaign to suppress all texts, including taking action as late as 1594 against 'John Bolt, yeoman' for transcribing the poem. Louise Imogen Guiney in *Recusant Poets* (London, 1938), p. 176, gives a full account of text printed by Stephen Vallenger on 16 May 1582: for which Vallenger, after having his ears cut off in the pillory, was imprisoned; he died in prison.

55 In his *Psalmes, Sonets, and Songs of sadness and pietie*, 1588 (*STC* 4253), no. 33.

56 Jessop, *One Generation of a Norfolk House*, p. 100.

57 Simpson, *Edmund Campion*, p. 462. Simpson lists in his Appendix IV the 'flood of publications' which followed his death; many like the *De persecutione Anglicana*, 1582, of Robert Parsons, in the library at Downside, contained engravings of the capture, torture and execution of Campion.

58 A. Nowell and W. Day, *A true report of the Disputation or rather private conference had in the Tower of London, with Ed. Campion Jesuite, the last of August, 1581. Set downe by the Reverend learned men themselves that dealt therein. Whereunto is joyned also a true report of the other three dayes conferences had there with the same Jesuite* 1st *January* 1983[4], fol. R.iv (*STC* 18744).

50 *STC* 4902.

Richard Topcliffe: Elizabeth's enforcer and the representation of power in *King Lear*

The name of Richard Topcliffe, one of the most notable figures of the last twenty-five years of Elizabeth I's reign, though familiar to Catholic historians, is noticeably absent from most mainstream history of the period. Many students have never heard of him, and even writers whose interests led them to discover quite a lot about him – among them Augustus Jessop, John Hungerford Pollen and, more recently, Alan Haynes and Charles Nicholl – have been reluctant to enquire at all closely into his career, relieved, one suspects, to sum him up in a phrase or two and be rid of him. With the exception of a skimpily researched, inaccurate apologia by A. L. Rowse, and an essay by Christopher Devlin, no one has attempted an account of Topcliffe's career, let alone an explanation of it, since Thomson Cooper wrote his article for the *Dictionary of National Biography*. Even his official position and standing has remained a mystery.[1]

On a Sunday night, 25 June 1592, Topcliffe and a posse of assistants, backed by a Justice of the Peace named Barnes, broke into Robert Bellamy's manor house, Uxendon, in the parish of Harrow-on-the-Hill, about ten miles north of London. There he found, as he knew he would, Robert Southwell, S. J., whom he arrested and took back to London, where he imprisoned him in his own house adjoining the Gatehouse Prison, Westminster. Early the next morning, after a brief preliminary interrogation, he wrote to the Queen, telling her of his capture and his plans for further interrogation under torture, and asking for her instructions. The Queen's reply does not survive, but, since Topcliffe tortured his prisoner so severely during the next day or so that he caused him severe internal injury, we can assume that he received the authorization he asked for.[2]

Topcliffe's letter, one of three from him to the Queen that remain in the large archive of his correspondence, is a remarkable document (see Appendix I below), surprisingly unceremonious, even informal. Its creepy mixture of candour, earnestness, self-congratulation and sinister jocularity reveals a writer long familiar, even friendly, with his correspondent. Yet it is a business letter, reporting a capture and asking for instructions, and the question is: why did Topcliffe write it to the Queen and not to the Council or one of its members? This is not a trivial question.

Most writers who mention the Tudors' use of torture point out that under English law it was, strictly speaking, illegal, and that, consequently, it was sparingly, even unwillingly used. John H. Langbein, who found eighty-one warrants for torture between 1540 and 1640, i.e., fewer than one a year, thought that some writers had exaggerated the use of it, and that others had been wilfully imprecise about what the word means. 'The jury standard of proof gave England', he wrote, 'no cause to torture' (78), and although his eighty-one cases 'constitute an incomplete data base' they 'do not drastically understate the total' (82). Even so, Langbein admits that 'The reign of Elizabeth was the age when torture was most used in England'.[3] James Heath's *Torture and English Law*,[4] a subtler and more thorough study, finds the same number of warrants, but enlarges the number of cases by drawing on other evidence, such as the famous 'Tower Diary' (printed by Dodd,[5] and attributed to Edward Rishton), as well as contemporary accounts of cases such as Southwell's for which either no warrants were issued or they have not survived.

Heath tracks the development of torture in late medieval England under the Lancastrians and the Yorkists, and shows that it entered the judicial system definitely, almost ordinarily, under Henry VIII. His account leads one to conclude, first, that torture developed as a result of the assertion of absolute power, first under the church; second, that its naturalization in England accompanied a new tendency to centralization and autocracy given voice and rationale by humanism, especially under the Yorkists; and third, that the assumption by the Crown of supreme spiritual as well as civil authority completed the process under Henry VIII, so that the real flood of cases came after the break with Rome. Torture, one concludes, was always inflicted under the royal prerogative, and justified by it, whether the jurists and theorists said so or not. Being ashamed of it, they kept quiet, and left the common lawyers to assert that torture had no place in the common law of England even while they assented to its use under prerogative – though Edward Coke, himself a torturer under Elizabeth, had second thoughts in his later years.

The association of torture and the royal prerogative returns us to the question: why did Topcliffe report his capture of Southwell to the Queen? First, though, there are some figures to be contemplated. Eighty-one torture warrants survive for the years 1540–1640, fifty-four of them (66 per cent) Elizabethan. Since some Privy Council registers are missing, the list of warrants should be a little longer. The surviving fifty-four Elizabethan warrants account for the torture of about ninety people. (It is hard to be exact, since the warrants themselves are often inexact.) Other sources, however, as Heath knew, enlarge the number of Elizabethan victims considerably. My own list, confined to cases of acute torture or the threat of it, has grown to between about 165 and 175 cases, or nearly double those accounted for by the warrants, and it is unlikely that this is a final number. Of those cases Richard Topcliffe was involved in at least about fifty between 1582 and 1599.

So who was he, and why did he tell Elizabeth I what he was planning to do to Father Southwell? Born in 1531, and so almost the same age as Elizabeth, Richard Topcliffe was a wealthy Lincolnshire gentleman whose sixteen heraldic quarterings so impressed his friend Burghley that Burghley sketched them for use in the decoration of his cloister at Theobalds. Through his mother Topcliffe was descended from Thomas, Lord Burgh, chamberlain of Queen Anne Boleyn's household, and ultimately from Hubert de Burgh, the Hubert of Shakespeare's *King John*. In that line he could also claim descent from the Nevilles and the Percys. His uncle Edward, son and heir of Lord Burgh, married, as his first wife, Katherine Parr. Topcliffe's father was Robert Topcliffe of Somerby, Lincolnshire, a family the heralds' visitations trace back six generations, to about 1400. When Robert died, Richard, his eldest son, who was only twelve, became a ward, and was placed in the guardianship of his uncle, Sir Anthony Neville. At his majority, in 1553, he entered into the possession of a large estate, with lands in northern Lincolnshire, Nottinghamshire and Yorkshire.[6]

At the very outset of Elizabeth's reign, as he told Robert Cecil in one of his later letters, Topcliffe entered the Queen's service,[7] though in what capacity is not clear. His name does not appear in the list of people provided for in the coronation procession nor in the surviving lists of salaried members of the Privy chamber.[8] In a Court of Requests suit of about 1589, however, Topcliffe is described as 'Esquire for the Body to her Majesty',[9] and it seems likely that this honorary, unsalaried office was the appointment mentioned in the letter to Cecil. To find the reason for it one probably has to look no further than the Burgh/Parr connection in his background, and the long wardship during which he may have come to know the Princess Elizabeth, as she then was.[10] Since he was one of the few male appointments to Elizabeth's predominantly female staff, we can infer that she knew him and liked him, and that he was a presentable young man: Elizabeth liked to have handsome, athletic men about her. As esquire for the body, an officer whose chief business, we are told in Edward IV's Black Book, was 'many secrets', Topcliffe first stepped on the historical stage carrying letters between Elizabeth and Leicester at the time of the Northern Rising, and it is as esquire that we find him, more than once, in the Queen's personal entourage on progress.[11] At the time of the Rising, by personally raising and equipping a force of thirty horsemen entirely at his own expense, he demonstrated his grasp of an esquire's obligation to defend the monarch's person; and as a reward for this service he asked for and received the stewardship of the forfeited Yorkshire estates of Richard Norton.[12] As he also told Robert Cecil in 1601, this was the time when his personal service to the Queen metamorphosed into service of the state.[13] The Rising, followed by the Papal Bull of Excommunication, seems to have caused that development. His stewardship of the Norton estates brought him in contact with centres of Catholic resistance, and by the mid-1570s he was recognized as an expert on Catholic activity. The period of his real power began about 1582; in that year a Catholic wrote of him, 'There is another now that far passeth the old rackmaster [i.e., Thomas Norton, Mr. Topcliffe].'[14] Significantly, one of the first priests he reported on (also in 1582), William Dean, was born on the Norton estates.[15] It seems likely, therefore, that Topcliffe's emergence as Elizabeth's chief anti-Catholic agent developed from his involvement in the Rising and its aftermath and from his – or her – interpretation of his duty, as esquire, to protect her.

From 1582 until 1597 Topcliffe was extraordinarily busy in the enforcement of the anti-Catholic penal legislation. At the peak of his power, 1588–95, one can compile an almost daily record of his activities, involved as he was in every stage of the judicial process. He hunted, captured and interrogated, usually with torture, sometimes in his own house, sometimes in the Tower or Bridewell; and he usually monitored, sometimes vociferously, the ensuing trials and executions. Of the fifty or so torturings he was involved in, a mere nineteen are accounted for by ten Privy Council warrants, leaving one to conclude that he operated with considerable autonomy under some other kind of blanket authorization. Heath, who links Topcliffe with William Waad and Richard Young as three figures who 'appear to have participated in torture interrogations as part of a much larger commitment to police activity', says of him that he was 'fanatically hostile to Roman Catholicism and successful in attaching himself to the highest centers of influence':

> he attained to a special working relationship with the Queen herself and came to occupy in the prosecution of Roman Catholics for politico-religious offences a position de facto resembling that of a justice of the peace, but without territorial limits being placed upon his authority within the realm, and to command from the Judicature more deference than any ordinary prosecuting justice would have received. Moreover, he found the funds to organize a considerable force of agents. He may be regarded, to this extent, as a primeval common ancestor of Pinkerton's and the FBI. (Heath, 138–9)

The funds for his operations came from his own pocket; like Walsingham, he ruined himself in the service of the Crown. As for his authority, there can be no doubt that it came from the Queen herself, and that it took the form of an open commission issued either under the signet or by the Council, empowering the bearer to enlist the assistance of local authorities in whatever search or seizure he judged necessary. A couple of such commissions, under the signatures of the Council, survive in the papers of Lord

Keeper Puckering.[16] Heath's implication that it was Topcliffe's special interests and abilities that recommended him to the authorities, though entirely
conventional in references to Topcliffe, is, as we have seen, mistaken. Topcliffe was an insider all his life, and he made no secret of his relationship
to the Queen. In conversation with one of his prisoners, Father Thomas
Pormort, he said that 'he did not care for the Counsell, for that he had his
aucthor[itie] from Her Majestie'. He even told Pormort that he was so
familiar with the Queen that she had allowed him to feel her breasts, legs
and belly, and 'said unto him, 'Be not thease the armes, legges and body of
King Henry?' To which he answered, 'Yea.' He also told Pormort that the
Queen gave him a present of white linen hose 'for a favour', and he made
very rude remarks about the Stanleys and Archbishop Whitgift.[17] It's unfortunate that those who have read Pormort's notes have not known of Topcliffe's position in the Queen's entourage, and that in their general shock
and incredulity at his words have missed the larger point, that whether or
not he was lying about his intimacies with the Queen, the whole object of
the conversation was to impress upon the priest the fact that his tormenter's
authority, his freedom of speech and action, came from the very top.[18] Two
or three years later James Rither, a kinsman of Topcliffe's imprisoned in the
Fleet, was in trouble with Lord Keeper Puckering for telling his fellow prisoners with cases pending in Chancery and Star Chamber that they should
petition the Queen directly through his cousin Topcliffe, and not waste their
time either in the courts or with the Council.[19]

Once one becomes aware of Topcliffe's royal backing, the Queen's personal interest in his activities becomes surprisingly clear in the documents.
On 2 May 1585, for instance, Sir Thomas Heneage wrote to Hatton, who
had a priest called Isaac Higgins in custody, and told him that it was
the Queen's pleasure he should send for information about the man to
Topcliffe.[20] When, in 1594, Topcliffe went north, apparently to check up
on the operations of the northern government, his visit coincided with the
capture of Henry Walpole, S. J., his younger brother and a solder called
Lingen as they landed at Flamborough. Topcliffe's long report to Puckering, 'to whome her Highness cheeffly referred mee in this my travell', points
out that:

> Mvche more lyethe hydden in theis toow lewde persons, the Ihezewit &
> Lyngen whiche wytt of man gevethe occacion to bee suspected that labor of
> man withowt furder avctorytie and conference then his Lordeshipp [i.e.,
> Huntington, the Lord President of the North] hathe here Can never bee
> digged ovt. And therfore as it is most honorrable for her Maiesties fayme,
> yt theis thinges whiche thus hathe beene gotten owt by his Lordeshipp with
> fayre counsell, & labor, & conversyon of the Sowle & body of yoing
> wallpoole, so the Ihezewit, & Lyngen, must bee dealt with in sume
> sharper Sort above, And more will burst ovt, then yett, or otherwise can bee
> knowen . . . *And so must I Saye, with all trewethe and hewmilytee to her*

Maiestie at my retvrne, when she shall vowchesayffe to heare mee. (my italics)

And he emphasizes the point about torture with a characteristic marginal note: 'Theis must bee gotten by her Maiesties power & your wisdomes.'[21]

Examples could be multiplied, but one more will make the point. Towards the end of his life and career, Topcliffe wrote in one of his letters to Robert Cecil, 'Inspeakeablye hathe her Blessed Maiesty Bovnde Mee with Her Sacredd Conceatte, & Her defence of my ovn Creddytt (the Comfortte of A treve Gentillman) In all Desperait tymes, Svtche As I have lyved in, who have lyved To See Six Rebellyons.'[22]

When, therefore, Topcliffe interrogated a prisoner, or was present and active at such scenes of carnage as the successive executions and dis-memberings of as many as seven victims at once (as in the case of the Babington plotters) or four (as when he attended the executions of Fathers Filby, Kirby, Richardson and Cottam, 30 May 1582), he was not present as an eccentric freebooter in the judicial system, pursuing a private obses-sion – which is the way most historians, with the exception of Heath, present him. He represented the power and the person of Elizabeth I, and there is no evidence that she ever disapproved of his activities or his methods. On the contrary, as his letter about Southwell's capture reveals, she participated in them by authorizing them.

Elizabeth I's cruelty is an aspect of her rule which virtually all histori-ans, with a few notable exceptions, ignore or deny, dazzled as they are by contemporary propaganda and subsequent English myth-making. Yet Elizabeth was personally responsible for, and gratified by, the vindictively cruel punishment of the population of the north after the Rebellion of 1569. In 1579 she was entirely responsible for the barbaric treatment of John Stubbs and his publisher. In 1583, when her agents in Scotland procured the arrest of Father William Holt, S. J., she was very keen to have him tor-tured, but, fortunately for Holt, the Scots ignored her demands. In 1586 she wanted special punishments invented for the Babington plotters, but Burgh-ley eventually persuaded her that the ordinary sentence for treason could be made sufficiently horrifying. When the London crowd showed its outrage over the cruelty of the first seven executions, Elizabeth, characteristically, backed down, and gave well-publicized orders that the second seven victims should be allowed to die before they were mutilated. What wasn't publi-cized was the fact that she had ordered the cruelty in the first place. As late as April 1602, when as a result of renewed enforcement of the penal laws, two priests were condemned, Fr Rivers wrote to Parsons, 'However, this much I am assured of, that the chief Justice [Popham] the day before their execution, going to the court to know the queen's pleasure, she wished him to proceed. Adding that she beshrewed his heart if he spared them or any of their coat.' But then her 'sacred conceit' of Topcliffe, and her defence of his 'credit' throughout the reign, to use his own words, are themselves evidence of her complicity in the worst actions of her government.[23]

The period of Topcliffe's greatest power, culminating in the mid-1590s, was a time of terror for many Catholics, and the very thoroughness and efficiency of the enforcement means that there is very little direct reflection of it in the mainstream literature of the period: plain speaking is to be found only in the work of migré writers such as Allen, Parsons and Verstegan, or in newsletters and pamphlets produced secretly in England – by Southwell and Garnet, for instance.[24] There are, however, sharp phrases in Shakespeare's work that must have found an echo in many spectators' minds, as when, in *Richard III,* Hastings calls the Tower a 'slaughter-house' (3.4.88), or when Salisbury in *King John* speaking of 'The uncleanly savours of a slaughter-house', says 'I am stifled with this smell of sin' (4.3.111–12). And it's surprising that commentators on Donne's satires have not realized the extent to which they reflect the frightening atmosphere of Elizabeth's later decades for Catholics. When Donne writes 'mee thought I saw / One of our Giant Statutes ope his jaw / To sucke me in' (Satyre 4, 131–3), it's important to remember that the purpose of those 'Giant Statutes', as members of the government admitted frankly enough in writing to each other, was to terrify Catholics, that is to say the majority of the population for the first twenty-five or so years of the reign, into submission.[25]

It is no wonder that, as historians have begun to acknowledge, whatever second thoughts the English began to have a few years later, they greeted James I's accession with relief and hope. Anxiety over the succession, which had driven so much of the previous government's action, disappeared, and with it the chief source of political and social tension. The peace treaty of 1604 ended the long war with Spain, and families whose religious and social allegiances had rendered them obnoxious to Elizabeth I and her advisers were once again welcomed at Whitehall. The Howards provide the most illustrious examples, but they were by no means the only ones.[26]

As we have seen during the past decade, a period of intense retrospection and reconsideration follows the passing of an oppressive regime. One remarkable sign of retrospection in Court circles in the first decade of James I's reign is James's own reinterment of his mother in Westminster Abbey, accompanied by a decidedly revisionist displacement of Elizabeth's body, fascinatingly recovered by Julia Walker in a recent article;[27] and another is the production at Court of *King Lear* by the King's own company of actors, a play which we know interested Catholic audiences and readers, and which is so profoundly and acutely retrospective as to be virtually a postwar play. The older assumption that the world portrayed in *Lear* was Shakespeare's allusive record of English disappointment with James has always been puzzling. After all, James had been on the throne barely two years when Shakespeare wrote *Lear*, and the play is quite specifically retrospective in some very obvious ways. The reiterated image of the play, as Caroline

Spurgeon discovered long ago, is of a tortured human body, and torture was an Elizabethan, not a Jacobean, practice.[28] The material of Edgar's simulated possession, taken from Harsnet's *Egregious Popish Impostures*, looks back to events in the 1580s, and Harsnet's book, though written 1602–3, was itself the culminating statement in a debate that began with the archpriest controversy and the episcopal campaign against Puritan exorcising in the late 1590s.[29] Cordelia's invasion of Britain backed by a French army realizes one of the worst nightmares of Elizabeth and her Privy Council.

These, however, are details. To see how the whole action of the play is retrospective requires a shift in one's historical perspective. King Lear is about the division of a kingdom, and the consequent eruption of personal and social disorder. Mainstream history, written from hindsight, congratulates Elizabeth and her government on preserving the unity of England through very dangerous times; but in fact Elizabeth's England was a profoundly divided country in which, from the outset of the reign, to be Catholic, that is to say to be one of the majority of the English people, was to be an alien in one's own native land, subjected to unremitting harassment rising finally to a terror intended to eradicate the religion once and for all – a policy which, largely owing to the activities of Richard Topcliffe, succeeded so well that by the end of the reign Catholics were a small, disarmed and virtually helpless minority. Elizabeth's unity was imposed by violence, and much of the danger to which the country was exposed arose from the government's divisive policy. After the arrival of Mary, Queen of Scots, in 1568, from the standpoint of many Catholics there were two queens in England, and, as Elizabeth and her Council understood, her final safety depended upon the killing of her rival.[30] After Walsingham succeeded in bringing that event to pass in 1587, to Elizabeth's Catholic subjects, as we learn from Robert Southwell's courageous pamphlet *An Humble Supplication to Her Majesty* (1591), Elizabeth was a *regina abscondita*, a missing queen.

Lear's divided kingdom, therefore, was a country familiar to English Catholics. As everyone knows, Shakespeare added to the main story of Lear and his daughters a subplot which he took, in outline, from an episode of Sidney's *Arcadia*. What a study of Richard Topcliffe's activities reveals, however, is that the story of Gloucester and his two sons, whatever its literary antecedent, has a close parallel in a notorious episode of Topcliffe's career.

The Fitzherberts of Derbyshire were a very old, wealthy Catholic family, and both they and Topcliffe, because of family allegiance and the situation of their estates, belonged in the affinity or field of influence of George Talbot. Earl of Shrewsbury. In 1561 Sir Thomas Fitzherbert, the head of the family, having refused to take the oath of supremacy tendered to him by the Crown's local commissioners, found himself (probably as a result of local rivalries) in prison. He was to spend the remaining thirty years of his life without trial in one prison or another, finally dying in the Tower in 1591. Since he was childless, his heir was a nephew, his brother John's eldest surviving son, Thomas. This John Fitzherbert, also Catholic, lived in his brother's manor of Padley, just outside Sheffield. In early 1587 John Manners, acting under instructions from the Earl of Shrewsbury, and on information probably supplied by Topcliffe, went to Padley to search for priests and to arrest John Fitzherbert. The raid failed, but then in 1588 Shrewsbury himself raided the house, caught two priests as well as John Fitzherbert, and took possession of the manor for himself.[31]

What had happened was that Topcliffe, who conducted a long vendetta against the Fitzherberts, had found Thomas Fitzherbert the heir in Derby jail, and persuaded him to throw in his lot with the government and turn informer, thereby saving his inheritance, otherwise almost certainly forfeit to the Crown; and it was on information supplied by the heir that his father was captured and imprisoned. In fact Thomas became for a time one of Topcliffe's chief henchmen; he was present at the arrest of Robert Southwell, and took the news of it to Court.[32] But Thomas went a great deal further than this. He entered into a bond to give Topcliffe £3,000 to procure the deaths of his father, his uncle Sir Thomas, and his uncle by marriage, William Bassett. Both his father and Sir Thomas died in prison, but Bassett – who protested vigorously against Topcliffe's persecution – survived. Consequently, arguing that his father and uncle had died natural deaths, and that Bassett was still alive, young Fitzherbert refused to pay. Topcliffe then sued him in Chancery, whereupon, according to Henry Garnet, the Council intervened.[33] Then, as we learn from his own letters to the Queen and Council, Topcliffe persisted in his claim, and told the Council he did not see why he should not have his £3,000 when the Lord Keeper (Puckering) and another Councilor (whom he doesn't name) had taken £10,000. The Council naturally construed this argument as contempt, and imprisoned him in the Marshalsea, taking away his commission in the process. Topcliffe, however, wrote two letters of protest to the Queen, and he was out of prison within about two or three weeks at the latest.[34] The Catholics, delighted to hear of his imprisonment, thought he had been made a scapegoat for the trial and execution of Robert Southwell (20–21 February 1595) which, to the chagrin of the presiding sheriff, had turned into a moral triumph for the victim; but the truth seems to have been quite otherwise.[35]

It appears, moreover, that Topcliffe was right about the Lord Keeper's £10,000. John Fitzherbert's son-in-law, Thomas Eyre, raised £10,000 to secure John's life and liberty. This was the bribe Topcliffe named, and, as one would expect, it was money wasted: John Fitzherbert died in prison.[36] To complete this picture of governmental gangsterism: Topcliffe had also persuaded young Fitzherbert to protect Padley manor by making it over to him as trustee. Then, as happened in the case of Shakespeare's mother's property and his uncle Edward, Topcliffe claimed the property as his own.

Thomas Fitzherbert sued him for it in Chancery, but the court confirmed Topcliffe in possession. Meanwhile, the Earl of Shrewsbury, himself a Privy Councilor at the time, who had already seized the manor in 1588 over Sir Thomas's protests, was in actual possession. Although the Queen saw to it that Topcliffe gained possession of the manor, once she was out of the way Shrewsbury's heir, Gilbert, ejected him, and returned the manor to its rightful owner, John Fitzherbert's younger son Anthony.[37]

To return to *King Lear*, Edmund's complicity in Cornwall's and Regan's brutal treatment of his father has a prototype in Thomas Fitzherbert, who procured the imprisonment and death of his own father. The story must have been fairly well known; both Henry Garnet and Robert Southwell publicized it, and Southwell was not alone in relating young Fitzherbert's behaviour to other cases of divided familes and to the miseries of a country under brutal government:

> Many children are rejected by their parents, and wives put from their husbands, because they are Catholics. Yea, many parents betrayed by their children and by their other heyres, as Sir Thomas Fitzherbert by his nephew . . . As they spoile us, so was England before this tyme never acquainted with so common beggery, the people never so needy, oppressed, on the one side, with raising of rents, paying fynes, and infinite devises of gentlemen to undo their tenants; on the other side, never so many subsidies exacted in three kings' tymes as in this only queene's, so many taxes, and fiftenes, one ever overtaking an other; and no peny being so soone warme in a poore man's purse, but the subsidie gatherer is ready to fetch it and this with such extremitie that, if there be no mony, they take cattle, selling them at halfe the price; and leaving many poore folkes and their children ready to famishe.[38]

Nor was Fitzherbert's behaviour unique, as another contemporary account makes plain:

> Husbands accused by their wives, fathers by their children *et e converso*. One Mr. Francis Rolson was apprehended and condemned to die by the procurement and evidence of his own son, but the precedent so bad he had his pardon. Mr. John Fitzherbert in like manner molested and troubled by his own son, imprisoned, and there dead. This imp also, Thomas Fitzherbert, hath sought by all means to take away the life of old Sir Thomas Fitzherbert, who made him his heir and brought him up from a child. He hath caused him to be suspected of statute treason, and to be committed to the Tower, where he continueth. He hath procured also divers of his uncle's tenants to be imprisoned in Stafford, and there some of them are dead.[39]

As for the nature of the 'molestation' and 'trouble' suffered by people such as the Fitzherberts and Shakespeare's Gloucester, yet another parallel appears in the Topcliffe papers, except that this time Topcliffe was an observer rather than a participant. There is an extra dimension of moral horror in Gloucester's blinding, in addition to its intrinsic brutality, because

Cornwall and Regan are at the time actually staying as guests in his house. In 1578 the Queen went on progress into East Anglia, and one of the houses whose hospitality she enjoyed was Euston Hall, Suffolk, belonging to Mr Rookwood. Topcliffe, as esquire of the body, was in the royal party and, in a letter to the Earl of Shrewsbury, described what happened when Rookwood came to take leave of the Queen. The house, said Topcliffe, was 'farre unmeet for her Highnes . . . nevertheles . . . her excellt Maty gave to Rookewoode ordenary thanks for his badd house, and her fayre hand to kysse.' This led to muttering among the men around the Queen, where-upon, in what can only have been a rehearsed move, the Lord Chamber-lain (Sussex) intervened, calling Rookwood before him, and asking how he, an excommunicate papist, 'durst presume to attempt her reall presence, he, unfytt to accumpany any Chrystyan person; forthewith sayd he was fytter for a payre of stocks; commanded him out of the Coort, and yet to attende her Counsell's pleasure; and at Norwyche he was comytted'. Then, on the pretext that a piece of plate was missing, the royal party searched Rook-wood's barn, and found in the hayrick a picture of the Virgin, which it seems likely had been planted there: 'for greatnes, for gayness, and woorke-manshipp, I did never see a matche', says Topcliffe. 'Her Maty commanded it to the fyer, wch in her sight by the cuntrie folks was quickly done, to her content, and unspeakable joy of every one but some one or two who had sucked of the idoll's poysoned mylke.'[40] So Rookwood, his house and hos-pitality insulted, found himself imprisoned in Norwich town jail which, if it was anything like other town jails in England, those of York or Derby for instance, was a disgusting and dangerous place. What he and Shake-speare's Gloucester have in common is that both found themselves the objects of an abrogation, committed by the royal governors of the country themselves, of the most fundamental rules of decent, civil order. And of course what Gloucester has in common with Rookwood, the Fitzherberts and other Catholic gentlemen of the period is that they are all suspected of dealings with domestic and foreign powers hostile to the ruling clique.

Thus aspects of Shakespeare's portrayal of illegitimate power in *King Lear*, which a long tradition of purely literary criticism has taught us to see as primarily figurative and theatrical, determined by the requirements of the genre, prove, when juxtaposed to the activities of Richard Topcliffe and the government he served so assiduously, to be remarkably true to the real con-ditions of life for Elizabeth's Catholic subjects.[41] Even the misery of the people of Lear's Britain, evoked in powerful speeches by both Lear and Gloucester, has its place in the play's field of retrospective Catholic refer-ence, since the sufferings of the English under the Elizabethan government were a constant theme of contemporary Catholic writing. For example:

For though a few persons in respect of the rest . . . are advaunced to riches and degree; and doe recken their present state, a terrestrial Paradise, feeling their owne wealth and not regarding other mens woe: yet in deed knowing as we doe, that the farre greater parte of our Countrie of al degrees are brought to ruine, miserie, or extreme danger and desolation, as wel them selves as their posteritie, for the raising of others unto this pleasure plentie and felicitie which they have now for some yeares enjoyed; we must needes confesse and testifie, that the bodie of the Realme generallie, was never in such extreme miserie.[42]

And what of Richard Topcliffe himself? Was he as so many writers have said, a sadist? As anyone who puts himself to the labour of reading thoroughly in the documents of English recusant history will discover, there is nothing that Topcliffe did that does not have its parallel in the behaviour of others. His role as chief enforcer of the Crown's policy, as well as his energy and enthusiasm for the work, rendered him particularly visible; but to call him a sadist saves the reputation of his employers by consigning him to an eccentric niche of his own. He certainly knew that his name had become a byword in his own time. When one of his nephews went travelling in Europe, he changed his name from Topcliffe to Cornwallis to protect himself from the opprobrium attached to the family name by his uncle's career;[43] and Topcliffe himself, in a letter to Cecil, regrets his reputation: 'And that is our [that is, his and his fellow commissioners'] greeffe, and myne especially, That we are often mistaken to bee Crewelle: But God is the wytness of Alle.'[44] In his own mind he was a man who had sacrificed his life and fortune in the service of Queen and country – as indeed he had. It would be unjust to judge him more severely than his Queen, than Burghley, Leicester, Walsingham, Hatton, Hunsdon, Heneage, or Knollys – or any of the others with whom he served out his long employment. Many of his contemporaries, however, were prepared to judge him and them severely, and William Shakespeare seems to have been one of them.

Appendix I

Lansdowne 72. No. 39. Monday 26 June 1592. Richard Topcliffe to Elizabeth I. Endorsed '26. Junii 1592 / Mr Topclif to ye Q / Maty / [space] wth ye examinacon of a preist / that will not confesse his / name

[recto]To yor most excellt / maty my graceoos / Sovereigne in / [space] great hast.'

> Most graceoos Sovereigne, Havinge fr: Robert Sowthwell (of my knowledge) ye Ihezut in my stronge chamber in westmr churche yearde. I have mayde him asseuered for startinge, Or hurtinge of hym self, By puttinge vpon his armes a pere of hande gyeves: & There & So cann keepe hym eather from vewe, or Conferrence wth any, But Nicolas ye vnderkeeper of the Gaythowse & my Boye. Nicolas beinge the mann yt ^cawsed me to^ tayke hym, by settynge of hym into my handes, xty myles from him /
> I have presewmed (after my lytell Sleepe) To rvnn over this Examon incloased, faythfully tayken, & Of hym fowlye, & Suspycioosly answered, &

Sumwhat knowinge the Natevre & doinges of the mann, may it please yor
maty to see my simple opynyonn. Constreigned in dewty to offer it //
Vpon this present taykinge of hym, It is good foorthewth to inforce him to
answer trewlye, & dyrectly, & So to proove his answers trewe in hast, To the
Ende, yt suche as bee deeply conserned in his treacherees have not tyme to
start, or mayke shyfte,
[flourish flourish]
To vse any meanes in common presons eather to stande vpon ^or ageinst^ the
wawle (whiche above all thinges Excedes & hvrteth not) will gyve warninge:
But if yor highs pleasor bee to knowe any thinge in his hartte, To stande
ageinst the wawle, His feett standinge vpon the grownde, & his handes But
as highe as he cann reatche ageinst ye wawle, lyke a Tryck at Trenshmoore,
will inforce hym to tell all, & the trewthe prooved by ye Sequelle;
1. The answer of him to ye Qvestyon of ye Countesse of Arrundell,
2. & That of father Parsons, discipherethe him / It may please yor maty to
    Consyde^r^ that
                                                            I never did

[verso]I did never tayke so weightye a mann: if he bee rightly vsed, yoinge
Anto Coplaye ye most desperayt yowthe yt lyvethe, & sume others, Bee most
famileare wth Sowthewell. Coplay did shoote at a gentilman the Last summer,
& killed an Oxe wth a mvskett, & in Horssam Churche threwe his dagger
at ye parishe Clarke & stvck it in a Seat in ye Churche. There Lyvethe not ye
Lyke I think in Engl: for sudden attemptes: Nor one, vpon whome I have good
grownde to have watchefuller Eyes for his syster Gaiges & his brother in Laws
Gaiges sayke, of whose pardons he Boastethe he is assawred.
So humbley submyttinge my selfe to yor mates direction in this, Or in any
servyce wth any hazzarde, I cease, vntill I heare yor pleasor, Heare at westmer,
wth my chardge, & Goastly father, this Munday ye 26 of June 1592.
                        yor mates faythefull servant
                        Ric: Topclyffe.

Appendix II

BL Ms. Harleian 6998, fol. 46. This is an 'open' warrant, with no commissioners
or officers named, and no places or suspects specified. A man such as Topcliffe could
go anywhere with this warrant or commission. In the same collection of papers associated with Lord Keeper Puckering, at fol. 137 there is a similar warrant, dated 24
February 1593, and signed by Puckering and Canterbury only.

Whereas the Bearers hereof are by the Quenes Matie speciallie appointed to
make search and to apprehende Certaine suspected persons accordinge to such
particuler direccion as they have in that behalfe received, Theis shalbe to will
and require yow and in her Maties name straightlie to charge and Comannde
yow and euery of yow to whome it shall appertayne to be by all good and
possible meanes aidinge and assistinge to the saide Bearers in thexecucion of
this service by enteringe into all such howses as they shall thincke mete and
hold suspected aswell within liberties as without, and in them and everie of

them to make due and dilligent search, and to sease all manner of letters, writinges, papers, bookes, and all other thinges Carryinge Note of suspicion, as also to apprehende and bringe before vs such persons as by direccions geven vnto them they are appointed, Wherein if they shall anie way require your further assistaunce yow maie not faile to yelde them the same with all dilligence and dexteritie Accordinge to the trust reposed in yow, and as yow will answere for your defaulte to the Contrarie at your vttermost perille. ffrom the Court at St. James this xxxth of March 1593.

> To all Iustices of the peace: mayors, Sheeriffes Bailiffes Constables headboroughes and to all other her Maiesties officers mynisters and lovinge subiectes to whom it shall appertaine and to euery of them.

Signed: John Cantuar
              John Puckeringe
              H Derby
              J Buckehurst
              J Wolley
              J Fortescue

Notes

1 Augustus Jessop, *One Generation of a Norfolk House* (London, 1879), treats Topcliffe in some detail in chapter 3; Alan Haynes, *Invisible Power: The Elizabethan Secret Services, 1570–1603* (New York, 1992); Charles Nicholl, *The Reckoning: The Murder of Christopher Marlowe* (New York, 1992); A. L. Rowse, 'The truth about Topcliffe', in *Court and Country: Studies in Tudor Social History* (Athens, 1987); Christopher Devlin, *Hamlet's Divinity and Other Essays* (London, 1963). S. T. Bindoff, 'Richard Topcliffe', in P. W. Hassler, *The House of Commons 1558–1603* (3 vols, London, 1982), vol. 3:513–15, provides some hitherto unpublished information, and describes Topcliffe's parliamentary career, but is mistaken in some important details. Of John Hungerford Pollen's many works, a student curious about Topcliffe should consult *Acts of English Martyrs* (London, 1891); 'Religious persecution under Queen Elizabeth', *The Month*, pp. 104.485 (November 1904), pp. 501–17; 'Religious terrorism under Queen Elizabeth', *The Month*, 105.489 (March 1905) pp. 271–87, and *Unpublished Documents Relating to the English Martyrs, 1548–1603* (London: Catholic Record Society, vol. 5, 1908).
2 Anthony G. Petti, ed., *The Letters and Despatches of Richard Verstegan* (London: Catholic Record Society, vol. 52, 1959), p. 77; BL Lansdowne 72.39.
3 J. H. Laugbein, *Torture and the Law of Proof* (Chicago, 1977), pp. 78, 82.
4 J. Heath, *Torture and English Law* (Westport, 1982).
5 Charles Dodd, *The Church History of England, With notes, additions, and a continuation by Mark Aloysius Tierney* (5 vols, New York, [1971]), vol. 3:148ff.
6 *DNB*, 'Richard Topcliffe'; *Notes and Queries*, 5th Series, vol. 7. pp. 33–2; Rowse, 'The turth', pp. 185–6; Bindoff, 'Richard Topchiffe', pp. 513; *Calendar of Patent Rolls, Edward VI*, vol. 5:393.

7 Manuscripts of the Marquess of Salisbury at Hatfield House (henceforth Hatfield Papers), 86/88. Topcliffe to Robert Cecil, 11 June 1601: 'Many Envyoos Eyes have beehelde my playne doinges, & would have beene gladd to have fownde sume iust cawse to have exclaymed ageinst mee To her Sacred Maiestye, Or to her honorrable Cownsell, that Eather In heatte, for Mallice; Or throwghe Covetoos Corrvpcyon, I hadd stvmbled, Bvt I (knowinge my ovne Innocencye from the fyrst) & at my Lxxth yeare of my Aidge; & at the Ende of my xliiijth yeare Service of her Sacred Maiesty & At the Ende of my xxxijty yeares service of this happy staite (In whiche I am a Simple freeholderr) I do defye the Mallice; & Cankerr'd haiteredd of the worlde, wherin None will Wronge mee, Bvt tratoroos papistes, Atheystes, or svtche As do Covntenance them for gayne presently, or for pollycy in Tyme to Cume.' Since Topcliffe was born on 14 November 1531, he was indeed in his seventieth year in June 1601; and if June 1601 came towards the end of his forty-fourth year of service to the Queen, and his thirty-second year of state service, then they began in 1558 and 1569 respectively.

8 For example, PRO LC2/4/3; BL Mss. Lansdowne 3, no. 88; 29, no. 68; 34, nos 29, 30, 31, 34; 59, no. 22; 104, no. 18. Topcliffe's name does not appear in the surviving rolls of new-year gifts, either (PRO C47/3/38 [1563], C47/3/39 [1577], C47/3/40 [1598], C47/3/41 [1602]).

9 PRO REQ 2/43/17.

10 Bindoff suggests that Topcliff came to know the Princess through his wife, Jane Willoughby, whose niece Margaret, later Lady Arundell, waited on the Princess at Hatfield. Unfortunately, the date of Topcliffe's marriage is unknown, and his own family connection through the Burghs offers a more likely explanation of his intimacy with the young Elizabeth.

11 David Starkey *et al.*, *The English Court from the Wars of the Roses to the Civil War* (London and New York, 1987), p. 34; PRO SP15/17/31, 15b. Topcliffe's nearness to the Queen on progress is recorded in his letter to the Earl of Shrewsbury from Norfolk (1578) in John Nichols, *The Progresses and Public Processions of Queen Elizabeth*, 3 vols (London, 1823), vol. 2:215–19, also in Ben Beard's account of his near-arrest of a priest during the progress at Basing (PRO SP12/248/102).

12 Leicester to Elizabeth, January 1570, PRO SP15/17/15b; Topcliffe's stewardship of Norton's lands can be traced in SP12/75/31, 32; 152/54, also REQ2/158/190; STAC5/T.5/14, STAC5/T.8/3, etc.

13 Hatfield Papers, 86/88.

14 Pollen, *Acts of English Martyrs*, p. 223.

15 PRO SP12/152/54.

16 BL Ms. Harleian 6998, fols 46, 137. See Appendix 2.

17 Printed in Petti, ed., *The Letters and Despatches*, p. 97. The holograph original is at Stonyhurst, Ms. *Anglia* I.68.119.

18 Pormort, who had suffered a rupture under torture supervised by Topcliffe, made notes of the conversation in order to discredit Topcliffe by repeating it at his trial. It is a sign of Topcliffe's standing and immunity that the attempt failed completely, even though Topcliffe was sufficiently rattled by the publicity that at the subsequent execution he kept Pormort standing on the ladder for two hours in his shirt on a cold February morning, trying to make him deny his

report of their talk. As to the credibility of Topcliffe's boast, it is hard to believe that either Pormort or Topcliffe made up the Queen's bizarre question about King Henry or her present of the white hose. Similarly, it is unlikely that the priest's report of Topcliffe's scorn for the Stanleys and Archbishop Whitgift (a Councillor since 1586) was anything but authentic. There was probably a foundation of fact to Topcliffe's boast about his intimacy with the Queen. Unlike her modern admirers, Elizabeth I was no prude; in old age she exposed herself to the French ambassador. For Pormort's rupture and James Younger's account of Topcliffe's behaviour at his execution see Stonyhurst Mss. *Anglia* vii.26, and *Anglia* vi.117, both printed in J. H. Pollen, *Unpublished Documents*, p. 292, and *Acts of English Martyrs*, pp. 118ff.

19 BL Ms. Harl. 6998, fols 180, 190, 192–4.

20 Sir Harris Nicholas, *Memoirs of the Life and Times of Sir Christopher Hatton, K. G.* (London, 1847), p. 426. Higgins was a bad lot, an unruly student, a trouble-maker at Wisbech and finally an apostate. See Godfrey Anstruther, *The Seminary Priests: I Elizabethan 1556–1603* (Ware, [1968]), pp. 166–7.

21 PRO SP12/247/21 (Richard Topcliffe to Lord Keeper Puckering, 25 January 1594).

22 Hatfield Papers, 90/2 (Richard Topcliffe to Robert Cecil, 24 December 1601).

23 Lacey Baldwin Smith, *Elizabeth Tudor: Portrait of a Queen* (Boston, 1975), pp. 65, 71–2; Philip Hughes, *The Reformation in England*, 3 vols (London, 1954), vol. 3:270–1, 327, n. 1; Pollen, 'Religious Terrorism', pp. 271–87. On the general question of cruelty under Elizabeth, one finds it often said – by Alison Weir, for instance, in her popular *Life of Elizabeth I* (New York, 1998), p. 367 – that it was 'normal practice . . . for the executioner to ensure that the victims were dead before disembowelling them'. 'Ensure' is very nice, but in fact this was not so. As the merciful intervention of the crowd at Henry Garnet's execution implies, the full sentence, which required live mutilation, was normally carried out. Looking over the accounts of priests' deaths, I have found only twenty cases of victims left to hang until they were dead, as opposed to forty-seven notes of live mutilation which, as the language used usually suggests, was the norm.

24 To give an idea of the efficiency of the enforcement: Patrick MacGrath and Joy Rowe, 'Anstruther analysed: the Elizabethan seminary priests', *Recusant History*, 18:1 (May 1986), pp. 1–13, estimate that 471 seminary priests were sent to England. Of them 115 fell into government hands within a year; 35 of them were taken at sea, arrested at the ports or captured within a few days of landing. So nearly one in four was taken before he had any chance to work; 165 served two years or less (35 percent of the total). 291 (over 60 percent) stopped operations five years after landing; 294 of the 471 were at some time in the government's hands, or over 62 percent. 'It is not always realised how successful the government was in tracking down the priests who came to England and how heavily the odds were loaded against the men from the seminaries.'

25 For estimates of the relative numbers of Catholics and Protestants see Hughes, *Reformation*, chapter 3.

26 Donne's friend Sir Henry Goodyer, who became a Gentleman of the Privy Chamber in the new reign, was another. It was a point in his favour with James

that his uncle, the elder Sir Henry, from whom he inherited his estates, had blotted his copybook at Elizabeth's Court by support for the King's mother, Mary, Queen of Scots (R. C. Bald, *John Donne: A Life* (New York and Oxford, 1970), p. 163.

27 'Reading the tombs of Elizabeth I', *English Literary Renaissance*, 26:3 (Autumn 1996), pp. 510–30.

28 Langbein, p. 135, is deeply puzzled that there was virtually no torture under the 'absolutist' Stuarts, and a great deal of it under the 'popular' Elizabeth. Heath, *Reformation* (pp. 148–54, 155–8) found only seven cases under James, three of them Gunpowder Plotters, and a mere two under Charles. All cases were political, and no blanket authority was given to the torturers. Both kings were reluctant to allow torture; neither Henry Garnet nor Felton, Buckingham's assassin, was tortured.

29 On Harsnet's book see F. W. Brownlow, *Shakespeare, Harsnett, and the Devils of Denham* (Newark, 1993). One explanation of Shakespeare's deeply engaged response to Harsnet's book might be found in Harsnet's contemptuous references to Shakespeare's kinsman Edward Arden, unjustly executed for treason in 1584, and to his schoolmaster's brother, Father Thomas Cottam, executed in 1582; also in the fact that one of the exorcizing priests, Richard Debdale, executed in 1586, was a Stratford man, and possibly a kinsman of Shakespeare (pp. 108–10).

30 Elizabeth I's poem on Mary, 'The doubt of future foes', written soon after Mary arrived in England, is an amazingly candid expression of a willingness, even an eagerness, to kill her. See Jennifer Summit, 'The arte of a ladies penne': Elizabeth I and the poetics of queenship', *English Literary Renaissance*, 26:3 (Autumn 1996), pp. 402ff.

31 For an account of the Fitzherberts under Elizabeth see J. Charles Cox, 'Norbury manor house and the troubles of the Fitzherberts', *Derbyshire Archaeological Journal*, 7 (1885), pp. 221–59, and Dom Bede Camm, O.S.B., *Forgotten Shrines*, second edn (London, n.d. [1936]), pp. 1–69.

32 Verstegan to Parsons, enclosing Henry Garnet's letter of 2 July 1592, n.s. (Petti, *The Letters and Despatches*, p. 67).

33 Stonyhurst Ms. *Anglia* A.I.82. Also printed by Foley, 4.49–50.

34 BL Ms. Harleian 6998, fols 184–87v. The Council imprisoned Topcliffe on Palm Sunday 1595 (3 April); he wrote to the Queen the next day, and again on Good Friday, and sent copies of his letters to the Council on 15 April. He was out of prison very soon. By 10 May Verstegan in Antwerp was telling Roger Baynes in Rome on the authority of an English letter dated 13 May (n.s., 3 May o.s.), that Topcliffe was free (SP12/252/15).

35 See for instance Petti, *The Letters and Despatches*, p. 232. Gossip, repeated by some modern writers, also circulated the figure of £5,000 for Topcliffe's bond, but £3,000 is his own figure in his letter to the Queen.

36 Cox, 'Norbusy', p. 247; Camm, *Forgotten Shrines*, p. 43.

37 Camm, *Forgotten Shrines*, p. 60; Lambeth Ms. 3198, fol. 456 (Sir Thos. Fitzherbert to George, Earl of Shrewsbury, 28 May 1589); Lambeth Ms. 3203, fol. 184 (Topcliffe to Gilbert, Earl of Shrewsbury, 20 February 1603/4).

38 Robert Southwell to Verstegan, between 2 July and 10 December 1591 (Stonyhurst, Ms. *Anglia* I.70, fol. 122, printed in Petti, *The Letters and Despatches*, pp. 6, 12).

39 John Morris, *The Troubles of Our Catholic Forefathers* (3 vols, London, 1872–77, rptd Farnborough, 1970, pp. 25–6. An interlined sentence, 'Old Sir Thomas now dead in the Tower', dates this account, since Sir Thomas died in the Tower on 1 December 1591.

40 John Nichols. *The Progresses*, vol. 2:215–19.

41 There has been some commentary on Edgar's sufferings as a reflection of the recusants' experiences. See, e.g., Peter Milward, *Shakespeare's Religious Background* (Bloomington, 1973), pp. 54, 72; *The Catholicism of Shakespeare's Plays* (Tokyo, 1997), pp. 86–7. Milward also mentions the Fitzherbert case.

42 William Allen, *A True, Sincere and Modest Defence of English Catholiques* [1584], pp. 170–1. See also Robert Southwell, *An Humble Supplication to Her Maiestie*, ed. R. C. Bald (Cambridge, 1953), 43.

43 Hatfield Papers, 79/52, fol. 2.

44 Hatfield Papers, 24/102. Topcliffe to Sir Robert Cecil, 17 January 1594/95.

Learned pate and golden fool: a Jesuit source for *Timon of Athens*

> Every grace of fortune
> Is smoothed by that below. The learned pate
> Ducks to the golden fool.   (*Timon of Athens*, 4.3.16–18)

Recent research on the possible Jesuit influence on William Shakespeare has opened an entirely new perspective on his life and his stage. Affinities between Catholic beliefs and his theatre have been explored in Stephen Greenblatt's book *Hamlet in Purgatory*; Richard Wilson's article 'Shakespeare and the Jesuits'; Alison Shell's essay on Campion's dramas; and indeed by other contributors to the present volume.[1] With this chapter I hope to add a textual dimension to the impressive results that have already been achieved in Shakespearean studies through this pioneering line of investigation. I would like to suggest that a Latin school play, preserved in manuscript in the Library at Dillingen in Bavaria, and entitled *Timon: Comoedia imitata ex dialogo Luciani qui Timon inscibitur* (1584), by the German Jesuit Jakob Gretser, is likely to have served as a previously unsuspected source for one of Shakespeare's most puzzling and controversial works: *Timon of Athens*.[2]

'*Timon of Athens* is still in most critics limbo, if not in an upper circle of hell',[3] it is generally believed. And while 'the opinions of critics regarding *Timon of Athens* have surely covered the whole critical spectrum, ranging from those who throw up their hands in despair to those who stoutly defend the play',[4] it is undoubtedly true that it is the detractors who have prevailed. Until today, commentators have been unable to agree upon even the authorship, let alone the date,[5] genre,[6] coherence, textual completeness[7] and, last but not least, the sources of Shakespeare's Athenian play.[8] Despite claims for Middleton, there is a consensus, none the less, that the work is by Shakespeare, and that he used Plutarch's *Lives of the Noble Greeks and Romans* in the translation by North. A minimum point of agreement, therefore, is that he took over all the episodes of the Timon story given in Plutarch's *Life of Alcibiades*, and more especially chapters 69 and

70 of the *Life of Antony*. Thus, editors accept that the dramatist adapted chapter 69 where it mentions Timon's retreat from the city; his cave surrounded by the sea; the ingratitude of his friends; and his hatred and disgust for all humankind. Likewise, he followed chapter 70 where it tells of Timon's origin as a citizen of Athens; hints at his two companions (in Shakespeare, Alcibiades and Apemantus);[9] reports of his wishing his friends hanged from his fig tree (in Shakespeare: 5.2.90–7); and describes Timon's grave on the desolate shore (5.5.67), recording his epitaph (71–8). Furthermore, the names Timon, Alcibiades and Apemantus, Lucilius, Hortensius, Ventidius, Flavius, Lucius and Philotus are all taken over directly from Plutarch's *Life of Antony*.

In addition to Plutarch, it is obvious that Shakespeare must also have known Lucian's *Timon* dialogue, as it is this text which depicts Timon the man-hater in most detail. Lucian begins with the poverty-striken Timon complaining to Jove about the Gods' incompetence and indolence in failing to support him. Looking back on his life of riches, he nostalgically describes the benevolence and generosity with which he had helped everyone in need. Now, in his bankrupt condition, nobody wants to know him, and he is forced to labour in the fields to make a living. All these details recur in *Timon of Athens*, although Shakespeare's Timon digs not for pay but for survival, and, most importantly, these events are not reported retrospectively but in the dramatic present. In Lucian, Jove then sends Plutus and Thesaurus to Timon, saying he does not want to behave as humans had done and leave Timon destitute. Timon finds gold, rejoices at it, and decides to buy the land on which he lives, stay there as a hermit all by himself and call himself *misanthropos* in order to take revenge on the people who rejected him. Shakespeare's Timon, who also finds gold, does not rejoice, however, but wants to use 'This yellow slave' (4.3.34) to destroy Athens. In Lucian (as in Shakespeare) the so-called friends return in order to acquire the gold from Timon. In the dialogue these are Gnathonides, who reminds Timon of his former banquets; Philiades, who once received a villa and 2,000 talents from Timon as a dowry for his daughter (in Shakespeare, the Old Athenian and Lucilius (1.1.124–56)); and the orator Demeas, who has been freed from prison by Timon (in Shakespeare: Ventidius (1.1.97–111)). The last visitor in Lucian's text is the philosopher Thrasicles, who is not mentioned by Shakespeare. But in both Lucian's dialogue and Shakespeare's play Timon drives the parasites away by pelting them with imprecations and rocks.

As this summary reveals, Lucian's *Timon* dialogue is undoubtedly the ultimate source for Timon's characterisation as *misanthropos*. It provided not only the basic plot, of a change from wealth to poverty, resulting in Timon's diatribes of hate, but also his aid to two friends; his discovery of gold; the parasites' sycophancy to him, and his repudiation of them with insults and stones. Clearly, to have composed *Timon of Athens*, Shakespeare must definitely have known Lucian's dialogue. The problem, however, is that there was no English translation available in his lifetime.[10] The earliest English translation of Lucian's complete works was published as late as 1684: *Lucian's Works*, translated by Ferrand Spence. And it was not until 1634 that even a selection of his works was edited under the title *Certain Select Dialogues of Lucian, translated into English by Francis Hickes*. Thus, to have had access to Lucian's *Timon*, Shakespeare could have used the Greek original, the Latin translation by Erasmus (1506), the French translation by Philibert Brétin (1582) or a dramatic version in Italian by Matteo Maria Boiardo (1487). Of these, it is easiest to exclude Boiardo's drama. Apart from the question of Shakespeare's knowledge of Italian, it soon becomes obvious that wherever Boiardo's comedy departs from Lucian's dialogue (and this is in quite a number of cases), Shakespeare never follows suit.[11] In the cases of the French translation by Brétin and the Latin translation by Erasmus, we have no evidence for or against Shakespeare having used them. Concerning the original Greek, T. W. Baldwin proposes that Shakespeare was likely to have learnt ancient Greek at Stratford Grammar School while reading the New Testament.[12] In his later school years, 'the curriculum stipulated that Isocrates, Theognis, Hesiod, Homer, Pindar, Lycophoron and Xenophon were to be read, followed by some of the tragedies of Euripides or of Sophocles, and a few of the comedies of Aristophanes. Lucian's dialogues may also have served a compositional turn.'[13] 'Lucian's *Dialogues* are mentioned for the third form in Winchester in 1530 and for the second at Eton in 1560 . . . In these instances a Latin translation was to be used . . . Thus Lucian's *Dialogues* in Latin translations were considered to rank with other dialogues in the second and third forms of grammar school.'[14] But while all these translations of Lucian's Timon dialogue might have been Shakespeare's source, editors conclude, 'it is impossible to say how Shakespeare knew it.'[15]

The text which scholars have always taken to be Shakespeare's most likely source in the Lucian tradition is the anonymous English *Timon* comedy, edited by Alexander Dyce for the Shakespeare Society in 1842. There can be no denying that this comedy is 'a long clumsy pedantic piece',[16] but it does share some similarities in plot and character-conception with Shakespeare's play. The anonymous author opens his drama with the wealthy Timon on stage lavishing his money on his friends. In the second scene he releases Eutrapelus from the hands of the usurer Abyssus, and later he releases the orator Demeas from prison by paying his debts for him. When his steward Laches warns him of his friends' parasitism, Timon banishes him from his household. Scene 1.3 initiates a farcical subplot around a boasting traveller and an idle fop who woos the fair Callimela. Laches returns, disguised as a soldier, to Timon's house, and he is accepted again. During a lascivious banquet Timon falls in love with Callimela and they marry. But then a soldier arrives and reports that all of Timon's ships (never previously mentioned) are sunk and he has lost his fortune. His wife leaves him at once, and Timon complains to the Gods. None of his so-called friends – Demeas, Eutrapelus, Gelasimus and Hermogenes – now admits to knowing him. Only Laches stays with his master. Timon invites them, however, for another banquet, at the end of which he throws stones painted like artichokes at them and banishes himself from human society. Later, Gelasimus meets Laches with Timon, digging without apparent reason, and stays with them wearing an ass's head. Timon and Laches find gold. Timon wants to drown it, but Laches advises him to keep it. The servant, who has cast off his disguise, is still not exempted from Timon's hate: 'Thou art man, that's wickednesse enough; / I hate the fault; I hate all humane kinde' (5.2.25). Timon nevertheless take his advice and keeps the gold. Consequently, his former friends reappear, before he drives them off with his spade: 'I curse / The ayre yee breathe: I loathe to breathe theat aire' (5.5.173). At the close, Timon remains alone on stage; but while he speaks the Epilogue, something completely unexpected happens: 'What's this? I feele throughout / A sodaine change; my fury doth abate / My hearte growes milde, and laies aside its hate . . . Timon doffs Timon' (Epilogue, 2–7).

The anonymous *Comedy* clearly stands in the Lucian tradition of the Timon plot but digresses from the Latin text in several crucial aspects. Most importantly, whereas the dialogue opens with the bankrupt Timon berating the Gods, and describing his wealth only retrospectively, the *Comedy* presents Timon on stage during his prosperity (Acts 1–3). It has always been thought to be the first text to do so. Then, while the anonymous author omits the dowry episode, he adds the symmetry of Timon's second mock banquet. Unfortunately, he also imposes a ridiculous Plautine subplot which takes up almost half the action, and explains the loss of Timon's wealth by the loss of his ships, thus cutting the causal and moral relations between Timon's prodigality and his poverty. Finally, he introduces the 'sodaine change' at the end of the story. The result is that commentators have found it very easy to dismiss the *Comedy* in derisive terms: 'The hero – who begins as Timon the Tosspot, goes on to figure as Timon in Love, and ends as a Lucianic man-hater – gets lost among a crowd of Jonsonian caricatures.'[17]

In spite of such disparagement, the *Comedy* has dominated accounts of the sources of *Timon of Athens*. And it is true that these two plays do share certain features. The most significant is that only the *Comedy* and Shakespeare's drama depict Timon in prosperity (or so it has been assumed), and this for a full three acts. Furthermore, the two English dramas both include the mirroring-effect of two banquets and foreground the faithful steward. Yet the *Comedy* does not include the dowry episode which is important in Lucian and figures in *Timon of Athens*. But what is really decisive is that the whole conception of the *Comedy* differs so markedly from Shakespeare's play. For the Timon of the anonymous play is free from every tragic trait: he does not exclude his faithful steward from his curses, but rather becomes a caricature of hatred and misanthropy who rails indiscriminately at everything which comes into his mind (5.2.47–58). Thus, the close of the *Comedy*, with its 'sodaine change', perfectly corresponds to its farcical and improbable plot, so unlike Shakespeare's unremitting tragedy, which concludes with Timon's absolute nihilism and the self-chosen solitude of the bitter end of his life.

Similar doubts attach to the English performance history of the Timon tale. One of the main problems in defining the relationship of Shakespeare's play with the earlier *Comedy*, for instance, is that there is no proof that the latter, which seems to have been designed for revels at the Inns of Court, was ever actually staged.[18] Furthermore even the date and occasion of the text are obscure, so that, as Ernst Honigmann concludes, 'an exact dating of the MS Timon may never be known'.[19] Recent scholarship on the *Comedy* has even moved towards the conclusion that it was in all probability written after *Timon of Athens*.[20] And, indeed, the likelihood that the *Comedy* is a derivative, rather than the source of Shakespeare's tragedy, which it postdates, seems to be clinched by the fact that it incorporates so many borrowings from other Shakespearean plays, including *The Merchant of Venice*, *A Midsummer Night's Dream*, *King Lear* and, most tellingly, *Coriolanus* (which most editors date after the Midland Rising of 1607), as well as from Jacobean dramatists such as Marston.[21]

As a result of the questions raised about its date and provenance, the anonymous *Comedy* can no longer be regarded as the intermediary text between Lucian's *Timon* and Shakespeare's *Timon of Athens*. But this is precisely where Jakob Gretser's *Timon* may have influenced the transmission of the story. Its author was born on 27 March 1562 in Markdorf, near Lake Constance.[22] On 24 October 1578 he joined the Society of Jesus. Having studied in Landsberg, Munich and Ingolstadt, he was called to Fribourg in 1584 in order to take over the newly founded sixth-form class in the Jesuit School which had been opened there in October 1582. After two years in Fribourg, Gretser was moved back to Ingolstadt, where he spent the rest of his life until his death on 29 January 1625. He wrote more than three hundred theological essays, and within the period from 1584 to 1600 composed no fewer than twenty-three dramas (*dialogi* and *comoediae*), of which twelve are still extant. Gretser's *Timon* is his only secular play, and we know that it was performed by the boys of his school in the marketplace at Fribourg on 15 October 1585, though with only moderate success: 'a discipulis nostris senatu populoque aequis animis . . . acta est' (It was received indifferently by both senators and people when it was acted by our pupils).[23]

Gretser's *Timon* begins with a dedicatory epistle to Petrus Lovaniensis, his headmaster at the Jesuit School. In this dedication Gretser apologizes to his employer for his too-rapidly composed work and explains that *Timon* is his first drama. Then a *prologus argumentativus* welcomes the audience and gives a short résumé of the play. The work ends with an Epilogue, the final part of which, unfortunately, is lost. Enough survives, however, for the speaker of the Epilogue to emphasize the moral uplift of the play and to summarize the plot. He asks the audience what lesson they have learnt from the play – but here the text breaks off with the word 'aurea' (golden). As becomes evident from the play as a whole, it is very likely that the Horatian *aurea mediocritas* [golden mean] is meant.

In its essential features of theme and plot, Gretser's *Timon* also stands clearly in the Lucian tradition. The Fribourg play opens with Timon in his days of prosperity, informing the audience about the extent of his wealth, his bountiful generosity and his abundant friends. He boasts of throwing so many banquets and his inability to refuse the wishes of his friends. In short, 'Vitam vivit Timon caelitam / Habeat Olympum Juppiter, terram mihi / Relinquat' (Timon lives as if he is in heaven. / Jove can keep Olympus, as long as he leaves the earth to me). In the second scene the two petitioners Ephestius and Philotimon come to pay suit, the former asking Timon for a dowry for his daughter, the latter begging money to pay his debts to a creditor. Timon helps both of them unstintingly. Then he invites his friends to a banquet which is presented on stage in masque-like splendour (including songs to Bacchus and Plutus and a balletic dance). As a consequence of so much prodigality, gluttony and worldly weakness, however, Plutus forsakes Timon, and Timon blames the God for his descent into poverty. Paupertas and Labour appear and attempt to persuade the fallen millionaire of the virtues of the life of the working man. Then, as in other versions, the erstwhile friends Ephestius and Philotimon pretend not to know their impoverished benefactor. In the third act the farmers Marsias and Getomus employ Timon to cultivate their field, and the parasites emerge once more. In the second half of his play Gretser follows Lucian very closely.[24] Thus, Timon complains to the Gods; Jove and Plutus discuss Timon's fate; and Jove states Timon's 'stultitia et inscientia' (stupidity and ignorance)[25] as the causes of his downfall. Jove and Plutus despatch Thesaurus to Timon, because Timon seems to have changed so much morally. Timon becomes rich again and rejoices at his wealth, but confirms his status as *misanthropos*. Finally, he drives off the Athenian parasites, whom he characterizes as 'pestes mortalium' (a human plague).

Gretser's *Timon* undoubtedly belongs to the Morality play tradition, as the names and personifications imply, although his protagonist is characterized in Renaissance terms as an individual. Nevertheless, it is obvious that Gretser fails in his own declared didactic aim. He follows the Horatian principle of instruction and delight and aims to vindicate the *aurea mediocritas* as the exemplary life. For this aim, however, the story of Timon is hardly apt. In order to convey a moral and didactic message to the audience, the prodigal Timon would have had to become an enemy to *himself* while remaining harmless to other people. By following his classical source so closely for the second half of his drama, and making Timon universally destructive, Gretser neglects this logical consequence.

What this summary of Gretser's *Timon: Comoedia imitata* of course reveals is a much closer affinity between the German play and Shakespeare's drama than can be claimed for the English comedy. In fact, although it may not yet be possible to prove decisively that it was this Jesuit work which served Shakespeare as a source for the Timon story, in respect of its plot and presentation of characters Gretrer's *Timon* is far closer to Shakespeare's *Timon of Athens* than any other text in the Lucian tradition which scholars have hitherto discussed as a source. And if the current thinking on the later Jacobean dating of the English play is correct, then it was Gretser who was, in fact, the first to put the wealthy Timon on stage, and this in no fewer than three acts. Thus, the German Jesuit would have been the first to rearrange the Greek plot into a chronological sequence and to create dramatic action out of Lucian's retrospective and dialogical narration (in Lucian there are only two monologues and one exchange between three characters). Gretser would also have been the first to present the two petitioners (Ephestius and Philotimon) and, most importantly for Shakespeare, to incorporate a spectacular banquet on stage.

Structural analysis of the similarities and differences between the anonymous *Comedy*, Gretser's *Timon comoedia* and Shakespeare's *Timon of Athens* produces the following salient points:

First, unlike Lucian, Gretser, the anonymous author and Shakespeare all present the rich Timon on stage in a chronological order of events.

Second, unlike the anonymous author, Shakespeare and Gretser include a dowry episode. The anonymous author shows two petitioners, both of them asking Timon to pay their debts to creditors. Gretser stages two petitioners, one asking Timon for a dowry for his daughter, the other asking for his own debts to be paid in order to be released from prison. Shakespeare also includes two petitioners: his Timon releases Ventidius from prison (1.1.97–111) and takes over the dowry for Lucilius' servant (1.1.113–51). Even if the amounts of money do not correspond, and even if Gretser's petitioner asks for financial help for his daughter and Shakespeare's for his servant, the dowry episode in *Timon of Athens* could have been taken over only from the Jesuit drama.

Third, unlike the anonymous author, Gretser and Shakespeare depict Timon's poverty as a consequence of his prodigality.

Fourth, unlike the anonymous author, Gretser and Shakespeare characterize their Timon as *misanthropos* to the end of the drama (their Timon does not feel a 'sudden change').

Fifth, unlike the anonymous author, Gretser and Shakespeare aim at conveying a moral message. Gretser makes this very clear throughout his drama, while Shakespeare's didactic manner has often been remarked by critics of his play.[26]

Sixth, unlike the anonymous author, Gretser and Shakespeare refer to Plutus (as in *Timon of Athens*: 'Plutus the god of gold / is but his steward' (1.2.275)).[27]

Seventh, unlike the anonymous author, Gretser and Shakespeare specifically name Timon a *misanthropos* (Gretser: 5.1.17 and 5.4.27; Shakespeare: 4.3.54).

Eighth, unlike the anonymous author and Shakespeare, Gretser and Shakespeare share some verbal allusions.

Ninth, unlike Lucian, Gretser emphasizes Timon's unwisdom as the reason for his fall, which might be repeated in Shakespeare's formulations: 'never mind / Was to be so unwise, to be so kind' (2.2.5), and 'Unwisely, not ignobly have I given' (2.2.178).

Tenth, unlike the anonymous author, Gretser explicitly aims to demonstrate the philosophical 'middle way'. Likewise, in *Timon of Athens* Apemantus tells Timon: 'The middle of humanity thou never knewest, but / the extremity of both ends' (4.3.100).

Despite the fact that the Jesuit *Timon* does not incorporate the masque structure of the double banquet, and omits the faithful steward, it should be clear that Gretser's comedy and Shakespeare's *Timon of Athens* share a number of fundamental characteristics which neither the anonymous *Comedy* nor the Latin and French translations of Lucian's dialogue include. And since the English drama has always been regarded with some scepticism as a source for Shakespeare's tragedy (and is, in any case, thought to be a probable parody, rather than the ur-*Timon of Athens*), it would seem that it is, in fact, Gretser's Fribourg entertainment which now has the strongest claim to be the step on the ladder up which Lucian's Timon story was passed to Shakespeare.

But if the Fribourg play was Shakespeare's primary source, two questions immediately arise. First, how could Shakespeare have become acquainted with a play by a south German Jesuit? And second, to what degree would he have been able to read and understand the priest's Latin? For as far as we know, Gretser's work was never translated into English. In any case, a printed copy of a Jesuit drama circulating in Elizabethan England would have been a dangerous possession.[28] As the parallels between Gretser's and Shakespeare's plays lie more in broader outlines than in details such as proper names or exact amounts of money, an oral transmission would seem more plausible. But it is, to say the least, highly unlikely that this occurred as a result of a personal encounter between Gretser and Shakespeare. As far as we know, Gretser never visited England, and there is, of course, no evidence that Shakespeare ever travelled to Fribourg! But the means of transmission could still have been through their mutual acquaintances. As the latest research suggests, lines of communication between the central European Jesuits and Shakespeare's intellectual milieu were numerous, and it comes as no surprise that in 1580 Edmund Campion travelled directly from Prague to Stratford-upon-Avon. Shakespeare, it is beginning to be clear, was a child of the European Counter-Reformation. But, among all these intriguing contacts, I would like to concentrate here on a few particular individuals connected with Jakob Gretser and institutions linked to Fribourg by means of which Gretser's *Timon comoedia* could have been transmitted to an English reader, and leave further discussion of these tantalizing connections to historians of Elizabethan Catholicism.

The first figure to notice with a view to a possible Shakespearean connection is Petrus, the college principal from Louvain, to whom Gretser dedicated his *Timon*. As is well known, the English Jesuits' novitiate in Louvain was founded by Robert Parsons in February 1607, but there were also long-standing publishing contacts between the English recusant presses and printers in Louvain, where Gretser's *Institutiones linguae Graecae* was printed in 1598. Unfortunately there are no documents, such as student rolls, for the period of our interest: 'Les tomes 12 et 13, les *Acta Universitatis* et *Acta Deputatorum* davril 1567 à décembre 1587 sont déjà renseignés comme perdus dans une liste qui est insérée dans le prémier tome des *Acta*. Cette liste fut probablement faite entre 1721–1729, vu que le dernier numéro renseigné est le tomus 32 qui embrasse ces années.'[29] It is also regrettable that the list of pupils in Fribourg for 1584–85 is lost as well: it is extant only for the year 1582 and from 1593. More helpful is the list of college officers, which includes all the Fribourg teaching staff from 1580 to 1585. As we know from this list and other historical events, there were three Englishmen closely concerned with the founding of the Jesuit College in the city. In 1580 the Jesuit General, Oliver Manare, sent Petrus Canisius to Fribourg to organize education there, after John Donne's uncle, Jasper Heywood, who was in Munich at this time, had refused to take on this task. In 1582 Canisius was succeeded as Headmaster by another Englishman, John Howlett, although the college list does not make clear whether he was still in Fribourg in 1584. Howlett died in Vilna, where yet other English Jesuits worked. Heywood was the only one of these Englishmen who returned to England, but since this was in 1581 he could not have seen Gretser's *Timon* in Fribourg. On the other hand, Gretser and Heywood are likely to have known each other personally, as they were both in Munich when Campion met Heywood there in 1580. But the most intriguing Englishman in Fribourg was Robert Arden, the Warwickshire Jesuit thought to be related to Shakespeare's mother, who joined Canisius in the city in 1580, fresh from a recruiting-drive around Stratford. In 1577 Campion had written to Arden from Prague, encouraging him to send his young Midland recruits towards 'the pleasant and blessed shore of Bohemia'. And although he ended his days as a Canon of Toledo, Arden may have remained long enough in Fribourg to consolidate the links between England and the territories of Rudolf II, and so to witness the performance, and even obtain a copy, of Gretser's *Timon*.[30]

An alternative route of transmission for the Jesuit *Timon* might have been through the English comedians themselves, but although they performed as far east as Gdansk, and regularly appeared in Heidelberg, Munich and Vienna, English acting companies seem not to have ventured to Fribourg. Much more likely as a medium of contact between Shakespeare and a Jesuit drama would have been one of the Inns of Court in London. Since these were organized not according to a strict curriculum (like that of Oxford and Cambridge) but rather by a laissez-faire system, they were the favourite residences of Catholics.[31] 'Here the old religion went underground', as Francis Cowper writes in his *Prospect of Gray's Inn*, and 'nowhere could there be a better hiding place than in an Inn of Court, where intellectual freedom, independence from outside interference and professional and personal comradeship were deep rooted traditions.'[32] The Inns of Court seem possible, too, as a link between Gretser's *Timon comoedia* and Shakepeare's *Timon of Athens* because of the origin of the anonymous *Comedy*, which was in all probability designed for the Inner Temple. As we have seen, both the dramas by the anonymous playwright and Shakespeare show parallels with Gretser's *Timon* drama, so that it seems very possible that a version of Gretser's play acquired by a Catholic member of the Inns of Court became the source for each of these later English adaptations. It is also noteworthy that a large number of the Elizabethan authors besides Shakespeare who mention the Timon figure were themselves members of the Inns of Court.[33] They include Thomas Lodge, Robert Greene's collaborator, who by the early 1590s was reported to be leaving the stage and turning to papistry, and Thomas Nashe, who 'actually announced his conversion in his pamphlet entitled *Christ's Tears over Jerusalem*'.[34]

Perhaps the most fascinating line of enquiry, and one which has been prompted by the recent work of Campion scholars such as Gerard Kilroy, Thomas McCoog and Alison Shell, is that the young Shakespeare had come into contact with the Timon story in the circle of the Jesuit martyr himself. Campion, who was fluent in Greek, was himself the author of a series of extant dramas, and is thought to have written others which remained unfinished or have not survived. His rosary was carried from England to Fribourg and presented to Canisius there as a *memento mori* in 1584. It would be tempting to infer some connection between the staging of Gretser's play and the memory of the martyr. But there is also the possibility that Campion, whose brilliant career turned into an exile like Timon's, had himself worked on an adaptation of Lucian's dialogue. In that case he might have inspired both the German and the English versions. Such speculation provokes other compelling lines of research. Did Shakespeare, for example, remember Campion in his retelling of the story? Or is there, perhaps, a version of *Timon* by Campion waiting to be discovered among his papers at Stonyhurst College and in the Jesuit records in Prague? As Peter Milward declares, the whole issue of the relationship of Shakespeare and Campion has been for too long 'glaringly omitted' from criticism, but can no longer be subject to 'coding and censorship'.[35] This is a project for a generation; but Kilroy's recent rediscovery of an epic poem by Campion in which he dooms London to burn like Troy shows how well the Timon plot fitted the martyr's bitterness towards the 'detestable town' (4.1.34). So, whether or not he rewrote the story himself, Campion's influence on the versions we do possess may be an instance of his fame. As Kilroy says, 'To contemporaries, who included a dazzling array of writers, he was a cult figure, "The observed of all observers" ', so there may be much more of Campion in their work than we are aware.[36]

If we assume that Campion somehow acquired knowledge of Gretser's Fribourg play, this recovery from the Jesuit archives could throw light on a number of the problems arrounding the form and composition of *Timon of Athens*.[37] For critics have too readily assumed that 'the play's survival and publication were probably an accident', and that its protagonist 'bores everyone, not excluding, apparently, the author'.[38] But if 'this rough work' (1.1.43) had a Jesuit source, commentators would be less inclined to wonder 'how Shakespeare with his unsurpassed artistic and psychological sureness, came to make such colossal a blunder', and would instead begin to consider *why* he chose a plot that seems to confound so many critical expectations.[39] For it is highly unlikely that Shakespeare would have chosen the subject of the Athenian exile without anticipating the final form of his play, or that he would have realized after no fewer than five acts that this plot was unmanageable and leave the work incomplete. It seems more probable that he knew exactly why he chose this topic and why he developed it in this particular form. And once the play's formal similarity to other Jesuit dramas is taken into account it becomes apparent that, in Ernst Honigmann's words, 'the vital fact that *Timon* appears to be an *almost* finished play has escaped the attention it deserved'.[40] Then, the text begins to look very like the mixed-genre theatricals acted by pupils at the Jesuit colleges, with their classical settings, large all-male casts, interludes of music and dance, rhetorical displays and disproportionate parts for prefects or teachers. Like *Timon*, these Baroque dramas break all rules of decorum, and read more like opera libretti than conventional playtexts. So, it may not be chance that the Shakespearean work that stands closest to *Timon of Athens* in language, setting, structure, sources, theme and date was officially recommended, we know, by Jesuit educators. *Pericles*, written in 1607 in collaboration with the Catholic George Wilkins, was the single secular text listed in their 1619 syllabus by the Jesuits of St Omer, and Willem Schrickx has argued that its apparently unfinished state might be a sign that it was written to be staged at the school.[41] Could *Timon of Athens* also have been designed for the students of one of the Jesuit colleges in Flanders or France? And, if so, would this account for its 'rough' experimental form?

A Jesuit commission for *Timon of Athens* would certainly explain why
so many critics have recognized Biblical allusions in the play or interpreted
it against a Christian background, the most influential being G. Wilson
Knight.[42] But even if the work was only indebted to the Jesuits, rather
having been specifically composed for them, there are certain features of
the drama that strengthen my thesis. First of all, Shakespeare's play shows
an implicit opposition to Calvinism, the orthodoxy of the Anglican Church
from the late sixteenth century to the accession of Charles I in 1625.[43] It
may be significant that the Jesuit College in Fribourg was deliberately
founded in reaction to Calvinist establishments in Geneva, Berne, Lausanne
and Basle ('ob vicinissimos potentes adversarios Calvinistas'),[44] and that
Gretser's dramas show a strong opposition to Calvinist theology.[45] In the
case of *Timon of Athens*, it is most obvious that, when in Athens, the
younger Timon is rich but not happy at all: every sign of his being one
of the elect proves false. What is more, at the very outset of the play the
Merchant (a character who never appears again and has therefore been
considered gratuitous) makes a direct appeal to Calvinist doctrine. In response, Apemantus offers a prediction that has almost choric status (and
incidentally makes it improbable that the play was written by a Protestant
such as Middleton). Coming so early, Apemantus' curse on those who
worship trade and profit looks like a framing device to provide spectators
with a perspective on the tragedy of one who is, indeed, confounded by
his commercial god:

> *Apemantus*:   Traffic confound thee, if the gods will not!
> *Merchant*:   If traffic do it, the gods do it.
> *Apemantus*:   Traffics thy god and thy god confound thee!   (1.1.236–8).

Even more telling is the fact that the plot of *Timon of Athens* so clearly
belongs with the literature of exile and self-exclusion which, as Shell has
demonstrated, comprised such an anguished genre of Catholic writing in
the 1600s.[46] Like *King Lear*, *Antony and Cleopatra*, *Coriolanus*, *Pericles*,
Cymbeline, *The Winter's Tale* and *The Tempest*, this is a play, moreover,
which stages the most acute dilemma of English Catholic refugees in the
early years of James I, of whether to continue to plot revenge on their homeland, as Timon curses Athens with death and destruction, or renounce violence, like Prospero, on the understanding that 'The rarer action is / In virtue
than in vengeance' (*The Tempest* 5.1.27). Without noticing a connection
with this émigré predicament, critics have long remarked the question of
self-ostracism in the play. Thus, Honigmann calls *Timon of Athens* 'a study
of different forms of loneliness (among other things)';[47] G. K. Hunter notes
that 'Timon is an outcast of society'; Cyrus Hoy calls *Timon* 'a tragedy of
alienation';[48] and R. Soellner observes that 'Timon's anger at mankind certainly is the manifestation of an intense suffering, and the pathos of his fall
is underlined by the servants' choric comments'.[49] Where *Timon* differs

from all the other Shakespearean representations of Jacobean exile, of course, is that its emigrant never plans to return or reconcile himself with his enemies. This is a tragedy uniquely targeted, it might therefore seem, at the most irreconcilable and militant wing of the Jesuit-educated English community abroad.

Connected to the topical Catholic theme of self-imposed exile in *Timon of Athens* are its figures of torture and dismemberment, which begin with the cannibalistic report on 'What a number of men eats Timon . . . so many dip their meat in one man's blood' (1.2.38–40), and develop into a fantasia on the Eucharistic connotations of hanging, drawing and quartering. Hanging is an obsessive metaphor (2.2.85; 2.2.97; 4.3.146–8; 5.1.130–3), but images of other horrific forms of execution recur, as when Flaminius condemns Lucullus: 'Let molten coin be thy damnation' (3.1.52). And critics such as Wilson Knight who interpret Timon as a Christ type base their reading on his exhilaration at his own martyrdom: 'Tell out my blood' (3.4.93); and 'Tear me, take me' (3.4.98). One scene of exile and execution certainly seems to reflect at length on papist persecution. This is the trial where Alcibiades pleads unsuccessfully for the life of the soldier who 'in hot blood / Hath stepp'd into the law' (3.6.11). The episode combines issues of friendship, justice and mercy in a debate that problematizes the legitimacy of a law that 'none but tyrants do use' (9), and there may be an allusion to those punished for their part in Essex's Revolt. In the comedies such a despotic verdict would, in any case, be overruled, as Theseus overturns 'the ancient privilege of Athens' (Dream 1.1.41; 4.1.176). But here, though Alcibiades pleads for pity (8), mercy (56), honour (83) and grace (95), the senators reiterate the death-sentence on the accused, and banish his champion for life. This judgement looks all the more arbitrary because, as Alcibiades laments, the defendant risked his life for the city when his judges merely 'let out / Their coin upon large interest' (3.5.108). In this society, we see, justice has 'gone, she's fled' as completely as from the Rome of *Titus Andronicus* (4.3.4). And there is one line that connects the plight of the Athenians inescapably with the atrocities inflicted on Catholic priests at Tyburn. This is Timon's perverted hope, as the worst fate he can imagine, for the 'sight of priests in holy vestments bleeding' (4.3.125). The fact that he should glory in this prospect, as a climax to the 'large confusion' he plots for Athens (127), confirms more than anything else in the play that what Shakespeare is depicting is the martyr-complex that colludes in the violence of its own end.

As its sacrificial symbolism makes clear, *Timon of Athens* can be read as a critique of the masochistic cult of martyrdom that gripped the Society of Jesus in his day. And, since the plot was determined by classical sources, it is interesting to see how the dramatist may have turned back upon the Jesuits a story they used against their foes. This tactic becomes apparent, for example, in the different representations of avarice and riches in Gretser and Shakespeare. Gretser's Timon can be seen to start out as a caricature Protestant, who believes in the deity of gold and is convinced he will gain fulfilment from it. He is cured of this idolatry by Paupertas and Labour, so that he leads a happy life of poverty while he is working in the fields. Because of this happiness he rejects the offer by Mercurius and Plutus to become rich again. But the god of traffic, Mercurius (a Vice type), persuades him to accept Thesaurus, in order not to become a Miso*theus*. By accepting Thesaurus, however, Timon falls back into the state of sin, drives Paupertas off and welcomes Desidies and Otium. He then subscribes to a whole catalogue of Morality sins, so that he has become much worse at the close of the play than at its beginning. In the end Gretser's Timon is rich *and* inhuman. His Timon has not gained any knowledge in a moral sense, but has become even more egoistic, and he is convinced he will become happy with the newly received gold without the necessity for friends. Thus, Gretser presents Timon as a character swinging between two extremes: on the one hand, he is a prodigal; on the other, he is induced by the false gods of traffic and money, Mercurius and Plutus, to keep possession of his wealth. With a clear thrust at Calvinism, Gretser's Timon is happy only while he is poor and working in the fields.

In contrast to Gretser, Shakespeare directs sympathy to Timon, who is characterized, in fact, in distinctly Jesuit terms, as one of 'so many like brothers commanding one another's fortunes' (1.2.97). This sympathy is enhanced by the comments of the steward, whom Shakespeare introduces to the story, and also by the Christian values of faith, hope and charity in which Timon believes: 'We are born to do benefits' (1.2.95). But while Shakespeare's Timon is blind to others, he perishes because of a fatal complicity between his self-destructiveness and the society around him. He belongs with Shakespearean characters such as King Lear and Coriolanus, who misjudge men and society, but go to their deaths bent on self-destruction. Thus, it is highly significant that, unlike Gretser's Timon, Shakespeare's squanders his money twice. At the start he does not know the world is poisoned by the avarice and egoism we see figured in images from the money market and the goldsmith's trade. So, he loses his fortune because he believes in brotherhood. Yet, after he learns how society is dominated by avarice and theft, he wastes his gold again, this time in order to destroy his homeland. He thereby shows himself to be deficient in the judgement – *discretio* – most highly prized by Jesuits. For, unlike Alcibiades, he does not know how to temper justice with mercy, 'the olive with the sword' (5.5.57). Shakespeare, in other words, foregrounds the vengefulness of Timon, which he doubles with the madness of his bounty. There are parallels here with the Biblical Job, who likewise lavished gifts on his friends, but found himself alone when Satan impoverished him. The difference, however, is that Job suffered in patience, and used his fortune wisely when it was restored. Timon, experiencing the same sequence of riches, poverty and return to riches, consumes himself in despair, the worst of Christian sins, symbolized in his appeal to the Judas tree (5.2.90–7). Editors have dated the play to between 1605 and 1608, and definitely after the Gunpowder Plot. This is important, because if *Timon of Athens* was a rewriting of a Jesuit drama for performance by pupils of the Order, it would be hard imagine a more apt staging of the suicidal violence of Catholic fundamentalism, or a more timely appeal to heal the wounds of the martyred body, so as to 'Make war breed peace':

> . . . make peace stint war, make each
> Prescribe to other as each other's leech.   (5.5.88)

Notes

1 Stephen Greenblatt, *Hamlet in Purgatory* (Princeton, 2001); Richard Wilson, 'Shakespeare and the Jesuits', *Times Literary Supplement*, 19 December 1997, pp. 11–13; Alison Shell, ' "We are made a spectacle": Campion's dramas', in Thomas McCoog, S.J. (ed.), *The Reckoned Expense: Edmund Campion and the Early English Jesuits. Essays in Celebration of the First Centenary of Campion Hall, Oxford (1896–1996)* (Woodbridge, 1996), pp. 103–18.

2 For further details see my doctoral thesis on this topic (in German): *Jakob Gretser, Timon. Comoedia Imitata (1584). Erstausgabe von Gretsers Timon-Drama mit Übersetzung und einer Erörterung von dessen Stellung zu Shakespeares 'Timon of Athens'* (Munich, 1994). It contains the first edition of Gretser's Latin play from the manuscript kept in the Library in Dillingen/Danube, a German translation and a discussion of about 250 pages on its relation to Shakespeare's *Timon of Athens*.

3 R. Soellner. *Timon of Athens. Shakespeare's Pessimistic Tragedy* (Athens, Ohio, 1979), p. 15.

4 David M. Bergeron, '*Timon of Athens* and Morality drama', *CLA Journal*, 10 (1967), p. 181.

5 Cf. John W. Draper, 'The theme of *Timon of Athens*', *MLR*, 19 (1934), Geoffrey Bullough (ed.), *Narrative and Dramatic Sources of Shakespeare*, vol. VI (London and New York, 1966), p. 235, and, more recently, Sandra Billington, 'Was *Timon of Athens* performed before 1604?', *NQ*, (Sept. 1998), pp. 351–3. Billington sees an allusion to a *Timon* play' . . . and the text of *Timon of Athens* best matches those allusions' (p. 353) in Marston's *Jack Drum's Entertainment* (1600).

6 Cf. esp. William E. Slights, 'Genera mixta and *Timon of Athens*', *Studies in Philology*, 74 (1977), pp. 39–62. Soellner, *Timon of Athens*, speaks of domestic tragedy (p. 20), Clifford Leech, 'Timon and after', in Leech (ed.), *Shakespeare's Tragedies* (London, 1950) and also Northop Frye in Robert Sadler (ed.), *Northop Frye on Shakespeare* (New Haven and London, 1986), see in *Timon* a precursor to the Romances. Muriel Bradbrook, *Shakespeare the Craftsman* (London, 1969), classifies *Timon* as dramatic show (p. 166), Derek Traversi, *An Approach to Shakespeare* (London, 1968–69), sees its affinity to a morality play, as do also Bergeron in '*Timon of Athens*', pp. 181–8, and Lewis

Walker, '*Timon of Athens* and the morality tradition', *Shakespeare Studies*, XII (1978), pp. 159–79. Oscar James Campbell, *Shakespeare's Satire* (New York, 1943), and Alvin Kernan, *The Cankered Muse: Satire of the English Renaissance* (New Haven, 1959), base their interpretation on the satiric traits.

7 Cf. esp. Una Ellis-Fermor, '*Timon of Athens*: an unfinished play', *RES*, XVIII (1942), pp. 270–83. Thomas M. Parrot, *The Problem of Timon of Athens* (London, 1923), and John M. Robertson, *The Baconian Heresy* (New York, 1913, repr. 1970), suggest Shakespeare's collaboration with Chapman. H. Dugdayle-Sykes, 'The problem of *Timon of Athens*', *NQ*, 5 (1923), pp. 83–6, was the first to introduce Middelton into the discussion. He was followed by many others, among them Stanley Wells and Gary Taylor in *William Shakespeare: A Textual Companion* (Oxford, 1987), and Marc Dominik, *Shakespeare-Middleton-Collaborations* (Beaverton, 1988), pp. 13–16.

8 Cf. Bullough (ed.), *Narrative and Dramatic Sources*, vol. VI (London and New York, 1966), and also W. H. Clemons, 'The sources of *Timon of Athens*', *Princeton University Bulletin*, XV (1903/4), pp. 208–23, and Georges Bonnard, 'Note sur les sources de *Timon of Athens*', *Etudes Anglaises*, VII (1954), pp. 59–69.

9 All references to *Timon of Athens* are to the Norton edition, ed. Katharine Eisaman Maus (New York, 1997), based on the Oxford edition.

10 Cf. S. F. W. Hoffmann, *Biographisches Lexikon der gesamten Literatur der Griechen*, vol. II (Amsterdam, second edn 1961), pp. 564ff.

11 L. Bergel, 'I due Timone: Boiardo et Shakespeare', in Guiseppe Anceschi (ed.), *Il Boiardo e la critica contemporanea* (Florence, 1970), p. 74.

12 T. W. Baldwin, *Shakesepare's Little Latin and Less Greeke*, 2 vols (Urbana, 1944).

13 Bullough, *Narrative and Dramatic Sources*, vol. II, p. 648.

14 Bullough, *Narrative and Dramatic Sources*, vol. II, p. 734.

15 Soellner, *Timon of Athens*, p. 206.

16 Bullough, *Narrative and Dramatic Sources*, p. 232.

17 Muriel Bradbrook, 'The comedy of Timon – a reveling play of the Inner Temple', *RED*, IX (1966), p. 85.

18 Cf. esp. *ibid.*, pp. 83–103.

19 Ernst Honigmann, *Shakespeare: The 'Lost Years'* (Manchester, 1985), p. 12, fn. 16.

20 'I incline to date the academic Timon after Shakespeare's play and after the publication of the first quarto of *King Lear* (1608)': Bullough, *Narrative and Dramatic Sources*, p. 235. Bradbrook, 'The comedy of *Timon*', (p. 103) refers to the revels at the Inner Temple in 1611 as the occasion of the comedy of Timon which burlesques Shakespeare.

21 Bullough, *Narrative and Dramatic Sources*, refers to Jonson's *Cynthia's Revels* (1600–1) and *Poetaster* (1601) and to Beaumont's *Knight of the Burning Pestle* (1608). Soellner, *Timon of Athens* (p. 86), refers to Heywood's *A Woman Killed with Kindness* (1608).

22 For his life and work cf. Anton Dürrwächter, *Jakob Gretser und seine Dramen: ein Beitrag zur Geschichte des Jesuitendramas in Deutschland* (Freiburg/ Breisgan, 1923) and R. DeBacker and H. Sommervogel, *Bibliothèque de la Compagnie de Jésus* (Brussels and Paris, 1842, repr. Brussels, 1969), vol. III, cols 1743–809.

23 Quoted in Dürrwächter, Jakob Gretser, p. 16.

24 He adds two more episodes in order to demonstrate right and wrong behaviour to his audience: In 4.4 Paupertas visits Timon and confirms him in rejecting the personified gold, Thesaurus. In 5.2 und 5.3 Paupertas, Desidies and Otium turn up and criticize Timon's attitude of misanthropy.

25 Lucian had not mentioned Timon's *inscientia*.

26 Spareness in characterization accompanied by an absence of complexity in the action have readily suggested also that Shakespeare was less than usually concerned with ordinary theatrical effectiveness and more with extraplating a moral idea. Peter Ure, *William Shakespeare: The Problem Plays* (London, 1961), p. 45: 'It seems . . . that in *Timon* Shakespeare was experimenting in a different, more didactic, kind of play than usual . . . he was drawn by the Lucianic source in the direction of a moral *exemplum*.' Bullough, *Narrative and Dramatic Sources*, p. 247: '*Timon* is too obtrusively didactic to be a tragedy.' Soellner, *Timon of Athens*, p. 24. Cf also: A. S. Collins, 'Timon of Athens: a reconsideration' *RES*, XXII (1946), pp. 96–108, and Lewis Walker, '*Timon of Athens* and the morality tradition', *Shakespeare Studies*, XII (1979), pp. 159–79.

27 Critics have regarded this utterance of the Second Lord as a proof of Shakespeare's knowledge of Lucian's dialogue; but references to Plutus are not uncommon (p. 20).

28 A. Allison and D. M. Rogers, *A Catalogue of Catholic Books in English 1558 to 1640* (Bognor Regis, 1956), list 276 items published from 1581 to 1610. Of that number 57 or about 21 per cent were written or translated by Jesuits. Parsons is responsible for almost a third (17). Thomas H. Clancy, *A Literary History of the English Jesuits: A Century of Books 1615–1714* (San Francisco and London, 1996), p. 8. J. M. Blom traces the Anglican readers of one particular German Jesuit, Jeremias Drexel, but this only from 1630. J. M. Blom, 'A German Jesuit and his Anglican readers: the case of Jeremias Drexelius (1581–1638)', in G. A. M. Janssens (ed.), *Studies in Seventeenth-century English Literature, History and Biography* (Amsterdam, 1948), pp. 41–51.

29 H. DeVocht, *Inventaire des Archives de l'Université de Louvain, aux Archives Générales du Royaume* (Louvain, 1927), p. 10, fn. 1.

30 Cf. Emil Herz, *Englische Schauspieler und englisches Schauspiel zur Zeit Shakespeares in Deutschland* (Hamburg and Leipzig, 1903), Anna Baesecke, *Das Schauspiel der englischen Komödianten in Deutschland* (Halle an der Saale, 1935, repr. Tübingen, 1974) and, more recently, June Schlueter, 'English actors in Kassel, Germany, during Shakespeare's time,' in John Pitcher (ed.), *Medieval and Renaisssance Drama in England* (London, 1998), pp. 238–61.

31 Wilfrid R. Prest, *The Inns of Court under Elizabeth and the Early Stuarts 1590–1640* (London, 1972), p. 168. Owing to this system, however, there are no residence records. It is impossible therefore to discover if or when a member came into residence, how long he stayed and when, if ever, he returned.

32 Quoted in Christopher Devlin, *The Life of Robert Southwell* (London, 1956), p. 218. H. Aveling, *Post Reformation Catholicism in East Yorkshire 1558–1790* (New York, 1960), calls the Jacobean Inns of Court a notorious haunt for Catholics (p. 27).

33 They were: John Lyly, *Euphues* (1578), Richard Mulcaster, *Positions* (1581), Robert Greene, *The Carde of Fancie* (1584–87), Edmund Spenser, *Daphnaida*

(1591), Thomas Nashe, *Christ's Tears over Jerusalem* (1593), Thomas Lodge, *Wit's Misery* (1596), Edward Guilpin, *Skialethia* (1598), Thomas Dekker, *Satiromastix* (1602). Guilpin is the first to characterize Timon explicitly as a man-hater, Dekker follows and Shakespeare takes Timon's hate to its extreme.

34 Devlin, *The Life of Robert Southwell*, p. 265.

35 'Wie freute sich der fromme Mann, als man ihm 1584 den Rosenkranz seines seligen Mitbruders Edmund Campion brachte, der drei Jahre zuvor in London seinen Glauben an die päpstliche Vollgewalt unter den grausamsten Peinen mit dem Blute besiegelt hatte!' O. Braunsberger, *Petrus Canisius: ein Lebensbild* (Freiburg am Breisgan, 2nd edn 1921), p. 285. Unfortunately, Braunsberger does not give a source for this episode. Edmund Campion to Robert Arden, 6 August 1577, reproduced in Richard Simpson, *Edmund Campion: A Biography* (London, 1896), pp. 120–1; Peter Milward, 'Catholicism and English literature, 1558–1660', *The Renaissance Bulletin: Tokyo*, 26 (1999), p. 26.

36 Gerard Kilroy, 'Campion's Virgilian epic', *Times Literary Supplement*, 8 March 2002, p. 15.

37 Probably less is known about *Timon of Athens* than about any other of Shakespeare's plays. Criticism of the play by scholars is often confused: F. Butler, *The Strange Critical Fortunes of Timon of Athens* (Ames, 1966), p. ix.

38 Bullough (ed.), *Narrative and Dramatic Sources*, vol. VI, p. 250; Hazelton Spencer, *The Art and Life of William Shakespeare* (New York, 1940), p. 350.

39 Ellis-Fermor, '*Timon of Athens*', p. 283.

40 Ernst Honigmann, 'Timon of Athens', *SQ*, 12 (1961), p. 14.

41 Willem Schrickx, '*Pericles* in a book-list of 1619 from the English mission and some of the plays special problems', *Shakespeare Survey*, 29 (Cambridge, 1989), pp. 214–18.

42 Peter Milward, *Biblical Influences in Shakespeare's Great Tragedies* (Evansville, 1987), Paul. N. Siegel, *Shakespearean Tragedy and the Elizabethan Compromise* (New York, 1957), R. V. Holdsworth, 'Biblical allusions in *Timon of Athens* and Thomas Middleton', *NQ* (June 1990), pp. 188–92; G. Wilson Knight, *The Wheel of Fire* (London, 1949) and *Shakespeare's Dramatic Challenge* (London, 1977).

43 John Stachniewski, 'Calvinist psychology in *Macbeth*', *Shakespeare Survey*, 20 (1988), p. 170.

44 Petrus Canisius in a letter to Eberhard Mercurian (16 July, 1580). Quoted in Ferdinand Strobel, S.J., *Der Regularklerus: die Gesellschaft Jesu in der Schweiz* (Helvetia Sacra VII) (Bern, 1976), p. 163, fn. 9.

45 Cf. Anton Dürrwächter, *Jakob Gretser und seine Dramen*, p. 32.

46 Alison Shell, *Catholicism, Controversy and the English Literary Imagination, 1588–1660* (Cambridge, 1999), pp. 175–87.

47 Honigmann, 'Timon of Athens', p. 16.

48 Soellner, *Timon of Athens*, p. 16.

49 *Ibid.*, p. 26.

Cymbeline and the sleep of faith

Sleep is not the sleep of reason in *Cymbeline*. There is indeed a toning down of watchfulness when the innocent Innogen's late reading of a not so innocent book puts her to sleep, but it is not a ghost that haunts her night, not a vision flitting across the gates of ivory, but a very real Iachimo who steps into her room and creeps to her bed (2.4). And when she wakes from her drugged sleep in the cave in Wales (4.2) it is a very real headless corpse she finds as a bedfellow. In both scenes Faith-in-love rather than reason is threatened by Innogen's sleep. That Innogen should be twice represented as a sleeper and more specifically the second time, when she chooses to call herself Fidele, cannot but point to a deliberate intention of allegorizing the issue of a failure in faith.[1] Sleep in *Cymbeline* is the sleep of faith. As to the third sleeping scene, it concerns Posthumus (5.3), whose dream vision of Jupiter admonishing his parents for their lack of faith is the beginning of his awakening to faith. The love story between Posthumus and Innogen – with insistence on the betrayal of faith as its major theme – cannot fail to appear as a cover for the more explicitly religious treatment of the theme.

Debora Shuger, after Roland Mushat Frye, reminds us that 'Protestant Englishmen did not seem very enthusiastic about staging the mysteries of faith'. The reformers' explicit intention of separating theology from the human arts manifested itself in the royal proclamations of the times warning against the confusion between pulpit and stage.[2] Reprobation lay on allegorization now that the Jesuits were trying to rehabilitate the medieval mode of allegorical interpretation.[3] The sleeping scenes in *Cymbeline* are the closest Shakespeare ever comes to an allegorization of a religious theme. The extra fact of using the tragi-comic genre theorized in Guarini's *The Compendium of Tragicomic Poetry* (1599) and so highly recommended by the Society of Jesus – Frei Luis da Cruz had published his *Tragicae comicae actiones a regio Artium Collegio Societatis Jesu* in 1605, in Lyon[4] – might offer an explanation for the mysterious laudatory assessment of *Cymbeline* as 'rare' by the English Jesuit in exile at Valladolid in charge of expurgating Shakespeare's 1632 Folio.[5]

Tragi-comedy was not of course the sole property of the Counter-Reformation artists,[6] and Shakespeare's use of the genre in his last plays follows the reformers' usual precepts of secularization of the religious issues by a constant reference to neoplatonic theology rather than to an explicitly doctrinal one. But the historical situation of the play at the moment of Christ's birth with its implicit allusion to the primitive church – so much of an issue in the works of the reformers' apologists – underlines the religious preoccupations of the play and its underlying polemical issue of the dialectics between faith and reason which was at the heart of many partisan debates.

This study is an attempt at explaining how it was that *Cymbeline* worked the high miracle of being a text equally readable by both antagonist parties, and how its form achieved the feat of putting it beyond the dangerously partisan spirit of the times.

Reason and faith

In the last plays the terms of the debate on the supremacy of faith over reason seem to reverse the sceptical attitude represented by Shakespeare's debt to Reginald Scot. Now scepticism attacks reason itself as the suspect source of many evils. We shall see how the influence of Montaigne's augustinism is paramount in Shakespeare's sceptical treatment of reason. Indeed, the influence of St Augustine, whom the Protestants and the Catholics were both keen to appropriate for themselves as an authority on the subject (the former refusing the adjunct of 'saint' to his name), becomes quite evident. The motto of the University of Wittenberg was (around 1511, when Luther became professor of biblical studies there), 'In the name of St Paul and Augustine'.[7] Whatever the conclusions reached regarding its authorship, the *Funeral Elegy* of 1612 is another illustration of the current obsession of the times on the growing dissatisfaction with an all-powerful reason that was trying to do without the promptings of faith. The elegy is out to prove that William Peter was murdered twice: once on the road to Exeter, and a second time when his name was slandered. But what is interesting is that the victim and his posthumous enemies embody the terms of the debate between reason and faith. William Peter's mind is described as 'a temple, in whose precious white / 'Sat Reason by Religion oversway'd' (59–60). His calumniators on the other hand are 'men . . . only led by Reason's law' (365) who too easily deduce from the mere formal chiasmic structure of the proverb, 'such as is the end, the life proves so', the rationality of their deadly claim against the young man. A lexical investigation into the elegy which can be supposed to find echoes in *The Two Noble Kinsmen* suggested similarities with a number of Shakespearean plays, *Cymbeline* in particular – which was composed and acted just before the events described in the elegy.[8]

The last plays seem to have been deliberately moulded to integrate such dialectics in their structure. Indeed the Baroque concept of 'meraviglia' pervades the romances, even though, as in *The Tempest*, wonder is shown to keep the humble place allotted to it by Aristotle as the first rung in the discovery of truth – a stage to be transcended maybe, but a necessary step albeit. Not only are the last plays mostly concerned with proving the necessity of 'overswaying Reason by Religion' but their actual form uses the fairytale structure of the happy ending that was, along with the extra bonus of pardon through grace for the wicked characters, ideologically compatible with a fideistic ideology.

Cymbeline falls short of tragedy because reason is overswayed by faith. The wager plot stages the destructive power of a reason bent on destroying faith in love: Iachimo is a perfect rationalist who props up his 'illegitimate constructions' with his highly sophisticated rhetorics. Whereas Innogen is an obvious allegory of Faith, Iachimo is an antithetical allegory of Reason, as his familiarity with the workings of the human mind shows. His speech in Innogen's bedroom illustrates the art of deduction such as could be found in Aristotelian philosophy. Iachimo has perfectly grasped how the higher faculties of man are all connected to one another, how the senses leave their impressions in the memory and how imagination brings them forth and how reason organizes them in a convincing and persuasive discourse. The rational deductions he inspires in Posthumus become the bases of the poisoning of the lover's mind against Innogen, whereas he can do nothing when he is confronted with Innogen's staunch faith in Posthumus (1.6). Against the tricks of Reason, Innogen remains adamant, thereby proving the supremacy of Faith.

Faith holds the faculties of the mind together. Such is the significance of Fidele's 'sleep of death' in Act 4, during which the bonds of faith are so much in danger of being loosened that Innogen is in a state of total confusion, verging on madness, suggestive of both Juliet's despair when she wakes up in the Capulets' vault and Ophelia's madness scenes – all three scenes being illustrative of the topsy-turvydom of the world repeatedly apparent in the fourth acts of most plays. In his comment on Hamlet's letter to Ophelia on the subject of faith in love, Freud, in *The Rat Man*, explains how, when faith is lacking in love, the doubt about love spreads over all the rest of one's life and contaminates it. The whole subtle construction of the mind is destroyed by doubt with the result that Ophelia's wits are made 'mortal as an old man's life' (*Hamlet* 4.5.16): her song 'How can I your true love know from another one' is her answer to Hamlet's letter. Innogen's confusion in the terrible ordeal of the 'discovery' of Posthumus's death, leading her to be unable to distinguish between her husband and the prince, is a first instance of the dulling of the senses that is a symptom of failing faith although, contrarily to Ophelia, she comes out victorious from this ordeal too.

In *Cymbeline* the issues relative to the Faith/Reason debate are concealed under the description of the psychological failings of the major characters.

No doubt because Augustinism and its stress laid on the supremacy of faith over reason were the major issues of the Council of Trent (1545–63),[9] they had led the reformers to pass for the champions of faith. Just two years after the end of the Council, however, in 1565, the Catholic Thomas Stapleton, the famous translator of Bede's *Historia ecclesiastica gentis Anglorum*, came up with a publication that showed how much the Catholics were most anxious not to let Faith become the personal property of the Protestants: *A Fortresse of the Faith, First planted among us Englishmen, and continued hitherto in the universall Church of Christ; The faith of which time Protestants call Papistry.*[10] John Murphy has pointed to the influence that this text had on the works of Parsons, and how *Cymbeline*, which, according to him, does not necessarily argue for the historical continuity between the British church and the Anglican Church, could well have been influenced by it. His most potent argument lies in the example used by Stapleton when he puts certain demands to Protestants as to the necessity of the continuity of a line of bishops:

> Let them bring forth the beginnings of their churches, let them reade unto us the rolle of their bishops. If they be not able . . . then undoubtedly they were not only all this time no true church, but no church at all, I saie no congregation at all except such a congregation as those headless heretikes called *Acephali* were, of whom we made mention even now.[11]

The reference is to two pages above (p. 93) where Stapleton tells us more about these *Acephali*: 'A sorte of heretikes there were about thirteen hundred yeares past, called *Acephali, quia sub episcopis non fuerant*, that his, headles heretikes bicause they were under no bishops.' For Murphy, the headless corpse of Cloten could be an allusion to these heretics of the past who were such a convenient metaphor for the Protestants who had got rid of the Pope. Donna Hamilton had also pointed to this possibility, quoting Bellarmine who accused the Protestants of 'cutting off the very head of the faith', but opted for the other hypothesis compounded from James I's discussion of the material from Revelation in which is to be found the description of the fall of Antichrist (the Church of Rome) who 'as a Milstone will be cast into the sea'.[12] In his lecture Murphy comments on this strange conflation of images in the following way: 'The savage farce might be to see the external body of the true church absolutely indistinguishable from the villainous false one, because the total face, brain, mind, in short the head is not there. I am surprised that criticism has not lingered on this vein of ore.'

The difficulty of pinpointing the historical significance of Cloten is enhanced by the name that Innogen gives the corpse she thought was her husband's. She endows him with the Frenchified version of a name which points to two different persons: Richard du Champ is the Stratfordian Richard Field, printer of *Venus and Adonis* and of *The Rape of Lucrece* (1561–24).[13] But, as Hamilton has shown, Richard Field is also the name of one of the greatest Protestant apologists of the period (1561–1616), who wrote the monumental *Of the Church* in five books, the latest published in 1610.[14] John Murphy convincingly comments on this homonomy by adding how ironical it was that Matthew Sutcliffe's 'Establishment' attack on Father Parsons's *Three Conversions* was published in 1606 by the Stratfordian Richard Field.

Shakespeare's puzzling intention to conflate the two homonymous figures in the gory corpse of Cloten seems to be an endeavour to confuse the issues deliberately after a misleading attempt at giving undeniable clues to the understanding of the character of Cloten. It is my contention that such a condensation of personalities in the same fictive character can mean only that Shakespeare is directing his audience to transcend the detective work he at first encourages in them, which is a way of transcending the polemics engendered by the gory wars of religion. The more one finds out about the reverend divine Dr Field, who was 'chaplain in ordinarie to James I', and sent to the conference at Hampton Court on 14 January 1603, the more we are tempted to think he was brought into the picture because he clearly rejected the accusation of being a polemicist. In his biography written by his son Nathaniel Field, where we find for instance that his surname was the occasion for puns on the part of the king, we find this insistence on his tolerant attitude:

> On the occasion of having delivered his first sermon in front of James, the King, descanting upon his name, sayd of him, Is his name Field? This is a Field for God to dwell in . . . He was one which laboured to heal the breaches of Christendome, and was readie to embrace Truth wheresoever he found it. He did not like those which are so much afraide of Romish errors, that they run into contrarie extremes. His desires, his praiers, his endeavours were for peace, to make up the Breaches of the Church, not to widen differences but to compose them.[15]

The polemical nature of *Of the Church* can however be testified to in chapters entitled for instance 'Stapletons reasons against our notes of the Church' (Book II, chapter 4), and that his works encouraged polemics is undeniable, witness the title of a book by the Catholic Theophilus Higgons printed in 1609, at the time of *Cymbeline*: *The First Motive of T H maister of Arts, and lately minister, to suspect the integrity of his religion: which was detection of falsehood in D. Humfrey, D. Field and other learned Protestants, touching the question of Purgatory, and Prayer for the Dead . . . An Appendix, intituled Try before you trust. Wherein some notable untruths of D. Field and D. Morton are discovered. Printed 1609.*[16] As for a famous sermon he preached before the King at Whitehall, on Friday 16

March 1604, Dr Field amply discusses St Augustine's position regarding purgatory, deliberately omitting the adjunct 'saint' which is one of the common transgressions of the Protestants that Higgons doesn't fail to underline. The extent of Field's tolerance is hard to determine in the heart of the raging debates of the time, and it remains to be understood whether Shakespeare might have used his name for the reputation he had of 'not . . . widen[ing] differences but . . . compos[ing] them', or whether he was just fascinated in the onomastics of these homonyms that had struck the King himself or maybe because this divine was another of these champions of faith. Was not the general intention of the sermon just quoted to talk about *the maintainance of faith* which he describes as follows: 'the name of faith signifieth the act or habite of beleeving, sometimes that sum of Christian doctrine, the conclusions whereof are not demonstrable by reason, but must be believed by faith'?[17]

Shakespeare and Montaigne's fideism

The last plays are heavily indebted to Montaigne certainly because of the latter's Augustinism. Florio's translation was ready by 1600 and had been licensed to E. Blount.[18] Its publication had been postponed till 1603 because of the French philosopher's earlier stoical phase. Even though *L'Apologie de Raimond Sebond* made it very clear that Montaigne had outgrown his vindication of the stoical reliance on human reason (since the middle 1570s), Florio had to find excuses for it in his dedication of the work to Sidney's daughter, the Countess of Rutland and to Essex's sister, Lady Rich.[19] Montaigne's scepticism towards reason was the basis of his fideistic attitude. It might seem surprising that Montaigne's fideism did not make him suspect to the Roman Catholic authorities. After all, fideism derived from the doctrine of the two truths that had had some influence on medieval nominalism. As Y. Bellenger remarks, Montaigne was not harassed by the Holy Office because it was only later at the time of the *Unigenitus* Bull in 1713 that fideism was sanctioned as heretical for the excesses it could lead to.[20] But in the sixteenth century Jansenism did not exist and Montaigne could freely build what were going to be Pascal's philosophical foundations no doubt because he had clearly disapproved of the Protestants' endeavour to change the rules and could pass for something of a conservative.

So, when Shakespeare turned to the Roman Catholic Montaigne as a major source of inspiration he wasn't only using his *Essays* as a pool of convenient topics. He was establishing transconfessional connections that had already been encouraged by the most liberal religious thinkers of the time. The possibility of such intellectual alliances between writers of different religions was the needed confirmation that liberal Catholics and liberal Protestants were waging their own war against the wars of religion.

Montaigne had condemned Protestantism but in many instances he might have been mistaken for one and he was respected enough by both parties to have played the part of a negotiator in the bitter religious feuds. David Daniell has recently argued that Shakespeare's indebtedness to Tyndale's plain and subjective style might be counted a proof of Protestantism.[21] But it might just as well be argued that Montaigne's use of a vernacular that was revealing a new conception of the subject was quite as convincing a source for Shakespeare's opening up of language to new perceptions of reality. As B. Copenhaver and C. Schmitt point out in their study of Montaigne in *Renaissance Philosophy*, '[Montaigne's] independence from the academy no doubt made it easier for him to write in the vernacular and thus to join Bruno, his contemporary, in inaugurating the transformation of philosophical language'.[22] The revolution in language was transconfessional. Montaigne, like Bruno, was one of these thinkers who represented a form of transconfessional wisdom which was making its way in those troubled times and preparing the first signs of the breakthrough in the seventeenth century. In *Giordano Bruno and the Hermetic Tradition* and in *Shakespeare's Last Plays: A New Approach*, Frances Yates showed how these brave politics of religious tolerance found an echo in Prince Henry, invested as Prince of Wales in 1611 and in whose honour *Cymbeline* was probably written.

The influence of Montaigne on *Cymbeline* appears in the play's undermining of the role of reason in the face of a growing reliance on grace and faith. It is no accident that Arviragus should be quoting directly from Montaigne (*Essais*, III, 5, 874c) when he says that 'Love's reason's without reason' (4.2.22) – a statement made famous by Pascal's appropriation of it in his famous 'pensée' 280. One of the consequences is the rejection of the stoical rationality that could be appealed to to exculpate acts of cruelty or hardness of heart. 'Pardon's the word to all' says the King (5.5.422), who, after a long phase of paranoid withdrawal and cruelty, proclaims his compassion and love for all, even though, as Richard Wilson has shown in *Will Power*, commenting on precisely this quotation from the play, 'the quality of mercy' at the beginning of the seventeenth century was only just another political move on the part of the monarch to leave his enemies in a state of mental subjection perhaps worse than the throes of bodily punishment.[23] Iachimo is not made to undergo the tortures that are promised Ambrogiuolo, his equivalent in Boccaccio's ninth tale of the second day in the *Decameron*. But the happy ending of the tragi-comedy must not conceal the pragmatic motivations that were behind it: one must not forget that it was the Portuguese and Spanish inquisitors who were so anxious for a hopeful ending, and this goes to consolidate Richard Wilson's thesis. But, however, the censors were not the only ones to indulge in a form of aesthetics that was highly popular. Nuccio Ordine has recently shown how Giordano Bruno was anxious to reverse Aristotle's view that the mixture of genres could only account for appearance, and his motto 'In tristezza hileris, in hileritate tristis' emphasized his involvement with tragi-comedy.[24] All must fall in the new pattern of the 'lieto fine' that emblematizes the aesthetics of a Christian theatre based on the reassessment of the three theologal virtues, faith, hope and charity, these supernaturally infused virtues, that a controversial character of the late plays, the Gonzalo of *The Tempest*, allegorizes. The question of these three virtues had already been considered as a moot point when in 1277, Etienne Tempier, the Bishop of Paris had condemned 219 theses deriving from the purely rationalistic, philosophical, Averroistic reading of Aristotle. Among these theses, centred on points of sexual ethics as Alain de Libera has shown,[25] the one concerning the questioning of the necessity of the theologal virtues is particularly relevant to the topicality of the late plays. That Shakespeare should choose to end his career with plays fashioned to put on stage the mysteries of faith in this way with a play that is from so many aspects so Protestant in its inspiration can be explained by the pervading Augustinism of the period and the way it could be appropriated by both Catholics and Protestants alike. In *Sources of the Self: The Making of Modern Identity*, Charles Taylor underlined St Augustine's achievement in having transcended all confessional differences in the sixteenth and seventeenth centuries.[26] In Letter 133 St Augustine advocates compassion and warns against the passion of revenge and pleads for the abrogation of torture. It is from such sources that Montaigne's essay *De la cruauté* derives (*Essais*, II, xi) and might well have influenced plays such as *Hamlet*.

> Celuy qui, d'une douceur et facilité naturelle, mespriseroit les offences receues feroit chose très-belle et digne de louange; mais celuy qui, piqué et outré jusques au vif d'une offence, s'armeroit des armes de la raison contre ce furieux appetit de vengeance, et après un grand conflict s'en rendrait enfin maistre, feroit sans doubte beaucoup plus. Celuy-là feroit bien, et cettuy-cy vertueusement; l'une action se pourroit dire bonté; l'autre vertu.[27]

Even though Montaigne goes on to praise the moral strength of the Stoics in the same essay, it is his growing questioning of stoical rationality which blossoms out in *The Apology of Raymond Sebond* that ends up by turning him into one of the recognized influences on the questioning of stoical values, according to W. R. Elton. Quoting from W. Lee Ustick's article 'Changing ideals of aristocratic character and conduct in seventeenth century England', he goes on to show how the ideals of *l'honnête homme* were changing in the seventeenth century and how, in the words of Ustick, 'one of the most notable traits of l'honnête homme of the late seventeenth century is his "good heart" '.[28] Innogen's 'compassion' speech in front of Belarius's cave (3.6), and the denunciation of Cymbeline's cold and cruel heart shed light on the more political speeches on tolerance at the end of the play. If this insistence on compassion comes from St Augustine, via

Montaigne's condemnation of some aspects of stoicism, then we might be inclined to interpret it as a genuine echo of those efforts to put an end to the wars of religion. Montaigne was precisely one of these liberal Catholics who took political measures in his lifetime to act as a negotiator between feuding parties. Moreover, as Frances Yates's analysis of *Cymbeline* in the light of Bruno's politics of tolerance and their influence on Prince Henry's European politics shows,[29] the questioning of the supremacy of reason in matters social and political passed through a revival of hermetic philosophy and neoplatonism. That Cymbeline's peace between Rome and Britain should be unequal and irrational and that the losers should be the winners appears as yet another example of the questioning of the supremacy of reason and of the nominalistic separation of the two levels of faith and reason that, after St Augustine, the reformers and the liberal Catholics alike were reviving. At this stage it is important to bear in mind what Debora Shuger tells us about the transformation undergone by the old fourth- and fifth-century Christian ideal of generous compassion which had given shape to what she calls 'the monastic construction of the self'. Compassion and the ideal of tolerance were slowly undergoing a process of interiorization and reappearing as a trope in literature – 'a transfer that parallels Foucault's description of the extension of monastic discipline to society as a whole'.[30] In this context plays such as *Cymbeline* or *King Lear* before where simply the channels operating this interiorization, while more cynical policies were being enacted outside the theatre.

Hermetic poetics

In Melanchthon's Wittenberg hermetic philosophy had become the medium through which faith could express itself in an educational system which had institutionalized the secularization of knowledge based on the radical division between reason and faith. A hermetic poetics come straight from Ficino's Florence was producing an almost infinite stock of images in which the mysteries of faith could be expressed without appearing to be explicitly religious.[31] And so, on the Protestant stage of James, *Cymbeline* could unashamedly make a display of the highly sophisticated medley of influences that make it the Baroque play it is, likely to be acceptable to a huge range of spectators belonging to the Protestant milieu but also to the remote reading rooms of the Holy Office at Valladolid. The immense symbolical wealth of the play – thirty-five mythological references have been assessed[32] – brings together an Augustinian inspiration, neoplatonism, Bruno's dream of a united Europe, Montaigne's fideism (through Florio who was acquainted with Bruno).[33] Religious hermetism was a common ground of agreement between the warring factions. This 'new philosophy' as the Catholic platonist Patrizi called it, was the only means of philosophizing about God since the *via moderna* had cut off the connection between reason and faith. 'You should cause this doctrine to be taught in the schools of the Jesuits', he said.[34] Anti-aristotelianism, an awareness of the danger of the supremacy of reason, brought all these otherwise more or less antagonistic currents together. Bruno had written severe attacks against Aristotle, so had Montaigne. In *Cymbeline*, Iachimo embodies a relentless rationality based on an Aristotelian theory of knowledge, involving the delicate balance between the faculties of the mind, memory and imagination but the knowledge he achieves so rationally is perfect falsehood. Behind this portrait of Iachimo we can read Bruno's contempt for 'the father of the sophistic kind' as he calls Aristotle in his *Art of Memory*, capable of deducing false truths.[35] Roughly the same attitude as Bruno's can be found in *L'Apologie de Raimond Sebond* by the fideist Montaigne:

> Pourquoi non Aristote seulement, mais la plupart des philosophes ont affecté la difficulté, si ce n'est pour faire valoir la vanité du subject et amuser la curiosité de notre Esprit, luy donnant où se paistre, à ronger cet os creux et descharné?[36]

In this anti-scholastic mood, philosophizing about God was no longer a central issue, and hermetic poetics were becoming a more acceptable means on disserting on the nature of God. The fashion for hermetic treatises which flourished in the seventeenth century corresponded with the need for an allegorical language which could transcend the stodgy polemical works of the Protestant divines and their Catholic interlocutors. The representation of God in *Cymbeline* is a case in point. P. Muñoz Simonds remarked that 'since the name of the Christian God could not by law be spoken of the English stage during the early XVIIth century, Jove is still a standard English euphemism for the deity'.[37] Whose God is Jupiter? As Gary Taylor pointed out, he responds to the intercession of dead souls.[38] In that he could be the God of the Roman Catholics. His presence on stage seems to forbid an assimilation with the *deus absconditus* of the fideists. And yet when Jupiter comes down from the heavens it is to admonish Posthumus's parents for their lack of faith (5.3.187–216). There is a passage in *L'Apologie de Raimond Sebond* that describes Montaigne's idea of God materialized in an image of Jupiter taken from the Greek obstetrician of the second century AD, Soranus, and which Montaigne had found in St Augustine's *City of God* IX, ii:

> De toutes les opinions humaines et anciennes touchant la religion, celle-là me semble avoir eu plus de vraisemblance et plus d'excuse, qui reconnaissait Dieu comme une puissance incompréhensible, origine et conservation de toutes choses, toute bonté, toute perfection, recevant et prenant en bonne part l'honneur et la révérence que les humains lui rendaient, sans quelque visage, sans quelque nom et en quelque manière que ce fût:
> *Jupiter omnipotens rerum regumque deumque*
> *Progenitor genitrixque.*[39]

In this passage Jupiter's power is that of an androgynous divinity, father and mother at the same time, an image that Shakespeare might have projected on to Cymbeline himself in the mysterious passage where the King sees himself as 'a mother to the birth of three' (5.5.370). In alchemical terms the apparition of Jupiter on an eagle symbolizes the long-sought-for union between the masculine and active principle of sulphur (spirit) and the feminine passive principle of mercury sometimes represented as an eagle (soul).[40] The alchemical phase of sublimation was often represented by Jupiter turning into an eagle and taking Ganymede upon his wings.[41] Before the wars of religion had actually started, emblems had been used as coded messages. Delio Cantimori has described the exchanges between the Catholic humanist Achilles Bocchi and Reginald Pole implying just such a scene of the abduction of Ganymede.[42] But the function of this particular choice here is to give a hermetic turn to the representation of God so that the endlessly polemical debates on the nature of God could be conveniently toned down. Frances Yates described how Catherine di Medici believed that the use of talismans in the Court pageants was a way of drawing the beneficial influence of the heavens down to earth and that their magic influence could literally check the progression of the wars of religion. One of the talismans she resorted to was precisely the figure of Jupiter on an eagle.[43] I have shown in the preface to a French edition of the play that the neoplatonic imagery of the play maps out a space for talismanic correspondences of this kind. The structure of the play brings out strange geometrical patterns involving mysterious perspectives that are more suggestive of hermetism than the diagrams of Alberti. Sonnet 24 reminds us that etymologically 'perspective' means 'to see through'. Three diagonals in the play (1.4.14–22; 3.3.11–13; 5.4.471–7) intersect the cross of the cardinal points, lead the spectators of *Cymbeline* to explore different layers of reality that range from the countries of the earth to the celestial beams that reach the stars. The strength of Innogen is that she 'think[s] of other place' (3.4.144). *Cymbeline* reflects a new geography of the world that was being materialized in James's dream of a Great Britain whose position would be central in Europe. The heirs to Cymbeline's throne have been brought up by a wise woman called Euriphile. This political vision was embedded in hermetic imagery as one of Michael Maier's emblems shows: a map of Europe is seen to be the privileged recipient of the celestial influx that reaches down from the sun through the mediation of the moon.[44] The image of Jupiter conflates all these codes emphasizing the play's involvement in issues that go far beyond a mechanical use of stage machinery.

Shakespeare's adoption of a hermetic language could seem to contradict his Augustinian inspiration since St Augustine's distrust of the Egyptians is to be found in a famous passage of *The City of God* (VIII, xxiii–xxvi).[45] But the literature of the emblems was in fact a way of moralizing the old mysteries, of christianizing them, as Ovid's *Metamorphoses* had been moralized. Shakespeare's use of such hermetic coding must not be laid aside. Peggy Muñoz Simonds has stressed the danger of reading a play such as *Cymbeline* with no reference to the emblematic codes that pervade the text: 'Such Romantic distortions appear continually in modern Shakespearean scolarship and tend to obscure much of what Shakespeare and his contemporaries were actually implying through their art'.[46] Another of these omissions consists in having more or less completely left out the very obvious alchemical connotations that shed light on some of its most puzzling passages.

Beyond contention: the alchemical narrative

In his sermon preached before the King at Whitehall in 1604 Dr Richard Field was anxious to defend himself against the accusation of encouraging dissension or the negative contention of those who 'blow the coales, and kindle the fire'. Taking his inspiration from the apostle Jude he endeavours to define in careful terms the only acceptable contention, that which is necessary 'for the maintainance of the faith'.[47] A major argument of the polemicists was the denial of a polemic discourse. In this context of contending parties trying to reach out for the true faith, hermetic imagery and alchemical allegorizing were an ideal medium for the conveyance of the idea that contentious parties could find some agreement, in a symbolical marriage of contraries.

   Cymbeline fits in perfectly with the alchemical narrative. The whole play is alive with alchemical connotations that are ingenious ways of bringing coded peaceful answers to the current polemical issues. It is daubed in black, white and red, the colours of the phases of the great work, *nigredo*, *albedo* and *rubedo*. The great birds of alchemy hover over the stage, the black crow (1.3.15; 3.3.12–13), the white swan (3.4.141) and the phoenix (1.7.17), the red bird named phoenix after the Phoenicians who invented the purple tincture. The play can be read as an alchemical allegory like the tale of Snow White from which it derives: Snow White's mother had dreamt of a child as white as snow, as red as blood, as black as ebony.[48] The aim of the great work is to bring opposites to coalesce, to work the union between the four elements, earth and water, fire and air, or between the eagle representing the cold and moist principle of passive and feminine mercury and the phoenix, illustrating its active male counterpart, hot and dry sulphur. The ultimate union between Innogen (the phoenix, 1.7.17) and Posthumus (the eagle, 1.2.70) symbolizes the last phase of the great work. *Cymbeline* is a 'great work', the *opus alchymicum*, in which warring factions are made to negotiate, in which male and female principles are made to marry, in which unequal forces are united.

   Alchemical symbolism makes its first appearance in the first act of the play at the moment of the separation of the lovers. When Posthumus dis-

appears from Innogen's view and fades into the distance in his love's mind's eye (1.3.15) he is compared to a crow. In the same way it is when Guiderius and Arviragus, growing aware of a desire of independence from their foster-father Belarius, climb the mountain that, looking down, they see him as a crow diminishing in the distance (3.3.12–13). The crow is the bird of the *nigredo*, the phase of *separatio* when the spirit must learn to separate itself from the body. Peggy Muñoz Simonds has shown that the crow is a symbol of fidelity in marriage and of political consensus,[49] but these interpretations must not obfuscate the alchemical one. The *nigredo* is also the stage of *putrefactio*. Cloten is a typical protagonist of this phase, standing for the gross *materia prima* undergoing putrefaction. A rank smell was a well-known feature of the stage of putrefaction. The first apparition of Cloten on stage is memorable for the mysterious and inelegant allusion to his smell on the part of the first lord (1.3 Arden, 1.2 Oxford).[50] Posthumus, Cloten and Belarius are all implied in this phase of incompleteness which is the necessary rite of initiation to the next stages of the great work. The alchemical reference to *nigredo* also sheds light on one of the most mysterious scenes in the whole of Shakespeare's drama: when the 'pale' Innogen wakes up beside the corpse of the gory headless body of Cloten, Shakespeare is staging another well-known phase of the *nigredo*, the chemical marriage between the red man and the white woman (4.2.291–332). The scene showing Innogen waking up by the corpse of the man who wanted to rape her is 'contra naturam' but appropriate in this phase of the *opus* which implies an inversion of what normally happens in nature.[51] It is not surprising to find such a scene in Act 4 which is in Shakespearean drama the usual 'place' where images of a topsy-turvy world can usually be found. One thinks of the airy Juliet in the earthy tomb of the Capulets, or the Malcolm–Macduff debate for instance, in which it is hard to distinguish what is foul from what is fair. The double nature of a poison which is also a medicine (an image of the versatile mercury) is also relevant to the same alchemical theme of inversion.[52] Innogen is placed in this uncannily incongruous position to illustrate the dire combat within the sexual bond of one sex over another, which the chemical marriage between the quarrelling red man and white woman is supposed to show. The implication is that male sulphur and female mercury must lie together in the grave (the alembic) before their spirits can escape from their bodies, and allow the reunion in the nuptial bed. In Johann Daniel Mylius's *Philosophia reformata* (1622) this double burial takes place in a crystal coffin,[53] emphasizing the alchemical interpretation of the tale of Snow White. When Innogen smears her face with the blood of Cloten (4.2.330), she becomes 'red head', symbolizing the consummation of the *opus*, and this is another example of the phenomenon of inversion.[54] The beheading of Cloten is of course another aspect of the phase of *separatio*: the head must be detached from the body to enable the perfect spiritualization of man who must detach himself from the heaviness of the body. Alchemically therefore, Cloten's beheaded corpse stands for the process of the spiritualization of the body which happens in the course of the chemical marriage. Innogen's paleness symbolizes the spirit. In one of the alchemist Mylius's plates from his *Anatomia auri* (1628) we can see the severed head of a crow emerging from the alembic with the mention *Caput Corvi Separatio animae a corpore* and the ensuing whitening of the black and stinking water.[55] When Innogen mistakes Cloten for Posthumus she is interpreting Cloten as a double of Posthumus, one of the forms that Posthumus must slough off before he can hope to reach a total spiritualization of his love. But besides this unintentional confusion between Cloten and Posthumus, Innogen deliberately adds another ambiguity by choosing to name the corpse Richard du Champ (4.2.377). That she should choose a homonym referring to two distinct contemporaries of Shakespeare as we have seen could be understood to mean to represent the stage of *multiplicatio*. But the name of du Champ for her dead companion could also be interpreted alchemically. A field is a common alchemical symbol. Two examples from Michael Maier can be used: one from *Atalanta fugiens* (1618) is emblem VI showing a farmer sowing gold in a field.[56] According to Jodocus Greverus in *Secretum* (1599), the operations of wheat farming can be compared to the operations of the *opus*.[57] In another of Maier's works, *Septimana philosophica* (1620), the field of wheat is shown between a garden and a forest and all three represent the vegetable realm seen as an adequate analogy for alchemy.[58] Further investigations should be made to account for the translation of the word into French, but we could suggest that, as elsewhere in Shakespeare's plays, French names are the occasions of puns implied by the conflation of a proper noun and a common one.

It appears highly significant that those scenes which are the hardest to decipher in terms of the contemporary issues should be deliberately even more obfuscated by alchemical imagery. It is not so surprising that it should be in the third and fourth acts of the play where the character of Belarius comes in that the alchemical allusions should be so numerous and involved. It is my contention that there is an intention of transcending the polemical issues in an attempt at neutralizing them. The aim seems to be in taking off the spectator's mind from a temptation to partisan reading. Yates has shown how involved the play was in the Protestant politics of the time but also how much it is full of the echoes of the old dream of finding 'some way to end the jars in religion'.[59] Muñoz Simonds has very convincingly shown how the eagle imagery could allude to the rebirth of the reformed church.[60] We have noted the debate around the significance of Cloten's headless corpse and the deliberately undecidable issues implied. Another example is the strange allusions to the burial rites which were such a subject of controversy at the time. Hamilton has singled out Belarius as liable to stand for one of those Catholics in the uncomfortable position that the Act of

Allegiance left them in.[61] It is Belarius who conducts the burial rites of Innogen and Cloten. He is very keen on the position of the bodies which was a way of identifying the religion of a dead person:

> *Guiderius*:   Nay, Cadwal, we must lay his head to the east,
>   My father hath a reason for 't.   (4.2.255–6)

Roman Catholics would usually insist on being buried with their heads to the west so that they would face the east at the Judgement Day. Archaeological excavations have been carried out in a medieval necropolis in France and it was discovered that out of fifty-three bodies, forty-eight had their heads to the west whereas only five had their heads to the east.[62] In the chancel of Trinity Church in Stratford Shakespeare himself lies with his head to the west. This came to be a point of acute controversy. Eamon Duffy comments on an Admonition to Parliament that complained of the superstitions used 'both in countrye and citie, for the place of buriall, which way they must lie'. The direction of the bodies was dismissed as superstition by the reformers.[63] In 1658 Sir Thomas Browne's *Hydriotaphia or Urn Burial* records that this east–west disposition had always been a point of controversy.[64] That the problem should be raised in *Cymbeline* might be understood as a way of emphasizing Belarius's Roman Catholic habits since he finds it all-important that Innogen should be buried according to a logic of his. But the position chosen is not the usual one, and Innogen would be facing west on the Last Day. Here again, as in all the crucial issues, if we allow the reference to the alchemical code, the allusion becomes meaningful. According to L. Abraham the east signifies the dry coagulating aspect (sulphur), while the west signifies the cold moist dissolving aspect (mercury).[65] Would this allusion be a simple reminder that Innogen's body in this scene has symbolized the two major operations of the *opus*, summed up in the famous formula: *solve et coagule*? It could be suggested that Innogen facing west (with her head to the east) would be looking forward to the necessary process of dissolution involving mercury (the converting of a solid body into a fluid substance – a spirit). After the terrible experience of the inversion Innogen is now ready to pass on to the stage of *albedo*. This must be the significance of another of Belarius's burial rites: he promises to bring midnight flowers and herbs that 'have on them cold dew o' th' night' (4.2.284). In alchemical terms this means that the body must be washed by the 'dew' of mercurial water before it can pass on to the next stage.[66] As she moves on her pilgrimage of faith, her vision whitens into the stage of *albedo*, which she had epiphanized by the vision of Britain as a 'swan's nest' (3.4.141).

The end of the alchemical narrative is achieved when the philosopher's stone is produced. It is symbolized by the orphan-child whose parents must die if he is to live and who depends on his foster parent the alchemist if he is to reach completude.[67] Guiderius, Arviragus and most of all Posthumus find themselves in such a position. That Posthumus should come across the two princes and their foster parent Belarius in the narrow lane episode emphasizes the necessary initiatory phases leading to the new births of the three young men.

Muñoz Simonds has shown how important it is in Renaissance studies to know 'whether the *topos* is being employed by a Catholic or a Protestant poet or painter'.[68] Alluding to the apparently inadequate comparison of Posthumus to an eagle (1.2.70), considering that the three characteristics of the eagle symbol hardly apply to the hero (keen vision, royalty, the ability to gaze into the sun),[66] she shows how important it is to explore the different uses each religious party made of the eagle *topos*. Regarding the capacity of flying into the sun it was, she says, used by Pico della Mirandola in his *Oration on the Dignity of Man* to show the Roman Catholic trust in the powers of reason to reach theological truths that the reformers considered as *hubris*.[67] Still, according to Muñoz Simonds, 'the Protestant Reformation added an important new element to the myth – the ideal of a reformed and renewed church'. In the Protestant Joachim Camerarius's *Symbola et emblemata* (1605) the eagle flying up into the sun burns off her feathers or her old clothes, and in his friend Nicolas Reusner's *Emblemata* (1581) the eagle imagery is used to emphasize once more the sufficiency of faith alone in salvation: 'For by steadfast faith he beholds the divine will'.[69] This reading of course points to the polemical use of emblems'. It seems to me however that in *Cymbeline* there is always an attempt to go beyond a partial reading and, to my mind, this is where the alchemical imagery comes in, with its constant and characteristic endeavour to coalesce contraries – as a deliberate effort at harmonizing the partisan imagery of the emblematists.

The soothsayer's vision of the eagle (Rome) being swallowed by the sun (Britain) sums up the dual operation of alchemy implying the union between opposites, sulphur (the sun, the fiery element implied in the phase of *coagulatio*) and mercury (the eagle, the liquid element implied in the phase of *dissolutio*). A striking alchemical engraving shows the union of the opposing principles of the alchemical *opus* as the head of a lion swallowing the head of an eagle. The head of the lion is related by the same serpentine body to the head of the eagle. This unique and double-headed body espouses the sun and moon placed one above the other in such a way as to allow the equation between eagle and moon and lion and sun. This engraving was used by Johann Daniel Mylius (1585–?1628) as one of the Seals of his *Opus medico-chymicum* (1618) to illustrate a Pythagorean motto: 'Sine igne nil operatur, ut nec bellator absq. armis' (without fire nothing will be wrought, as no warrior should be without arms).[70] Mylius, incidentally, enjoyed the patronage of the leaders of the Protestant party, Maurice and Frederick Henry of Nassau, to whom he dedicated his *Philosophia reformata* (1622).[71] It appropriately illustrates the context of the wars between

Rome and Britain. Cymbeline is the lion, or the sun of the sulphurous fire swallowing up the mercurial Roman eagle but the unequality of this balance is counteracted by the communion of the unique serpentine body common to both heads and illustrates perfectly the type of union that the play is expounding between the two giants at war. The use of alchemical imagery once more aims at making the point, that the necessity of one party being necessarily victorious over the other does not entail an intrinsic superiority of one over the other, since, as in the alchemical marriage two *unequal* forces are *equally* essential to the production of the philosopher's stone. The essentially paradoxical nature of alchemical imagery would help to express the desire to ease the way to a peaceful issue between contending parties.

Incongruity

The 'incongruity' that Dr Johnson diagnosed in 1756 as the origin of the 'unresisting imbecility' of the play is rather an effect of the *materia prima*, that terrible dark confusion of matter that the play, read as an *opus alchymicum*, is in the process of sublimating. Its apparently irreducible confusion is the condition for the beauty of its sublimation. Moreover, its resistance to partisan investigation and the way it encourages a balanced view of both warring factions makes of *Cymbeline* a vital juncture in the process of an interiorization of the wars of religion that would eventually take place. Its hermetic imagery, obstrusive only to modern readers, is in fact a highly political language, allowing for the perception of a solution to the religious crises that could hardly have been imagined at the outset of Shakespeare's career. It is no wonder then that the alchemical connotations become more and more explicit from *King John* to *Romeo and Juliet* to *Cymbeline* where they bloom in their Baroque splendour.

In October 1610, a few months after the assassination of Henry IV (14 May), possibly at the time when *Cymbeline* was being composed, the French Protestant Casaubon sailed to England in order to settle there. He had played the uncomfortable part of the umpire in the Fontainebleau conference which had been opened under the auspices of Henry IV in 1600. There he had chaired the debate between the liberal Catholic Cardinal du Perron – a convert from Calvinism and a key figure who had obtained the reconciliation of Henry IV and the Pope in 1595 – and Duplessis Mornay, a Protestant, highly influenced by hermetism.[72] The Catholics had come out more or less victorious, and for a long while Casaubon had been suspected of not having been partial enough to his own party.

In 1612 Cardinal du Perron wrote from Paris to Casaubon in England. His letter speaks of his wish that King James I could pretend to the title of Catholic:

I assure myself, he would not thinke it strange that I should wish him the title of Catholike: but would also wish and desire it himself, and put himselfe in state to obtayne it both to himselfe, and his: I meane, he would to his other Crownes adde also this, that he would become a Mediatour for the reconciliation of the Church which would be unto him a more triumphant Glory than of all Alexanders and Cesars: and it would obtaine no lesse honour to his Iland, to have bene the place of his birth, then to have brought forth the great Constantine, the first deliverer and pacifier of the Church of Christ.

I beseech the infinite goodnes of God, that he would vouchsafe one day to increase with this, the other graces, which he hath given him, and to graunt in this behalfe, the prayers of the happy deceased Queene his Mother, whose not only tears, as did those of s Augustines Mother; but also her bloud doth make intercession, and cry unto heaven for him: and allwayes preserve you in health and safety. FINIS.[73]

And so the Cardinal makes the audacious point that James is as happy in his mother as St Augustine was in his. The explicit assimilation of James with the Father of the Church via the intercession of Mary, Queen of Scots, comparable to St Monica shows in a most striking way how near these liberal negotiators came to expressing the dream of a faith such as St Augustine had defined it, which would be the common reference of Europe. He who had brought about the reconciliation of Henry IV and of Pope Clement VIII (1592–1605) was no doubt dreaming of a similar reconciliation between James and Paul V (1605–21), under the holy patronage of the most transconfessional holy figure whom both parties could appropriate for themselves.

It is this old dream of religious peace expressing itself through the language of hermetic philosophy going back to the Protestant Melanchthon's (1497–1560) years at Wittenberg, to the hidden messages of the Catholic emblematist Alexander Bocchi, to Bruno's cryptic symbols left as leaven in all the cities of Europe, and later to the more directly political endeavours of Cardinal du Perron and Duplessis Mornay to establish religious peace, that is behind much of the complex and 'incongruous' imagery that makes of *Cymbeline* the parable of an awakening from the sleep of faith.

Notes

1 P. Muñoz Simonds, *Myth, Emblem and Music in Shakespeare's Cymbeline: An Iconographic Reconstruction* (Wilmington, 1992), pp. 119–29. Simonds gives a mythical (not allegorical) account of the sleeping figure of Innogen, whom she compares to the reclining body of Ariadne abandoned by Theseus and about to be awakened by Dionysus. 'The sleep of faith' was a subtitle to a paragraph in my preface to a French edition of *Cymbeline* (trans. J-M. Déprats, Paris, 2000).

2 D. Shuger, 'Subversive fathers and suffering subjects: Shakespeare and Christianity', in D. Hamilton and R. Strier, *Religion, Literature and Politics in*

Post-Reformation England, 1540–1688 (Cambridge, 1996), p. 46. R. Mushat Frye, *Shakespeare and Christian Doctrine* (Princeton, 1963), pp. 69–90.

3 G. P. Norton, ed., *The Cambridge History of Literary Criticism, The Renaissance*, vol. III (Cambridge, 1999), p. 105.

4 P. Muñoz Simonds, '*Cymbeline* as a Renaissance tragi-comedy', in *Myth*, p. 31. Guarini's text can be found in Allan H. Gilbert, *Literary Criticism, Plato to Dryden* (Detroit, 1940, 1962), pp. 504–33. Reference to the Jesuits' influence on literary genres: Ugo Serani, 'Gil Vicente ou la commedia dell'arte au service de la cour', in O. Kleiman, G. Logez and R. Horville, eds, *Théâtre de cour, théâtre de ville, théâtre de rue* (Lille, 2001), p. 58.

5 Frye, *Shakespeare*, p. 277.

6 Muñoz Simonds, *Myth*, p. 44.

7 Allan D. Fitzgerald, O.S.A., *Augustine through the Ages, an Encyclopedia* (Grand Rapids, Mich., 1999).

8 D. W. Foster, *W[illiam] S[hakespeare] Elégie Fun èbre* (trans. into French by L. Carrive) (Paris, 1996), p. 72.

9 H.-I. Marrou, *Saint Augustin et l'augustinisme* (Paris, (1955), 1997), p. 166.

10 T. Stapleton, *A Fortresse of the Faith* (Aldershot, 1973), p. 163.

11 J. Murphy, '*Hamlet* and *Lear*: resolution in *Cymbeline*', paper delivered at the Lancastrian Shakespeare Conference, at Hoghton Tower, July 1999.

12 D. B. Hamilton, *Shakespeare and the Politics of Protestant England* (New York, 1992), p. 146.

13 J. M. Nosworthy, ed., *Cymbeline*, Arden Shakespeare (London, 1955), note to 4.2.377, p. 138: Field (1579–1624) had a French wife and liked to call himself Ricardo del Campo. Field: an anagram of Fidel. Quote by R. J. Kane, *Shakespeare Quarterly*, IV (1953), p. 206. In the 1998 Oxford World's Classics edition, Roger Warren repeats this information (p. 214) and doesn't mention the other Richard Field (1561–1616) whom D. B. Hamilton, *Shakespeare*, sees as a possible reference.

14 Hamilton, *Shakespeare*, p. 134. *Of the Church, / Five Bookes. / By Richard Field, Doctor of / of Divinitie. / At London, / Imprinted for Simon Waterson. 1606. The fifth Booke / Of the Church. / Together with an Appendix, containing a defense of such partes and passages of the former / Bookes, as have bene either excepted against, or / wrested, to the maintenance of Romish / errours. / By Richard Field, Doctour / of Divinity. / London, / Printed by Nicholas Okes for Simon Waterson, / and are to be sold at the signe of the Crowne in / S. Paules Church-yard. / 1610.* (Cambridge University Library: Syn 5. 61. 10).

15 *Some short / Memorials / concerning the / Life / Of that Reverend Divine / Doctor Richard field, / Prebendarie of Windsor, / and / Dean of Glocester, / The Learned Author of Five Books of / the Church. / Written by his Son Nathaniel Field, Rector of / Stourton in the Countie of Wilts. / Published from the Original by / John Le Neve, Gent. / London: Printed by H. Clark, for / Henry Clements at the Half-Moon / in St Paul's Church-Yard. / 1716–7.* (Cambridge University Library: N. 25. 74).

16 Facsimile English Recusant Literature 219, Ilkley, 1974.

17 *A / Learned Sermon / preached before the / King at Whitehall, on / Friday the 16 of March: by / M. Doctor Field: Chaplaine / to his Maiestie. / At London, /*

Printed by Iames Ro-/berts, for Ieffry Chorl-/ton. 1604. (Cambridge University Library: Peterborough. 76-3414. H. 2. 10).

18 F. B. Yates, *John Florio: The Life of an Italian in Shakespeare's England* (London, 1968), p. 213.

19 *Ibid.*, pp. 106, 223.

20 Y. Bellenger, *Montaigne, une fête pour l'esprit* (Paris, 1987).

21 D. Daniell, 'Shakespeare and the Protestant mind', lecture delivered at the International Shakespeare Conference, Shakespeare and Religions, Stratford-upon-Avon, 30 July–4 August 2000.

22 B. Copenhaver and C. Schmitt, *Renaissance Philosophy* (Oxford, 1992), p. 251.

23 R. Wilson, *Will Power* (Hemel Hempstead, 1993), pp. 144–51.

24 N. Ordine, in a lecture on Giordano Bruno delivered at the Sorbonne, Paris, 2 May 2000.

25 A. de Libera, *Penser au Moyen Age* (Paris, 1991), p. 199.

26 C. Taylor, *Sources of the Self: The Making of Modern Identity* (Cambridge, Mass., 1989), p. 141.

27 M. Rat, ed., *Montaigne, oeuvres complètes* (Paris, 1967), *Les Essais*, II, xi, p. 400a.

28 W. Lee Ustick, 'Changing ideals of aristocratic character and conduct in seventeenth century England', *Madern Philology*, XXX (1932), pp. 147–66, quoted by W. R. Elton, *King Lear and the Gods* (San Marino, (1966), 1968), p. 97.

29 F. B. Yates, *Shakespeare's Last Plays: A New Approach* (London, 1975), pp. 20–1.

30 D. Shuger, 'Subversive fathers', p. 56.

31 D. Cantimori, 'Défis à la foi traditionnelle', in M. Brion, ed. *La Renaissance* (Paris, 1974), trans. from the English edition, ed. M. Grant (London, 1969), p. 198.

32 Ann Thompson, 'Philomel in *Titus Andronicus* and *Cymbeline*', *Shakespeare Survey*, 31 (1978), p. 29, n. 2, quoted by Muñoz Simonds, *Myth*, p. 66.

33 Yates, *John Florio,* chapter 5: 'Florio and Bruno'.

34 F. B. Yates, *Giordano Bruno and the Hermetic Tradition* (London, (1964), 1978), pp. 181–5.

35 Copenhaver and Schmitt, *Renaissance Philosophy*, p. 296.

36 Rat, ed., *Montaigne*, p. 488b.

37 Muñoz Simonds, *Myth*, p. 294.

38 G. Taylor, 'Divine [ ] sences', lecture delivered at the International Shakespeare Conference, Shakespeare and Religions, Stratford-upon-Avon, 30 July–4 August 2000.

39 Rat, ed., *Montaigne*, p. 493 and note.

40 L. Abraham, *A Dictionary of Alchemical Imagery* (Cambridge, 1998), p. 64: 'eagle'.

41 *Ibid.*, p. 110: 'Jupiter'.

42 Cantimori 'Défis', p. 206.

43 Yates, *Giordano Bruno*, p. 176. The influence of Ficino: pp. 72–3.

44 S. Klossowski de Rola, *The Golden Game: Alchemical Engravings of the Seventeenth Century* (London, 1988) (paperback ed. 1997), p. 163.

45 Yates, *Giordano Bruno*, p. 9.

46 Muñoz Simonds, *Myth*, p. 312.

47 *A Learned Sermon . . . by M. Doctor Field . . . 1604*, p. 28.

48 A. Teillard, *Le Symbolisme des rêves* (Paris, 1944), pp. 212–13. She expatiates on the symbolism of the fairy tale: the seven dwarves are the seven metals. The Queen delivers Snow White to the Green Hunter who is asked to murder her. After an apparent death, she is saved by Prince Charming who is no other than Philosophical Mercury.

49 Muñoz Simonds, *Myth*, pp. 207–13.

50 Abraham, *Dictionary*, p. 184: 'smell'.

51 *Ibid.*, p. 108: 'inversion'. p. 139: 'opus contra naturam'.

52 *Ibid.*, p. 208: 'venom'.

53 Klossowski de Rola, *Golden Game*, p. 174.

54 *Ibid.*, p. 96: 'red head'.

55 Klossowski de Rola, *Golden Game*, p. 203.

56 Klossowski de Rola, *Golden Game*, p. 74.

57 Klossowski de Rola, *Golden Game*, p. 98.

58 Klossowski de Rola, *Golden Game*, p. 164.

59 Yates, *Shakespeare's Last Plays*, p. 19.

60 Muñoz Simonds, *Myth*, pp. 221–4.

61 Hamilton, *Shahespere*, pp. 159–60.

62 P. Racinet, 'Pratiques funéraires de deux monastères picards', in CAHMER (Paris XIII) et CREDHIER (Université catholique de Lille), eds, *Histoire médiévale et archéologie: moines et moniales face à la mort* (Lille, 1993) (I am indebted to J. Longère (CNRS) for this reference).

63 E. Duffy, *The Stripping of the Altars: Traditional Religion in England 1400–1580* (New Haven, 1992), p. 578 (I am indebted to G. Kilroy (Lancaster University) for a discussion on the subject that led to this reference).

64 C. A. Patrides, ed., *Sir Thomas Browne, The Major Works* (Harmondsworth, 1977), p. 294.

65 Abraham, *Dictionary*, pp. 186–7: 'solve et coagule'; p. 65: 'east and west' p. 65.

66 *Ibid.*, p. 53: 'dew'.

67 *Ibid.*, p. 139: 'orphan'.

68 Muñoz Simonds, *Myth*, p. 16.

69 Muñoz Simonds, *Myth*, 'The hero as molting eagle': pp. 213–17.

70 Klossowski de Rola, *Golden Game*, p. 148: plate 261 and p. 154.

71 *Ibid.*, p. 133.

72 Yates, *Giordano Bruno*, p. 176.

73 *A / Letter / written / From Paris, / by the / Lord Cardinall of Peron, / to / Monsr. Casaubon / in England. / Translated out of the French corrected / Copie, into English. / Anno M. DC. XII* (Aldershot, 1971) (Cambridge University Library: 9100 b (336)).

Shakespeare and Catholicism

The topic of Shakespeare and religion has been visited and revisited many times over the past century. Scholars have examined Shakespeare's uses of the Scripture and of the official Book of Homilies,[1] as well as his allusions to Christian beliefs and practices in the plays and poems.[2] Particular plays have been related thematically to the immediate context of Christian feast days relevant to their first performances: for example, *King Lear* with St Stephen's Day, *The Comedy of Errors* with 'Innocents-Day' or *Twelfth Night* with the Feast of the Epiphany.[3] Recently, as historical scholars have renewed their attention to early modern religion, some have taken a fresh look at Shakespeare's relation to general and specific issues of Protestant reform,[4] while others have readdressed the topic of Shakespeare's possible Catholicism – this time in terms of his early years in Stratford and the 'lost years' before his emergence as a player and playwright in London.[5] Any discussion of religion and Shakespeare is an overdetermined one, related, as it is, to the emotionally invested ideological or confessional appropriations of that author as well as to the underlying schemes of cultural and literary history that have been constructed to contain his writings and those of other early moderns.

Where are we now? While Catholic apologetics may have led to a clumsy attempt at appropriating Shakespeare,[6] recent historical re-examinations of early modern English Catholic history by such scholars as Christopher Haigh, John Bossy and Eamon Duffy[7] have helped demolish the Protestant–Whig narrative into which Shakespeare and other early modern writers have been inserted in literary history, though a Protestant/liberal-democratic master narrative still underlies some sophisticated cultural-historical accounts. The new historicist and cultural materialist occlusion of religion as a topic or treatment of it as a mystification of economic and political relations has led, not surprisingly, to a resurgence of scholarship dealing with the centrality of religion in early modern culture: I include, of course, such work as Lowell Gallagher's study of casuistry, Debora Shuger's intellectual-historical studies and Frances Dolan's book on Catholicism and gender.[8]

In dealing with the topic of Shakespeare and Catholicism, I begin with several assumptions: first, Shakespeare's family background was Catholic, but his religious education and acculturation were mixed; second, Shakespeare's audiences (in the public theatre, at Court and in other venues) included Catholic spectators; third, both the censorship of religious controversial material in the drama and the danger of expressing dissident religious opinions encouraged Shakespeare to use indirection and ambiguity in handling both general and specifically topical religious subject matter; fourth, Shakespeare's temperament was sceptical and intellectually exploratory – with regard to religion as well as to other subjects – so that his texts are more 'open' than those of, say, Ben Jonson or John Webster, more receptive to spectators' wishful projections, ideologically malleable, 'as you like it', 'what you will'.

Peter Milward's argument for Shakespeare's Catholicism, Donna Hamilton's reading of selected plays as religio-political allegories and Huston Diehl's delineation of a Protestant didacticism in selected Shakespearean dramas all present insights and analyses that are relevant and useful, but all three critics too firmly fix the religious points of view of the plays and oversimplify audience response.[9] They generally ignore the fact that, in Shakespeare's time, there was a great muddled middle in English Christianity, a broad terrain occupied by 'church papists'[10] and by what Christopher Haigh has called 'parish Anglicans',[11] the mass of culturally conservative Christians in which rigorist reformist doctrine and practice only took slowly. Haigh maintains that 'For much of the reign of Elizabeth, the Church of England was a prescribed, national Church with more-or-less Protestant liturgy and theology but an essentially non-Protestant (and in some respects anti-Protestant) laity'.[12] Especially in rural areas, the transformation from Catholic to Protestant culture was a slow one, so the situation of the Stratford of Shakespeare's youth and early manhood was, in some respects, quite typical, that of a religiously hybridized and confessionally ambiguous local culture with a necessary latitude for toleration of religious difference, despite the legislative and governmental acts and actions meant to enforce a new Protestant conformity. Furthermore, household religion and public worship, or domestic education of the young and grammar school and parish catechetical, scriptural, and moral education could be quite different realities for particular individuals, especially for Catholics. The religious majority was allergic both to hardline Counter-Reformation Catholicism and to Puritanism. To the extremes, the middle was morally and doctrinally compromised: Counter-Reformation activists called church papists 'schismatics' and tried to 'reconcile' them; Puritans regarded conservative Protestants as 'papistical' and used the same anti-Catholic language against them that they directed against Roman Catholics.

Aside from those accommodationist Catholics and church papists whose religious commitments might have been loose or ambiguous, there were obviously many people who had converted to or drifted into the English Protestant Church, but whose background and kin were Catholic. Except for those converts such as Anthony Tyrrell, John Gee or James Wadsworth, who publicly (and suspiciously) performed their change of religion,[13] those who had made the transition had good reasons for wishing a less antagonistic relationship between Protestants and Catholics, even a more ecumenical vision of Christianity. As historians of the period have noted, there was a large difference between folk Catholicism or residual Catholic culture and the more sharply distinguished political and hardline Counter-Reformation Catholicism that was defined in polemical engagements, religio-political crises such as the Armada and Gunpowder Treason and political problems such as the succession crisis of Elizabeth's last years. One obvious split in the English Catholic population, and in its clerical leadership, was between the more militant recusants who hoped or worked for a change of monarch and of the state religion (an enterprise that effectively died with the accession of James – except for the fanatics who planned and bungled the Gunpowder Plot) and those Catholics who hoped for toleration (who were also disappointed early in the Jacobean period when it was clear that the King was not able or willing to grant it). The Armada crisis was not, actually, an event that sorted out these two groups from one another, since even most hardline Catholics were patriotic English opposed to foreign invasion. More telling was the behaviour of some church papists and of the opposing sides in the 'archpriest controversy'[14] of the late 1590s and the Oath of Allegiance controversy of 1606 and following.[15] The first was a dispute between pro- and anti-Jesuit factions occasioned by the naming of the (Jesuit-nominated) secular priest George Blackwell as supreme local religious authority for England. The second was a Protestant – Catholic debate over whether Catholics could, in good conscience, subscribe to an oath that acknowledged the King's authority in both secular and religious spheres. In the second controversy, at least initially, some accommodationist Catholics were willing to take the oath: ironically, the same George Blackwell initially opined that it was licit for Catholics to do so.[16] In the aftermath of the Catholic-terrorist Gunpowder Plot there was a redrawing of the lines between hardline and accommodationist Catholics and between practising Catholics and religious conformists (who may have initially been church papists). Ben Jonson, converted to Catholicism in prison in 1597, moved away from his new religious affiliation in this period (histrionically rejoining the official church in 1610 by enthusiastically draining the Communion cup).[17] The religio-political events and crises and the harsh penal legislation of this period not only put enormous pressure on English Catholics to join the established church but also made it increasingly difficult for them to separate political loyalty from religious conformity. It became more and more obvious that to be a good English man or woman was incompatible with being a Roman Catholic.

Shakespeare's upbringing was *both* Catholic and Protestant: he may have had Catholic instruction at home from his mother and been influenced by his Catholic schoolmasters in the King's New School,[18] but he also attended church services, read the Geneva Bible and used it for academic translation exercises, absorbed the language and content of the official Book of Homilies, and was regularly catechized.[19] The religious environment of Stratford and Warwickshire, however, in which the processes of Protestant reform were more retarded than in many other areas of England, was mixed. Shakespeare grew up in an atmosphere of practical toleration for Catholics not only on a local level, where the need to preserve social harmony militated against the sharpening of sectarian religious differences, but even in more urban, courtly and cosmopolitan political milieux. As Anthony Milton has recently argued, it is a mistake to extrapolate actual social conditions from the rhetorical excesses of polemical literature or even from the ubiquitous nationalistic anti-Catholic language and codes.[20]

We have, then, a vocabulary problem when it comes to discussing Shakespeare's religion: 'Protestant' and 'Catholic' are too rough as categories – especially if we consider the possible divergence between devotional inclinations and pious beliefs, on the one hand, and religiously inflected political loyalty to the state, on the other. Just as there were Protestant reformist subversives (presbyterians or more radical separatists about whom the Elizabethan government fretted in the late 1580s and 1590s, and Puritans in the Jacobean period whose religious and foreign-policy agendas were at odds with the King's), there were also Catholic subversives (exiles abroad fighting for Spain in the Low Countries or working actively for the restoration of Catholicism in England, martyrdom-seeking missionaries and lay people at home deeply alienated from the official Protestant polity, rebels and would-be assassins and fanatics associated with plots and treasons, including the most shocking and desperate one, the Gunpowder Plot). But, like their Protestant-nationalist compatriots, most Catholics were loyalists:[21] their patriotism and local allegiances prevented their collaborating with potential foreign invaders or with domestic rebels, assassins and terrorists.

In his biography of Shakespeare, S. Schoenbaum calls the playwright 'a tolerant Anglican'.[22] Gary Taylor has him a 'church papist',[23] though he claims that no one is likely to prove conclusively that Shakespeare was a Catholic. He argues that the fascination Shakespeare had with characters who are pretenders is related to his disguised religious commitment. Referring to Shakespeare's self-protectiveness and the elusiveness of his personality in literary biography, Taylor says 'Shakespeare's apparent invisibility is not a simple fact; it is an *act*. Which is to say: it is a motivated action, and it is a performance. There may be many motives for such self-erasure; any act so bizarre and so sustained must have been overdetermined. But the desire to protect yourself from those who would "pluck the heart of

[your] mystery" is perhaps understandable in adherents of a religion which was defined by law as treason.'[24] In E. A. J. Honigmann's *Shakespeare: The 'Lost Years'*, a book that emphasizes the importance of the Lancaster connection, Shakespeare is portrayed as a Catholic who turned against the religion of his youth in response to Catholic conspiracies and the Armada invasion, who was outraged by the Gunpowder Plot, who used anti-Catholic codes and language in a number of his plays, but who often reverted to Catholic ways of thinking. Whatever Shakespeare's beliefs and religious or emotional attachments and inclinations, like the vast majority of his compatriots he was a loyalist.[25] In *Henry V*, in contrasting the mercenary traitors he condemns from traitors and assassins who act out of religious motives, the King sarcastically refers to the latter:

> devils that suggest by treasons
> Do botch and bungle up damnation
> With patches, colours, and with forms, being fetched
> From glist'ring semblances of piety.   (2.2.111–14)[26]

When Shakespeare alludes to assassins taking the sacrament as a prelude to their evil deeds,[27] he attacks the treasonous Catholic fanaticism that motivated such assassins and would-be assassins as the killers of William of Orange, of Henry III and Henry IV of France, and the Gunpowder Plotters. As for politically scheming churchmen, the plays certainly demonstrate that Shakespeare was put off by popes and prelates playing at power politics.[28]

Shakespeare's Catholic background and the especially perilous position of Catholics in late Elizabethan and early Jacobean England led him to be especially careful in handling religious issues in his drama – in fact, to resort to forms of ambiguity that marked a real difference between his plays and the more Protestant nationalistic dramas of the time.[29] Shakespeare was keenly aware of contemporary religious doctrinal controversies – in *Measure for Measure*, for example, the cynical Lucio alludes to a crucial Protestant–Catholic dispute when he says 'Grace is grace despite of all controversy' (1.2.23)[30] – but, for whatever reasons (his family's Catholic background, his political prudence, his scepticism, his wish to appeal to a religiously heterogeneous audience), Shakespeare chose to occlude or blur them. If we compare Shakespeare's plays with those of Marlowe, Dekker, Webster and Middleton, all of whom reproduce in strong form the anti-Catholic codes circulating in the culture, one can see obvious differences. Marlowe's anti-fraternal and anti-papal satire in *Doctor Faustus* and his sick-joke dramatization of atrocities associated with the St Bartholomew Day Massacre (in *A Massacre at Paris*); Dekker's lame-brained anti-Catholic allegory, *The Whore of Babylon*; Webster's tragic-satiric assault on Catholic ceremonialism, ecclesiastical corruption, and superstition in his tragedies; Middleton's tragedies and his anti-Spanish and anti-Catholic *A*

Game at Chesse – these are all closer to the propagandistically Protestant-nationalistic norm than, for example, Shakespeare's *King John* and Shakespeare's and Fletcher's *Henry VIII*. When it came to the international politics of religion, however, Shakespeare, of course, utilized some of the relevant anti-Catholic codes to affirm national loyalty and identity – though he certainly avoided using some of the cruder polemical caricatures such as the images of evil Catholic Spaniards associated with the 'Black Legend,' except, perhaps in the case of Iago in *Othello*.[31]

King John adopts a post-Armada, invasion-scare tactic of upholding English nationalism and of arguing for the importance of loyalty (including Catholic loyalty) in the face of foreign threats to England's sovereignty.[32] Both English king and French dauphin in the play reject the papal claims of temporal supremacy (3.1.73–86 and 5.2.78–108); the play portrays the crudeness of the papacy's political threat of excommunication and not only its attempt to break off subjects' bonds of allegiance to the monarch but also its sanctioning of assassination (3.1.98–105); there are attacks on church wealth and on the papacy's commercial use of a spiritual pardoning or indulgence;[33] the play suggests a connection between the wrecking of the French supply ships with the providential defeat of the Spanish Armada (3.4.1–3), and between the monk Jacques Clement, who assassinated Henry III of France, and the monk who poisoned King John.[34] This history play, however, dangerously suggests a parallel not only between John's concern about the threat posed by a rival claimant to the throne, Arthur, and Elizabeth's former worries about her cousin, Mary Queen of Scots, but also between John's blaming of Hubert for the death of Arthur and Elizabeth's scapegoating of her Secretary of State, William Davison, for the execution of Mary.

Given its marked religio-political difference from the Protestant nationalist *The Troublesome Raigne of King John*, it is not surprising that Shakespeare's *King John* has become a central piece of evidence in the discussion of Shakespeare's religious inclinations. John Henry de Groot, in his evidence-rich, but tendentious, *Shakespeare and the 'Old Faith'*,[35] proposes this history play as strong evidence of Shakespeare's Catholic point of view. Donna Hamilton, however, reads *King John* as a politically oppositional play written out of sympathy for the radical Protestant critique of royal absolutism. Although her analysis is rich in suggestive contextual information, one might find it problematic – not only because of the tenuousness of the connection between Shakespeare and those who sympathized with Presbyterianism but also because, as Gary Taylor has pointed out, Catholics shared the same desire as radical Protestants for limited monarchy and for protection of dissent.[36] In the period radical Catholics and radical Protestants were, in fact, both associated with resistance theory.[37] The portrayal in Shakespeare's plays of particular monarchs as morally flawed, politically illegitimate or tyrannical could have been motivated as easily by Catholic as by radical Protestant sympathies. In any event Shakespearean drama is open to interpretation by religiously and politically different audience members in very different ways.

Shakespeare's comic portrayal of Sir John Oldcastle in his *Henry IV* plays has been read as a heterodox treatment of a proto-Protestant (Lollard) 'martyr', to which his descendants so strongly objected that the playwright had to rename him Falstaff and a rival company answered with the hagiographical *Fortunes of Sir John Oldcastle*.[38] In his discussion of the name change of Oldcastle to Falstaff in the *Henry IV* plays, however, David Kastan suggests that a mockery of Falstaff would, in the late 1590s, have been perceived less as a Catholic denigration of a Protestant martyr than as an establishment-Protestant criticism of a Lollard precursor of contemporary radical Protestants:

> Shakespeare's audience in 1596 or 1597 was far more likely to see the lampooning of Oldcastle as the mark of a Protestant bias rather than a papist one, providing evidence of the very fracture in the Protestant community that made the accommodation of the Lollard past so problematic. Lollardy increasingly had become identified not with the godly nation but with the more radical Puritans . . . that had tried and failed to achieve a 'further reformation' of the Church of England. If in the first decades of Elizabeth's rule the Lollards were seen (with the encouragement of Foxe) as the precursors of the national church, in the last decades they were seen (with the encouragement of Bancroft and other voices of the Anglican polity) as the precursors of the nonconforming sectaries who threatened to undermine it.[39]

This may be one valid interpretation, but Shakespeare's audience probably did not perceive this dramatic material in a uniform way. John Chamberlain's comments on those eager spectators who thronged to Middleton's *A Game at Chesse* in 1624 is a reminder of the mixed character of public theatre audiences: 'people old and young, rich and poore, masters and servants, papists and puritans, wise men etc . . . churchmen and statesmen . . . and a world besides'.[40] If the Globe audience of Middleton's rabidly partisan play contained Catholics as well as conservative and radical Protestants, then the no less heterogeneous audience of Shakespeare's histories would have responded to the Oldcastle satire in a variety of ways.[41] In discussing the second Henriad, Maurice Hunt points to Shakespeare's 'syncretic' fusing of Protestant and Catholic vocabularies, for example, in the depiction of the outcome of the battle of Agincourt, of the Protestant notion of deliverance with the Catholic one of miracle.[42]

At the end of his career, in *Henry VIII* (alternately entitled *All Is True*), Shakespeare offers multiple perspectives on religion. In her recent analysis Annabel Patterson sensibly associates Shakespeare with religious irenicism, perceiving the case for religious toleration as a subtext in the drama – a recurrent dream of accommodationist Catholics throughout the period, one that was threatened, but not destroyed, by the Gunpowder Treason. Patterson associates Shakespeare's 'all is true' attitude with regard to religious struggle with the moderate position of Holinshed, who, in his *Chronicles*, conflated both reformist Protestant and Catholic sources – for example, in the account of Cardinal Wolsey.[43]

One of the interesting things about this play is that it treats the Catholic, foreign queen quite positively: Katherine of Aragon is not only admirably honest and assertive, but also noble in her suffering. Furthermore, to dramatize her death, Shakespeare utilizes the Catholic modality of the mystical dream or vision: in one of the play's many spectacle-moments, angelic 'Spirits of peace' (4.2.83), as Katherine names them, symbolically crown her as a saint. In her interesting analysis of the drama in its immediate religio-political contexts Donna Hamilton might have considered the fact that the contemporary Catholic, foreign Queen Anne might have affected the way in which Henry's first queen is presented.[44]

Even though *Henry VIII* rehearses familiar Protestant criticisms of Roman Catholicism, embodying in Wolsey and the visiting Cardinal Campeius papal and ecclesiastical political coercion, economic exploitation and materialism, the play's Protestanism is somewhat blurred. Apart from the very positive portrayal of Thomas Cranmer – whom the villainous Stephen Gardiner's nastily calls a 'heretic' (3.2.103),[45] 'arch heretic' (5.1.45) or 'sectary' (5.2.104) (he also calls Anne Boleyn a 'spleeny Lutheran' (3.2.100) – the drama seems to play down Catholic/Protestant differences, preferring to hold out a model of Jacobean irenicism in Henry's forcing a final reconciliation of Cranmer and Gardiner. The drama avoids the kind of anti-Spanish rhetoric that might have been employed in relation to Henry's divorce negotiations: after all, it was Spanish and Imperial pressure that forced the Pope to deny Henry's petition for divorce.[46] Shakespeare seems to find the religious, irenic programme of King James more congenial than the more oppositional, activist line with which Donna Hamilton associates him through the Pembroke faction: Shakespeare's taking an irenic stance on religio-political matters did not mean affiliating himself with the Earl of Northampton and the Howard faction.

Shakespeare's religious politics, then, were both nationalist and irenic. Not surprisingly, he avoided bold allusions to a most sensitive topic, the persecution of Catholics in the period. A half century ago Graham Greene mused about some of the gaps in Shakespeare:

> isn't there one whole area of the Elizabethan scene that we miss even in Shakespeare's huge world of comedy and despair? The kings speak, the adventurers speak . . . the madmen and the lovers, the soldiers and the poets, but the martyrs are quite silent . . . One might have guessed from Shakespeare's plays that there was a vast vacuum where Faith had been – the noise and bustle of pilgrimages have been stilled . . . An old Rome has taken the place of the Christian Rome – the pagan philosophers and the pagan gods seem to

have returned. Characters speak with the accent of stoics, they pay lip service
to Venus and Bacchus. How far removed they are from the routine of the
torture chamber.[47]

There are, however, at least a few intimations of the persecution and execution of Catholics in Shakespeare's plays. In *Titus Andronicus*, in which,
as John Klause points out, there are more uses of the word 'martyr' and its
cognates than in any other Shakespeare play, there may be, in the third
scene of the fourth act, a reference to the fate of the Catholic lay petitioner
to the Queen, Richard Shelley, who was thrown into prison and died.[48] In
The Comedy of Errors the reference to 'the melancholy vale, / The place of
death and sorry execution, / Behind the ditches of the abbey here' (5.1.121–3)
has been connected to Shoreditch (near Burbage's playhouse, the Theatre),
the execution place of the priest William Hartley in 1588.[49] In *Love's
Labour's Lost* the reference to 'love's Tyburn, that hangs up simplicity'
(4.3.49) alludes to the usual place where condemned priests were hanged
for 'treason'. Antony's funeral speech for Caesar in *Julius Caesar*, which
suggests that a sympathetic 'commons' might 'kiss dead Caesar's wounds,
And dip their napkins in his sacred blood' (3.2.127, 129–30), evokes the
spectacle of Catholic relic-hunters at executions.[50] Sonnet 124's reference
to the 'fools of Time, / Which die for goodness, who have lived for crime'
(13–14), in registering the influence of Robert Southwell's *An Humble Supplication to the Queen*, may allude to Catholic martyrs.[51] The hanging of
Bardolph in *Henry V* for stealing a pax[52] is a strange reversal of gallows
punishment for violating, rather than upholding, the older religious order.
In *Measure for Measure* Escalus is ready in the last act to arrest the
Friar/Duke and put him on the rack, the favourite torture appliance used
on Catholic priests.[53] Edgar's fugitive status in *King Lear*, Stephen Greenblatt suggests, may have been seen as a reference to the plight of hunted
missionary priests,[54] and Kent's line early in the play – 'Freedom lives hence,
and banishment is here' (1.1.181) – might have spoken strongly to Catholic
members of the audience. Perhaps, also, the 'Come. Let's away to prison'
speech (5.3.8–19) may reprise some of the themes of Catholic consolation
literature aimed at members of the faith who were imprisoned or in danger
of being jailed.[55] Finally, in *Macbeth*, where the negative valence of the word
'equivocation' (which also earlier appears in *Hamlet* (5.1.127)) ties the play
topically to the aftermath of the Gunpowder Plot and to the trial of the
author of 'A Treatise of Equivovation', the subsequently executed Jesuit
Henry Garnet, there is also a short dialogue between Lady Macduff and
her son that suggests a very different point of view of hanging the 'traitor'
who 'swears and lies' (4.2.46, 47).[56]

   Although at times Shakespeare shared some nationalistic sentiments with
militantly Protestant writers, when it came to attitudes toward and the aesthetic influence of residual English Catholic culture, he could be markedly

different. Like so many of his contemporaries, Shakespeare was haunted by the symbols, rituals and beliefs of a culturally repressed Catholicism. In a recent study of early modern English culture Elizabeth Mazzola observes that 'the Protestant world is coated with symbolic residue':

> sacred symbols and practices still powerfully organized the English moral imagination in the sixteenth and seventeenth centuries, continued to orient behavior and arrange perceptions, and persisted in specifying to believers and non-believers alike the limits of the known world . . . These powerful relics come to inhabit a "separate cognitive zone".[57]

Both print culture and the Protestant reorientation of the human perceptual apparatus towards the written and spoken word (with the iconoclasm and/or iconophobia that accompanied it) may have worked to change the ways people took in information and knew both the world and themselves, but the change from an older oral and visual culture was anything but instantaneous. Older modes of apprehending reality remained, 'symbolic residue' of the 'old religion' was all about, the culturally repressed returned, again and again. Mary Douglas's complaint about what she calls the 'anti-ritualist prejudice' inscribed in the work of British (Protestant) anthropologists, the inability to appreciate the fact that 'it is impossible to have social relations without symbolic acts',[58] applies to most studies of early modern English literature and culture. A Protestant aesthetic of 'less is more', Enlightenment rationality and cultural-materialist abstraction have combined to denigrate or ignore what Michael O'Connell has called the 'incarnational aesthetic'[59] of the older, but residual, Catholic culture whose 'symbolic residue' was everywhere in Shakespeare's England.

Shakespeare's relation to an earlier religious culture was conflicted – sometimes nostalgic and elegiac, sometimes haunted and disturbed. While, for aesthetic, dramatic, religious or emotional reasons, he seems to have remained attached to certain ceremonies and doctrines associated with his and his country's Catholic past (to prefer an 'incarnational aesthetic'), at other times, he treated the elements of the Catholic culture he internalized as bad introjects (Diehl's discussion of *Othello* suggests this, as do many discussions of *Hamlet*).[60] Peter Milward, John Henry de Groot and others have sought to underscore the features of Shakespeare's Catholicism by pointing to linguistic evidence (such as his repeated use of the word 'holy'),[61] and they have noted that, despite the occasional portrayals of morally flawed bishops and cardinals, nuns, monks and friars were not, for him, figures of corruption, superstition, and the diabolical, as they were in Protestant polemic and plays promoting radical Protestant reform.[62] Given the tradition in Protestant anti-Catholic drama of presenting evil or diabolical characters in clerical garb[63] – which Marlowe follows in having Mephistophilis appear as a Franciscan monk – it is noteworthy that Shakespeare's monks and friars are generally kindly personages.[64] Milward claims: 'Behind all such references to Catholic priests and religious there appears a feeling of nostalgia for the Catholic past of England, now dissolved and fallen into ruin like the medieval monasteries.'[65] Gary Taylor seems to agree: 'Shakespeare . . . made the past real . . . But the past he made real . . . was a royalist past: a past of bishops and kings. Adherents of "the old religion" were, not surprisingly, often nostalgic.'[66] In *As You Like It* the offstage hermit-priest by whom the evil Duke Frederick 'was converted / Both from his enterprise and from the world' (5.4.150–1) is a figure from England's Catholic past: he recalls the older Marian clergy in hiding in the Warwickshire of Shakespeare's youth.[67] Certainly, unlike Spenser, whose Archimago poses as a hermit-priest, Shakespeare does not portray such a figure negatively. Such non-normative representations would have been somewhat surprising.

Sometimes it seems that Shakespeare deliberately used Catholic doctrinal allusions or aesthetically Catholic theatricality to disorient his religiously heterogeneous audience, if not also, as Diehl argues, to invite them to critique the very modes of representation he employs. For example, in *Hamlet*, the Ghost (whose role Shakespeare himself may have played)[68] comes from a Catholic purgatory. If those audience members who are knowledgeable and committed Protestants interpret it as a devil-in-disguise, a possibility entertained by Hamlet himself before the play-within-a-play scene (3.2), the action forces them to revise their initial opinion, as it rehabilitates, for dramatic purposes, a rejected Catholic belief. But the play also incorporates, as Mark Matheson has noted, a Wittenberg-educated hero who undergoes a conversion experience after which he speaks 'a specifically Protestant discourse of conscience and of God's predestinating will'.[69] With its Catholic purgatory[70] (and reference to the Catholic sacrament of extreme unction (1.5.77)) and its Protestant suggestion of predestination, *Hamlet* sends mixed confessional signals.[71] Also, given the fact that one of the possible interpretations of the figure of the malcontent is that he may be, as (the Catholic convert) Thomas Lodge put it in *Wits Miserie* (1596), 'a counterfait Catholike',[72] the religious signals seem even more confusing.[73]

The notorious dramatic crux at the end of *Measure for Measure*, the Duke's proposal to Isabella and her (non-)response, might be interpreted in an interestingly ambiguous religious context. One of the sharp differences between Protestantism and Catholicism (at least for Protestant polemicists) concerned the relative value placed on marriage and celibacy. Catholicism, reading St Paul's 'it is better to marry than to burn' (1 Corinthians 7:9) as a relegation of marriage to second-class status, idealized virginity and celibacy as preferable for those wishing to lead a morally rigorous Christian life. Protestants, advocating a married clergy and the social and religious superiority of marriage to celibacy, celebrated Christian marriage as the higher state. At the conclusion of Shakespeare's play the on-stage spectacle presents the Duke, still dressed as a friar (with his cowl down), inviting Isabella, clad as a novice nun, to become his wife. In one sense this is a kind of religious joke, the pairing of an apparent priest and nun; in another it is a serious bit of inconclusiveness that men and women, Catholics and Protestants, in the audience could read in different ways. Whether or not the spectators would have seen an allusion to Martin Luther and his spouse (Katherine von Bora, an ex-nun), they would certainly have found it difficult to see the scene either as a celebration of marriage in the manner of the romantic comedies or as an endorsement of clerical religious celibacy – although a feminist desire to see Isabella rejecting the Duke may be a modern translation of the wish to escape from the marriage market some women fulfilled by taking the veil.

The erotic pairing of friar and nun (imagined satirically in Protestant anti-Catholic polemic and in close fit of 'the nun's lip to the friar's mouth' (2.2.23–4) alluded to by the Clown in *All's Well*) does not work here in the usual way. Neither potential partner reveals sexual desire. The Duke might as well be a celibate clergyman and Isabella is an anachronism, a cultural holdover from an earlier era, belonging more to the world that the early sixteenth-century prioress Isabella Shakespeare[74] inhabited or that to which English Catholic young women and widows escaped in Continental Catholic countries whose convents served as religious safe havens. The ultra-rigorous order that Isabella attempts to enter in the play, the Poor Clares, in fact, sent fund-raising letters to England advertising their austere way of life, which they hoped English Catholics would financially support.[75] What was on the periphery, however, could, for fervent English Catholics, be at the centre of their world view: a family's religious commitment and identity could be strengthened by the presence of some of its members in convents or seminaries abroad. Such vocations, such places could be at the ideological heart of an embattled English Catholicism, especially since, in a de-Catholicized English landscape and a Protestantized local church, zealous Catholics would have found it hard to identify with an English locus for their practice of religion. Their religion was underground, surreptitious, shielded from an increasingly secularized public world, perhaps fostered in aristocratic great houses, but not materially present in the way it had been in the pre-Reformation era.

So, Isabella in *Measure for Measure* is both a misfit, a figure from a Catholic past and an allusion to an embattled Catholic present – both belonging and not belonging to the dominant culture. But, despite her minor moral inconsistency in consenting to the bed-trick, she is, in this drama of hypocrisy and devious manipulation, a centre of moral integrity and strength – not assimilable, despite the dramatic and closural pressure to draw her into the social network of the marital couples of the play's conclusion. It is as though Shakespeare were asking at the end of this play 'Where does Isabella belong?' and leaving the audience with no easy answer.

One of the regular charges that Protestant writers levelled against Catholic priests, especially Jesuits, was that they passed off theatre and trickery as supernatural manifestations and miracles. Samuel Harsnett thus debunked exorcisms as fraudulent religious spectacle.[76] Anti-Jesuit writers offered examples of staged apparitions meant to deceive naive believers into accepting the spiritual (and financial) guidance of those missionaries.[77] In the theatre, plays not only incorporated apparitions, visions and other supernatural phenomena in their actions but also frequently exposed them as artistic and/or villainous contrivances. But, as the story of the extra on-stage devil in a performance of Marlowe's *Dr. Faustus* testifies,[78] in the theatre (as well as in the everyday world) there was an epistemological instability, an uncertainty about the boundary between the real and the illusory related to the culture's transitional state between a previous era in which religion was much more imbued with superstition, magic, and the miraculous and an emerging modern culture of scripturally centred faith and secular rationalism.

Shakespeare composed both tragedies and tragi-comedies that contain non-satiric expressions of some of the very experiences of the miraculous and wondrous that Protestant polemicists and rationalists were debunking as part of the old religion's supposed superstition and trickery. In one sense Shakespeare (like many conservative Protestants) might have been trying to salvage for a post-Catholic English culture some of those emotionally powerful features of medieval Catholicism that broadened the range of religious experience and perception, preserving a sense of the mysteriousness and wondrousness of both the natural and supernatural worlds. Rather than restricting the workings of mystery, wonder and miracle to the mind or heart of the fervent protestant believer or to those historical events that could be coded as povidential deliverances, Shakespeare did not wish to separate himself absolutely from the older ways of perceiving the mysterious, the miraculous and the wondrous as immanent in a broad range of human experience.[79] He was not willing (if only for good dramaturgical reasons) to abandon these sources of power. This is clear in a play such as *A Midsummer Night's Dream*, where the political and intellectual authority of Theseus is compromised by his opposition not only to 'fairy toys' (5.1.3) – an objection that associates him with Protestant polemicists[80] – but also to 'imagination' (5.1.8) in both its aesthetic and its amorous manifestations.

As Stephen Greenblatt and Louis Montrose have argued, the English Renaissance theatre captured some of the power of the old religion in absorbing some of the very features purged from it by Protestant reformers.[81] Repeatedly Shakespeare asserts the validity of experiences not accounted for by a strict standard of rationality. Although, as Huston Diehl maintains, Shakespeare often metadramatically analysed the illusion-making power of the theatre, he nevertheless rescued from an older culture, and from the 'old religion' specifically, those very modes of perception and belief that were under attack (as Catholic 'superstition') by polemical Protestant writers and by rationalistic sceptics (such as Reginald Scot). Diehl's argument that Elizabethan dramatists developed a *Protestant* way of seeing and interpreting visual images is a needed corrective to those who, like Montrose and Greenblatt, draw too sharp a line between Protestant iconoclasm and theatre. I am uncomfortable, however, with her reliance on the theory, rather than the practice, of dramatic representation and with her assumption that dramatists such as Marlowe and Shakespeare are being programmatically didactic.[82] In Shakespeare's case I think it misleading to concentrate on the ways in which this dramatist's metadramatic devices school the audience in critical Protestant interpretation of theatre magic, since this is only one component of Shakespearean practice and metadramatic consciousness can also, paradoxically, *increase* audience wonder and preserve the sphere of the marvellous from relentless rational assault. La Few's oft-cited comment in *All's Well* critiques such wholesale demystification: 'They say miracles are past, and we have our philosophical persons to make modern and familiar things supernatural and causeless' (2.3.1–3).[83]

One of the points of dispute between Protestantism and Catholicism, of course, was miracles: the age of miracles had passed, according to the Reformers, and any contemporary miracle-mongering was priestly trickery and/or diabolical deception. In his plays Shakespeare expresses contradictory attitudes towards supernatural manifestations and signs, the first sceptical, if not mocking,[84] the second receptive and admiring. In the romantic and problem comedies and in the histories, supernatural manifestations are usually associated with delusion and self-delusion: Shakespeare satirizes Joan La Pucelle's mystical self-aggrandizement in *1 Henry VI* and Glendower's in *1 Henry IV*; in *The Comedy of Errors* and *Twelfth Night* he portrays exorcism as deceit. In the romances they are taken seriously – in, for example, the theophany in *Pericles* (5.1),[85] the dream vision in *Cymbeline* (5.4) and in the statue scene in *The Winter's Tale* (5.3).[86]

Huston Diehl has a brilliant discussion of the relationship of Protestant iconophobia and gynophobia, especially in Stuart love tragedy, pointing out the connections between Protestant fears of antitheatricality and of idolatry. But, earlier in her book, she points to a very different set of connections when she treats the way the playwright 'directs attention to "God's workmanship"'. She says that

> By embracing the notion, cherished by Calvinists, that the visible world is itself a 'magnificent' theater created by the great 'Artificer', Shakespeare deflects his own capacity to inspire wonder onto a deity Calvin calls the 'wonder-worker'. Shakespeare's remarkable achievement redeems art, rescuing theater (at least temporarily) from antitheatrical threats by transforming (before our very eyes in *The Winter's Tale*) the bewitching image – painted and stony, dead and man-made – into a living person, wrinkled by time.[87]

But Hermione as a Giulio Romano statue is treated very differently from those seductive, bewitching heroines of Stuart love tragedy Diehl discusses or the ridiculous dancing statues Middleton inserts in *A Game at Chesse* (5.1) as an example of Roman Catholic trickery and idolatry.

Shakespeare's romances or tragi-comedies reflect a sensibility closer to the Catholic Providentialism and paganism of Giambattista Guarini, the early modern inventor of pastoral tragi-comedy, than to the witty rationalism of John Fletcher. Julia Reinhard Lupton, for example, reads the pastoral polytheism of the Bohemian scenes of *The Winter's Tale* as 'rustic English paganism, the country remains of Catholic syncretism'.[88] What Shakespeare might easily demystify, he remystifies and makes ambiguous, participating in a rehabilitation of magic and the visual that is elaborated in the Stuart Court masque. Though he was alert to the intellectual and political complexities and ambiguities of his world and he may have outwardly conformed to the official state religion, Shakespeare could not, and apparently did not wish to, sever his or his culture's ties to a Catholic past and its residual cultural presence.

Notes

Earlier versions of this chapter were presented as papers at the 1999 Shakespeare Association of America national convention and at the July 1999 conference Lancastrian Shakespeare at the University of Lancaster.

1 For a recent inventory of biblical and liturgical references in Shakespeare's plays of see Naseeb Shaheen, *Biblical References in Shakespeare's Plays* (Newark and London, 1999).

2 See, for example, Roland Mushat Frye, *Shakespeare and Christian Doctrine* (Princeton, 1963); Roy Battenhouse (ed.), *Shakespeare's Christian Dimension: An Anthology of Commentary* (Bloomington and Indianapolis, 1994); Debora Shuger, 'Subversive fathers and suffering subjects: Shakespeare and Christianity', in *Religion, Literature, and Politics in Post-Reformation England, 1540–1688*, ed. Donna B. Hamilton and Richard Strier (Cambridge: Cambridge University Press, 1996), pp. 46–69; John Cox, *Shakespeare and the Dramaturgy of Power* (Princeton, 1989); and Judy Kronenfeld, *King Lear and the Naked Truth: Rethinking the Language of Religion and Resistance* (Durham and London, 1998). The last three criticize new historicist and cultural materialist readings of a nascent modern radicalism in the drama by pointing to both older and contemporary Christian thought that underlay various forms of resistance and political critique.

3 Leah Marcus, *Puzzling Shakespeare: Local Reading and its Discontents* (Berkeley, Los Angeles, and London, 1988), pp. 148–59; J. Chris Hassel, *Renaissance Drama and the English Church Year* (Lincoln and London, 1979), pp. 38–41.

4 See, for example, Donna Hamilton, *Shakespeare and the Politics of Protestant England* (New York, London, etc, 1992), and Huston Diehl, *Staging Reform,*

Reforming the Stage: Protestantism and Popular Theater in Early Modern England (Ithaca and London, 1997).

5 See E. A. J. Honigmann, *Shakespeare: The 'Lost Years'*, 2nd edn (Manchester and New York, 1998); Richard Wilson, 'Shakespeare and the Jesuits', Times Literary Supplement, 19 December 1997, pp. 11–13.

6 See, for example, H. Mutschmann and K. Wentersdorf, *Shakespeare and Catholicism* (New York, 1952).

7 Christopher Haigh, *English Reformations: Religion, Politics, and Society under the Tudors* (Oxford, 1993); John Bossy, *The English Catholic Community 1570–1850* (New York, 1976), and Eamon Duffy, *The Stripping of the Altars: Traditional Religion in England 1400–1580* (New Haven and London, 1992).

8 Lowell Gallagher, *Medusa's Gaze: Casuistry and Conscience in the Renaissance* (Stanford, 1991); Deborah Kuller Shuger, *Habits of Thought in the English Renaissance: Religion, Politics, and the Dominant Culture* (Berkeley and Los Angeles, 1990), and *The Renaissance Bible: Scholarship, Sacrifice, and Subjectivity* (Berkeley, Los Angeles and London, 1994); and Frances Dolan, *Whores of Babylon: Catholicism, Gender, and Seventeenth-century Print Culture* (Ithaca and London, 1999).

9 Peter Milward, *Shakespeare's Religious Background* (Chicago, 1973); Hamilton, *Shakespeare and the Politics of Protestant England*; Diehl, *Staging Reform*.

10 See Alexandra Walsham, *Church Papists: Catholicism, Conformity and Confessional Polemic in Early Modern England* (Woodbridge and Rochester, 1993).

11 Haigh defines this term at length: ' "anglicans", because of their stress on the Prayer Book and insistence that "there is as good edifying in those prayers and homilies as in any that the preacher can make"; and "parish" because of their emphasis on the harmony and vitality of the village unit, at play and at worship. Their model minister was not the divisive godly preacher, but . . . the pastor who read services devoutly, reconciled quarrellers in his parish, and joined his people for "good fellowship" on the ale bench. These "parish Anglicans" and their favoured clergy had not been moved by the evangelistic fervour of the Protestant Reformation – indeed, in the sense that they knew little of doctrine and rejected justification by faith and predestination they were not Protestants at all. But, despite some similarity between their views and those of their pre-Reformation forebears, they were no longer Catholics: they had been neglected by the missionary priests, and they attended the services of the Church of England and demanded obedience to its liturgy . . . Although theirs was a residual religion, and they were the spiritual leftovers of Elizabethan England, they should not be dismissed as "mere conformists", for in their defence of ceremonies and festivities they formed a factor to be reckoned with. Indeed, it was their demand for some ritual in their services which made possible – even made necessary – the drive for liturgical uniformity carried out by Whitgift and Bancroft. Later, their kind would provide the parochial foundations upon which the Laudian Church was built, and a considerable body of support for Caroline ceremonialism and Arminian doctrine' ('The Church of England, the Catholics and the people', in *The Reign of Elizabeth*, ed. Christopher Haigh (Basingstoke and London, 1984), (pp. 218–19). Haigh 205 (9.1) uses the term 'mere conformists' to designate Catholics and conservatives within the Church of England who were, in effect, 'anti-Protestants' (p. 218).

12 *Ibid.*, pp. 196, 198.

13 The first was a priest arrested at the time of the Babington Plot who published a sermon recanting his Catholicism in 1589, the second an ex-Catholic who wrote anti-Catholic, anti-Jesuit works in the early 1620s (e.g. *The Foot out of the Snare* (1624)), the third a Jesuit-educated son of the (Catholic) English ambassador to Spain who printed *The English Spanish Pilgrim* (1630) as evidence of his reconciliation to the Church of England.

14 See Thomas Graves Law, *A Historical Sketch of the Conflicts between Jesuits and Seculars in the Reign of Queen Elizabeth* (London, 1889), Arnold Pritchard, *Catholic Loyalism in Elizabethan England* (Chapel Hill, 1979), pp. 120–74, and Peter Milward, *Religious Controversies of the Elizabethan Age* (London, 1977), pp. 116–24. Using problematic verbal evidence, David Kaula has argued Shakespeare's interest in this intramural Catholic dispute in *Shakespeare and the Archpriest Controversy* (The Hague and Paris, 1975).

15 See Peter Milward, *Religious Controversies of the Jacobean Age* (Lincoln and London, 1978), pp. 89–119.

16 *Ibid.*, pp. 90–1.

17 See *Conversations with* [William] *Drummond* [of Hawthornden], in *Ben Jonson*, ed. C. H. Herford and Percy Simpson, vol. 1 (Oxford, 1925), p. 141.

18 See Park Honan, *Shakespeare: A Life* (New York and Oxford, 1998), pp. 51, 63–4, on Simon Hunt, Thomas Jenkins and John Cottom.

19 Honan, *Shakespeare*, p. 32, points out that catechizing was required of everyone over six and under twenty for one hour a day, and school exercises in translation into Latin from the Geneva Bible were standard (p. 49).

20 Anthony Milton, 'A qualified intolerance: the limits and ambiguities of early Stuart anti-Catholicism', in *Catholicism and Anti-Catholicism in Early Modern English Texts*, ed. Arthur F. Marotti (Basingstoke and London and New York, 1999), pp. 85–115.

21 See Pritchard, *Catholic Loyalism in Elizabethan England*.

22 *William Shakespeare: A Compact Documentary Life* (New York, 1977), p. 61.

23 'For much of his life-particularly in his first two decades in Stratford – he was almost certainly a church papist; in those years he could easily have acquired his evident familiarity with the homilies. Once he began dividing his life between London and Stratford, he might have become a recusant, or he might have continued the caution of occasional conformity. Certainly, like the vast majority of English Catholics, he had no appetite for martyrdom' ('Forms of opposition: Shakespeare and Middleton', *ELR*, 24 (1994), p. 298).

24 *Ibid.*, p. 314.

25 See James Shapiro, 'Revisiting *Tamburlaine*: *Henry V* as Shakespeare's belated Armada play', *Criticism*, 31: 4 (Fall 1989), pp. 351–66, for a discussion of Shakespeare's history in relation to invasion fears of 1599.

26 Here and elsewhere I quote from the Oxford edition of Shakespeare's works as reproduced in *The Norton Shakespeare*, ed. Stephen Greenblatt *et al.* (New York and London, 1997).

27 See, for example, *1 Henry VI* 4.2.28; *Richard III* 1.4.191; *King John* 5.2.6; and *Richard II* 5.2.97–9.

28 Jeffrey Knapp, 'Preachers and players in Shakespeare's England', *Representations*, 44 (Autumn 1993), pp. 29–59, discusses Shakespeare's aversion to 'episcopal militarism' (p. 36).

29 See Andrew Gurr, *Playgoing in Shakespeare's London* (Cambridge, pp. 1987), 148–9, on Henslowe's company's production of militantly Protestant 'Elect Nation' plays. See also Margot Heinemann, *Puritanism and Theatre: Thomas Middleton and Opposition Drama under the Early Stuarts* (Cambridge, 1980), and Paul Whitfield White, 'Theater and religious culture', in John D. Cox and David Scott Kastan (eds), *A New History of Early English Drama* (New York, 1997), pp. 145–6.

30 Cf. Falstaff's comment in *1 Henry IV* about a partner in crime, 'O, if men were to be saved by merit, what hole in hell were hot enough for him?' (1.2.94–6). In *Love's Labour's Lost*, the Princess uses a metaphor that sarcastically refers to the new Protestant orthodoxy that rejects salvation by works (or 'merit'): 'See, see, my beauty will be saved by merit! / O heresy in fair, fit for these days' (4.1.21–2).

31 For this particular religio-political mythology see William Maltby, *The Black Legend in England: The Development of Anti-Spanish Sentiment* (Durham, 1971). Anti-Hispanic dramas include, in addition to Thomas Kyd's post-Armada *The Spanish Tragedy*, Peele's *Battle of Alcazar* (1594), Dekker's *Lust's Dominion* (1599), and (Anon.), *The Weakest Goeth to the Wall* (1600), *A Larum for London* (1602) (subtitled *The Siege of Antwerp*) – see a discussion of these and of other anti-Catholic dramas in Rainer Pineas, *Tudor and Early Stuart Anti-Catholic Drama* (Nieukoop, 1972). For connections between Shakespeare's characterization of Iago (and Roderigo) and of an anti-Hispanism reactivated by the 1604 peace negotiations with Spain see Eric Griffin, 'Un-sainting James: or, Othello and the "Spanish Spirits" of Shakespeare's Globe', *Representations*, 62 (Spring 1998), pp. 58–99. Cf. Diehl's chapter on *Othello* (pp. 125–55) and Robert N. Watson, '*Othello* as Protestant propaganda', in *Religion and Culture in Renaissance England*, ed. Claire McEachern and Debora Shuger (Cambridge, 1997), pp. 234–57.

32 See, for example, 5.7. pp. 112–18.

33 The monasteries and abbeys are taxed to support the Crown's military needs (3.2.17–19).

34 In John Foxe's *Actes and Monuments* (*Book of Martyrs*), one of the woodcuts illustrates the latter scene. In his Arden edition of *King John*, 4th edn (London, Cambridge, Mass., 1954), E. A. J. Honigmann points out that Pandulph's promise (3.1.102–5) in the play of 'canonization for regicide' might have reminded Shakespeare's audience of the papal Bull of Excommunication of Elizabeth, but, more specifically, of the Catholic League's campaign to have Clement canonized, which was 'the burning question in 1589–90' (p. xlvi).

35 New York, 1946, pp. 180–224.

36 'Forms of opposition', p. 299.

37 For a discussion of Catholic resistance and resistance theory see Peter Holmes, *Resistance and Compromise: The Political Thought of Elizabethan Catholics* (Cambridge, 1982).

38 See *The Oldcastle Controversy*, ed. Peter Corbin and Douglas Sedge, The Revels Plays Companion Library (Manchester and New York, 1991). Reminding his

readers of the Catholic character of Elizabethan Lancaster, in reviving discussion of the possible connection between N. D.'s [Robert Parsons's] *A Conference About the Next Succession to the Crowne of Ingland* and Shakespeare's dramatization in the second tetralogy of material relevant to the sensitive question of the succession, Richard Dutton, 'Shakespeare and Lancaster', *SQ*, 49:1 (Spring 1998), p. 17, contextualizes John Speed's comment on the dramatization of a 'ruffian' Oldcastle by Persons and Shakespeare, '"the papist and his poet"'.

39 'Killed with hard opinions: Oldcastle, Falstaff, and the reformed text of *I Henry IV*', in *Textual Formations and Reformations*, ed. Laurie E. Maguire and Thomas L. Berger (Newark and London, 1998), pp. 211–27; at 217. Kristen Poole, 'Saints alive! Falstaff, Martin Marprelate, and the staging of Puritanism', *SQ*, 46:1 (Spring 1995), pp. 47–75, similarly argues that Shakespeare, in the context of 1590s anti-Puritan satire, satirizes Oldcastle as a carnivalesque Puritan and that the name change from Oldcastle to Falstaff was occasioned by the hostile response of that sector of his audience that wished to perceive Oldcastle as a Lollard martyr.

40 Cited in the Revels edition of Thomas Middleton's *A Game at Chesse*, ed. T. H. Howard-Hill (Manchester and New York, 1993), p. 205.

41 Mary A. Blackstone and Cameron Louis, 'Towards "A full and understanding auditory": new evidence of playgoers at the First Globe Theatre', *MLR*, 90:3 (July 1995), pp. 556–71, discuss the disruptive behaviour of a group of recusant theatergoers at the Globe in 1612 in relation to the different point of view such spectators might have brought to the Catholic elements of a play such as Webster's *The Duchess of Malfi*. See I. J. Semper, 'The Jacobean theater through the eyes of Catholic clerics', *SQ*, 3 (1952), pp. 45–51, for a discussion of evidence that both Catholic clergy and lay people regularly attended performances at the public playhouses.

42 'The hybrid reformations of Shakespeare's second Henriad', *Comparative Drama*, 32 (Spring 1998), pp. 176–206.

43 '"All is true": negotiating the past in *Henry VIII*', in *Elizabethan Theater: Essays in Honor of S. Schoenbaum*, ed. R. B. Parker and S. P. Zitner (Newark and London, 1996), pp. 147–66. Walter Cohen states: 'Fletcher's sections of the play arguably have a more pro-Protestant outlook than Shakespeare's relatively balanced and uncommitted treatment of religious controversy. And the distinction may even extend to the title, with *All Is True* representing Shakespeare's evenhanded view and *The Famous History of the Life of Henry the Eighth* Fletcher's celebration of the king who broke with Rome' (*Norton Shakespeare*, 3118).

44 Hamilton, *Shakespeare and the Politics of Protestant England*, pp. 163–90.

45 In *The Winter's Tale*, Paulina refers to heretic-burning in a critical way in language that evokes John Foxe's perspective, 'It is an heretic that makes the fire, / Not she which burns in't' (2.3.115–16). John Kerrigan, 'Revision, adaptation, and the Fool in *King Lear*', in Gary Taylor and Michael Warren (eds), *The Division of the Kingdoms: Shakespeare's Two Versions of* King Lear, p. 223, dates the revision of the play in 1609–10 and thus has the Fool's line 'No heretics burned, but wenches' suitors' (3.3.83) written before the last heretic burnings in the era, those of the Socinian religious radicals Legate and Wightman.

46 G. R. Elton, *Reform and Reformation: England, 1509–1558* (Cambridge, Mass., 1977), pp. 103–11, notes that the coincident sack of Rome, which resulted in the Pope's becoming a virtual prisoner of the Holy Roman Emperor, Charles V (Queen Katherine's nephew), doomed the divorce petition from the start.

47 Introduction to John Gerard, *Autobiography of a Hunted Priest*, trans. Philip Caraman (New York, 1952), p. x–xi.

48 John Klause, 'Politics, heresy, and martyrdom in Shakespeare's Sonnet 124 and *Titus Andronicus*', in *Shakespeare's Sonnets: Critical Essays*, ed. James Schiffer (New York and London, 1999), pp. 219–40, at 224–6. Klause suggests that *Titus* "must have spoken with a special force to a certain part of [Shakespeare's] audience, moderate lay Catholics who might have seen the play even in its initial productions by the acting company of Lord Strange, a suspect Protestant whose ambience was Catholic. For many of them, who wished to preserve an integrity of conscience but did not yearn for the glory of martyrdom, both the Machiavellianism of the Goths and the austere *Romanitas* of Titus were cause for dismay in reminding them of the religious politics of their own time" (p. 235).

49 Milward, *Shakespeare's Religious Background*, p. 69.

50 See the note to 3.2.135 in the (second) Arden edition of this play: William Shakespeare, *Julius Caesar*, ed. T. S. Dorsch (Cambridge, Mass., 1955), pp. 83. The 'bloody napkin' (4.3.92) in *As You Like It* may have similar resonance.

51 Klause, 'Politics', pp. 222–32.

52 A pax or 'paxbread' was, as Duffy, *The Stripping of the Alters*, p. 125, explains, 'a disk or tablet on which was carved or painted a sacred emblem, such as the Lamb of God or the Crucifix. This pax was . . . taken [after being blessed by the priest at Mass] by one of the ministers or . . . by the clerk, to the congregation outside the screen, where it was kissed by each in turn . . . [It was] clearly a substitute for the reception of communion.' See See Knapp's discussion, 'Preaches and Players', pp. 39–40, of Bardolph's stealing of the pax in relation to Protestant criticisms of Catholic materialism and political manipulation. Lisa Hopkins has recently argued ('Neighbourhood in Henry V', in *Shakespeare and Ireland: History, Politics, Culture*, ed. Mark Thornton Burnett and Ramona Wray (Basingstoke and London, 1997, pp. 9–26) that there is a strong emphasis on Catholicism in *Henry V*.

53 See Battenhouse, *Shakespeare's Christian Dimension*, p. 164.

54 *Shakespearean Negotiations: The Circulation of Social Energy in Renaissance England* (Oxford, 1990), pp. 121–2 – but this was noted much earlier by Henry Bowden (1899), as indicated by Battenhouse, p. 5. Greenblatt discusses *King Lear* as Catholic allegory in relation to its performance, along with *Pericles*, in a recusant house in Yorkshire in 1609/10. Cf. John L. Murphy, *Darkness and Devils: Exorcism and King Lear* (Athens, 1984), pp. 93–118, on the recusant theatre company, the Simpsons, and their legal troubles for staging for recusant audiences (in addition to *King Lear*, *Pericles* and *The Travels of the Three English Brothers*) a St Christopher's play with a disputation between a Protestant minister and Catholic priest which the latter wins.

55 See Cecile M. Jagodzinski, *Privacy and Print: Reading and Writing in Seventeenth-century England* (Charlottesville, 1999), p. 33.

56 See Gary Wills, *Witches and Jesuits: Shakespeare's* Macbeth (New York and Oxford, 1995), and Leeds Barroll, *Politics, Plague and Shakespeare's Theatre: The Stuart Years* (Ithaca and London, 1991), pp. 235ff.

57 *The Pathology of the English Renaissance: Sacred Remains and Holy Ghosts* (Leiden, Boston, and Cologue, 1998), pp. 7, 3.

58 *Purity and Danger: An Analysis of Concepts of Pollution and Taboo* (London and Henley, 1966), p. 62.

59 Michael O'Connell, 'The idolatrous eye: iconoclasm, antitheatricalism, and the image of the Elizabethan theater', *ELH*, 52 (1985), pp. 279–310. O'Connell has recently argued for the influence of the Coventry Corpus Christi dramas on the young Shakespeare and, generally, for a greater scholarly acknowledgement of the vital connections between medieval religious drama and the professional theater of the late sixteenth century – 'Vital cultural practices: Shakespeare and the Mysteries', *Journal of Medieval and Early Modern Studies*, 29:1 (Winter 1999), pp. 149–68. These essays are incorporated in O'Connell's recent book, *The Idolatrous Eye: Iconoclasm & Theater in Early-modern England* (New York and Oxford, 2000). Cox argues for the influence of an Augustinian 'political realism' (p. xii and *passim*) on Shakespeare by way of medieval religious drama. Cf. the chapter, 'Shakespeare and the Mystery cycles', in Emrys Jones, *The Origins of Shakespeare* (Oxford, 1977), pp. 31–84, which emphasizes the influence of the dramatization of the Passion in the mysteries on Shakespeare's tragic dramaturgy.

60 Diehl, *Staging Reform*, pp. 125–55, 81–92.

61 Milward, *Shakespeare's Religious Background*, pp. 24–5. See also the account of Catholic language, practices and beliefs in Mutschmann and Wentersdorf's *Shakespeare and Catholicism*.

62 See Paul Whitfield White, *Theatre and Reformation: Protestantism, Patronage, and Playing in Tudor England* (Cambridge, 1993), for a discussion of reformers' use of theatre for religious instruction.

63 Pineas, *Tudor and Early Stuart Anti Catholic Drama*, p. 23. Honan, Shakespeare, p. 23, notes that 'Sodomismus in Bale's *Thre Lawes* appears as a monk (B2v), Flattrie as a friar in *Thrie Estaits* (l. 746), and Satan as a Catholic hermit in *The temptacyon of our lorde* (D3v). In *The Divils Charter*, a devil appears dressed as the pope (A2v), and Cacurgus in *Misogonus* . . . is probably dressed as both a fool and a monk.'

64 Examples include the Abbess in *Comedy of Errors* and the Friar in *Romeo and Juliet* (both figures of parental affection). Helena visits a Franciscan hostel in *All's Well* and Roy Battenhouse observes: 'No other Elizabethan dramatist dared stage friars in a favorable light as this play does' (*Shakespeare's Chirtian Dimension*, p. 163). Honan, *Shakespeare*, p. 205, citing the computer studies of Donald Foster, suggests that Shakespeare himself might have acted roles such as Friar Lawrence in *Romeo and Juliet* and the Friar in *Much Ado About Nothing*.

65 Milward, *Shakespeare's Religious Background*, p. 78.

66 Taylor, 'Forms of opposition', p. 311.

67 Milward, *Shakespeare's Religious Background*, p. 37. '[C]onverted' and its cognates are important recurrent terms in Shakespeare. See, for example, *As You Like It* 4.3.135, 5.4.150, 5.4.173; *Timon* 4.3.140; *Hamlet* 3.4.119; *Much Ado*

2.3.20 and 3.4.76; *Merchant of Venice* 3.5.29; *Henry VIII* 1.3.43; and *King John* 5.1.19. The 'holy man' or priest with whom Olivia enters the scene in *Twelfth Night* 4.3 is going to perform the marriage ceremony of Olivia and Sebastian in a place coded as Catholic, a 'chantry' (4.3.23–4).

68 This information comes by way of Nicholas Rowe (1709), cited in E. K. Chambers, *William Shakespeare: A Study of Facts and Problems*, 2 vols (Oxford, 1930), 2:265.

69 Mark Matheson, '*Hamlet* and "a matter tender and dangerous"', *SQ*, 46 (1995), pp. 383–97; at 390. Matheson sees in the play a mixture of such 'specific religious discourses' as those of 'Roman Catholicism, neo-Stoicism, and Protestantism . . . Religious discourse is integral to *Hamlet*, but Shakespeare's representation of religion in the play is oblique and inconsistent.' Cf. Peter Iver Kaufman, *Prayer, Despair, and Drama: Elizabethan Introspection* (Urbana and Chicago, 1996), pp. 7–9, 103–49, for a discussion of the play in relation to Calvinistic self-scrutinizing piety. Janis Lull suggests that text of the play in the First ('bad') Quarto is a de-Protestantized one suitable to specifically Catholic audiences – for example, in affirming 'the ethics of the post-feudal honor culture, especially the value of heroic individualism, whereas the F[olio] text shows Hamlet accepting the newer Protestant ethic by subordinating his individual will to divine providence . . . By selectively forgetting parts of *Hamlet* that allude to Protestant ideology, Q1 reinterprets the play, making it affirm the very warrior values that the F version calls into question' ('Forgetting *Hamlet*: the First Quarto and the Folio', in *The* Hamlet *First Published [Q1, 1603]: Origins, Form, Intertextualities*, ed. Thomas Clayton (Newark, London and Toronto, 1992), pp. 137–50, at 137 and 149.

70 For a recent cultural analysis of subject of purgatory in relation to this play see Stephen Greenblatt, *Hamlet in Purgatory* (Princeton, 2001).

71 There is a similar mixing of vocabularies in *The Tempest*. See David N. Beauregard, 'New light on Shakespeare's Catholicism: Prospero's epilogue in *The Tempest*', *Renascence*, 12:3 (Spring 1997), pp. 159–74. Richard Wilson, 'Voyage to Tunis: new history and the old world of *The Tempest*', *ELH*, 64 (1997), pp. 333–57, discusses the connections of *The Tempest* to the career of the renegade Catholic aristocrat Robert Dudley and to plans for a marriage of Prince Henry to the Catholic daughter of the Grand Duke of Tuscany.

72 Quoted in James Biester, *Powerful Insinuations: The Rhetoric of Lyric Wonder* (Ithaca and London, 1997), p. 17.

73 Dorothea Kehler, 'The First Quarto of Hamlet: reforming widow Gertred', *SQ*, 46 (1995), pp. 398–413, suggests that the religiously conservative portrayal of Hamlet's mother in the First Quarto in that version of the play was most suited for performance in Catholic households or parts of the country that had a high Catholic population.

74 Milward, *Shakespeare's Religious Background*, p. 22.

75 See, for example, the letter from Sister Mary Goch of the Poor Clares convent at Graveling, a copy of which is preserved in the Archives of the Archdiocese of Westminster Mss. 8: 89–90. The Poor Clares were banned in England in 1540 along with the other religious orders. An English Poor Clares convent was established at Gravelines in the Low Countries (between Calais and Dunkirk) around 1575. They left Gravelines and resettled in the Flemish Poor Clare Convent at

St Omer (Mary Winefride Sturman, O.S.U., 'Gravelines and the English Poor Clares', *London Recusant*, 7.1 (1977), pp. 1–8).

76 *A Declaration of Egregious Popish Inmpostures* (1603), a work Greenblatt, *Shakespearean Negotiations*, pp. 94–128, discusses in relation to *King Lear*.

77 See, for example, John Gee, *New Shreds of the Old Snare* (1624), pp. 1–8, 10–25.

78 See E. K. Chambers, *The Elizabethan Stage*, vol. 3 (Oxford, 1923), p. 424. See Arata Ide, '*Doctor Faustus* and the appearance of the Devil', in *Japanese Studies in Shakespeare and his Contemporaries*, ed. Yoshiko Kawachi (Newark and London, 1998), pp. 11–24.

79 This is O'Connell's argument in 'The idolatrous eye'.

80 See François Laroque, *Shakespeare's Festive World: Elizabethan Seasonal Entertainment and the Professional Stage*, trans. Janet Lloyd (Cambridge, 1991), pp. 21–6.

81 Louis Montrose, *The Purpose of Playing: Shakespeare and the Cultural Politics of the Elizabethan Theatre* (Chicago and London, 1996), p. 25, argues that 'Popular and liturgical practices, ceremonial and dramatic forms were not systematically suppressed by the royal government but were instead selectively appropriated' – for example, for royal progresses and Accession Day festivities.

82 In the case of Marlowe, Diehl reads *Doctor Faustus* as an enactment of and elucidation of the wrong kinds of theatricality, rather than, for example, as the manifestation of a characteristically Marlovian aesthetic sadomasochism in which a cynical artist and gullible spectators are both pleasured by and punished for enjoying dazzling dramatic trickery.

83 See Marco Mincoff, *Things Supernatural and Causeless: Shakespearen Romance* (Newark London and Toronto, 1992); Peter G. Platt, *Reason Diminished: Shakespeare and the Marvelous* (Lincoln and London, 1997; and T. G. Bishop, *Shakespeare and the Theatre of Wonder* (Cambridge, 1996).

84 In 2 *Henry VI* (2.1) Shakespeare dramatizes a false 'miracle' claimed for the Shrine of St Albans. Honan, *Shakespeare*, p. 140, says of 1 *Henry VI*: 'Shakespeare's French hardly seem Catholic, except for an allusion to Joan's Mariolatry, and he does not refer to Catholic repression. His satire is that of a moderate Anglican.'

85 F. D. Hoeniger's Arden edition of *Pericles* emphasizes the connection with the miracle play form (pp. lxxxvii–xci – citation from Milward, *Shakespeare's Religious Background*, p. 36 and note). Taylor, 'Forms of opposition', p. 293, notes the evidence that Shakespeare composed the play with the Catholic George Wilkins and that it was played along with *King Lear* at an English recusant house in Yorkshire in 1609/10, but one does not have to go to Yorkshire to find Catholic spectators for Shakespeare's play, since they were in the London theatres. The play also appears on a book-list of mostly devotional and polemical work from the Jesuit college at St Omer in 1619, confirming its Catholic resonance: Willem Schrickx, ' "Pericles" in a book-list of 1619 from the English Jesuit mission and some of the play's special problems', *Shakespeare Survey*, 27 (1976), pp. 21–32, suggests that the play was probably performed at the Jesuit college.

86 See O'Connell's discussion of this in 'The idolatrous eye', *Staging Reform*, pp. 304–5.

87 Diehl, pp. 86–7.

88 *Afterlives of the Saints: Hagiography, Typology, and Renaissance Literature* (Stanford, 1996), p. 197.

The cultural politics of Maybe

Maybe it isn't exactly ethical to read other people's mail, but as we relish the licensed voyeurism of scholarship we can comfort ourselves, morally, with the knowledge that early modern Europeans never depended on the confidentiality of their correspondence. Even diplomatic correspondence. In 1620 the Venetian ambassador to London informed his superiors that 'no letters have arrived from Italy this week by the ordinary of Antwerp. It is thought that they have been intercepted . . . This sort of thing may happen frequently.'[1]

The Venetian ambassador's mail was apparently intercepted on its way through Antwerp, and the private letters I am going to open and read were all sent through Antwerp; indeed, they were sent to the man most likely responsible for intercepting that Venetian diplomatic correspondence. For more than a decade the English diplomat William Trumbull was 'resident agent of his Majesty King James' to the Court of the Archduke and Archduchess in Brussels; he controlled an extensive network of spies and informants throughout the Low Countries and the balkanized sub-states of the old Holy Roman Empire.[2]

Trumbull himself never showed the least interest in Shakespeare, but some of his correspondents did. One of them was an Oxford scholar and translator who wrote one of the commendatory poems which preface the first edition of *Mr William Shakespeares Comedies, Histories, and Tragedies*. His given name was James; his family name was usually spelled Mabbe (or Mebbe), but he at least apparently pronounced it 'Maybe'; his regular pseudonym 'Puede-Ser' means 'maybe', and is apparently a pun on his surname.[3] So I will call him, as he wished to be called, 'Maybe'.

Maybe's letter to Trumbull was written on 23 October 1622, about a year before publication of Shakespeare's *Comedies, Histories, and Tragedies*; it has never been published.[4] From the first sentence of this letter we can deduce that Maybe was replying to an earlier letter from Trumbull, and that the two men had never met; they struck up a correspondence

because Maybe was tutoring Trumbull's son at Oxford. But the real interest of this letter is what it tells us about Maybe's own political and religious
convictions. In fact this letter leads us into an unexplored network of letters
and documents; it links the publication of the Shakespeare First Folio to
the most contentious religious and political issues of early modern Europe;
and it raises epistemological anxieties which are as pressing for us as they
were for Shakespeare and his contemporaries. How can I know what
someone else believes? How can I know what to believe? Does it matter?

But before we can tackle these grand questions of history and theory, we
need to peek over someone's shoulder, and read Maybe.

> Sir.
>   Your Letters found mee at Oxforde, wch were very wellcome vnto mee,
> who haue long since wisht all good fortunes to followe you, more out of the
> knowledge of your worthe, then your person. W^{ch} as yet I haue not had the
> happines to inioye. But I hope to see you settled at lengthe in your owne
> Couuntrie, & to receiue the deserued recompence of ye long and faithefull
> seruices you haue donne his Matie. I can not tell whether I should impute yt
> to my discretion (though yt please you to stile yt so) or my destinie, that after
> a six yeares imployment abroad, I should retyre my selfe to my Cell. I can
> assure you I enuye none of your greate ones heere in Courte, but doe pitie
> some; & would not change my poore but contented present life, wth that w^{ch}
> the Marques

That is, the Marquess of Buckingham, the favourite of King James, and the
second most powerful man in England

> would not change my poore but contented present life, wth that wch the
> Marques leades, to inioy all his favours. I haue seene the stormes in forraine
> Courtes, & some in our owne. As allso obserued in Ministers abroad, how
> slowly moste of them are rewarded, & how sone exception taken. And that
> one oblique Action (& that not so in ytselfe; but by others interpretation, &
> malitious construction, where they intend to crushe) hathe ouerthrowne the
> painefull & faithfull indeuours of many yeares tedious wattchings & toylings.
> Had I beene forsaken of my noble Lord –

(The letter itself does not identify which 'noble lord' Maybe is talking
about; this is an important issue, but for the moment is must remain in
suspension.)

> Had I beene forsaken of my noble Lord for my falsehood, or showd myselfe
> careles & negligent in his seruice, & so forced to thruste my selfe into a corner,
> & to shunne the lighte, I should haue held my selfe of all men the moste mis-
> erable. But for that I knowe my Lord will abonar my true loue & seruice,
> and that my retyrednes was out of election, & not constraint, I holde yt no
> small happiness vnto mee, that I am, as I am: And I am glad that my resid-
> ing in Mag: Colege hathe brought the sonne of so deseruing a father to my
> Knowledge,

I will spare you Maybe's long paragraph praising Trumbull's son. His description of the boy's academic progress leads to the subject Maybe himself knew best: Spanish language and literature.

> Wee are now entred vpon the Spanishe. And for I am acquainted wth. the Spanishe fleagme, & how things goe on there muy de espacio, I hope he shall runne ouer the Spannishe, before that Spanishe Lady come ouer.

That 'Spanishe Lady' is an allusion to the Infanta, the younger sister of King Philip of Spain; England and Spain had for many years been negotiating the terms of a marriage between the Infanta and Prince Charles, the so-called 'Spanish Match', which was the key to the diplomacy of King James in the early 1620s. James believed that such a marriage, by creating an alliance between the ruling families of Catholic Spain and Protestant England, would force Spain to intervene in Germany on behalf of James's Protestant son-in-law, Frederick, the Elector Palatine, who by October 1622 had been completely driven from his territories by Catholic troops. The negotiations for this marriage and alliance were primarily entrusted to the English ambassador to Madrid, Sir John Digby, the Earl of Bristol; Maybe had in fact apparently been part of Digby's entourage during his 'six years' employment abroad'. Having segued from tutorials in the Spanish language to 'that Spanishe Lady', Maybe continues on the subject of the proposed marriage, and expresses considerable doubt about the wisdom of the King's policy.

> And so my Lorde of Bristoll, & his Companie were well at home, lett them go on with as muche leysure as they liste themselues. For I doe not see vpon what hinge can well hang, the Matche wth. Spaine, and y^e. losse of the Palatinate. Besides, his Matie. heere, subsists of himselfe, and hathe no diuerticula, or starting holes to flye to; whereas the Catholic King, hathe many euasions yf hee liste; As to please ye Popes vnwillingness, & hardnes to bee drawne to yeelde to suche a Matche. And ye distaste his owne Cleargye take thereat. And for the Palatinate, hee will putt that ouer vpon y^e. Emperour, & hee will poste y^e. same ouer vpon Bauaria. So that betweene these stooles, wee may plainely see whose tayle is like to goe to ground. But wheth^r doe I roue? This is not a marke for suche arrowes as are taken out of the Vniuersities quiuer. I will therefore vnbend my bowe, leaste (as yt is in ye prouerb) I mighte seeme to shoote my bolte.

The proverb being, of course, 'a fool's bolt is soon shot'.

> I will leaue therfore the construction of these things to your selfe, & other publick Ministers abroad, who are able to make a nimble apprehension of theyr good or badd intentions ...

Maybe was remarkably prescient about the eventual failure of the Spanish Match. The Spanish did indeed prolong the negotiations by seeking approval from the Pope – which was of course given only upon conditions which the English could not accept. King James wanted the King of Spain to pressure his Habsburg kinsman Ferdinand, the Holy Roman Emperor, to restore the territories of the Palatinate to Frederick; but King Philip knew, better than King James, that Ferdinand would pay very little attention to Spanish requests, and that the conquest of the Palatinate had in fact been driven by Ferdinand's most important military ally, Maxmilian, Duke of Bavaria. Even if it had been consummated, the Spanish Match would not have untangled the military and political problems of central Europe. In the end there was no Spanish Match, and no restoration of the Palatinate, and England was sucked into the whirlpool of the Thirty Years War.

But from our perspective Maybe's prescience is less important than his ideology. His criticisms of the Spanish Match were those which had been voiced, for more than two years, by increasingly exasperated and worried Protestants, in England and abroad. In April 1622, only six months before this letter was written, one of Maybe's Oxford colleagues had been arrested after delivering a sermon which appeared to justify resistance to the King's policies; he was still in the Fleet prison, as were many other Protestant critics of the Spanish Match. In August 1622, the King's 'Directions concerning Preaching' effectively silenced ecclesiastical resistance, or at least drove it underground.[5] Maybe's letter of October 1622 not only voiced the dissent of the English Protestant opposition; it did so at a particularly dangerous time, in a letter to one of the King's own ministers. Indeed, Maybe's attitude to the Spanish Match almost perfectly corresponds to the policy of William Herbert, the Earl of Pembroke, the leader of the anti-Catholic faction in the Privy Council – and, of course, a man to whom the Shakespeare First Folio was dedicated. Could it be that the Shakespeare First Folio was promoted by a coalition of opposition Puritans?

But before we sell the film rights to Oliver Stone, we need to read another unpublished letter to Trumbull: not a letter by Maybe but a letter about him. This letter, dated 5 July 1622, was written by George Abbot, Archbishop of Canterbury, a regular correspondent of Trumbull, and probably his most important political ally and patron; also, the most powerful Calvinist in England, and a fierce opponent of the Spanish Match.[6]

Good m^r Trumbull, I thanke you for all your love, as well expressed to mee by your brother as otherwise. There is reason of forbearance of letters, till some things bee setled, wherevnto I pray God to give a good ende, to the strengthening of the Gospel, and comfort of those who truly love religion and their countrey. When your sonne goeth to Oxon~, I shall recommend him in the best fashion that I can.

Of Mebbe I must say this to your selfe, and afterward other things for him. Hee lived long in Italy and Spaine, and as time showes, brought home many vices with him. Pretending a desire to bee reformed in religion (whiche bothe in him and others hath often catched mee, and cost mee great summes of mony) I intertained him, and approving his good parts, after one yeere I

tooke him into my chamber. His plenty made him wanton, idle, and machi-
nating mischeefe, and afterward I founde that hee served Diegos and the
Jesuites turnes vpon mee. I had advertisement out of Italy that I had a
perpetual spy vpon mee who gave intelligence of the most minute matters
concerning mee, and all to evill. Vpon the best advice that I could take, it
fell properly vpon Mebbe, and to make triall of it, I called him privately vnto
mee, and after a fewe wordes, I put my hande into his pocket to see what
papers hee had there. I founde diverse strange attempts of his machinations
vnder his owne hande, suche as could not bee but in a scholar of the Jesuites,
and one that had bene in Italy. Above the rest I founde one paper in
Spanishe, & some part of it in cipher, the rest in Turke wordes wherein were
related diverse things whiche hee heard from the LL. whispering one to
another at Starre chamber, the like at the Court, in my chamber, at my table,
all to make discord betweene great persons, & muche of it fained.

I questioned him about it, & promised him pardon if hee would deale truly
with mee, who set him on worke. Hee refused it, & I turned him out of my
doores. This came so vnexpected on him, that hee knew not whiche way to
turne him, but after a moneth taking ill counsel, hee gave the kinge two or 3.
sheetes of paper against mee, wherein some fewe wordes were lewde inoughe.
The kinge acquainted mee with it, and I prayed that his my. would commend
the examination of all things, to mr Secretary Naunnton, and mr Secretary
Calvert. They heard it, & reporting all to the king and among the rest his plot
to bee a Spy vpon his my, in a service of my L. of Buckingham whiche hee
then aimed at, by his my^s. direction he was laide vp close prisoner in the
Gate-house, & there continued 3. q~rs of a yeare till hee had made a good
submission vnto mee whiche I accepted yet chained him with bondes that hee
should bee forth-coming, whiche now hee hath broken. In the meane time
being there with you, hee hath discovered another mans villany against mee
who probably is as false a varlet as hee himselfe was. [sidewise along the left
margin:] I must take this as a mercy of God vpon mee, who so discovereth
Satans practises against mee, whiche avise I thanke God without my desert,
but for my constant opposing popery, and some other factious proceedings.
And of these machinations I have had stoure, by all, that for Christ & conscience sake, I have intertained out of Italy, yea by Spalato him selfe.

In this last phrase Abbot is referring to Marcantonio de Dominis,
Archbishop of Spalato, who had come to England as a convert to Protestantism, in what had seemed at the time a major propaganda victory; he
had been joyously welcomed by King James, Archbishop Abbot and many
others, but this political honeymoon was quickly followed by mutual ideological disillusionment, and earlier in 1622 Spalato had returned to Italy.
Abbot is thus comparing Maybe to a man Middleton would later immor-
talize, in *A Game at Chess*, as 'yon greasy turncoat gourmandizing prelate'
(2.2.54).[7] He has been so disllusioned by such men that he declares he will
no longer believe any such converts.

And of these machinations I have had stoure, by all, that for Christ &
conscience sake, I have intertained out of Italy, yea by Spalato him selfe. So

that I have now done with them, and will be wary of them as of a dragon or a Serpent. But for Mebbes parte (whome I vsed as my sonne rather than as my servant) I pray you do not beleeve all that hee saithe. ffor his protestations are with equivocation, as our eyes heere have assured vs; and hee meaneth, that of some particulars hee was not guilty, but another man did the like as hee did, whiche I now beleeve to bee true.

Concerning that whereof hee lately advertised mee, I pray you do this. Let him see no letters of mine, but by worde of mouth tell him, that I take well that whiche hee sent vnto mee, and in token thereof do both forgive him all his former errours, and pray God to blesse him, whiche I do not doubt but hee will do, if hee serve him and daily pray vnto him. Adde to this, that whereas hee writeth of a conspiracy whiche was two or three yeeres since against mee, I will bee glad to knowe what hee meaneth, and who those were that had hand in that wicked plot. Lastly tell him, that I shall take a time, God willing, to sift that party, whome hee hath in ielousy.

It should by now be clear that Abbot himself was the 'noble lord' that Maybe mentioned in his own letter to Trumbull. ('Had I beene forsaken of my noble Lord for my falsehood, or showd myselfe careles & negligent in his seruice, & so forced to thruste my selfe into a corner, & to shunne the lighte, I should haue held my selfe of all men the moste miserable.') Maybe did not know, of course, that Trumbull had already received the full story directly from Abbot; he did not know it, because Abbot gave Trumbull explicit directions on what to reveal to Maybe, and what to keep hidden. Abbot told Trumbull to lie to Maybe (or at least, to withhold the whole truth), so that Maybe would continue lying to Trumbull, unaware that Trumbull could see through all his 'equivocations'. By the time Trumbull received Maybe's letter of 23 October, Abbot had taught him how to read it.

Maybe and Abbot cannot both be telling the truth, and it is hard to avoid the conclusion that Maybe is the one lying. The vague philosophizing of Maybe's account contrasts strikingly with the circumstantial specificity of Abbot's narrative, supported by references to other figures – Naunton, Calvert, the King – who could easily confirm or deny its veracity; Trumbull corresponded with all three. Moreover, Abbot had no reason to deceive his trusted ally Trumbull, but Maybe had every reason to deceive his new acquaintance. And Abbot's charges are intrinsically plausible, given Maybe's lifelong love-affair with all things Spanish: after all, Maybe's first book, published within a year of this letter, includes the sentence 'O *Spaine, Spaine*, my beloved Countrey, Faith's true keeper, God vphold thee with his hand'.[8] Maybe could claim that he was just translating his Spanish author; but, given the freedom of other translations, he could easily have left out such phrases, and few English readers would have complained.

In the light of Abbot's letter, we are forced to read Maybe's letter rather differently. His reflections on the ingratitude of monarchs to their ministers

and diplomats, and on the insecurity of ministerial favour, not only exculpate himself, by explaining away his own retirement from Court; they also
reveal more than an apolitical Oxford don might be expected to know
about the government's repeated tardiness in paying Trumbull's salary and
expenses, and they intimate that Trumbull should not place too much confidence in his own political allies and superiors. Of course, if a badly paid
diplomat, uncertain of his own future, begins to doubt the integrity of his
superiors, he may eventually be persuaded that his own integrity is unap-
preciated, and that he might as well hedge his bets by playing both sides of
the game. Maybe's criticisms of the Spanish Match are equally cunning.
Given Maybe's previous associations with Abbot, Digby and Trumbull's
own son, he must certainly have known that Trumbull shared the general
Protestant unease with the King's policy. It cost Maybe nothing to tell
Trumbull what Trumbull already believed, about the inexpediency and probable failure of the Spanish negotiations; by doing so, he ingratiated himself
with Trumbull, while simultaneously presenting himself as an expert on
Spanish issues, and the sort of blunt, honest chap who says what he thinks
even when it is dangerously impolitic to do so.

Thus, what at first glance looked like the sincere expression of an
ardently Protestant and nationalist political position turns out to have been
a very sophisticated piece of political equivocation by a Catholic spy, trying
to ingratiate himself with an important English diplomat. Moreover,
Maybe's letter is not just an instance of personal dishonesty; there needs no
ghost come from the grave, no letter come from the archives, to tell us that
human beings lie from time to time. As Abbot's reference to 'equivocation'
demonstrates, Maybe's letter belongs to a historically specific, systematic
pattern of behaviour rationalized by an embattled ideology. Catholics under
Protestant regimes – like Protestants under Catholic regimes, or Jews and
atheists under Christian regimes – were forced to find ways to combine
outward conformity with inward resistance and spiritual integrity. Maybe's
letter illustrates Perez Zagorin's thesis, in his book *Ways of Lying*, that 'The
phenomenon of dissimulation rationalized by doctrine was so extensive that
it was like a submerged continent in the religious, intellectual, and social
life of early modern Europe'.[9] The systematic cultivation of ambiguity and
equivocation in Shakespeare's writing – celebrated by so many modernist
critics as evidence for the trans-historical complexity and objectivity of his
art – clearly belongs to the same programmatic double consciousness as
Maybe's 'I am that I am', or Iago's 'I am not what I am'. And Shakespeare's
occasional gestures toward religious conformity mean no more than
Maybe's criticism of the Spanish Match.

But that is not the end of the paper trail, or the end of the story. Because
Maybe also figures in a third letter written to Trumbull in the second half
of 1622. This letter was written by the chief publisher of the Shakespeare
folio, Edward Blount.[10] Like the other letters from Blount to Trumbull

which I am about to read, this manuscript was first noticed by E. A. J. Honigmann, who quoted some excerpts from it in 1965;[11] but Blount's letters have never been published in full, and Blount's own politics have never been investigated. Of course publishers have personalities and ideologies and canons, just as authors do. Like an author, a publisher simultaneously reflects and shapes a culture, transforming it in the process of transmitting it. The 1623 folio of *Comedies, Histories, and Tragedies* is Blount's work, as well as Shakespeare's works. And in the *longue durée* of European culture, what Blount made of Shakespeare has been far more visible, and far more important, than what Shakespeare himself believed. So, knowing what you now know about Maybe, listen to what Blount had to say about Maybe on 8 November 1622 (two weeks after Maybe's own letter to Trumbull):

> I must needes come in wth a Postscript too, and tell y^t your sonne is well, and a great proficient in the spanishe tongue, by the meanes of m^r. James Mabbe, of Magdalen College who takes as muche delight in reading to him and other gentlemen of that howse; as they take in that their desyre.

Six months later, Blount mentions Maybe in another letter to Trumbull, dated 30 May 1623 – only a few months before publication of the Shakespeare folio.

> Worthy S^r.
> A strickt charge was layed vpon me by my good freind mr. Mabb to send this inclosed safe to you: I am bound to obserue his Comand, and serue you: yesternight he did remember your health in a glasse of Canarye, wch was plighted by D^r. Fox, m^r. Rob: Dallington and my self. This morning he is gone for Oxford. And hath made half a promise to see Bruxells this somer if his Gout will giue him leaue and hath preuailed wth me to keepe him companye in that Iourneye. Here is litle newes worthy your self: Only I send you by this messenger, the History of Xenophon: and the Catholick moderator: wch are all the newe bookes come forth this tearme.

One of the two other men Blount mentions in this letter was Robert Dallington. Blount had published Dallington's *A Survey of the Great Dukes State of Tuscany* (STC 6200, 1605), which has been described as 'the first useful account of Italy since William Thomas's *History of Italy* of 1549',[12] and secondly *Aphorismes Civill and Militarie: Amplified with Authorities, and exemplified with Historie, out of the first Quarterne of Fr. Guicciardine* (STC 6197, 1613). According to his only modern biographer, Dallington was an important 'promotor of a more attractive image of Italy and mediator of a wider artistic culture which helped to overcome the aesthetic narrowness of the Elizabethan Protestant tradition'.[13] In other words Dallington was as closely associated with Catholic Italy as Maybe was with Catholic Spain. And one of the two books Blount mentions here – *The*

Catholic Moderator[14] – was an English translation of an original French text by the English recusant poet Henry Constable.[15]

Why is Edward Blount consorting with, and recommending to Trumbull, a Catholic spy like James Maybe? And why is he sending Trumbull a book written by a Catholic? Blount's first publication was a French poem, translated by an English merchant living in Catholic Brussels. He next published a book of French and Italian songs, with a French title-page.[16] He published dictionaries of Italian, Spanish and Latin works translated out of French, Italian, Spanish and neo-Latin European histories and European travel books.[17] A large majority of the foreign authors he published were Catholic. Moreover, by contrast with most English printers and publishers of the time, Blount devoted little of his attention to polemical or devotional Protestant texts. For instance, for the decade and a half before he formed a business partnership with William Barrett in 1608, he did not publish a single sermon, although that genre was very popular and profitable; moreover, the sermons which Blount and Barrett published together were always registered for copyright in Barrett's name only. Barrett, one might suspect, was Blount's cover, preventing anyone from noticing the remarkable absence of Protestantism in his career as a publisher.

We might begin at this point to suspect that the Shakespeare First Folio was promoted not by a conspiracy of opposition Puritans but by a conspiracy of underground Catholics. After all, 1623 was the high-water mark of Counter-Reformation publishing in English.[18] Look at the four men who wrote commendatory poems for the *Comedies, Histories, and Tragedies*. Both James Maybe and Leonard Digges were notorious hispanophiles; Hugh Holland was openly Catholic; Jonson had been a Catholic for a decade, and although by 1623 he might qualify as some sort of Protestant he openly loathed the aggressive Calvinist wing of the English church. After these Catholic or crypto-Catholic preliminaries, the Folio begins with *The Tempest*, a tragic-omedy which dramatizes the resolution of inter-state rivalry and political conflict through a dynastic marriage – like the proposed marriage between Prince Charles and the Catholic Infanta. And why does the volume end with *Cymbeline* – a play singularly inappropriately placed in the genre of tragedies? Perhaps because *Cymbeline* ends with the happy re-union of Britain and Rome. Is it simply a coincidence that the only known foreign purchaser of the Shakespeare First Folio, when it was new, was the Catholic Spanish diplomat Count Gondomar?

Maybe it *is* only a coincidence. Listen to another unpublished letter from Blount to Trumbull, this one written on 15 June 1621. Blount is obviously responding to a request, from Trumbull, to describe a theological debate which had taken place in London earlier that year:

> For your second demand or postscript, Concerning the priuate Conference
> betwee [*sic*] our englishe diuines and ministers and that dangerous Champion

Muskett; Thus. it is true y^t suche meetings ther were betweene D^r. Featly whome I suppose you well knowe to be a worthy learned Scholler, and the sayed Muskett, the occasion of these meetings were well grounded and iustly, but to long to relate two of theis meetings was att M^r. Bills howse, wher, by ye neerenesse of freindship, I was allowed to come my self and to bring 2· or 3· of my freinds, I carried m^r Dallington for one who was desyrous to be ther some others I gott in by fauor. Ther were many Schollers and gentlemen of the one syde, and many Catholick gentlemen and learneder priests then Muskett on ye other syde two priests for scribes of Musketts syde, .2· schollers for scribes of D^r. Featlyes syde but not to hold you long wth what is not worthy writing, I neuer heard nor knewe a more simple ignorant audacious shame-lesse foole then Muskett; such an one as I dare vndertake to finde in euery Colledge of Oxford and Cambridge, that haue not yett taken degree of m^r. of Art. 6. that shall make a Asse of him; for he had nothing in him but meere sophistry, and would neuer abyde to followe or counter an Argument. in a word, it was (as m^r. Dallington sayth) the vnequalest matche at Cock-fight that euer he was at. for the muche better scholler had the best cause, and the poorest leanest scholler had worst cause to defend.

I could devote several pages to identifying the various people mentioned in this paragraph, but instead I want to analyse for a moment Blount's own position. Of course, the obvious sectarian bias of his conclusion – that the Protestants had both the 'much better scholar' and 'the best cause' – could easily be dismissed, on the grounds that Blount is dissimulating, just as Maybe had dissimulated: both simply told Trumbull what Trumbull wanted to hear. But we can convict Maybe of a cover-up, because we found the smoking gun; for Blount there is no smoking gun. We can be certain about Maybe; but Blount is not so straightforward. How can we know whether Blount was lying, or telling the truth? After all, Blount's personal history is very different from Maybe's, or Shakespeare's. He was born and raised in London, in the few most consistently Protestant square miles in the kingdom; he lived his entire life in St Paul's churchyard, in the small community of the Stationers Company, where nonconformity of any kind would have been conspicuously visible, and would almost certainly have disqual-ified him from elevation to the guild's livery (in 1611) and the Court of Assistants (in 1622). Unlike Shakespeare, unlike Maybe, Blount was never, to my knowledge, accused of being a Catholic. Of course, maybe my knowl-edge is defective; maybe Blount, like his twenthieth-century namesake, was a remarkably cunning ideological mole. The fourth man.

Maybe. Maybe not. How can we know?

Maybe, in our pursuit of a question we cannot answer, we are over-looking the purloined letter in front of our faces. We will almost certainly never be certain of Blount's real verdict on the debate between the Jesuit Fr George Muschet and the Calvinist Dr Daniel Featley. But we can never-theless describe, with absolute certainty, Blount's position in relation to that debate. Blount positioned himself as a spectator. The great conflict between Catholic and Protestant, between Reformation and Counter-Reformation, the struggle which had already disturbed the political and psychological peace of Europe for more than a century – that world-historical *agon* had become, for Blount and his friend Robert Dallington, a spectator sport – like cockfighting: a very exclusive performance in a private home, an event not advertised or open to the general public, seating limited, admission by invitation only.

The disputation described here by Blount was not an isolated event. Dr Featley himself, the Protestant champion on this occasion, had starred in another such Catholic–Protestant disputation nine years before, in Paris.[19] Ben Jonson had been in the audience.[20] And Featley appeared again in another disputation in London two years later, excitedly described by the Cambridge letter-writer Joseph Meade, on 11 July 1623: 'This day sennight was a conference begun at S[r] Humfrey Lynes in Shore lane nere Temple-barre, where were many present of quality & some of honour. It began between D[r] Featley & Iesuite Fisher, held 5 houres, but Fisher would not answere one argument.'[21] Both sides published accounts of this debate.[22] The same Jesuit, Fr Fisher, had already been involved in two other 'private' debates, in January and May of 1622, staged for the benefit of the Count-ess of Buckingham, accompanied by the Lord Keeper Bishop Williams, the Marquis of Buckingham and his wife, and King James himself. The King had always been interested in theological debating; one of the first sub-stantive acts of his reign was the Hampton Court conference in January 1604, where the King met his bishops first 'in an inner withdrawing chamber . . . in a very private manner', and then 'in his privy chamber, in the presence of his privy council only' he 'in most excellent and extraordi-nary manner, disputed and debated' with several 'of the most learned of the preciser sort', from eleven in the morning till four in the afternoon, and 'confuted their objections'.[23] The King's participation in another private theological debate, in 1622, is thus hardly surprising in itself.[24]

The fate of the soul of the Countess of Buckingham matters less to me, I am afraid, than perhaps it should. What interests my critical self is: what do such debates imply about the culture in which they occur? Did Blount's faith hang upon the outcome of that debate between Dr Featley and Fr Muskett? If it did, then the occasion demonstrates the fragility and fungi-bility of the categories Catholic and Protestant; after all, many men and women in early modern England, in early modern Europe, moved from one category to another. Shakespeare's patron Southampton, however Catholic he may have been in 1593 and 1594 – or at least however Catholic he may have appeared to someone like Shakespeare who in 1593 clearly didn't really know him personally at all – that Catholic young man Southampton had publicly become Protestant by 1603, and probably by the late 1590s.

But what if, as seems to me more likely, Blount's faith did not hang on the outcome of that debate between Featley and Muskett? What if his attendance did not express a deep spiritual crisis, but something closer to mere intellectual curiosity? Contrast the relaxed wit of Blount's account – 'the unequalest match at Cockfight that ever he was at' – with the breathless earnestness of that precise Cambridge Protestant, the Reverend Joseph Meade: 'Dr Featly was to shew where our Church was before Luther &c Fisher was wholy confounded as well as confuted. Dr White should haue followed to proue the Pope not Head of the Church against Iesuite Sweet but the Iesuites could not by any meanes be brought to buckle with him, though before they had giuen out, he durst not dispute with them.' Contrast Blount's chatty nonchalance with the moving sixteenth-century descriptions of the suffering of men and women for whom such issues were literally worth dying for.

For Blount, in 1621, the debate between Catholic and Protestant was not a spiritual crisis, with souls hanging by the thread of a theological argument. Noticeably, Blount says nothing whatever about the actual theological content of the debate; he cannot be bothered to rehearse the arguments Tyndale and Campion had died to make. Instead, Blount describes the scene, the actors, the narrative of their interaction. For Blount, the only authority that matters is what Robert Weimann has described as 'the authority of performance'.[25] Maybe, to Blount, it didn't matter whether James Maybe, or Ben Jonson, or Hugh Holland, or William Shakespeare, was or was not a Catholic; maybe their authority as writers depended on linguistic performance, not religious belief. Maybe Blount published Maybe because Maybe was, as twentieth-century critics agree, one of the greatest English translators of any European language, and indeed one of the great English prose stylists of the seventeenth century.[26] Maybe Blount published John Earle, not because Earle was a Protestant bishop, but because his *Microcosmography* was the apex and epitome, in English, of the entire tradition of 'character' writing. Maybe Blount published Shakespeare, not because he was Catholic or Protestant, but because he was the most successful English playwright of Blount's generation.

In part, Blount's position as a spectator judging verbal performers is a natural consequence of his sixteenth-century humanist education. Blount was born two years before Shakespeare, and apparently attended the Merchant Taylors' School, where his education would have been organized around pedagogical exercises which routinely taught students to argue *'in utramque partem'*– on both sides of any question.[27] But what Joel Altman describes as 'the Tudor play of mind', or 'the moral culture of ambivalence', was not simply aesthetic, not ideologically neutral, in sixteenth-century Europe, so ferociously divided by theological binary oppositions. That pedagogy enabled the masterful evasiveness of men such as Shakespeare and Maybe.

And Marlowe. In the 1590s, Blount published Marlowe, not Shake-speare. We know from other sources that, before his death, Marlowe had made friends among the stationers in St Paul's churchyard, but the only sta-tioner ever publicly identified as Marlowe's friend, by himself and by others, was Edward Blount. In his preface to *Hero and Leander*, Blount described himself as the executor of his dead friend's literary estate. What does it mean to describe yourself as the executor of the most famous atheist in six-teenth-century England? What does it mean that the publisher of that puta-tive English atheist also published the first English translation of the most influential sceptic of sixteenth-century France, Montaigne, and the most influential demythologizer of seventeenth-century Spain, Cervantes? What does it mean that he also published the first English translation of Jose de Acosta's *Natural and Moral History of the Indies*, which Anthony Grafton has described as 'the most original and influential of all histories of the New World'– original in part because of its scepticism about ancient authority, its methodological empiricism, its cultural relativism?[28] What does it mean that the publisher of Marlowe, Montaigne, Cervantes and Acosta also pub-lished, soon after it appeared in France, the first English translation of Pierre Charron's 'scandalous book' *De la sagesse*, 'Of Wisdom'. Starting from the scepticism of Montaigne, Charron created, as Tullio Gregory has shown, one of the foundational texts of post-Christian philosophical atheism.[29] What does it mean that this most consistently secular publisher of early modern London, the literary executor of notorious sceptics and putative atheists, also published Shakespeare?

Maybe it means nothing. In the century after Luther nailed the Catholic church, the Reformation and the Counter-Reformation debated each other into permanent disequilibrium; each side deprived the other side of its authority, its legitimacy; each relentlessly and repeatedly exposed the other, until what had been *habitus* was transformed into a visible self-conscious contested ideology. Moreover, those visibly contested ideologies created a strong incentive for individuals to render their own ideology invisible. Maybe Blount is a Catholic or an atheist; maybe he is not; how can I know? But this epistemological question is directly related to others. Maybe the Catholics are wrong; maybe the Protestants are wrong; how can I know? Indeed, how can I know whether either of them is right? Maybe they are both wrong. How can I know? The sixteenth-century fissuring of Chris-tendom, the debates between and within denominations, are decisive ele-ments of 'the new histories of atheism' being written by historians such as David Wootton and John Sommerville, and literary critics such as Celia Daileader.[30] In the debate between Fr Muskett and Dr Featley, Blount was watching the play of ideology, and reporting it from a position which seemed outside of ideologies, a position which could somehow judge that one side or the other had the best debater and the best argument. That posi-tion – the position of the proudly impartial observer, the scientist, the journalist, the artist, the literary critic – becomes, of course, the dominnat paradigm of a new secular culture, the culture of Edward Blount, like ourselves a reader and transmitter and interpreter of texts – but also a businessman, working in the heavily capitalized and technologized world of early modern European text-production and text-marketing.

For a businessman, for men such as Heminges and Condell and Blount, the religion of a customer is irrelevant; a Catholic penny is worth no more, and no less, than a Protestant penny. Catholics and Protestants continued to do business with one another, across national and denominational boundaries, throughout the sixteenth century, and were accordingly distrusted by ideologues on both sides. From the point of view of business, another person's religion belongs to the category of *adiaphora*, things indifferent, matters about which members of a religious community – or a business community – were permitted to disagree. That theological category, the category of *adiaphora*, was introduced as a way of mediating and avoiding disputes; but the deeper and more persistent the divisions between Christians became, the more important and extensive the category of *adiaphora* had to become, until in the end 'indifference' or 'disinterestedness' was itself canonized as the most important social, cultural and intellectual virtue. In a world of apparently irresolvable difference, which created massive incentives for dissimulation, how could one confidently know the religious beliefs of a customer, or a playwright, or a bookseller? And if one could not know, if such beliefs made no discernible difference, then maybe matters of belief could be relegated, should be relegated, to the ever-expanding category of *adiaphora*. Medieval Catholicism was thus transformed into 'universality'; a religious claim to all-inclusiveness morphed into a commercialized aesthetic claim that 'One Bard Fits All'.

I have argued elsewhere that the early modern theatre was distinguished from all earlier forms of Western drama by the 'routinized commodification of affect'.[31] If we are to believe the moving stories told elsewhere in this volume, the emotional sources of *Hamlet* and *King Lear* are the tragedies of Elizabethan Catholic martyrs. But what is surely the most salient fact about those plays is not that an erudite modern scholar can crack the code of their secret Catholic referents and meanings; no, surely the more important fact, historically and culturally, is that any Catholic meanings they may have had were encrypted, simultaneously buried and made cryptic. Historically and culturally, the more important fact is that Shakespeare transformed all that real grief, real pain, real loss, real sacrifice, all that individual and collective religious trauma, into an apparently secular affective commodity.

As scholars, we pounce triumphantly upon each little glimpse of religious allegiance, in the way that committed believers pounce upon each little glimpse of God's intervention in a seemingly godless world, like a single flower erupting through a fissure in a square-mile concrete parking lot. And we are right to insist that any purely secular representation of Shakespeare's life or world, any account of the Renaissance which ignores the religious passions of the Reformation, is a falsification. But that falsification, that misrepresentation, begins with Shakespeare himself. If Shakespeare has been the god of our idolatry for four centuries, it is because he created the scripture for an emergent secular world. Maybe what Shakespeare believed matters less than what he did. Maybe we should not believe Hamlet, or Shakespeare, when he tells us 'I have that within which passeth show'. Middleton did not believe him.[32] Middleton answered Shakespeare, as DeFlores answered Beatrice-Joanna: 'You're the deed's creature.'[33] What is within does not matter, if it does not come out; the secret subjectivity that you imagine for yourself is irrelevant, by comparison to the substantive social and material identity created by what you have actually done. You are created by, and a slave to, your actions, not your self-regarding fantasies. Deflores refuses to flatter the would-be transcendentalism of the ego. The gospel according to Middleton is less comforting than the gospel according to Shakespeare. Maybe that is why I believe Middleton, and doubt Shakespeare.

Maybe. Maybe not.

Notes

1 *Calendar of State Papers Venetian*, XVI (1910), p. 434 (Girolamo Lando to the Doge and Senate, 11 October 1620). 'God grant that they contain nothing of moment. They also think that some despatches of those already sent to Venice have also been intercepted.'

2 Sonia P. Anderson, 'The elder William Trumbull: a biographical sketch', *The British Library Journal*, 19 (1993), pp. 115–32.

3 Arthur W. Secord, 'I.M. of the First Folio Shakespeare and other Mabbe problems', *Journal of English and Germanic Philology*, 47 (1948), pp. 374–81; Leslie Hotson, *I, William Shakespeare, Do Appoint Thomas Russell, Esq.* (New York, 1938), pp. 238–50, 255. The *Oxford English Dictionary* records 'mebbe' as a dialectal spelling of 'maybe'.

4 British Library Additional Ms. 72364, fol. 93, letter to Trumbull '23 of October 1622 from Mr James Mab'.

5 See Thomas Cogswell, *The Blessed Revolution: English Politics and the Coming of War, 1621–1624*, Cambridge Studiese in Early Modern British History (Cambridge, 1989), pp. 6–54.

6 British Library Additional Ms. 72242, item 44: George Abbot, Archbbishop of Canterbury to William Trumbull, from Lambeth, 5 July 1622.

7 Quotations from Middleton refer to *The Collected Works*, gen. ed. Gary Taylor (Oxford, forthcoming).

8 *The Rogue*, trans. Mabbe, I, 210.

9 *Ways of Lying: Dissimulation, Persecution, and Conformity in Early Modern Europe* (Cambridge, Mass., 1990), p. 14.

10 In asserting Blount's centrality to the publishing of the First Folio I am drawing upon research in progress, which has been partially reported in papers circulated in two seminars at Shakespeare Association of America conferences (1997, 1998), in a paper delivered at a Modern Languages Association conference (1997) and in a paper delivered at a University of Georgia Shakespeare symposium (1999). I expect to publish a book on Blount, in the near future.

11 E. A. J. Honigmann, *The Stability of Shakespeare's Text* (London, 1965), pp. 34–5.

12 Robert Hill, 'Works of art as commodities: art, patronage, and the career of Sir Dudley Carleton 1610–1625' (unpublished University of Nottingham Ph.D. thesis, 1999), p. 46, note 31. I am grateful to Dr Hill for giving me advance access to his work, the first extended account of Carleton's career.

13 Karl Joseph Holtgen, 'Sir Robert Dallington (1561–1637): author, traveller, and pioneer of taste', *Huntington Library Quarterly*, 47 (1984), pp. 147–77.

14 Entered in the Stationers' Register on 15 May 1623, only two weeks before Blount's letter.

15 *The Catholic Moderator; or a moderate examination of the doctrine of the protestants. Proving . . . that we ought not to condeme the protestants for heretikes. First written in French by a catholike gentleman (H.C.) and now translated*; By 'W. W.' (printed by Eliot's Court Press for Nathaniel Butter). The original (*STC* 5638.7) was published in London in 1589 under a false imprint (actually printed by John Wolfe). This English translation (*STC* 5636.2) was reprinted twice in 1623 (*STC* 5636.4, 5636.6), and again in 1624 (5636.8).

16 Charles Tessier's *Le premier livre de chansons et airs de court tant Enfrancois qu'en Italien et Gascon*. Blount's third publication was John Florio's *A World of Words, or most copious dictionarie in Italian and English*.

17 Blount stressed the European credentials of his books. In 1600, for instance, he dedicated a translation of Conestaggio's *History of Portugal* to the Earl of Southampton (Shakespeare's patron), describing it as 'a thing first and excellently writen in Italian; then translated into French, and generally receiued in both those toongs through all christendome for a faithfull, elegant, sinewie, and well digested historie' (A2).

18 A. Allison and D. M. Rogers, *Catalogue of Catholic Books*, in *Biographical Studies*, III (1955–56), pp. 822–3 (tabulation of recusant books published by year).

19 The Paris debate is described in Featley's *The great sacrilege of the Church of Rome . . . together with two conferences: the former at Paris* (1630), *STC* 10733, and *The Relation of a conference touching the reall presence* (1635), *STC* 14053/22814; also see *STC* 10740.

20 C. H. Herford, Percy Simpson and Evelyn Simpson, ed., *Ben Jonson*, 11 vols (Oxford, 1925–52), vol. I, pp. 65–7; L. A. Beaurline, *Jonson and Elizabethan Comedy* (San Marino, 1978), pp. 226–30.

21 British Library, Harleian Ms. 389, Joseph Meade to Sir M. Stuteville, fol. 346v.

22 See Featley, *The Fisher catched in his own net* (1623), *STC* 10732, reprinted and expanded as *The Romish Fisher caught and held in his own net* (1624), *STC* 10738, and Henry Rogers, *An Answer to Mr. Fisher the Jesuit* (1623), *STC* 21177); for the Catholic point of view see Fisher, *True relation of sundry conferences* (1623), *STC* 10916.5.

23 'Bishop Matthew's report on the Hampton Court conference, 1604', in *Religion and Society in Early Modern England: A Sourcebook*, ed. David Cressy and Lori Anne Ferrell (London, 1996), pp. 123–5.

24 In January Father Fisher debated one of the royal chaplains, Dr White; in May he debated William Laud, the future Archbishop, and – at least from the perspective of the most important member of the audience – the Jesuit defeated the Protestant doctors: the Countess of Buckingham voted with her faith, and remained Catholic.

25 See the complex and nuanced argument in Robert Weimann, *Authority and Representation in Early Modern Discourse*, ed. David Hillman (Baltimore, 1996).

26 See for instance Dale B. J. Randall, *The Golden Tapesty: A Critical Survey of Non-chivalric Spanish Fiction in English Translation (1543–1657)* (Durham, 1963), pp. 15–16, 22, 27, 32, 33, 114, 116, 176, 181, 228.

27 Joel Altman, *The Tudor Play of Mind: Rhetorical Inquiry and the Development of Elizaberhan Drama* (Berkeley, 1978), pp. 31–106.

28 Anthony Grafton, *New Worlds, Ancient Texts: The Power of Tradition and the Shock of Discovery* (Cambridge, Mass., 1992).

29 A. Gregory, 'Pierre Charron's "Scandalous Book"', in Michael Hunter and Wootton, *Atheism from the Reformation to the Enlightenment* (Oxford, 1992), pp. 87–110.

30 Michael Hunter, 'The problem of atheism in early modern England', *Transactions of the Royal historical Society*, 5th ser., 35 (1985), pp. 135–58; Michael Hunter and David Wootton, *Atheism from the Reformation to the Enlightenment* (Oxford, 1992); John Sommerville, *The Secularization of Early Modern England* (London, 1992); Celia R. Daileader, *Eroticism on the Renaissance Stage: Transcedence, Desire, and the Limits of the Visible* (Cambridge, 1998).

31 Gary Taylor, 'Feeling bodies', in *Shakespeare in the Twentieth Century: Proceedings of the Sixth World Shakespeare Congress*, ed. Jonathan Bate *et al.* (Newark, 1998), pp. 258–79.

32 On the contrast between Middleton's religious politics and Shakespeare's see Gary Taylor, 'Forms of opposition: Shakespeare and Middleton', *English Literary Renaissance*, 24 (1994), pp. 283–314, and 'Divine [ ]sences', *Shakespeare Survey 54* (Cambridge, 2001), pp. 13–30.

33 *Hamlet* 1.2.85; *The Changeling* 3.4.140.

Index

Note: main entries are given in **bold**.

Abbot, George, Archbishop, 245–7
Acton, John, Stratford schoolmaster, 21
Acton, John, Lord, Catholic historian, 6
Agazzari, Alfonso, 119
Alençon, Duke of, 120
Alfield, John, Catholic controversialist, 87
Allen, William, Cardinal, 21–2, 26, 58–60, 66–7, 87, 94, 111, 130, 133, 167
Alleyn, Edward, actor, related to Hoghtons, 22
Althusser, Louis, 1
Altman, Joel, 253
Anderton, Roger, Lancashire exile, 134–5
Anne of Denmark, as Catholic, 225
Antwerp, Catholic refuge, 21, 27, 87–104, 124, 133–5, 242
Aquaviva, Claudio, 119–20
Arden, Edward, alleged plotter, 7–10, 14, 61, 110–12, 117, 169
Arden, Robert, Warwickshire Jesuit, 27, 187
Arden family, 7–10, 16–17, 27, 30, 60–1, 110, 117

Cheshire and Lancashire branch, 20, 134
Arnold, Matthew, 4
Ashton-under-Lyme, Cheshire, 21
Aspinall, Alexander, Stratford schoolmaster, 21, 26, 58
Aston, Margaret, 41
Aubrey, John, 8–9, 21, 60

Babington Plot, 137, 166
Bacon, Sir Francis, 13
Bacon, Sir Nicholas, 105–7
Baker, Oliver, 25
Baldwin, T. W., 24, 181
Bale, John, reformer, 55, 94
Barker, Francis, 15
Barrett, William, publisher, 250
Bassett, William, prisoner, 169
Bate, Jonathan, 12–13, 112
Becon, Thomas, iconoclast, 77
Beeston, Christopher, 21, 60
Beeston, William, 21, 60
Bellamy, Anne, recusant, 143
Bellamy, Robert, recusant, 161
Bellarmine, Robert, Cardinal, 96
Bellenger, Yves, 202
Berry, Philippa, 31
Bevington, David, 75

Bidermann, Jakob, Jesuit dramatist, *Cenodoxus*, 73–6

Blackwell, George, archpriest, 220

Blount, Edward, as Catholic publisher, **248–55**

Blundell, William, 49–50

Bodin, Jean, 88, 120

Boleyn, Anne, 29, 163, 225

Bond of Association (1584), 11–12

Borromeo, Carlo, Cardinal, 10–12, 61

Bossy, John, 11, 27, 30, 118–19, 218

Bourdieu, Pierre, 2, 4

Bowden, Henry, 13

Bradbrook, Muriel, 152

Breight, Curtis, 112

Brooke, Arthur, 109

Browne, Sir Thomas, *Urn Burial*, 211

Brownlow, Frank, **161–78**

Bruen, John, Cheshire Puritan, 48

Bruno, Giordano, 203–6, 214

Buckingham, George Villiers, Marquess, later Duke of, 243

Bullingham, Nicholas, 46

Burgess, Glen, 87–8

Burgh, Thomas, Lord, 163

Burlace, Jane, 47, 51

Burleigh, William Cecil, Lord, 7–8, 65, 76, 89, 105–8, 111–12, 140, 144, 155, 163, 166

Byrd, William, as Catholic composer, 40, 154

Camden, William, 93
 Britannia, 89, 91

Campion, Edmund, 10–12, 14, 21–7, 29–30, 59, 62–8, 73, 87, 93, 95, 108–9, 111–12, 118, 120, 122, 133, 140, 144, 148, 151–6, 187–9
 Ambrosia, 25, 76–82
 Decem rationes, 78–9
 History of Ireland, 78

Canisius, Petrus, Jesuit educator, 187–8

Carey, John, 6

Carroll, David, 3–4

Catesby, Robert, 10, 17, 61, 137

Catesby, Sir William, 10, 61

Catesby family, 10, 16, 30

Cecil, Sir Robert, 3, 124, 152, 163–4

Cervantes, Miguel, 254

Chamberlain, John, 224

Chambers, E. K., 24–6

Chapman, George, 101, 136

Charles I, 54, 101, 190, 244, 250

Cheshire, Catholicism in, 48

Chettle, Henry, Protestant rabble-rouser, 15

Charnock Richard, Lancashire, 62, 132, 134

Cholmeley family, Yorkshire recusants, 23–4

Claxton, William, antiquarian, 51, 56

Clement VIII, Pope, 214

Clitheroe, Margaret, Catholic martyr, 95

Clubb, Louise, 83

Clyff, George, monk of Durham, 51

Coke, Edward, 90–1, 162

Collinson, Patrick, 11, 81

Constable, Henry, Catholic poet, 250

Cooper, Thomas, 88–9, 93, 161

Cottam, John, Stratford schoolmaster, 17–18, 21, 25–6, 58–9

Cottam, Thomas, priest, 17–18, 30, 166

Cottam family, Lancashire recusants, 21, 23

Cotton, Sir Robert, 54

Cranmer, Thomas, Archbishop, 77, 225

Cromwell, Oliver, 127

Daileader, Celia, 254

Dallington, Robert, Catholic travel-writer, 249–50, 252

Daniel, David, 203

Davies, John, 134

Davies, Richard, 5, 69

Dean, William, priest, 164

Debdale, Robert, Stratford priest, 17–18, 30, 58, 67–8
Dekker, Thomas,
  The Virgin Martyr, 83
  The Whore of Babylon, 222
Derby, Ferdinando Stanley, Lord Strange, 5th Earl of, 20, 23, 26–7, 64, 125, 132, 136–7
Derby, Henry Stanley, 4th Earl of, 19–20, 26
Derby, William Stanley, 6th Earl of, 19
Devlin, Christopher, 15–17, 161
Diehl, Huston, 219, 228, 230–1
Digby, Sir Everard, 147
Digby, Sir John, ambassador, 244
Digges, Leonard, as Hispanophile, 250
Dilworth, Lancashire, 59–60
Dimocke, Anne, 139
Dolan, Frances, 218
Donne, John, 6, 19, 101, 167, 187
Douai, Catholic College at, 17–19, 21, 24, 58–9, 66–7, 108, 130
Douglas, Mary, 227
Doyle, Ian, 53
Duffy, Eamon, 40–57, 145, 148–9, 211, 218
Duncan-Jones, Katherine, 31, 151
Durham, Catholicism in, 50–1
Dutton, Richard, 117
Dyce, Alexander, 181

Eagleton, Terry, 30
Earle, John, 253
Eliot, George, historicism of, 6
Elizabeth I, 11–12, 14, 28–9, 69, 76, 81, 130, 134–7, 140, 152, 161–78
Elton, W. R., 204
Enos, Carol, 130–42
Erasmus, 181
Essex, Robert Devereux, Earl of, 3, 17, 124, 191, 202
Everett, Barbara, 148
Eyre, Thomas, recusant, 169

Featley, Daniel, Calvinist controversialist, 250–2
Ferdinand, Holy Roman Emperor, 245
Field, Nathaniel, 201
Field, Richard, name of two persons, 200–1
Fielitz, Sonja, **179–96**
Fitzherbert, Thomas, informer, 169
Fitzherbert family, recusants, 168–9
Flaubert, Gustave, and authorial disinterest, 2, 4
Fletcher, John, 232
Flynn, Dennis, 19
Foucault, Michel, 15, 18, 29–31, 205
Foxe, John, Protestant martyrologist, 61, 88–92, 94–5
Francisci, Jacomo, model for Jacques, 137–9
Fraser, Antonia, 11
Frederick, Elector Palatine, 244
Freud, Sigmund, 199
Fribourg, and Jesuit drama, 183–90
Frith, John, Warwickshire priest, 65, 147
Frye, Roland Mushat, 149, 197
Furnivall, Frederick James, 2–3, 6

Gallagher, Lowell, 218
Galli, Tolemeo, 119
Gardiner, Samuel, historian, 6
Garnet, Henry, priest, 47, 87, 169–70
Gdansk, English players in, 188
Gee, John, apostate, 220
Gerard, Sir Gilbert, Lancashire notable, 134
Gerard, John, priest, 73, 143–4, 146–7
Gilbert, George, Catholic plotter, 122
Gillam, Fulk, Chester player, 24–5, 60
Gillam, Thomas, Chester player, 25
Gondomar, Count, purchaser of First Folio, 250
Grafton, Anthony, 254
Grant, John, Catholic plotter, 16
Gregory XIII, Pope, 119

Greenblatt, Stephen, 12, 23, 31, 179, 226, 230
Greene, Graham, 14–15, 28, 225–6
Greene, Robert, 20, 65, 188
  A Groatsworth of Wit, 62
Gretser, Jakob, priest and playwright, 179–96
Greville gang, Stratford persecutors, 14
de Groot, John Henry, 223, 227

Habington, Thomas, 47
Haigh, Christopher, 145, 218–19
Hale, Thomas, recusant, 49
Hall, Edward, *Chronicle*, 22, 110
Hall, Hugh, priest and informer, 110
Hamilton, Donna, 87–104, 200–1, 210, 219, 223, 225–6
Harding, Matthew, 81
Harrison, William, *Description of England*, 47
Harsnet, Samuel, 230
  Declaration of Egregious Popish Errors, 67, 78–9, 146, 168
Hathaway family, 18, 65
Hatton, Sir Christopher, 137, 165
Haynes, Alan, 161
Heath, James, 162, 165
Henry, Prince of Wales, 203–5
Henry III of France, assassination of, 222
Henry IV of France, 213–14
Henry VIII, 162, 223–6
Hesketh, Richard, 136–7, 140
Hesketh, Sir Thomas, 24, 26, 60, 64–6
Hesketh family, 21, 136
Heywood, Jasper, Jesuit educator, 187
Hicks, Leo, S.J., 122
Higgins, Isaac, priest, 165
Higgons, Theophilus, Catholic polemicist, 201–2
Hill, Christopher, 6
Hoghton, Alexander, 20–2, 24–6, 60–1, 65, 108, 133

Hoghton, Richard, 62, 109, 132–6
Hoghton, Sir Richard, conformist, 22, 133–4, 141
Hoghton, Thomas, Catholic exile, 21, 59–60, 66–7, 130, 132–6, 140
Hoghton, Thomas, priest, 133
Hoghton, Thomas, 24–6
Hoghton family, 54, 66, 117, 132–6
Hoghton Tower, Lancashire, 20–1, 31, 58, 61, 107–8, 117, 133
Holden, Anthony, 31
Holland, Hugh, recusant poet, 250, 253
Holleran, James, 146, 151
Holt, William, priest, 166
Honan, Park, 147
Honigmann, Ernst, 20–3, 25–7, 117, 183, 189–90, 222, 249
Hooker, Richard, 81
Howard, St Philip, 48–9
Howard family, 101, 106, 167, 225
Howlett, John, Jesuit educator, 187
Hoy, Cyrus, 190
Hughes, Anne, 11
Hughes, Ted, 27
Hugo, Herman, 97
Hunt, Maurice, 224
Hunt, Simon, priest and Stratford schoolmaster, 17, 21, 58–9, 108
Hunter, G. K., 190

Inns of Court, as Catholic enclaves, 188–9
Isabella, Infanta and Archduchess, 97, 124–5, 242

James, Mervyn, 17
James I, 3, 23, 69, 87, 90–2, 95–6, 101, 167–8, 190, 201–9, 213–14, 220, 225, 242–6
Jenkins, Thomas, Stratford schoolmaster, 21, 58–9
Jessop, Augustus, 161

Jesus, Society of, 17–18, 23–5, 28–9, 58, 61–5, 68, 71–86, 97, 111, 116–20, **179–96**, 197

Jewel, John, iconoclast, 77, 81

Jocelyn, John, 93

Jones, Inigo, 40, 101

Jones-Davies, Margaret, **197–217**

Jonson, Ben, as Catholic, 21, 60, 101, 219–20, 250, 253

Joyce, James, and 'Catholic Shakespeare', 13, 74

Kastan, David Scott, 224

Keen, Alan, 22

Kent, Catholicism in, 41–2

Kilroy, Gerard, 18–19, **143–60**, 188–9

Kirby, Luke, priest, 166

Klause, John, 226

Knollys, Sir William, 124

Lambarde, William, 41, 55, 69
  The Perambulation of Kent, 41–2

Lancashire, Catholicism in, 19–27, 30, 49–50, 54, 58–65, 94, 105, 108, 146–7, 222

Langbein, John, 162

Latimer, Hugh, 77

Laud, William, Archbishop, 54

Leicester, Robert Dudley, Earl of, 3, 66, 76, 95, 108, 112, 153, 155

Leland, John, 88, 93

Leslie, John, Bishop, 94, 112
  Treatise of treasons Against Queen Elizabeth, 105–8

Levi, Peter, 21–2

Lincolnshire, Catholicism in, 46, 53

Lipsius, Justus, 90, 97

Little Crosby, Lancashire, 49

Lodge, Thomas, 188, 228

London, Catholicism in, 42–5, 61, 188, 251–2

Long Melford, Suffolk, 51–2

Louvain, Catholic university, 187

Loyola, Ignatius, 71–2, 93, 98, 120
  Spiritual Exercises, 62–3

Lucian, *Timon*, 180–5

Lucy, Sir Thomas, persecutor and pupil of Foxe, 7–9, 13, 61, 110

Luis de Granada, Catholic divine, 110

Lupton, Julia Reinhard, 232

Luther, Martin, Shakespeare's possible depiction, 229

Mabbe (Maybe), James, publisher and spy, **242–58**

McCabe, William, S.J., 71

McCoog, Thomas, S.J., 188

McManaway, James, 12

Maier, Michael, 207–10

Malone, Edmund, 10, 61

Malvern Priory, 47

Manning, Roger, 11

Marlowe, Christopher, 231, 254
  Doctor Faustus, 11, 75–6, 222, 227, 230
  Massacre at Paris, 222

Marotti, Arthur, 19, **218–41**

Martin, Randall, **105–15**

Martin, Roger, Suffolk recusant, 51

Mary Queen of Scots, 94, 105–6, 123, 168, 214

Marvell, Andrew, 'double heart' of, 6

Massinger, Philip, *The Virgin Martyr*, 83

Matheson, Mark, 228

Mayer, Jean-Christophe, **116–29**

Mazzola, Elizabeth, 227

Meres, Francis, 132

Meyer, Oskar, 151

Middleton, Thomas, as Protestant playwright, 179, 190
  The Changeling, 256
  A Game at Chess, 222–4, 246

Mildmay, Sir Walter, priest-hunter, 109

Milward, Peter, S. J., 27, 58–70, 127–8, 139–40, 188–9, 219, 227–8

Miola, Robert, 31, **71–86**
Mirandola, Pico della, 212
Montaigne, Michel de, 198, 202–5, 254
Montgomery, Philip Herbert, Earl of, dedicatee of Catholic works, 87, 96–7, 101
Montrose, Louis, 230
More, Sir Thomas, 29, 68
Morwen, John, Catholic propagandist, 44
Munday, Anthony, 87
Munich, as Jesuit centre, 71, 73, 75–6, 183, 187–8
Murphy, John, 200–1
Muschet, George, Jesuit controversialist, 250–2

Nashe, Thomas, 20, 84
  Christ's Tears over Jerusalem, 188
Neale, Sir John, 11
Nicholl, Charles, 161
Northampton, Henry Howard, Earl of, 93, 101, 225
Northamptonshire, Catholicism in, 61
Northern Rebellion 1569, 3, 21, 46, 112, 163–4
Norton, Thomas, dramatist and rackmaster, 8, 164
Nuttall, A. D., 147–8

O'Connell, Michael, 227
Oxford University, Catholicism in, 18, 21, 24, 59, 117

Pace, John, Stratford recusant, 18
Parker, Archbishop Matthew, 43, 88, 93
Parr, Katherine, 163
Parsons, Robert, 11, 26, 58, 87, 96–7, 101, **116–29**, 137, 139, 166–7, 200–1
  Christian Directory, 127

Conference about the Next Succession, 90, 122–8
Epistle of the Persecution of Catholics in England, 80
Treatise of Three Conversions, 90
Pascal, Blaise, 202
Patterson, Annabel, 224–5
Patterson, W. B., 96
Paul V, Pope, 214
Pembroke, William Herbert, Earl of, dedicatee of Catholic works, 87, 96–7, 101, 225, 245
Philip II of Spain, 90, 123–4, 130–1
Philip III of Spain, 244–5
Pibush, John, Catholic exile, 143
Pilkington, James, reformer, 43–5, 77, 81
Pius V, Pope, 123
Plutarch, *Life of Alcibiades*, 179–80
Pole, Reginald, 207
Pollen, John Hungerford, 118, 161
Pormort, Thomas, priest, 165
Porteman, Karel, 97–8
Pounde, Thomas, recusant patron, 59
Prague, 10, 18, 24–5, 27, 64, 140–1, 151, 186–8
Preston, Lancashire, 62
Puckering, Sir John, 165–6, 169
Puttenham, George, 84

Quarles, Francis, 97
Quiney, Adrian, 46
Quiney, Richard, 13

Rasmussen, Eric, 75
Rishton, Edward, prison diarist, 162
Rither, James, prisoner, 165
Rites of Durham, 50–1, 53
Roche, William, Stratford schoolmaster, 21, 58
Roche Abbey, 46
Rogers, Thomas, iconoclast, 77
Rookwood family, 171

Roper, Margaret, Catholic matriarch, 68

Roscarrock, Nicholas, 47, 51

Rossall, Lancashire, 58

Rowington, Warwickshire, 62

Rowse, A. L., 161

Rudolf II, Holy Roman Emperor, 25, 187

Rufford, Lancashire, 21, 26, 62

St Paul's Cathedral, 43–4

Savage, Thomas, of Rufford, Globe shareholder, 26

Schoenbaum, Samuel, 6, 10, 221

Schrickx, Willem, 189, 231

Scot, Reginald, religious writer, 198

Shakeshafte family, Preston, 27

Shakespeare, Anne, née Hathaway, 65

Shakespeare, Hamnet, 65

Shakespeare, John, 9–13, 21, 27, 45–6, 61, 65, 130

Shakespeare, Judith, 65

Shakespeare, Mary, née Arden, 7, 27, 110, 169

Shakespeare, Robert, 110

Shakespeare, Susanna, 65

Shakespeare, William
  All's Well That Ends Well, 66–7, 229, 231
  Antony and Cleopatra, 29, 190
  As You Like It, 42, 63, 66–7, 69, 130–42, 228
  Comedy of Errors, 59, 218, 226, 231
  Coriolanus, 183, 190, 192
  Cymbeline, 63, 69, 190, 197–217, 231, 250
  A Funeral Elegy, 198
  Hamlet, 7–8, 11–15, 18, 29–30, 63–4, 68, 110, 143–60, 199, 204, 226–8, 254–5
  1 Henry IV, 112, 224, 231
  2 Henry IV, 112, 126, 224

  Henry V, 3, 63–4, 123, 126–7, 222, 224, 226
  1 Henry VI, 3, 29, 231
  2 Henry VI, 3, 7, 61, 121
  3 Henry VI, 3, 29, 105–15, 120–2
  Henry VIII, 3, 223–5
  Julius Caesar, 23, 226
  King John, 3, 7, 69, 163, 167, 223–4
  King Lear, 13, 15, 17, 28, 30, 59, 64, 67–9, 78–9, 146, **161–78**, 183, 190, 192, 205, 218, 226, 254
  Love's Labour's Lost, 20, 29, 69, 226
  Macbeth, 16, 29, 105, 209, 226
  Measure for Measure, 222, **226–9**
  Merchant of Venice, 11, 29, 61, 68–9, 183
  Merry Wives of Windsor, 61
  A Midsummer Night's Dream, 4, 13–14, 16, 29, 68, 183, 191, 230
  Much Ado About Nothing, 68
  Othello, 28, 29, 223, 227
  Pericles, 7, 189–90, 231
  Phoenix and the Turtle, 26
  Rape of Lucrece, 22
  Richard II, 3, 67–8, 124–6, 147
  Richard III, 3, 20, 22–3, 125, 167
  Romeo and Juliet, 13, 22–3, 63, 68–9, 209
  Sonnet 33, 29
  Sonnet 73, 40, 53–6
  Sonnet 124, **29–30**, 229
  The Tempest, 13, 29, 63, 199, 204, 250
  Timon of Athens, **179–196**
  Titus Andronicus, 19, 66, 191, 226
  Troilus and Cressida, 64
  Twelfth Night, 24, 65, 190, 218, 231
  Two Noble Kinsmen, 198
  Venus and Adonis, 15–16, 22

The Winter's Tale, 24, 27, 29, 190, 231–2
Shakespeare in Love, 5
Shell, Alison, 18, 25, 81, 179, 188
Sherbrook, Michael, Anglican rector, 52–3
Shottery, Warwickshire, Catholicism in, 59
Shrewsbury, George Talbot, Earl of, extortioner, 170
Shuger, Debora, 197, 205, 218
Sidney, Sir Philip, 1, 83, 95, 151, 202
Arcadia, 168
Simonds, Peggy Munoz, 206–8, 210–12
Simons, Joseph, *Mercia*, 82–3
Simpson, Richard, 1–13, 26–7, 31, 29, 139
'Snow White', source of *Cymbeline*, 208–9
Soellner, R., 190
Somerville, John, alleged terrorist, 7–9, 30, 16, 61, 109–12, 117
Sommerville, John, 254
Southampton, Henry Wriothesley, 2nd Earl of, 24
Southampton, Henry Wriothesley, 3rd Earl of, 59, 112, 252
Southwell, Robert, priest and poet, 6, 15–17, 26, 143–4, 146, 153–4, 161, 169–70
Humble Supplication, 226
Speed, John, 127
Theatre of the Empire of Great Britain, 116
Spelman, Sir Henry, antiquarian, 56
Spenser, Edmund, 228
Spurgeon, Caroline, 167–8
Stanley, Sir William, 136–7, 140
Stanley family, 20, 26
Stapleton, Thomas, Catholic translator, 89, 200
Stonyhurst College, Lancashire, 188

Stow, John, historian, 42, 51, 53, 56
Survey of London, 42–3
Stratford-upon-Avon, Catholicism in, 5, 7–13, 17–18, 30, 45–7, 58–9, 110, 130, 218–21
Straton, Jan van, 149
Strype, John, historian, 131
Stubbs, John, controversialist, 166
Suffolk, Catholicism in, 51–2

Taylor, Charles, 204
Taylor, Gary, 1, 15, 17, 26, 31, 206, 221–3, 228, **242–58**
Throckmorton, Edward, Catholic zealot, 17–18
Throckmorton family, 7, 17–18, 11, 30, 117
Thurston, Herbert, S.J., 12
Topcliffe, Richard, Rackmaster, **161–78**
Trigge, Francis, reformer, 53
Trumbull, William, ambassador, 242–50
Trussel, John, Catholic publisher, 16–17
Tyndale, William, 203
Tyrrell, Anthony, apostate, 220

Valladolid, Jesuit centre, 197, 205
Vaux family, 16, 139–40
Verstegan, Richard, 87–104, 131–2, 167
Vienna, English players in, 188
Vilnius, English Jesuit mission, 187

Waad, William, torturer, 164
Wadsworth, James, apostate, 220
Walker, Henry, Puritan publicist, 127
Walpole, Henry, poet and priest, 95, 154–5, 165
Walsingham, Francis, 144, 164, 168
Walsingham, pilgrimage site, 42, 48–9
Waugh, Evelyn, 24

Webster, John, 219, 222
  The Duchess of Malfi, 41
Weever, John,
  Ancient Funeral Monuments, 54–5
  Epigrams, 22–3
Weimann, Robert, 253
Weston, William, priest, 58–9, 67, 73
Whitgift, Bishop John, 43, 165
Wickersley, Yorkshire, 52
Wilkes, Thomas, priest-hunter, 110
Wilkins, George, recusant dramatist,
  189
William of Orange, assassination of,
  222
Wilson, John Dover, 13, 20
Wilson, Richard, 1–39, 108–9, 117,
  179, 203
Wilson, Scott, 28–9
Wilson Knight, G., 190–1

Windsor, Edward, Catholic conspirator,
  137
Wittenberg, Protestant University, 198,
  205, 214, 228
Wolsey, Cardinal, Shakespeare's
  depiction, 225
Woolf, Daniel, 87
Wooton, David, 254
Worcestershire, Catholicism in, 47
Worden, Blair, 30
Wroxall, Warwickshire, 62

Yates, Frances, 203–5, 210
Yorkshire, Catholicism in, 52–3, 61–2,
  65, 69
Young, Richard, torturer, 164

Zagorin, Perez, 248